Harvard Economic Studies, Volume 145

The studies in this series are published under the direction of the Department of Economics of Harvard University. The Department does not assume responsibility for the views expressed.

The Economics of Multi-Plant Operation

*An International
Comparisons Study*

*F. M. Scherer
Alan Beckenstein
Erich Kaufer
R. Dennis Murphy
with the assistance of
Francine Bougeon-Maassen*

Harvard University Press
*Cambridge, Massachusetts
and London, England*
1975

Copyright © 1975 by the President and Fellows of Harvard College
All rights reserved
Library of Congress Catalog Card Number: 74–33697
ISBN 0–674–23340–9
Printed in the United States of America

Acknowledgments

Except in substituting a strong plot line for glorious color, this volume resembles a Hollywood epic: a huge cast of actors (many, alas, playing anonymously) and an equally extravagant list of credits. Here we attend to the latter.

Concerning the authors, all that requires mention is the division of labor. Erich Kaufer was primarily responsible for writing Chapter 4, Dennis Murphy for Chapter 5, Alan Beckenstein for Chapter 8, and F. M. Scherer as senior author for the other chapters along with entrepreneurship, homogenization of styles, and final editing. Francine Bougeon-Maassen had no chapter assignment, but she was solely responsible for the French research program.

We have enjoyed much valuable collaboration at key stages in the effort. The late Jacques Houssiaux laid the plans for our French research before his tragic death in 1970, and his reputation contributed to the success of the French interviewing campaign. Frank W. Steere served as research assistant in the early literature search period; Johan Lybeck located and translated numerous Swedish documents and helped make company contacts; and James M. Kennedy performed statistical analyses and much other yeoman service during 1971 and 1972. Cheryl Zello typed some early chapter drafts, Nancy Matthews the entire submission manuscript, and Betsy Williard the final footnote revisions.

Extremely valuable critical comments on the entire manuscript came from Leonard Weiss and Richard Caves. Much help was received from two University of Michigan doctoral dissertation committees, including Michael Klass, W. G. Shepherd, and Franklin Moore for the work underlying Chapter 5 and Sidney Winter, Frank Stafford, and H. Paul

Root for the thesis version of Chapter 8. Paul Kleindorfer commented critically on Chapter 2, Aubrey Silberston on Chapter 4, and an anonymous *Review of Economics and Statistics* referee on parts of Chapter 3. W. G. Shepherd and Jürgen Müller helped locate foreign source material. Edward Margolin of the Interstate Commerce Commission staff made seminal suggestions on the transportation cost measurement methodology adopted in Chapter 5. The ideas and advice of Richard Soland were indispensable to the development of Chapter 8.

Financial backing came from a number of sources. The primary research effort was covered by National Science Foundation grant GS-2809. Foreign travel was made possible through a grant from the University of Michigan Program in Comparative Economics, funded in turn by the Ford Foundation. The University of Michigan Institute of Public Policy Studies helped free chunks of the senior author's time for research between 1970 and 1972. His writing and manuscript revision activities from August 1972 to June 1974 were generously supported by the International Institute of Management, whose funds came from the German Federal Government and the City of Berlin Senate. Some of Professor Kaufer's research time was covered by a grant from the Deutschen Forschungsgemeinschaft.

By far the most distinctive and important facet of the research underlying this book was the set of 128 interviews with manufacturing companies in the United States, Canada, Germany, France, Sweden, the United Kingdom, and Japan. John B. Heath and John Pinder helped arrange interviews in the U.K.; Bengt Rydén, Fredrik Neumeyer, and Erich Dahmén in Sweden; and Thomas A. Wilson in Canada. Our greatest debt is to the many company officials who took time from busy schedules to discuss their firms' operations, usually with remarkable candor. That they must remain unnamed in no way reflects a lessening of our gratitude.

As usual, the authors alone accept responsibility for errors and misguided value judgments.

The manuscript was completed in February of 1974, nearly a half year before Messrs. Scherer and Murphy joined the staff of the Federal Trade Commission. This book is consequently not an F.T.C. staff report, nor does it necessarily reflect the Commission's views.

F. M. Scherer, Washington, D.C.
Alan Beckenstein, Charlottesville
Erich Kaufer, Saarbrücken
R. Dennis Murphy, Washington, D.C.

November 1974

Contents

Tables

Appendix Tables

Figures

The Economics of Multi-Plant Operation

1

Introduction

This book is our response to a puzzle first identified by Joe S. Bain. In 1966 Bain published a comparative study of plant sizes, plant concentration, and leading company concentration covering eight nations.[1] One prominent finding was that the average size (measured in employment terms) of the largest plants outside the United States was considerably smaller than the size of plants in comparable U.S. industries. Letting average employment in the largest 20 U.S. plants of any given industry be indexed at 100, Bain derived the following median relative plant size indices for his eight nation sample:[2]

Nation	Median 20-plant size index
United States	100
United Kingdom	78
France	39
Japan	34
Italy	29
Canada	28
India	26
Sweden	13

1. *International Differences in Industrial Structure* (New Haven: Yale University Press, 1966).
2. Ibid., p. 38.

The differences are clearly impressive. Using U.S. cost-scale relationships estimated in an earlier study as a bench mark, Bain discovered that the relatively small scale of leading plants outside the United States implied widespread acceptance of production scale economy sacrifices. The proportion of industries in which more than 30 percent of all employees worked in plants sufficiently small to bear unit cost penalties of 5 percent or more ranged from 32 percent in the United Kingdom, he estimated, to 82 percent in Sweden and 91 percent in Italy.[3]

One further finding heightens the puzzle. Comparing the fraction of sales originated by the three or four largest *companies* in each industry with the share of employment contributed by the three or four largest *plants*, Bain compiled a crude index of the minimum possible number of plants operated by the leading sellers—or, in other words, a rockbottom index of multi-plant operation. The mean and median estimated company/plant concentration multiples were:[4]

Nation	$\left(\dfrac{\text{Sales share of N largest companies}}{\text{Employment share of N largest plants}}\right)$	
	Mean value	Median value
United States	3.6	3.2
United Kingdom	2.6	1.9
France	4.3	3.0
Japan	3.9	2.5
Italy	3.6	2.0
Canada	2.0	1.8
India	4.3	4.4
Sweden	1.7	1.5

In several countries the indices of multi-plant operation appear to be of roughly the same magnitude as in the United States. And in all, a fair amount of multi-plant operation is suggested.

Now our query: Why on the average should firms outside the United States operate multiple plants, presumably of suboptimal scale, when they might produce the same output at lower unit cost in a single large-scale plant? This is the puzzle which stimulated the research underlying the present book. Although he proposed several tentative explanatory hypotheses, Bain concluded his international comparisons study admitting that "we are really more or less at a loss to explain . . . the failure of these anticipated intercountry differences [in the extent of multi-plant operation] to develop."[5]

One possible set of reasons for the relatively small average size of

3. Ibid., pp. 55–64.
4. Ibid., p. 132.
5. *International Differences in Industrial Structure*, p. 151.

non-U.S. plants is that optimal plant sizes abroad are smaller because of lagging technological sophistication; factor price ratios discouraging the use of large, capital-intensive production processes; or higher-cost transportation systems. If this were true, multi-plant operation might reflect efficient choices even though plant sizes fell substantially below the threshold required to achieve all scale economies by U.S. standards. A second possibility is that the plant size distributions of the 1950s studied by Bain were heavily influenced by the persistence of units embodying the obsolescent technology of the 1920s and 1930s, whose replacement was delayed by World War II and the burdens of postwar recovery. Or third, firms may have knowingly built inefficiently small plants in the past, perhaps under a protective umbrella of cartel arrangements. To the extent that any of these conjectures is valid, we should expect to see the obsolete and inefficiently small plants disappear as nations grow, modernize, implement new anticartel laws (as most Western European countries have since the mid-1950s), and stimulate cross-border competition by joining trade blocs like the European Common Market and the European Free Trade Association. Fourth, plant size decisions outside the United States may have been a rational response to special product differentiation or other market characteristics. It is generally believed, for example, that Europeans demand greater product variety than Americans, and to the extent that similar degrees of product specialization within plants exist, European plants will tend to be correspondingly smaller. Another possibility is that Bain's data present an inaccurate picture of actual plant size and multi plant operation patterns. The difficulties in obtaining accurate data directly comparable across a wide sample of industries and nations are great; sample sizes were necessarily limited; and the variance from industry to industry in size and multi-plant indices for industries studied by Bain was substantial. Estimation errors could have intruded because of defective raw data, sample bias, or deficient methodology.

Last but not necessarily least, it is conceivable that the coexistence of small plants and multi-plant operation stems from conscious, rational, tradeoff decisions. Operating plants too small to realize all scale economies imposes unit production cost sacrifices. But such sacrifices might be compensated if there are economies attributable to multi-plant operation, for example, from achieving close proximity to customers or production inputs at different points on the map; from specializing plants in the production of narrow, easily manageable product line segments; or from spreading production risks.

If in fact multi-plant operation offers advantages sufficiently compelling to warrant scale economy sacrifices at the individual plant level, conventional wisdom receives a severe jolt. It is generally believed that production scale economies are realized predominantly within individual plants and that the savings attainable by multiplying plants are negligible. However, the evidence on this point is extremely tenuous. Much of what is known on the subject comes from another pioneering study by Bain.[6] His analysis is almost exclusively empirical, drawing upon interviews with and questionnaires from firms in twenty U.S. manufacturing industries. The theoretical logic of why production and physical distribution cost savings might be gained through multi-plant operation is scarcely considered. Perhaps because of this, Bain's respondents evidently had trouble distinguishing among various possible scale economy dimensions, and especially between physical distribution and sales promotional economies. Usable responses were obtained for only twelve of the twenty industries surveyed. And even within this restricted sample, some of the responses were contradictory. Thus, at least one steel firm claimed that unit costs could be reduced by 2 to 5 percent through operating up to eight plants as compared to one efficient-sized plant, while other respondents denied that any economies of multi-plant operation existed.[7] Given these difficulties, Bain's conclusion is appropriately cautious: "The economies of large multi-plant firms are left in doubt by this investigation. In half the cases in which definite estimates were received, such economies were felt to be negligible or absent, whereas in most of the remainder of cases they seemed slight or small. Perhaps the frequently expressed suspicion that such economies generally are unimportant after all is supported, and perhaps we are justified in saying that we have had difficulty in accumulating convincing support for the proposition that in many industries production or distribution economies of large firms seriously encourage concentration."[8]

Certainly the question is far from settled. The paucity of knowledge is a serious barrier to formulating sound public policies, particularly in the antitrust realm. There is considerable evidence from the work of Bain, Ralph Nelson, and John Blair that the leading firms in U.S. industries typically maintain multiple plants and hence owe their market

6. "Economies of Scale, Concentration, and the Condition of Entry in Twenty Manufacturing Industries," *American Economic Review*, 44 (March 1954), 15–39; and *Barriers to New Competition* (Cambridge: Harvard University Press, 1956), esp. chap. 3. See also C. F. Pratten, *Economies of Scale in Manufacturing Industry* (Cambridge, Eng.: Cambridge University Press, 1971); and Aubrey Silberston, "Economies of Scale in Theory and Practice," *Economic Journal*, 82 (March 1972, Supplement), 369–391. The Pratten-Silberston study, though a most important extension of Bain's plant scale economies work, deals only peripherally with economies of multi-plant operation.

7. *Barriers to New Competition*, pp. 88 and 254.

8. "Economies of Scale," pp. 38–39. See also *Barriers to New Competition*, p. 89.

positions at least in part to multi-plant operation.[9] The justification for higher seller concentration in industrial markets may therefore depend on the extent and character of the scale economies attributable to multi-plant operation. If they are minute, it will be hard to make a strong case on efficiency grounds for the existence of many industrial market power concentrations. If they are substantial, recurrently advanced proposals for breaking up large multi-plant firms in concentrated industries lose some of their appeal.[10] It is important therefore to know more about the economies of multi-plant operation. Filling that knowledge void and explaining why plants have been built at apparently suboptimal scales in so many industries are the dual and in many respects complementary goals of this study.

Chapter 2 develops an economic theory of plant size and multi-plant decisions, stressing the spatially dispersed nature of real-world markets and the incentives for plant specialization flowing from product line complexity. Chapters 3 and 4 analyze the statistical and qualitative evidence on factors affecting plant size decisions. There follow four chapters examining the extent of multi-plant operation, its statistical correlates, and the economies actually or potentially realizable from various modes of multi-plant operation. We conclude by drawing implications of our findings with respect to antitrust policy, foreign trade policy, developments in the scientific management of business enterprise, and the general state of knowledge concerning industrial organization.

Methodology and Data

Methodologically, our approach in this book spans all three activities Joseph Schumpeter viewed as the core of economic analysis[11]—the building and manipulation of abstract theoretical models; the assembly of quantitative data and statistical testing of hypotheses; and "history," or

9. See Bain, "Economies of Scale," pp. 34–35; and *Barriers to New Competition*, pp. 84–85; Ralph L. Nelson, *Concentration in the Manufacturing Industries of the United States* (New Haven: Yale University Press, 1963), pp. 59–77; and John M. Blair, *Economic Concentration* (New York: Harcourt Brace Jovanovich, 1972), pp. 101–107.

10. See G. W. Stocking and M. W. Watkins, *Monopoly and Free Enterprise* (New York: 20th Century Fund, 1951), pp. 553 and 563–564; Carl Kaysen and Donald F. Turner, *Antitrust Policy* (Cambridge: Harvard University Press, 1959); the *Report of the White House Task Force on Antitrust Policy* (the so-called Neal Report) (Washington, July 5, 1968), reprinted in the *Journal of Reprints for Antitrust Law and Economics*, 1 (Winter 1969), 633–826; the Democratic party national platform adopted July 12, 1972; and the text of the Industrial Reorganization Act introduced by Senator Philip A. Hart, *Congressional Record*, 118 (July 24, 1972), S–11494–11501.

11. *History of Economic Analysis* (New York: Oxford University Press, 1954), p. 7.

the analysis of qualitative evidence on static structural relationships and dynamic changes.

Much less orthodox are the data analyzed and the methods by which they were collected. Attacking Bain's puzzle required that the research embrace a cross section of nations. It was recognized that serious problems would be encountered in obtaining accurate, comparable data on the industrial structures of different nations. This consideration urged a selective, intensive approach. It was also clear that if new light were to be shed on the economies of multi-plant operation, the research would have to probe even more perceptively into the actual operations of industrial firms than Bain's pathbreaking twenty-industry study did. This in effect necessitated going directly to companies with some type of interview technique. To be sure, extensive use has been made of industrial census documents, trade journals, and similar published materials. But the critical distinguishing methodological feature of our research was to be in-depth interviews with businessmen actively involved in plant size and multi-plant operating decisions.

Interviews are costly in terms of both money and research time. At the outset it was estimated that 120 company interviews spanning twelve industries and five nations would just about exhaust the investigators' capacity to master technological and market detail, not to mention their tolerance for travel. Given these target parameters, the goal was to choose a sample of nations, industries, and firms which maximized the variance of characteristics expected a priori to affect plant size and multi-plant decisions.

The sample in fact includes six nations—Germany, France, the United Kingdom, Sweden, Canada, and the United States—one more than originally planned. In one important respect the sample choice minimized rather than maximized the variance of a potentially important characteristic: technological maturity. All six nations were by 1965 quite clearly mature in Walt Rostow's sense of being able to apply a broad array of the most modern technologies virtually at will.[12] This restriction was imposed deliberately in the belief that dealing simultaneously with the problems of less developed countries would have complicated the research effort formidably. Language skills were a second key constraint. Coinvestigators F. M. Scherer and Erich Kaufer were capable of conducting interviews in both English and German, hence the choice of three English-speaking nations plus Germany. Sweden was included in part because of the (correct) expectation that Swedish businessmen could converse fluently in either English or German. France was added when Jacques Houssiaux of the University of Paris agreed to direct a parallel

12. *The Stages of Economic Growth* (Cambridge, Eng.: Cambridge University Press, 1961), esp. p. 10.

interview and quantitative data collection program. Following his tragic death at an early stage in the project, his research assistant, Francine Bougeon, ably completed the French research phase. Inclusion of Japan in the sample would have been desirable, but this was precluded by language barriers and a limited travel budget.[13] Subject to these technological maturity, language, and budgetary constraints, an attempt was made to select nations of widely divergent size, population density, rates of post-World War II industrial growth, degrees of openness to international trade, cartelization histories and policies, and aspects of what is commonly understood to be "culture."

The Industry Sample

The twelve industries selected for intensive interview research are listed in Table 1.1. Column (1) gives the short designation used in many subsequent references, column (2) the principal U.S. Census classification (S.I.C.) codes covered, and column (3) a more comprehensive definition.

Several explicit criteria guided the choice of these twelve. One important deliberate bias was toward industries characterized by moderate to extensive multi-plant operation among leading firms, at least in the United States. This was done to maximize the amount of information gained from interviews on the nature and rationale of multi-plant operation. Nevertheless, to provide a reference point for comparison, two industries with low multi-plant operation in the U.S.—cigarettes and refrigerators—were also chosen.[14] As column (4) of Table 1.1 shows, the average number of plants per company operated by the three leading U.S. cigarette and refrigerator producers in 1970 was 2.0 and 2.33 respectively. At the other extreme were fabric weaving and shoes, with thirty and twenty eight plants per Big Three member.

Another conscious bias was toward industries whose production technology was neither extremely complex nor subject during the 1960s to major technological revolutions. This limitation was a necessary evil, given our desire to develop reliable information on the relationship between plant scale and manufacturing costs. Thus, the sample provides no insight into industries with technologies as complex and dynamic as, say, electronic computers.

Within this broad framework, an attempt was made to maximize the

---

13. As a by-product of a 1973 visit to Japan, however, the senior author was able to explore with several academicians and three firms certain questions on which the main interviewing program had shown Japanese experience to be particularly interesting or unique.

14. In refrigerators there is also little multi-plant operation in the other countries studied. However, considerable multi-plant operation exists in the cigarette industries of some nations.

Table 1.1. Salient Characteristics of the Twelve Industries Selected for

(1)	(2)	(3)	(4)
Industry	Principal U.S. S.I.C. codes	Description	Average number of plants, top three U.S. producers
Brewing	2082	Brewing of beer, ale, and other malt liquors	6.33
Cigarettes	2111	Manufacture of cigarettes; tobacco stemming and drying and production of cigars or pipe tobacco excluded	2.00
Weaving	2211 2221	Weaving of cotton, linen, and synthetic fabrics; secondary attention to spinning of fibers and finishing of cloth	30.33
Paints	2851	Manufacture of paints, varnishes, stains, and lacquers; resin and pigment production excluded	9.67
Petroleum refining	2911	Refining of gasoline, fuel oil, etc. from crude oil; lubricant blending and special asphalt plants excluded	8.00
Shoes	3131 3141 3142	Production of leather and related shoes and slippers; all-rubber and rubber-canvas shoes, wooden clogs, and tanning excluded	28.33
Glass bottles	3221	Mechanized production of glass bottles and related containers; glass tableware and other blown glass products excluded	13.00
Cement	3241	Production of portland and other hydraulic cements	13.00
Steel	3312	Production of carbon steel from pig iron and scrap and rolling of basic steel shapes; special alloy steel works excluded	9.67
Bearings	3562	Production of ball and roller antifriction bearings	7.33
Refrigerators	3632	Assembly of refrigerators and freezers for household use	2.33
Storage batteries	3691	Production of lead-acid storage batteries, with emphasis on automotive and marine starter, lighting, and ignition types	12.67

Sources: Cols. (8) and (9), U.S., Bureau of the Census, *Census of Manufactures, 1967*, vol. I: *Summary and Subject Statistics* (Washington: USGPO, 1971), chaps. 1 and 9; other information, interview research.

Intensive Research.

(5) Type of technology	(6) Type of product	(7) 1963 U.S. transport cost per dollar of value, 350- mile haul	(8) 1967 U.S. value added (millions of dollars)	(9) 1967 U.S. four-firm concentration ratio
Process	Consumer	7.8	1546	40
Assembly[a]	Consumer	0.7	1640	81
Assembly	Producer- intermediate	0.7	2546	36
Assembly[a]	Half consumer, half producer	2.2	1319	22
Process	Consumer	8.9	4745	33
Assembly	Consumer	0.4	1729	26
Process	Producer- intermediate	9.9	842	60
Process	Producer- intermediate	44.6	812	29
Process	Producer- intermediate	7.5	8910	48
Machining & assembly	Producer- intermediate	0.9	833	54
Machining & assembly	Consumer	1.7	797	73
Assembly	Consumer	2.4	259	61

[a]Classification arguable.

variance among several characteristics potentially relevant to plant size and multi-plant decisions. As column (5) of Table 1.1 suggests, five of the industries can be classified as having predominantly "process" technologies, those in which significant chemical or physical transformations of raw material inputs are effected. At least five and perhaps seven have an assembly and/or metal machining orientation. Six sell their products primarily for end consumption, five primarily for use directly or as intermediate goods by other producers, while the paint industry caters almost equally to end consumers and industrial firms. The relative importance of outbound transportation costs varies widely between industries, as revealed in column (7), presenting an index of transportation cost per dollar of product value on a standardized 350-mile haul under 1963 U.S. conditions.[15] For shoes, outbound freight costs on such a shipment amounted to 0.4 cents per dollar's worth of goods shipped F.O.B. plant; for cement, 44.6 cents.

Applying these criteria and after a preliminary screening of probable data availability, some 30 possible industry sample candidates were identified. Following a more thorough check into information sources, the list was narrowed to 20. The final selection of 12 industries was determined partly on the basis of further data availability checks, including judgments on which industries access to key companies seemed likely; partly on the basis of maintaining balance among the high- vs. low-multi-plant, technology type, product market type, and transportation cost characteristics; partly after consideration of geographic accessibility;[16] and in part on the basis of several "intrinsic interest" attributes.[17] To elaborate on the last set of criteria, all of the industries selected are fairly large and prominent. Of the U.S. representatives, none had 1967 value added of less than $250 million. The 12 industries include fewer than 4 percent by number of the 422 four-digit manufacturing industries identified in the U.S. Standard Industrial Classification, but they originated 10.4 percent of 1967 U.S. manufacturing value added. Although not by overt choice, the industries selected also tend to be slightly more concentrated than U.S. manufacturing generally, with a simple average 1967 four-firm national concentration ratio of 47 com-

15. Details of the derivation are presented in Chaps. 3 and 5.

16. Thus, the sawmill industry was eliminated because the main producers are typically located far from industrial centers, and to reach them for interviews would have imposed a disproportionate strain on a tight travel budget.

17. Industries eliminated in the final screening from 20 to 12 were soaps and detergents, electric lamps, automobile tires, metal cans, synthetic fibers, flour milling, farm tractors, and metal-cutting machine tools. The earlier dropouts were nuts and bolts, typewriters, sewing machines, automobiles, flat glass, matches, synthetic rubber, industrial gases, thread mills, and sawmills.

pared to 39 for all 411 industries on which such ratios have been published.[18] Five of the included industries were also covered by Bain's 1950s' study of plant scale and multi-plant economies.[19] This overlap reflected a deliberate compromise between maintaining some benchmarks against which to compare our findings and adding fresh evidence to the stock of industrial knowledge. Finally, the passenger automobile industry was excluded in part because it has been so thoroughly studied, so the characteristics of its multi-plant structure are well known, and partly because the scope and complexity of its production operations are so vast that a thorough reinvestigation would have consumed a disproportionate quantity of research time.

In sum, the sample of twelve industries is neither random nor fully representative of its parent population. Yet it clearly spans a broad range of economically interesting characteristics. And as Chapter 3 will show, it exhibits quantitative attributes quite similar to those observed for a larger, less deliberately selected sample of industries studied by Bain.

The Company Interview Sample

Given this twelve industry, six nation framework, an attempt was made to maximize diversity over relevant characteristics of the companies interviewed. The broad strategy was to interview at least three U.S. firms in each industry, including at least one with considerable multi-plant operation and another with only one or a very few plants. For each of the other five nations, the goal was to interview at least one firm in each industry, with heavier sampling where plants were particularly small, multi-plant operation especially pronounced, and/or a recent history of structural change was evident. Although there were some deviations due to access difficulties and deliberate decisions to pursue certain questions further than originally planned, in general the sampling objectives were satisfied quite successfully. For only one nation-industry cell, involving the Swedish glass container monopoly, was no interview secured.[20] The number of interviews conducted in each nation and the number of interview requests rejected were:[21]

18. The difference in means is not statistically significant at the 0.05 level.
19. *Barriers to New Competition.*
20. In one other cell no interview was conducted domestically, but interviews at the headquarters of two multi-national firms dealt with the special problems of their subsidiaries serving that market.
21. Not counted are three 1973 interviews with Japanese firms. Included in the interview count are one with a trade association official who had previously been president of a small company and one with a recently retired vice-president of a company which had declined to be interviewed directly. When more than one semi-

Nation	Interviews completed	Interview requests rejected
United States	41	7
Canada	16	3
United Kingdom	18	6
Sweden	13	6
France	20	2
Fed. Rep. of Germany	17	8
Total	125	32

The comparatively low Swedish batting average probably reflects an interaction between modest language barriers and approaching companies by mail from only a narrow base of domestic contacts. The high frequency of German rejections was largely due to an unmistakable bias toward secrecy, even in some companies which did grant interviews.

Certain corporate interviewees were assured that their identity and hence participation would not be disclosed. To minimize the risk of disclosure no complete nation-industry interview frequency matrix can be presented. However, aggregated over the six nations, the completion and rejection tallies by industry were:[22]

Industry	Interviews completed	Interview requests rejected
Brewing	12	2
Cigarettes	9	0
Weaving	11	6
Paints	11	4
Petroleum refining	11	1
Shoes	13	5
Glass bottles	7	2
Cement	11	3
Steel	12	1
Bearings	8	3
Refrigerators	10	2
Storage batteries	10	3
Total	125	32

autonomous branch of a multi-national or multi-industry company was interviewed, each such interview is counted separately. Excluded from both columns are two U.S., one British, one Swedish, and two French interviews which were agreed to by the companies but had to be canceled by the interviewers owing to schedule conflicts.

22. One interview with a company supplying a critical high-scale economy input to a sample industry is assigned to the sample industry. Not counted in the tabulation are one bearing industry and two steel industry interviews in Japan.

The only noticeable pattern was for rejections to be relatively more frequent in industries which were monopolized or cartelized, and perhaps therefore apprehensive, and those which were being buffeted by unusually strong competitive forces. The latter typically pleaded either demoralization and unwillingness to discuss their problems or lack of organizational slack to accommodate interviewers.

The companies interviewed covered a wide spectrum of sizes. Twenty-three had total corporate sales of $1 billion or more in 1970, although in several such cases the interview locus was a division accounting for only a fraction of that total. Included were nine members of *Fortune's* list of the fifty largest U.S. industrial corporations in 1970 and eight from the comparable compilation of non-U.S. enterprises. At the other extreme were a paint manufacturer with four employees and a storage battery maker with forty employees. Most of the companies tended to be large enough to engage in at least some multi-plant operation. Out of seventy-two possible nation-industry cases, the interviews included forty-one firms leading their industry in sales.

Interview Methodology

The interview research phase began in the spring of 1970, peaked during the summer and fall of 1970, and trickled on into the summer of 1972. In the first round of interviews, the goal was to visit at least one company in each industry in the United States to pin down the details of industry technology, obtain a first approximation to the contours of the long-run cost function, and explore the main patterns and rationale of multi-plant operation. Eleven of the twelve industries were actually covered before attention shifted to Europe for three months of intensive interviewing. Sweden was canvassed by coinvestigators Scherer and Kaufer in June 1970; England by Scherer, Kaufer, and Bougeon in July. This collaborative venture helped build methodological skill and knowledge of industry technology before Bougeon and Kaufer turned to solo interviews in France and Germany, respectively. To supplement the intrinsically limited verbal communication of interviews, an effort was made to inspect at least one plant in each industry. This objective was accomplished fully, with perhaps unfortunate consequences for Wassily Leontief's definition (in a 1959 theory course lecture at Harvard) of an industrial organization economist as a person who has never been inside a factory. In fact, twenty-seven physical plant inspections were conducted by the senior author, six accompanied by one or both of the other interview team members. Six additional inspections were made during solo interviews by Bougeon and Kaufer. During the autumn of 1970 the Canadian research phase was initiated and additional interviews were scheduled in the United States, in both instances on a solo basis by the senior author. Through these and continuing interviews in Germany, data obtained in the early stages were verified or modified, new leads were explored, and greater depth of understanding was sought. The general sequence during the two-year interviewing period was for progressively less attention to be devoted to basic technology and market institutions, with a correspondingly increased intensity of focus on what were coming to be recognized as the critical variables in plant size decisions and multi-plant operation. In other words, a good deal of learning occurred, precipitating some changes in research questions.

The interview phase had been preceded by nearly a year of library research by the senior author and an assistant, plus shorter efforts by Kaufer and Bougeon to locate and digest existing scholarly and governmental studies of the sampled industries, identify the leading firms in each nation's industries, assemble quantitative data on plant sizes and market structure, and track contemporary industry developments in trade journals and newspapers. This undertaking was invaluable, though far from completely successful; subsequent field work brought to light much relevant published material which had escaped the initial screen. Whenever possible, the annual reports of a company for several previous years were studied before an interview request was made. The objective was to find out as much as possible in advance about the firm's operations: where its plants were located; in what products they specialized; what plants the firm had recently opened, expanded, and closed; who the firm's major competitors were; what its market position and profitability record had been; and how much it expended on sales promotion and research.

This work underlay the very heart of our interview strategy: to deal with concrete plant structure decisions and to avoid getting bogged down in broad philosophical discussions. Favorite questions included: Why did you build a plant at that particular location? Why didn't you build it bigger or smaller? How did its opening affect the pattern of regional and product specialization at plants B and C? What are the advantages of concentrating the production of product X at plant B? What penalties in the way of higher transport costs, strike risks, and the like does this production assignment decision impose? Why does your firm allocate such a large share of its advertising budget to local spot television messages? How large a discount can your firm obtain in purchasing raw material Y, compared to companies operating only one good-sized plant? This approach not only minimized the tendency for interviewees to spout platitudes but enhanced rapport. For in most instances, once they had taken the first crucial step and agreed to cooperate in an interview obviously aimed at specifics, most company representatives evidently enjoyed talking about concrete operational patterns and problems. Questions aimed at eliciting generalizations, when posed, were saved until a solid base of rapport and facts had been established.

Formal requests for interviews were generally made by letter, often preceded or accompanied by personal contacts with acquaintances or friends of friends in the company contacted. For the first round of U.S. contacts, a separate and rather lengthy list of questions was dispatched. This appeared to do more harm in discouraging cooperation than good in focusing eventual discussion, so subsequent contact letters included a single paragraph with six to twelve pointed questions bracketing the areas of interest. Their main role was to suggest what sorts of company representatives could most usefully cooperate and to show that the interviewers already had appreciable knowledge of the industry and company, so that the discussion could proceed on a relatively sophisticated plane.

Some interviews involved a series of separate conversations with diverse functional specialists, but the more prevalent pattern was for several company representatives to attend a single comprehensive meeting or (less often) for one executive to handle the entire interview. As one would expect, there was an inverse relationship between company size and the level in the corporate hierarchy of persons interviewed, though there were also some illuminating exceptions to this tendency. A rough tabulation of the position held by the most senior person with whom substantive discussions were held is:

Position	Number of interviews
Chairman, president, managing director of company, or vice-chairman	29
Executive vice-president; operational vice-president or general manager of division	24
Staff vice-president or comptroller; director of corporate staff function	43
High-level divisional staff member	9
Plant manager	2
Third-tier corporate staff member	16
Other	2
Total	125

The interviews ranged from thirty minutes to six hours in duration, with most clustering between one and three hours. As a rule, notes were not taken during the interviews, although key numbers and names were sometimes recorded on the spot. This tactic was chosen in the belief that good rapport and thoroughgoing exploration of key issues were more important than detailed reproduction of the points discussed. Points which later proved to be unclear were frequently rechecked through telephone calls or follow-up letters. Also, subsequent interviews provided an opportunity to check critical data items. Immediately following each interview, significant factual information was recorded in a set of rough notes. Later, usually within twenty-four hours, a full summary of the interview was written. The interview reports total nearly 500 single-spaced pages, excluding exhibits, brochures, and the like supplied by interviewees. The reports are and will continue to be treated as strictly confidential.

In most cases interviewees were assured that information provided on specific company operations would be held in confidence and not released without explicit clearance. This appeared to be a necessary condition for obtaining the insights desired, especially into the character of multi-plant economies. It has several drawbacks. First, the names of companies interviewed are for the most part not identified in this volume except where failure to do so would cause a serious sacrifice of insight.[23] Second, quantitative data are generally aggregated sufficiently to prevent the compromise of individual company information. Third, when making a point fully understandable appeared to hinge on linking an interviewed company's name to information not in the public domain, or on presenting sufficiently detailed factual material that a well-informed reader could guess the source, approval to publish the passage was sought from the relevant interviewee. Roughly 100 such clearances were requested. Most were granted, often accompanied by information on new developments subsequent to our interviews. But in a few cases interviewees insisted that certain passages be truncated or (in still fewer instances) that references to a specific point be eliminated altogether. At worst, this imposed only a minor constraint on our ability to report research findings.

During final revisions, some 200 pages were eliminated from the original book manuscript. Hardest hit in these cuts was detailed interview evidence in Chapters 4 and 7 (including much material which had

---

23. Readers eager to penetrate this veil of secrecy are warned that specific references to companies not in our interview sample are about as frequent as references to interviewed firms. The information on noninterviewed firms was obtained both from interviewees and public sources. When there were doubts about accuracy, letters quoting the material and asking for critical comments were sent to the noninterviewed companies. We did not, however, consider ourselves bound by any objections so raised.

survived the clearance process) plus an appendix on the technological bases of plant scale economies. For scholars interested in seeing the full-length cleared version of Chapter 7 and the scale economies appendix, bound copies have been deposited in the following reference libraries:[24] The Library of Congress, Washington, D.C.; Central Library, the Federal Trade Commission, Washington, D.C.; Library of the Department of Trade and Industry, London; Commercial Reference Library, Guildhall, London; Library of the International Institute of Management, Berlin; and Library of the Institut für Weltwirtschaft, Kiel, Germany.

24. F. M. Scherer, *Economies of Scale at the Plant and Multi-Plant Levels: Detailed Evidence* (Berlin: International Institute of Management, 1974). The plant scale economies appendix is also available in limited supply as F. M. Scherer, "The Technological Bases of Plant Scale Economies in Twelve Manufacturing Industries," Preprint I/74-6, International Institute of Management, Griegstrasse 5, 1 Berlin 33, Germany.

2

The Pure Theory
of Multi-Plant
Operation

Two questions predominate in this volume—why firms frequently operate plants seemingly too small to attain all economies of scale, and why they operate numerous plants, often small, rather than one or a very few large plants. One possible set of explanations emphasizes historical legacies or pathological behavior. These cannot be ignored. But multi-plant operation and the maintenance of small plants may also reflect rational, calculated responses by firms seeking to maximize profits in the face of special market conditions. This chapter articulates several theoretical models identifying conditions under which such responses are consistent with profit maximization or cost minimization. They will provide the basis for quantitative tests and qualitative explorations in subsequent chapters.

Our approach proceeds from two empirical premises commonly ignored in standard expositions of the theory of the firm, but obvious to even the most casual observer of real-world industries. First, production and the physical distribution of products take place in geographic space. Inputs must be assembled from diverse locations and outputs must be shipped to customers at a host of points on the map. When the geographic territory served is large, it *may* be more profitable to operate several spatially dispersed plants rather than a single larger centralized plant. Choices of this nature are a standard topic of location theory, upon which we shall draw heavily. Second, firms in real-world industries (including those defined narrowly enough to satisfy the economist's ideal construct of an "industry") often supply a multiplicity of products, each requiring its own special production process adaptations. The multi-product firm must decide whether to concentrate its production in a single plant or to operate multiple smaller plants specializing in some particular product or narrow range of products. The economic logic of such plant specialization choices is not nearly as well developed in the literature as the classic "plant location" problem. Therefore, a coherent theory must be synthesized from various fragments, drawn mostly from the field of management science.

A third crucial premise implicit in the two stated above must be made explicit. It is not obvious that a firm must serve all of a nationwide or multi-national market if doing so optimally requires the operation of multiple, geographically decentralized plants. Regional specialization by single-plant firms is conceivable. Likewise, when there are advantages to having plants specialize in a narrow range of products, an industry might well be organized with single-plant, narrow-line specialists rather than multi-plant, broad-line firms. The rationale for multi-plant operation cannot be found solely in the advantages of geographic decentralization or product segment specialization; there must be interaction effects which give the multi-plant producer some advantage not available to single-plant specialists. In this chapter and in some of the statistical analyses which follow we shall for the most part simply *assume* that such compulsions toward full-line nationwide operation exist. Not until Chapter 7—the longest in the book—will we probe deeply into their character.

The Static Size and Location Model

The simplest static model of a firm serving markets covering geographic space will serve as a starting point. Complications will then be added step-by-step.

Economies of Scale

A key concern is the extent to which firms realize economies of scale in production. Scale economies at the plant level are conceptualized by the long-run unit cost function, represented graphically in Figure 2.1 as the cost curve LRUC, sometimes also called the "planning curve." It reflects the locus of unit costs attainable by building plants of varying sizes and actually operating them in the neighborhood of their planned outputs.[1] When economies of scale exist, long-run unit cost falls as larger and larger plants are built and operated. The unit cost reductions

---

1. The long-run cost curve is the lower-bound envelope of all short-run cost functions. As such, it does *not* describe what unit costs will be if a plant is built and then operated well below or above its planned output. By "planned output" is meant that output at which a short-run cost curve is tangent to the long-run envelope curve.

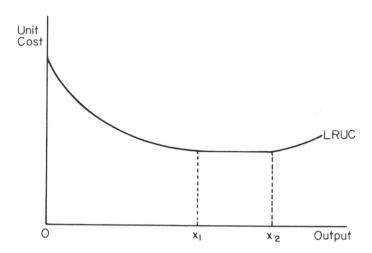

Figure 2.1.   Long-run Unit Cost Function.

associated with increasing plant size can have numerous causes: increased specialization of machinery and labor; indivisibilities making it worthwhile to spread the cost of lumpy equipment and special skills over a large output; technological relationships permitting equipment to be scaled up at less than a proportional increase in investment outlays; economies gained in high-volume purchasing and shipping; and "massed reserves" advantages permitting a large plant to retain proportionately fewer repair men and backup machines to hedge against randomly occurring breakdowns.[2]

Nevertheless, the economies of large-scale plant operation are not necessarily inexhaustible. Normally, there will be some plant scale at which all relevant advantages of large size are attained and at which unit costs reach their minimum value. That plant scale at which the long-run unit cost curve first attains a global minimum—that is, at output OX_1 in Figure 2.1—is called the *minimum optimal scale* or MOS, or sometimes the minimum efficient scale (MES). Beyond the MOS, unit costs

2. Abundant illustrations are contained in the separately published appendix to the present volume, F. M. Scherer, "The Technological Bases of Plant Scale Economies in Twelve Manufacturing Industries," Preprint I/74-6, International Institute of Management (Berlin, 1974). The classic reference on the theory of scale economies continues to be E. A. G. Robinson, *The Structure of Competitive Industry*, rev. ed. (Chicago: University of Chicago Press, 1958). An outstanding collection of empirical studies is found in C. F. Pratten and R. M. Dean, *The Economies of Large-scale Production in British Industry* (Cambridge, Eng.: Cambridge University Press, 1965); and C. F. Pratten, *Economies of Scale in Manufacturing Industry* (Cambridge, Eng.: Cambridge University Press, 1971).

may be constant as larger plants are built and operated, as in the range X_1X_2, or they may rise due to diseconomies of scale, as in the range to the right of OX_2.

All else equal, economic efficiency requires that production take place at minimum unit cost; that is, in plants of at least the minimum optimal scale. Bain's work revealing that plant sizes fall short of this ideal on a widespread basis provided the initial inspiration for this study. One possible explanation is the existence of monopoly pricing power in markets so small or so fragmented owing to product differentiation that marginal revenue falls into equality with long-run marginal cost at an output below the minimum optimal scale. The theory is well known; the relevant evidence will be considered in subsequent chapters.

Outbound Transportation Costs

The "all else equal" assumption of the preceding paragraph is often violated, especially when transportation costs are significant. Then the criterion for cost minimization is not attainment of the lowest possible unit *production* costs only, that is, at or beyond the minimum optimal scale, but rather, minimizing the sum of production plus physical distribution costs. Figure 2.2 provides an introduction to the problem. Consider first the costs of transporting output from a plant to customers. If customers are distributed over geographic space, selling the output of increasingly large plants requires shipment to customers at greater and

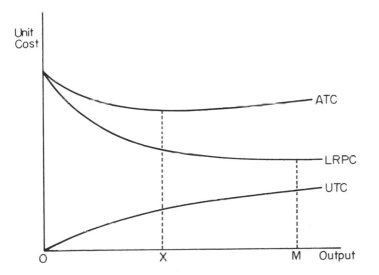

Figure 2.2.   Unit Production and Transportation Costs.

greater distances, ceteris paribus. This means that the average cost of distributing one's output rises with increasing plant size, as shown by the unit transportation cost curve UTC in Figure 2.2. *Total* unit cost ATC is found by summing vertically the UTC curve and the long-run unit production cost curve LRPC. For the curves illustrated, average total cost is minimized at plant size *OX*—well below the minimum optimal scale of production alone *OM*. If the unit transportation cost curve has any persistent positive slope, the least-total-unit cost plant will necessarily be smaller than the MOS plant. For a given LRPC function, the steeper the unit transportation cost curve is, the more the ATC-minimizing plant size will fall below the minimum optimal scale, defined in terms of production costs only.

Upon what does the slope of the UTC curve depend? Common sense can provide most of the answer.[3] One element is the structure of transportation charges, varying with the commodity, medium, and distance shipped. Shipping eggs costs more per hundredweight than shipping crude oil; shipping by tank truck costs more per ton mile than by 250,000 ton deadweight tanker; and shipping 1000 miles costs more (though perhaps not proportionately more) than shipping 100 miles, ceteris paribus. Second, for a given cost per ton mile shipped, unit transportation cost will rise more rapidly in relation to unit production costs for commodities like cement, whose unit production cost per pound is low, than for high-value commodities like miniature ball bearings and quality shoes.[4] Third, the geographic distribution of potential customers matters. If demand is distributed evenly over the map, transportation costs will rise less than proportionately with volume sold, ceteris paribus, since shipping cost is related to the radius of shipment while the amount of patronage is related to the square of the radius, that is, to the area served. If, on the other hand, customer density declines sharply with increasing distance from

3. This discussion is drawn with only minor changes from F. M. Scherer, *Industrial Market Structure and Economic Performance* (Chicago: Rand McNally, 1970), p. 78.

4. E.g., suppose the cost of shipping a ton of some commodity one mile is 10 cents, and transport costs rise linearly with distance shipped. To sell 100 tons per day of the product requires an average shipping distance of 100 miles. Increasing sales to 200 tons per day raises the average shipping distance to 140 miles. Thus, average transportation cost per ton is $10.00 for a plant producing 100 tons daily and $14.00 for a plant twice that size. But what matters in choosing minimum-ATC plants is the change in UTC *in relation to* the change in LRPC. If doubling plant size leads to a 10 percent decrease in unit production cost, the fall in the LRPC curve will be 5 times the rise in UTC if the cost of production in quantities of 100 tons per day is $200 per ton. But if the unit production cost at a scale of 100 tons per day is only $20 per ton, the $2 decline in LRPC from doubling production will be more than offset by the $4 rise in UTC, and expansion to a scale of 200 tons per day would not be economical.

one's plant, transport costs per unit may even rise more than proportionately with volume sold. A fourth consideration is the nature of the pricing system. Transportation costs borne by the producer rise with output only if they cannot be passed on to customers in the form of higher prices. This will occur when prices are uniform in all markets, or when the price at more distant sales locations is set by more advantageously located rival producers. A final factor is the size of the plant in relation to the size of the market served. If the plant supplies only a small fraction of total market demand, it may be able to increase sales substantially without expanding its geographic spread by reducing its mill net price slightly. But if the market is oligopolistic, as most of the industries covered by our interviews were, respect for mutual interdependence is likely to discourage price cutting to gain market share, and the costs of expanding through farther shipping may be an important plant size constraint.[5]

The problem can be formulated rigorously by invoking the location theorist's common (but heroic) assumption that a plant with a market share of S serves a circular market area with a radius of R miles, homogeneous demand density of D units per square mile, and a uniform cost T of shipping one unit of output one radial mile.[6] Using the method of cylindrical shells, and letting Z be the distance any given unit of output is shipped, it can be shown that the total transportation cost $\tau(R)$ is:[7]

$$(2.1) \qquad \tau(R) = \int_0^R 2SDT\pi Z^2 \, dZ = \frac{2}{3} SDT\pi R^3.$$

When the total quantity produced is Q units and the number of units sold per square mile is SD, the total number of square miles served must be:

$$(2.2) \qquad \frac{Q}{SD} = \pi R^2.$$

5. For an interesting attempt to integrate the theory of oligopoly pricing with location theory, see Melvin L. Greenhut, *A Theory of the Firm in Economic Space* (New York: Appleton-Century-Croft, 1970).

6. Assuming quadrangular, fractional circular, or hexagonal markets leads to no fundamental change in the relationships. See Herbert Mohring and Harold F. Williamson, Jr., "Scale and 'Industrial Reorganisation' Economies of Transport Improvements," *Journal of Transport Economics and Policy*, 3 (September 1969), 9–10.

7. See George B. Thomas, Jr., *Calculus and Analytic Geometry*, 3rd ed. (Reading, Mass.: Addison-Wesley, 1962), pp. 230–232. For an intuitive proof based upon the geometry of conic sections, see Mohring and Williamson, "Scale and 'Industrial Reorganisation' Economies," p. 10.

Solving (2.2) for R, substituting into (2.1), and dividing through by Q, we find transport cost per unit to be:

$$(2.3) \qquad UTC = \frac{\tau(Q)}{Q} = \frac{2T\sqrt{Q}}{3\sqrt{SD\pi}}.$$

To minimize the average total cost of production plus transportation, the absolute value of the LRPC curve's slope must be set equal to the slope of the UTC function, which is:

$$(2.4) \qquad \frac{dUTC}{dQ} = \frac{T}{3\sqrt{SD\pi Q}}.$$

Under the assumptions stated and given $d\,LRPC\,/\,dQ < 0$ (implying the presence of production scale economies), the average total cost minimizing plant size will be larger, the smaller is the cost of transporting a unit of output a given distance, the larger is the plant's share of the market, and the more densely packed demand is over geographic space. These relationships will prove to be crucial in our subsequent statistical investigations of observed plant sizes.

It must be emphasized that in assuming sales per square mile to be fixed at SD, we are ignoring inter alia the effect price variations have on the quantity demanded. This is not a realistic assumption when firms possess considerable latitude in setting prices, for example, when they have a well protected monopoly position or where they can ignore the effects of their prices on rival prices and outputs. But when respect for mutual oligopolistic interdependence is strong, it is fairly realistic to assume that prices will be set on the basis of strategic considerations (at the level required optimally to restrain new entry) and that sellers will participate in the demand at any locality in proportion to more or less historically determined market shares.

The Multi-Plant, Multi-Market Model

This simple one-plant model provides important preliminary insights into the incentives for multi-plant operation. It is obvious that to serve a given total demand distributed over some geographic space, the plants operated will be smaller and there will be more of them if transport costs are large in relation to unit production cost and if demand per square mile is low than if transport costs are relatively modest and/or demand density is high. The single-plant analysis does not, however, provide a complete solution to the plant size, numbers, and location problem. There are three related reasons.

For one, the decisions concerning plant sizes are interdependent. If a plant in Chicago is expanded by assigning to it more customers in Ohio and western Pennsylvania, the size of a sister plant in New Jersey may have to be contracted, causing a sacrifice of scale economies which may, even after taking into account the reduction in outbound freight charges from New Jersey, lessen total company profits. To minimize company wide production plus distribution costs (which, given the assumption of fixed prices and demands, is tantamount to maximizing profit) an intra-company general equilibrium problem must be solved.

This would pose no particular analytic difficulties were it not for a second complication: the existence of production scale economies. Then the orthodox rule from calculus that marginal costs be equalized among plants is not sufficient to ensure that total costs are minimized, since, if a situation exists in which plants' marginal production plus transportation costs are still falling at the output levels prevailing, a small increase in output at, say, plant A would require that plant to incur additional costs lower than those at which the other plants had been producing and delivering their last units of output. If more can be saved by expanding some plants than is added by contracting others, cost minimization may require that some plants be closed down altogether. The correct "corner solution" can be ascertained under these circumstances only by comparing the *total* costs of widely varying (non-marginal) output assignment alternatives.[8]

The third problem is a practical one. Real-world analogues of the unit transportation cost curve in Figure 2.2 are apt to be ill-behaved and kinky owing to discontinuities in the geographic distribution of demand. West of Kansas City is to the modern U.S. market density and transportation cost analyst what the western Atlantic Ocean was to pre-Columbian European navigators. If one is to do more than extract heroic abstractions concerning the plant size and location problem, one must confront Mother Nature's lumps along with her curves.

Thus, the standard operational approach to the problem now emphasizes mathematical programming.[9] The state of the art has not progressed sufficiently to permit quantities demanded to vary with price,

8. See Don Patinkin, "Multiple-Plant Firms, Cartels, and Imperfect Competition," *Quarterly Journal of Economics*, 61 (February 1947), 173–205; and the comment by Wassily Leontief and reply from Patinkin, *Quarterly Journal of Economics*, 61 (August 1947), 650–657.

9. See, e.g., Tjalling Koopmans and Martin Beckmann, "Assignment Problems and the Location of Economic Activity," *Econometrica*, 25 (January 1957), 53–76; Thomas Vietorisz and Alan S. Manne, "Chemical Processes, Plant Location, and Economies of Scale," in A. S. Manne and Harry Markowitz, eds., *Studies in Process Analysis* (New York: Wiley, 1963), pp. 136–158; and E. Feldman, F. A. Lehrer, and T. L. Ray, "Warehouse Location under Continuous Economies of Scale," *Management Science*, 12 (May 1966), 670–684.

so some sort of oligopolistic price rigidity and exogenous market share determination mechanism assumption is an analytic necessity. Usually, this is done by identifying a set of m discrete market territories, demand in the jth territory being fixed (or estimated) as d_j. N possible plant locations are assumed, the output from the ith plant shipped to the jth market being X_{ij}. There is a matrix T of transportation costs from each plant site to each market, t_{ij} being the cost of shipping one unit of output from plant i to market j. Where

$$c_i \left(\sum_{j=1}^{m} X_{ij} \right)$$

is the total production cost function for plant i, the problem is to minimize with respect to the matrix of plant output and shipping assignments X the sum of all production and transportation costs:

(2.5) $\text{Min } TC = \sum_{i=1}^{n} c_i \left(\sum_{j=1}^{m} X_{ij} \right) + \sum_{i=1}^{n} \sum_{j=1}^{m} t_{ij} X_{ij};$

subject to constraints:

(2.5a) $\sum_{i=1}^{n} X_{ij} \geq d_j$ for all j, and

(2.5b) $X_{ij} \geq 0$ for all i and j.

If the production cost function $c_i(\cdot)$ is linear and homogeneous, the total cost minimization problem can be solved by straightforward linear programming methods. However, the more interesting cases are those with economies of scale in production; that is, with $d^2 c_i / dX_i^2 < 0$ over at least some extensive output range. Then the problem is one of concave programming, whose state of the art is still primitive and whose models in generalized form permit few analytic insights. The strength of such models is their ability to accommodate real-world complexity; the price paid is analytic intractability. Therefore, at this point it is not possible to go beyond the generalizations suggested by our simple single-plant model of the production cost-transportation cost tradeoff. Further insight will be provided through numerical analysis in Chapter 8.

The Role of Input Transportation Costs
    Plant numbers, locations, and sizes may also be influenced by the locations and costs of transporting raw materials and other inputs. This complication can be introduced into a programming model without great difficulty. Where R_{khi} is the quantity of the kth input from the hth source used by the ith plant, t^*_{khi} is the cost of transporting a unit of input k

from source h to plant i, a_k is the quantity of input k needed to produce a unit of output at any plant, and, assuming for simplicity that input F.O.B. prices are invariant with respect to source,[10] we merely add to previous equation (2.5) an input transportation cost term, so the firm minimizes with respect to the input source choices and the plant output and delivery assignments:

$$(2.6) \qquad Min\ TC = \sum_{i=1}^{n} \sum_{k=1}^{v} \sum_{h=1}^{w} t^{*}_{khi} R_{khi} + \sum_{i=1}^{n} c \left(\sum_{j=1}^{m} X_{ij} \right) + \\ \sum_{i=1}^{n} \sum_{j=1}^{m} t_{ij} X_{ij}.$$

In addition to constraints (2.5a) and (2.5b), the production requirement and nonnegativity constraints must be introduced:

$$(2.6a) \qquad \sum_{h=1}^{w} R_{khi} \geq a_k X_i \qquad \text{for all } k \text{ and } i, \text{ and}$$

$$(2.6b) \qquad R_{khi} \geq 0 \qquad \text{for all } k, h, \text{ and } i.$$

This is much too general to yield any economically interesting insights. Somewhat more concretely, location theory reveals that the choice of any given plant's location is the resultant of directional pulls from the various raw material sources and end product markets, the strength of each pull being proportional to the weight of the input (or output) per unit of output times the shipping cost per unit of weight.[11]

Further enlightenment comes from recognizing certain important distinctions. One is between localized inputs, those like diamonds and high-grade nickel ore which are available only at a small number of geographic locations, and inputs distributed more or less ubiquitously over geographic space. Another is between weight-losing production processes, in which the weight of the finished output is significantly less than the weight of key raw material inputs, and weight-increasing processes, where output weighs more than the sum of the input weights. Weight-increasing processes are almost always pulled toward end product markets, other things being equal, and when outbound transportation

10. Otherwise we should have to disentangle input usage costs from the production cost function c_i (·) or recast that function in terms of inputs as opposed to outputs. Scale economies in the use of inputs or the existence of substitution relationships among inputs whose prices vary from source to source would complicate matters formidably.

11. The classic reference is August Lösch, *The Economics of Location*, 2nd ed., trans. W. H. Woglom (New Haven: Yale University Press, 1956), esp. chaps. 4, 8, and 21. For a succinct and informative survey, see Martin Beckmann, *Location Theory* (New York: Random House, 1968), chap. 2.

costs are substantial in relation to production cost, multi-plant operation is likely if a geographically vast market is to be supplied. With weight-losing processes the problem is more complex. If the inputs are localized, plants will tend to be pulled toward the location of the principal input, and multi-plant operation is likely to be constrained by the paucity of input sources.

This conclusion may be modified, however, if transportation costs per unit of weight for outputs exceed those for inputs by more than the ratio of input to output weight, for example, because low-cost bulk shipping media are available for the inputs but outputs are bulky or fragile (like light bulbs). Likewise, if inputs are localized but there are many of them, none of dominant importance, and the sources are highly dispersed, pulls toward input sources may neutralize one another and multi-plant operation may emerge as a result of end product market pulls or other influences. If key inputs into a weight-losing process are ubiquitous, the input locational pull will be insignificant and outbound transportation cost or other considerations will dominate the plant size and numbers decision. Finally, if there are numerous dispersed input source locations for a weight-losing process but each is of very limited capacity relative to total requirements, multi-plant operation may emerge in response to the pull toward input locations. An example might be tomato canning, in which damage in shipping and spoilage raises raw material transportation costs and leads to the multiplication of canneries in close proximity to superior growing centers.

We find then a rich menu of possibilities. In only one case—highly localized key resources plus a weight-losing production process—are tendencies toward multi-plant operation associated with relatively high output transportation costs definitely counteracted. In other cases input pulls are neutralized, while in still others they may encourage geographically dispersed multi-plant operation.

For purposes of this volume, the important question is whether input transportation costs exert sufficient locational pull to modify the generalizations emerging from our model analyzing only production scale economies and the costs of shipping final output to demand nodes. It is useful to digress from the theoretical argument and examine the evidence for the twelve intensively studied industries.

Most of the production processes covered by our interview research are weight-losing in the sense that some materials waste occurs. But for the most part the weight losses are small and are more than compensated by freight rates and in-transit inventory carrying costs that are higher on end products than on raw materials. This is the case for woven fabrics, paints and varnishes, shoes, glass bottles, antifriction bearings, refrigerators, storage batteries, and (less clearly) for cigarettes. Ubiquity or heterogeneity of raw material sources also helps nullify raw material locational pulls in many of the same industries. Cement manufacturing on the other hand is fairly strongly weight-losing, requiring inter alia roughly 1.5 tons of limestone for every ton of cement produced. But with only a few notable regional exceptions (such as New England and Scotland), limestone is virtually ubiquitous. Its locational influence is confined for the most part to determining the *specific* site of a cement works; it is seldom strong enough to override a general pull, reflecting high end product shipping cost, toward centers of demand. Beer brewing is also weight-losing, in the sense that the typical brewer uses between seven and twenty times as much water for cleaning and other functions as the volume of beer shipped. Yet popular mythology to the contrary notwithstanding, modern chemistry has made water a nearly ubiquitous resource for the brewer, so brewery locational decisions tend to be market-oriented. And if scarcity or high transportation costs significantly raised the price of water to brewers, investment in recycling equipment would surely become profitable, greatly reducing the weight loss coefficient. Thus, the prevalent pattern in ten of the twelve industries is for outbound transportation costs to dominate plant-size and numbers choices, at least to the extent that transport costs have any significant influence at all.

Steel and petroleum refining constitute the principal exceptions. For both the locational equilibrium determinants are extremely complex. The blast furnace stage of an integrated steel works is severely weight-losing. A typical U.S. blast furnace operation of the late 1960s used about 1.6 tons of iron ore, 0.4 tons of limestone, and 0.63 tons of coke (characteristically produced on the mill site from 0.9 tons of coal) to turn out a ton of pig iron. Limestone, as noted before, is virtually ubiquitous, but good ore and coking coal deposits are localized. Since suitable ore and coal are seldom found at the same sites, their locational pulls are to some extent conflicting. Also, the pulls are attenuated by the fact that ubiquitous steel scrap is added to pig iron in substantial quantities to produce steel and also by the existence of much higher freight rates on finished steel products than on iron ore. Thus, the average cost of shipping beneficiated iron ore from the western shore of Lake Superior to Cleveland by ore boat in 1970 was about $1.20 per ton, while in 1963 the cost of shipping representative steel mill products in an average rail-truck mix from Cleveland to Chicago, a much shorter distance, was about $8.00 per ton. Such shipping cost disparities are sufficient to impart a strong element of final market orientation to steel mill location decisions. When good deep-water transportation from coal and especially iron ore sources is available, the most common pattern is for integrated steel mills to be relatively "footloose" with respect to raw materials over a wide array of alternative sites. Choices among these locations and on how many works to operate are then made on the basis of market proximity vs. scale economy tradeoffs. Yet diverse patterns also exist because of differing technologies (for example, electric arc furnaces accepting nearly ubiquitous steel scrap charges are more footloose than blast furnace shops); because of unique raw material or transportation medium availability conditions; or because locational decisions made long ago in response to quite different technologies and price stimuli are difficult to escape.

The crude oil input/product output weight ratio for U.S. refineries averages about 1.09; variations depend mainly on whether volatile fractions are burned for fuel or converted into petrochemical feedstocks. The locational balance is therefore tipped by relative input vs. output shipping costs. When deep-water port facilities are available, they exert a strong locational pull, since crude oil can be transported in very large (250,000 deadweight ton) tankers at a per ton cost about half that of the largest tankers practical for refined product shipment. If several such ports are available, markets may pull toward multi-refinery operation, scale economies permitting. When port channels are too shallow to accommodate supertankers (as was the case on the U.S. East Coast up to 1973)[12] or when markets far inland must be served, the availability of pipeline facilities can become a crucial consideration. Costs per ton mile transported vary more with the size of the pipeline than with the type of input or output transported, so much depends upon what pipelines have been built, which in turn may reflect various historical accidents. The central and south central United States are richly interconnected with both crude oil and product pipelines. As a result, decisions on whether to install refining capacity near crude oil fields or near markets are nearly a toss-up, hinging on numerous special factors. When crude shipping facilities are superior to product pipelines, as was the case in western Canada until the early 1970s, refinery locations are pulled toward markets. When on the other hand there are larger product pipelines, as between the Texas Gulf and the U.S. East Coast in the 1960s, refineries tend to be pulled toward crude oil sources. In short, the pattern is highly varied.

To sum up, for the majority of the twelve industries, the simple model emphasizing scale economy vs. outbound transport cost tradeoffs pro-

12. See "No Superports for Supertankers," *Business Week*, May 20, 1972, pp. 108–110.

vides a good first approximation to the location-theoretic determinants of plant-size and numbers decisions. Petroleum refining and steel may be exceptions, but even in those input-oriented industries, end product market pulls play a significant role under many circumstances.

The Special Economies of Labor Inputs

In focusing on the weight contributions of production inputs, what for most industries is the most important single input—labor—tends to be overlooked. In a simple-minded sense, labor is available ubiquitously. But special skills may be highly localized. And perhaps more important, workers' subjective locational preferences and other immobilities prevent wage levels from being equalized at all points on the map. Wage rates for a given set of skill qualifications tend to be lower in certain regions or localities than in others. Or, as many of the interviewees emphasized, workers in less urbanized areas are often willing to work harder and more conscientiously for a given wage. Such low-wage and high-productivity centers exert a pull on plant location decisions, with possible implications for both plant size choices and the extent of multi-plant operation.

One source of low-wage pull is a whole region which is underdeveloped, underindustrialized, and/or experiencing an unusually large exodus of persons from low productivity farming. The southeastern and south-central states of the United States provide a classic example. Also, in all the nations covered by our study, with the possible exception of Sweden, there appeared to be a tendency for wage rates to be lower in small, relatively remote towns than in and around the larger cities, ceteris paribus.

This latter phenomenon has important implications. Plants are attracted to small towns by the prospect of paying low wages or experiencing a favorable work ethic. But small towns by definition have small labor forces. A plant of substantial size is almost inevitably a monopsonist in the small-town labor market. The labor supply curve it faces slopes upward perceptibly for at least two reasons. First, to hire more intensively within the town, ceteris paribus, it must draw workers away from leisure pursuits or alternative occupations of ascending (and perhaps rapidly ascending) opportunity cost. Or second, it may seek to expand its hiring extensively by drawing workers from outlying areas, but it can do so only by paying transportation costs rising with the distance commuted. And unless the plant can practice monopsonistic wage discrimination, which as a rule is difficult, the increase in the wage paid to *marginal* workers is likely to raise average wages not only through its direct contribution but also by driving up the wages of inframarginal workers demanding equal treatment. Thus, the more workers the plant hires, the higher will be its average wage. In large labor markets this monopsony effect is absent or minimal. The general wage level may be higher than in small towns, but average wages are not apt to be affected much by any single plant's hiring decisions.

The effect of labor market monopsony on plant size decisions is exactly analogous to the effect of outbound transportation costs, as illustrated in Figure 2.2. It is only necessary to relabel the UTC curve, calling it an "average wage premium curve." Then the more rapidly the average wage premium curve rises, reflecting an increasing degree of labor market monopsony, ceteris paribus, the smaller will be the size of the average total cost minimizing plant in comparison to that output volume which yields all technological economies of scale. And for a firm of given size which chooses to locate its plants in small towns, the more extensive will be its degree of multi-plant operation.

A complication reinforces this conclusion. Just as monopolists must worry about setting prices which encourage the entry of competing sellers, small-town plants must be concerned with the potential entry of competitors for their labor supply. Setting high wages can discourage such entry, but defeats the purpose of locating in a small town. If the plant exercises great restraint in its hiring, it is apt to keep wages sufficiently low and labor supply sufficiently slack that a rival plant is invited to enter, with potentially adverse effects on wage levels and operating flexibility.[13] Fearing this, companies operating plants in small towns normally take pains to avoid having their plants employ a very large fraction of any single local labor force, thereby holding their vulnerability to competitive entry within acceptable bounds. This too constrains plant sizes and encourages multi-plant operation.

Of the twelve industries in our interview sample, shoes and weaving exhibited by far the strongest propensity to locate plants in small towns in order to take advantage of low wage rates. A weaker tendency was evident in the antifriction bearings industry, at least for new plants, although skill agglomerations at such traditional bearing manufacturing

13. To be sure, entry may be deterred by potential entrants' fear of a wage-rate war. Potential entrants' recognition that entry on any appreciable scale can have a significant "percentage effect" may contribute to the persistence of low wages in small towns. Interviews with low-wage companies revealed that industries customarily paying somewhat higher wage levels were considered to pose the most serious threat of entry into monopsonized labor markets. Operating at a productivity disadvantage (analogous to a production cost disadvantage in the theory of sellers market entry deterrence), the original low-wage plant is not able profitably to deter entry over the long run. See Scherer, *Industrial Market Structure and Economic Performance*, pp. 219–230; and Darius W. Gaskins, Jr., "Dynamic Limit Pricing: Optimal Pricing under Threat of Entry," *Journal of Economic Theory*, 3 (September 1971), 306–322.

centers as Schweinfurt, Germany; Gothenburg, Sweden; Paris; and Canton, Ohio exerted a partly countervailing pull. U.S. cigarette plants have been located exclusively in Virginia, North Carolina, and Kentucky to take advantage of relatively low wages and permissive work attitudes, but the preferred locations have been moderately large cities, not small towns.[14] No similar attraction toward low-wage areas could be detected in the five other national cigarette industries covered by our research. There was also some indication that refrigerator manufacturing gravitated toward medium-sized towns in low-wage areas (such as the south-central United States and northern Italy) and in a few cases (most strikingly, Amana of Amana, Iowa; 1970 population 550) in small towns. But numerous counterexamples exist, such as General Electric's Chicago plant and the AEG-Linde plant in the heavily industrialized Frankfurt, Germany, area. In the remaining seven industries, systematic wage differentials frequently influenced the specific choice of a plant location (for example, between Dallas and Fort Worth), but only when other considerations such as access to markets and availability of raw materials were essentially equal. They were not sufficient to pull plants far from what, given wage parity, would otherwise have been optimal locations. Thus, in only two or at most five of the twelve industries did the attraction of small-town, low-wage labor significantly constrain plant sizes and encourage dispersed multi-plant operation.

Since all firms presumably desire to reduce costs when they can, why should only certain industries be drawn toward a plant strategy taking advantage of low-wage or high-productivity labor supply pockets? What distinguishes the various industries in this regard? Three main characteristics appear relevant.

One is an emphasis on skills which can be acquired quickly, without a costly investment in on-the-job training. This emphasis minimizes both the costs of starting up without a trained labor force and the human capital losses should new labor market entry occur, depleting one's work force. Thus, a farm girl who knows how to sew can become proficient in the main operations of shoe assembly in a very few weeks. The small-town youth who has built a hot rod requires not much longer to learn how to operate an automatic screw machine, one of the most complex machines in a ball bearing plant. Still this characteristic, although important to locating in a small rural town, is clearly not a sufficient explanation, since many plants with even lower on-the-job training requirements remain in the large cities.

14. The pull of locally grown leaf tobacco was said to be unimportant compared to labor market considerations.

A more compelling factor may be a technology such that the minimum optimal scale involves a relatively small work force—one small enough not to impinge heavily on a small town's labor supply. Or at least, the scale economy sacrifice owing to building a small plant must be sufficiently modest that it does not consume the wage savings small-town operation permits. That is, the long-run unit production cost curve must be fairly flat beyond that scale of operation compatible with small-town labor supply conditions. This argument, it must be noted, comes dangerously close to ensnaring us in circular reasoning, since the shape of the long-run production cost curve and hence the value of the MOS may depend upon the height and elasticity of the labor supply function assumed. Caution is therefore advised.

Third, transportation costs matter. Locating in a low-wage area makes little sense if the savings are frittered away transporting raw materials from distant sources. Or more important for the twelve-industry sample, outbound shipping costs high in relation to product value are likely to pull production toward markets even though lower wages beckon elsewhere. Remote low-wage locations will in general attract only those industries with transportation costs modest in relation to product value. This is a prominent and common feature of the shoe, weaving, bearing, and cigarette industries—the only ones with plants drawn strongly toward low-wage areas. Furthermore, experience in the first three industries suggests, low product transportation costs not only *permit* location in low-wage areas, they may actively *encourage* it. For if tariff barriers are moderate, the penetration of imports from low-wage nations is relatively easy if transport costs constitute only a small fraction of product value even on long shipments. Thus, competitive pressure may drive producers to seek low-wage sites to the extent that other conditions permit.

It is important to note that the MOS labor force requirement and transport cost factors are apt to interact in their effect upon the extent of multi-plant operation. When a large labor force is needed and outbound shipping costs are high in relation to F.O.B. mill values, plants will be decentralized to urban locations near demand nodes. With a large labor requirement and low shipping costs, plants may gravitate toward cities in low-wage regions, as in the U.S. cigarette industry. In both cases, wage patterns per se should have no strong systematic effect on the extent of multi-plant operation; the main consideration will be the trade-off between scale economies and transport costs. The lower transport costs are, the stronger will be the agglomerating forces and the less likely will be the operation of multiple small plants, ceteris paribus. When plants require only a small labor force and product transport costs are high, production will be drawn toward demand centers, settling in low-wage peripheral towns if they exist. Nationwide producers in geographically vast countries will then operate numerous plants. Finally, when the required work force is small and product transportation costs are low, multi-plant operation may be a direct consequence of firms' attempt to spread production over numerous small towns to avoid monopsonistic labor market repercussions.

The Dynamics of Plant Size and Multi-Plant Decisions

The analysis thus far has been largely static, implicitly assuming that firms move freely along long-run cost functions to optimal plant structures. This is a fair first approximation, but no more than that. Dynamics makes a difference because factories, major processing units, and production lines are often lumpy. Movement to points on the long-run production cost curve may therefore take place in jumps, and, once such a jump is made, it constrains the options open in future choices. Thus, a 4 million ton per year pig iron works built in four 1 million ton capacity blast furnace stages is not the same, nor does it enjoy as low unit costs, as an installation with two 2 million ton furnaces. Lumpiness problems of this nature are particularly important in the steel, petroleum refining, cement, bottle, and refrigerator industries, but they also occur in attenuated form elsewhere. For instance, it is a fairly simple matter to knock down a wall, pour new concrete, and install twenty-four new looms at a textile plant, but certain complementary machines (such as sizing units) can be added only on a scale large in relation to the volume of a minimum optimal scale plant. For a closer approximation to the determinants of plant size, plant efficiency, and multi-plant operation, therefore, it is necessary to examine the dynamics of plant investment.

The Single-Plant Investment Size Decision

The essence of the problem is that investment occurs in discrete lumps, providing an increment of capacity which will satisfy growing demand for some time to come. The larger the investment lump, the longer will be the time interval before a further plant expansion is required. Economies of scale exist, so building larger capacity increments leads to lower capital costs per unit of capacity. But building a very large unit means that an outlay is incurred immediately for capacity which will not be needed until later, and whose provision might be deferred, freeing funds for alternate remunerative uses. Or in a more complex case, building a very large unit may involve accumulating a capacity deficit and incurring premium costs to satisfy or suppress current demands by other means. The decision-maker must trade off achieving scale economies against the cost of carrying excess capacity temporarily or sustaining a temporary capacity deficit. The question is, how large shall each capacity increment be and, hence, given some rate of demand growth, how long shall the interval between capacity expansions be?

Our approach to this problem is based, with only minor amendments, on the work of Alan S. Manne and associates.[15] Manne et al. devise an infinite recursion algorithm for comparing investments with differing time profiles. Its fundamental assumption is that each capacity expansion is precisely like the one before it in size and timing. This pattern will be exactly optimal if demand grows by a constant absolute amount per year and the scale economy technology is invariant over time.[16] Thus, the time lapse T between investments is the same for each cycle. If then capacity equals demand (in Manne's terminology, reaches a regeneration point) every T years, and if the absolute growth in demand per year is G, the size of each capacity increment will be GT. The present value of the investment costs associated with a capacity increment of size GT installed at time $t = 0$ is $f(GT)$.[17] The present value of the investment costs of *all* capacity increments over all time is defined as $c(G, T)$. $c(G, T)$ is to be minimized with respect to the decision variable T, the cycle length between investment increments. If a decision-maker were to project himself T years into the future, when the next cycle begins, the present value of all remaining investment costs from *that* vantage point (that is, at time $t = T$) is also $c(G, T)$. To be sure, one cycle has passed, but one cycle more or less at the end of an infinite chain discounted to present value is literally nothing. Now if the present value of all costs from T on as of vantage point T is $c(G, T)$, the present value of that stream viewed from $t = 0$ is $c(G, T) e^{-rT}$, where r is the appropriate discount rate. The present value of costs over all time from $t = 0$ is obviously the present value of costs associated with the first cycle plus the present value of costs following that cycle:

(2.7) $c(G, T) = f(GT) + c(G, T) e^{-rT}$.

Rearranging and solving for $c(G, T)$, we obtain:

(2.8) $c(G, T) = \dfrac{f(GT)}{1 - e^{-rT}}$,

15. See esp. Alan S. Manne, ed., *Investments for Capacity Expansion* (Cambridge: M.I.T. Press, 1967).

16. Assuming that demand grows geometrically (at a constant percentage rate) rather than arithmetically does not change the constant cycle time assumption under plausible conditions. See the proof by T. N. Srinivasan in Manne, *Investments*, pp. 151–156.

17. We assume infinite plant lives. On the relaxation of this assumption, see Manne, *Investments*, pp. 39–40.

which is to be minimized with respect to the cycle duration T. The derivative of (2.8) with respect to T is uninteresting unless specific content is given to the $f(GT)$ function. A simple but realistic approach is to assume that total investment cost is a power function of the amount of capacity installed, thus:

(2.9) $f(GT) = \alpha(GT)^\beta$,

where under the "two-thirds" scale economy rule we might expect β to be on the order of 0.67.[18] Substituting (2.9) into (2.8) and differentiating $c(G, T)$ with respect to T, we obtain the first order condition for a total investment cost minimum:

(2.10) $\beta = \dfrac{T_{opt}\, r\, e^{-rTopt}}{1 - e^{-rTopt}}.$

Even for this simplest case no easily interpretable solution emerges, although the optimal value of T is readily found by numerical methods. Before explicit examples are presented, however, it is important to note that neither G nor α appears in (2.10). The optimal cycle time T_{opt} depends upon the scale economies parameter β and the discount rate r.

To illustrate a typical case, let us assume (invoking the two-thirds rule) that $\beta = 0.67$, $r = 0.12$, demand increases by $G = 1000$ units per year, and $\alpha = \$1000$. Operating costs can also be taken into account. Let us assume that they are $50 for each unit produced. Unless they are subject to economies of scale, they do not affect the optimal cycle length, which is therefore determined solely by condition (2.10).[19] Figure 2.3 shows the present value of total investment plus operating costs for various values of T. Discounted total costs are minimized when plants are built or plant expansions are carried out every 6.3 years, the optimal capacity increment being $6.3 \times 1000 = 6300$ units.

It can be shown that for all but the special case of $\beta = 1$, a unique cost minimum exists at some positive cycle time T under the assumptions

18. Cf. John Haldi and David Whitcomb, "Economies of Scale in Industrial Plants," *Journal of Political Economy*, 75 (August 1967), 373-385.

19. Cf. Manne, *Investments*, p. 39. When there are economies of scale in operating costs associated with investing in larger steps, the optimal time between investments tends to be increased, all else equal. For example, letting the unit operating cost function be characterized as $UOC = \$25 + 222.73\,(GT)^{-.25}$, which lets unit operating costs equal $50 with capacity increments of 6300 units, leads to an increase in the optimal cycle time from 6.3 to 19 years. It is worth noting that when such operating cost scale economies are realized, increases in the demand growth parameter G lead to reductions in the optimal T, unlike the simpler case characterized by condition (2.10). Numerical analyses revealed that this effect is stronger at low values of β than at high values.

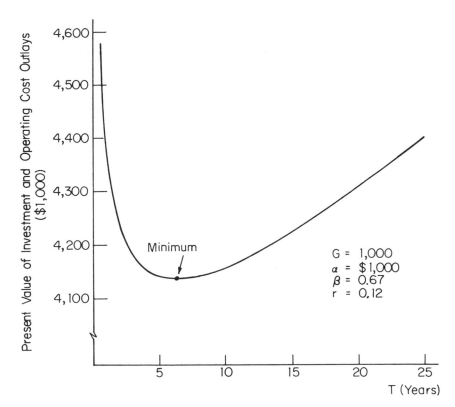

Figure 2.3. Present Value of Investment plus Operating Outlays for Alternate Cycle Times.

stated. As noted earlier, the optimum depends solely upon the values of β and r. Figure 2.4 demonstrates how the optimum varies with these parameters. For $1 > \beta > 0$, the higher the discount rate is, the shorter will be the interval between expansions and hence the more scale economies will be sacrificed, ceteris paribus. The higher β is, that is, the weaker the scale economy effect is, the shorter the interval between expansions will be. When $\beta = 1.0$ and investment occurs at constant unit cost, the interval falls to zero. Investment then takes place continuously in pace with the expansion of demand, since the absence of any unit cost advantage from building large finite increments leaves no justification for accepting temporary periods of excess capacity.

To repeat, the rate at which demand increases G does not affect the optimal interval between investments T in this model. This does not mean that the size of the capacity increments is invariant with G. On the contrary, for given values of β and r, the optimal T is determined,

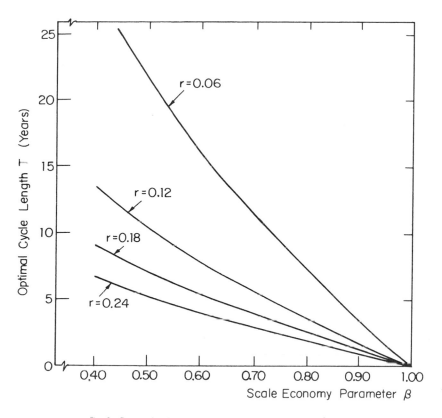

Figure 2.4. Cycle Length Optima for Various Values of r and β.

and for a given optimal T the absolute size of the capacity increment GT is larger, the larger G is. Thus, firms experiencing substantial annual demand growth (owing to having a large sales base to begin with or a high percentage rate of growth or both) will construct larger plants and plant increments than firms which experience small absolute growth, all else equal.

In at least one important respect, however, the size-invariant cycle result is unrealistic. The optimal T does not vary with G because equation (2.9) assumes no proportional diminution of the scale economy advantages from investments of increasingly large scale. Doubling the size of a 200,000 barrel per day petroleum refinery is assumed to yield the same percentage decrease in investment per unit of capacity as doubling the size of a 10,000 barrel per day refinery. But this is implausible. Sooner or later diminishing returns are likely to set in; thus, β is an increasing function of GT. The firm enjoying large values of G will probe this stage of diminishing returns more deeply than the firm with little annual demand growth, ceteris paribus. As $\beta \to 1.0$ for the firm making large expansions, the incentive to build still bigger increments and accept a commensurate temporary excess capacity burden attenuates. Therefore, the firm with large annual demand growth is likely to have shorter optimal intervals between expansions than low demand growth firms, all else equal. Its capacity increments will still be larger than those of the low G firm, since for an investment of the same size as that of the low G firm the high G firm will confront the same value of β, not yet having been held back by a rising β. They will simply not be larger in proportion to the difference in G values.

Single-Plant Decisions Allowing Capacity Deficits

Thus far it has been assumed that new capacity increments are brought on stream just in time to ensure that growing demands are satisfied. Excess capacity exists immediately after investment occurs, declining to zero just before the next investment jump takes place. The path described by the firm's capacity under these assumptions is shown by the heavy line in Figure 2.5a, while $D(t)$ traces the growth of demand over time, and the shaded area between the demand and capacity trajectories identifies the amount of excess capacity.

Frequently, however, producers choose to build up a capacity deficit before bringing a new increment on stream. This type of strategy is illustrated in Figure 2.5b. At time $t = 0$, capacity and demand are exactly in balance, that is, a regeneration point is attained. Rather than expanding its plant immediately, the firm allows a capacity deficit (horizontally shaded area) to accumulate. After Z years have passed from the point of regeneration, a sizeable capacity increment is added, ushering in a period of excess capacity (vertically shaded area). The excess capacity dwindles as demand grows until capacity and demand come into balance at time T and a new cycle begins.

During the capacity deficit period the firm cannot fully satisfy effective demand. Excess demand might be choked off by raising price, but this option is assumed to be precluded—in Manne's analysis focusing on nationalized enterprises in India, apparently because overall demand is highly price-inelastic or under some unarticulated "just price" rationale. For Western European and North American enterprises it seems more reasonable to assume that price is fixed on strategic grounds, for example, at the level which optimally deters new entry by outsiders, and hence is not available as a short-run capacity vs. demand balancing instrument. Interview evidence to be considered later suggests that such an assumption is not altogether unrealistic, though it is also much less than a perfect

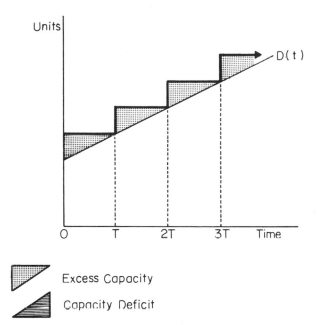

Excess Capacity

Capacity Deficit

Figure 2.5a. Investment with No Capacity Deficit Allowed.

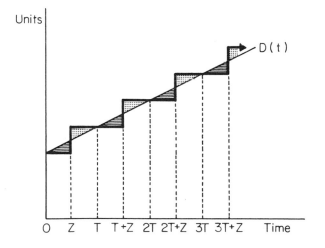

Figure 2.5b. Investment with Periodic Capacity Deficits.

approximation to reality.[20] We assume also that demands cannot be shifted over time; thus, orders unfilled during the capacity deficit period cannot be backlogged for completion after an expansion has created excess capacity. During the capacity deficit period, then, the producer must either satisfy its customers by obtaining additional supplies from outside through imports or purchases from competitors, or it must default on some orders, letting customers turn to competitors or go unsatisfied. In either case it incurs a penalty cost p for every unit of demand not satisfied from its own production capacity. Manne and his associate Donald Erlenkotter assume that imports are the sole source of deficit-covering supplies and define p to be the difference between the C.I.F. import price, adjusted to reflect the correct shadow price of foreign exchange reserves, and the domestic operating cost per unit. For a private sector firm, p might more appropriately measure the difference between the prices charged by rivals for deficit supplies and the marginal cost of internal production, the profit foregone on orders not filled, or the profit immediately foregone plus a discounted sum of future profits lost as dissatisfied customers switch their patronage more or less permanently to rival suppliers.

We proceed now to formulate an investment model incorporating these capacity deficit assumptions. Time $t = 0$ is calibrated as the first regeneration point, when capacity exactly equals demand. As demand grows penalty costs begin to mount. Their discounted present value during the first cycle is

$$\int_0^Z pGt\, e^{-rt}\, dt,$$

assuming that the next capacity increment comes on stream Z years after the regeneration point. The investment outlay at $t = Z$ (occurring by simplifying assumption instantaneously) depends upon the size of the increment GT, as in equation (2.9). To bring it back to present value, it must be multiplied by the discount factor e^{-rZ}. The capacity lump GT is sufficient to satisfy all previously unmet plus new demand until $t = T$, when a new cycle begins. By the recurrence logic of equation (2.7), total investment plus penalty costs over all such cycles can be written:

(2.11) $c(T,Z,G) = \int_0^Z pGt\, e^{-rt}\, dt + e^{-rZ}\alpha(GT)^\beta + e^{-rT}\, c(T,Z,G).$

$\quad = \quad$ (first cycle $\quad + \quad$ (first cycle $\quad + $ (all subsequent
$\quad\quad$ penalty cost) $\quad\quad$ investment cost) $\quad\quad$ cycle costs).

20. For a quite different approach emphasizing the effects of diverse market structures and pricing policies on plant sizes in a comparative statics framework, see Yoram Barzel, "The Evolution of Industrial Structure," paper presented at the meetings of the Econometric Society, December 1971.

Integrating, rearranging, and solving for $c(T,Z,G)$, we obtain:

$$(2.12) \qquad c(T,Z,G) = \frac{\frac{pG}{r^2}(1 - e^{-rZ} - rZe^{-rZ}) + e^{-rZ}\alpha(GT)^\beta}{1 - e^{-rT}}.$$

This is to be minimized with respect to the two policy variables Z (reflecting the length of the capacity deficit period) and T (reflecting the total cycle length). By a proof too intricate to reproduce here,[21] Donald Erlenkotter has shown that when the penalty cost p is a constant, the optimal values of Z and T are uniquely related by the function:

$$(2.13) \qquad Z_{opt} = \frac{r\,\alpha(GT_{opt})^\beta}{p\,G}.$$

Substitution of (2.13) into (2.12) permits some simplification, but the resulting cost function and its derivatives are too complicated to yield simple analytic solutions. We therefore bypass the additional manipulations and proceed to summarize the insights provided by Erlenkotter through numerical analysis.[22]

One point can be seen merely by inspecting (2.13). As the penalty cost tends toward infinity, the optimal value of Z tends toward zero, implying no capacity deficit at all. It follows obversely that when the penalties associated with buying from other suppliers or leaving some customers' wants unfilled are *not* prohibitive, it generally pays to accumulate at least some capacity deficit before bringing a new capacity increment on stream.

A second very important point is closely related. When penalty costs are finite, the optimal investment cycle and hence the optimal capacity increment size GT are always larger than they would be if no preinvestment capacity deficit were tolerated. The lower the penalty cost p is, the longer will be the optimal cycle length, ceteris paribus. This means inter alia that easy access to backup supplies during deficit periods is conducive to the achievement of scale economies.

Erlenkotter also shows that when p has low values, it is no longer true that the optimal cycle length increases monotonically with decreases in the scale economy parameter β and the discount rate r. It was shown earlier that as $\beta \to 1.0$ the optimal cycle length approaches zero because, with little or no scale economy advantage to be gained from building a large plant, there is little incentive to commit one's money to

---

21. See Manne, *Investments*, pp. 166–170.
22. Ibid., pp. 162–166.

investments well in advance of demand. However, when deficit-filling supplies can be obtained outside at low penalty cost, an increase in β and hence a diminution in the percentage cost saving from constructing large units may lead to a prolongation of the cycle not because large units are so attractive, but because the scale economies realizable internally are so meager that it is worthwhile relying on outside supply sources for a long time before undertaking a (large) investment. In other words, the interaction between low penalty cost and modest scale economies tilts the "make vs. buy" tradeoff decision increasingly toward buying. Likewise, when penalty costs are quite low, increases in the discount rate beyond 10 or 15 percent induce increases in cycle length, not decreases. This is evidently so because the combination of a high discount rate and low penalty cost greatly attenuates the discounted cost of heavy reliance on outside suppliers in the later years of a protracted deficit period, again tilting the decision toward extended "buying," with corresponding deferral of investment in one's own production facilities.

Note that in attempting to explain the common sense of the Manne-Erlenkotter p, β, r interaction results, we have stressed the outside purchase cost premium interpretation of p. This is a crucial point. For alternative interpretations it is probably quite unrealistic to assume that p is a constant. Thus, the longer customers are left dissatisfied owing to capacity deficits, the more likely they are to defect more or less permanently to rival suppliers, and hence the greater will be the future sacrifice of quasi rents on lost sales. In this case p becomes an increasing function of Z. This may also be true in the case of outside purchases, for the longer and more heavily a firm remains dependent upon rivals for supplies of its product, the more vulnerable it becomes to foreclosure by, and/or defection of customers to, the rival source. Consequently, even when the penalty cost variable p is low during the early stages of a capacity deficit period, it will in a rivalrous situation tend to rise with the length and size of the deficit, thereby nullifying the tendency for the optimal cycle time T to increase with increasingly high values of β and r.

To sum up, the Manne-Erlenkotter analysis of optimal dynamic investment choices indicates that firms will build larger production units, and hence take fuller advantage of scale economy opportunities, the larger the absolute annual demand growth they experience and the lower are the cost and customer defection penalties from permitting capacity deficits to develop. Also, but less confidently, larger capacity increments are likely to be chosen, the lower is the rate at which firms discount future cash flows and the stronger and more pervasive are the opportunities for reducing cost through large-scale investment, ceteris paribus.

Multi-Location Investment Dynamics

Thus far we have said nothing about the geographic location of investments made. Implicitly, a single plant site has been assumed, but unless early investments include overhead facilities making it possible to add later stages at lower incremental cost,[23] a firm might well locate successive investments at different sites in the same general market area, in which case a pattern of multi-plant operation will gradually emerge. When product transportation costs are appreciable, the firm might deliberately disperse its successive capacity increments over the geographic submarkets it serves.

When this possibility is recognized, it is natural to suppose that there might be some best way to phase investments among the diverse sites so as to minimize combined capital, operating, penalty, and transportation costs. On this point Manne and Erlenkotter have also made major analytic contributions which we now summarize.

One possible approach is to assign each plant a market territory by some procedure similar to the static production cost vs. transport cost tradeoff analysis presented earlier and then to make each plant respond to demand growth autarkically. Thus, suppose a firm decides that transport costs warrant operating two geographically separated plants, one serving market 1 and the other market 2. Demand grows at the rate of 100 units per year in market 1 and at 50 units per year in market 2. For plants built in either territory the discount rate is 12 percent, the scale economy parameter $\beta = 0.67$, unit operating costs are invariant with plant size or location, and we tentatively assume capacity deficits are precluded. Under these simplifying assumptions, the interval between investments does not depend upon the demand growth parameters G_1 and G_2. From Figure 2.3 we ascertain that the cost-minimizing $T \simeq 6.3$ years. Every 6.3 years a capacity increment of 630 units will be added at plant 1, and plant 2 will be expanded by 315 units.

This strategy requires each plant to bear its own burden of excess capacity. When a capacity increment of GT units is added, the amount of excess capacity in annual units borne during the first investment cycle is the number of units available per year GT times the number of years T less the amount of capacity for which there is (growing) demand

$$= \int_0^T Gt \, dt.$$

Thus, excess capacity

(2.14) $E = T(GT) - \int_0^T Gt \, dt = GT^2 - \tfrac{1}{2}GT^2 = \tfrac{1}{2}GT^2.$

23. On the analysis of this problem, see Manne, *Investments*, pp. 95–101.

For plant 1 this is 1984.50 annual units before full capacity utilization is achieved and for plant 2 it is 992.25 units, making a total of 2976.75 annual units.

By coordinating investments and incurring transportation costs it is possible to reduce this excess capacity burden. Let us consider first the simplest alternate strategy, which Manne calls a "two-phase investment cycle." We assume provisionally that the same optimal value of T exists for both plants; that is, every 6.3 years plants 1 and 2 will add $6.3G_1$ and $6.3G_2$ units respectively to their capacity. What differs from the previous "single phase" strategy is the timing. We begin by calibrating time $t = 0$ at a regeneration point when capacity exactly equals demand at each plant. To meet growing demands, a capacity increment of $G_1T = 630$ units is built at plant 1. No investment is made yet at plant 2. Plant 1 uses its newly added capacity to accommodate not only its own demand, growing at the rate $G_1 = 100$ units per year, but also the excess demand in plant 2's assigned territory, growing at $G_2 = 50$ units per year. This involves a transportation cost of s_{12} for every unit shipped from plant 1 to market 2. With demand in the two markets together growing by 150 units per year, the plant 1 capacity increment will be fully utilized in $630/150 = G_1T/(G_1 + G_2) = N = 4.2$ years. Only then, at $t = N = 4.2$, is the capacity increment of 315 units installed at plant 2. Plant 1 then stops shipping output to market 2, freeing $G_2N = 50 \times 4.2 = 210$ units of capacity to meet the still growing demand in its own territory. Of plant 2's 315 unit capacity increment, 210 units are utilized immediately to cover what had been plant 1's contribution, the balance of 105 units being available to satisfy future local demand growth. These temporary excess capacity levels of 210 units at plant 1 and 105 units at plant 2 then decline linearly until $t = T = 6.3$, when demand has risen to equality with capacity at each site and a new cycle begins.

It is a simple matter to compute the total amount of excess capacity in the system with this modified investment phasing scheme. Between $t = 0$ and $t = N$, excess capacity at plant 1 declines linearly from 630 to zero at a rate of 150 units per year. That component of the total is $\frac{1}{2}(G_1 + G_2) N^2 = \frac{1}{2} \times 150 \times 4.2^2 = 1{,}323$ annual units. From $t = N$ to $t = T$ excess capacity at plants 1 and 2 is $\frac{1}{2}G_1(T - N)^2 = \frac{1}{2} \times 100 \times 2.1^2 = 220.5$ and $\frac{1}{2} \times 50 \times 2.1^2 = 110.25$ units, respectively. Total excess capacity during the cycle with a two-phase strategy is $1323 + 220.5 + 110.25 = 1653.75$ annual units. This is a substantial reduction from the 2976.75 annual units with an autarkic single-phase strategy.

Reducing excess capacity through some such phasing scheme exercises its favorable effect on cost by deferring investments as long as possible. Against the savings in excess capacity carrying costs is offset the transportation cost incurred shipping increasing amounts of output from plant 1 to market 2 between time $t = 0$ and $t = N$. During the first cycle this is

$$\int_0^N s_{12} \, G_2 t \, dt.$$

If shipping cost per unit s_{12} is quite high, total transportation costs may outweigh the savings attributable to reduced excess capacity, and discounted *total* cost will be minimized by letting each plant serve its territory and carry out its expansion investments autarkically. Manne found that two-phase cycles saved less than one percent of total discounted investment, operating, and transportation costs relative to optimal single-phase cycles in the Indian cement industry, with rail transport costs amounting to roughly 36 percent of plant costs on a shipment of 350 miles.[24] On the other hand, when unit shipping costs are more modest, substantial savings can result from coordinated two-phase cycles. For the Indian caustic soda industry, with transport costs on a 350-mile shipment amounting to less than 10 percent of an MOS plant's unit production cost, Manne found discounted total costs using two-phase strategies to be 9 to 10 percent lower than with comparable single-phase autarkic cycles.[25] This inverse relationship between unit shipping costs and investment phasing savings is almost surely not monotonic, however, since with very low transport costs, dispersed end-market-oriented plants may no longer be optimal. In this case, any savings are more apt to be attributable to concentrating investments at a single plant complex than to phasing and cross-shipping among regionally decentralized plants.

Two complications must now be introduced. First, in addition to reducing excess capacity, optimally coordinated multi-region, multi-plant investment phasing also increases the optimal cycle time T, leading to more complete exploitation of potential scale economies, ceteris paribus. Given a set of regionally decentralized plants experiencing growing demand, the lower unit transport costs are, the more interplant shipping there will be, the longer the investment cycle will be, and the larger will be the capacity additions installed, ceteris paribus.[26] Transportation costs are in effect traded off against the realization of scale economies as well as the reduction of excess capacity. In this respect the unit transport cost variable s_{ij} is directly analogous to the capacity deficit penalty p in the earlier analysis of single-site investments. The less expensive it is to "import" deficit-covering supplies, from *either* outside

24. Manne, *Investments*, pp. 108–113.
25. Ibid., pp. 77–85.
26. Manne, *Investments*, pp. 66–68 and 202–205.

sources or one's own more remote plants, the more advantageous it will be to accumulate a substantial temporary deficit and then build a really big plant.[27]

Second, when the investment phasing problem is formulated in a less constrained form, it is no longer correct to speak of *the* optimal cycle length T. Rather, each plant may have its own optimal cycle interacting in complex ways with the cycles of other plants. Finding the optimal set of investment cycles and interterritorial product flows then becomes an extremely difficult mathematical programming problem combining the static features of equation systems (2.5) and (2.6) with the dynamic aspects emphasized in this section. Manne and Erlenkotter sought numerical solutions for specific cases in three different ways: through a heuristic algorithm, integer programming, and dynamic programming.[28] With the heuristic approach one can never be sure the optimum has actually been attained, while computational requirements with the programming formulations increase explosively when the number of regions considered exceeds three or four. Finding exact solutions for larger problems would overstrain the capabilities of even the largest digital computers. Yet even "nearly optimal" solutions imply attractive payoffs. Relative to the best two-phase solutions, Manne was able, using his heuristic algorithm, to find complex investment phasing programs yielding discounted cost savings of 4.6 percent for the Indian cement industry and 8.4 percent for the caustic soda industry.[29] And for the caustic soda industry, we recall, the two-phase solution was in turn substantially less costly than the best autarkic single-phase strategy.

These, to reiterate, are economies realized by coordinating the investments of multiple plants over both time and geographic space. In other words, they are economies of multi-plant operation. To the extent that they are available uniquely to multi-plant firms, such firms should be expected to enjoy lower excess capacity costs and greater production scale economies than single-plant firms, all else equal. The actual importance of these multi-plant economies in our twelve-industry sample will be assessed later.

27. Note the emphasis on *either*, since buying outside and shipping from one's own plants may be substitute policies. This point will assume critical importance in Chap. 7.

28. Manne, *Investments*, pp. 193–236.

29. Ibid., pp. 229–235. A newer dynamic programming method yielded nitrogeneous fertilizer industry investment plans with discounted costs 7 to 10 percent lower than Manne's heuristic algorithm, which in turn had found a solution with costs 14 percent lower than the best single-phase strategy. Donald Erlenkotter, "Capacity Planning for Large Multilocation Systems," Western Management Science Institute Working Paper No. 197, University of California at Los Angeles, February 1973.

Run-Length Economies, Inventory Policy, and Plant Specialization

Up to this point we have been concerned with scale economies resulting from building whole plants or plant additions of substantial size, without regard to the mix of products manufactured within those plants. We shall call such economies, whose analysis dominates the U.S. industrial organization literature on scale economies, *plant-specific* economies. There is, however, another set of scale economies embedded not in overall plant sizes but in the lengths of production runs for individual products. These will be called *product-specific* scale economies.

The simplest case occurs where many different items are produced on a given machine or assembly line and fixed costs must be incurred to reset the machine or change the line over from one product to another. For example, setting up a roller printing press to print cotton or synthetic dress cloth takes about two hours. Once the press is ready, a 10,000 yard run, more or less standard among U.S. producers, can be completed in roughly eight additional hours. Thus, the fixed costs of setup account for approximately 20 percent of total machine and attendant time. If the run is only 5,000 yards, which is more typical in the smaller Canadian dress goods market, setup time rises to a third of the total time requirement. The shorter the run, the higher is the setup cost per unit.

When production is not on a strict to-order basis, decisions on how long a run to authorize involve a tradeoff between minimizing unit setup costs vs. minimizing inventory carrying costs. The logic is illustrated by the simplest variant of the classic "economic lot-size" problem.[30] Let D be the quantity demanded per unit of time (that is, per week). The fixed cost of setting up a run is F dollars; the variable cost of production is assumed to be constant at C dollars per unit; and the cost per week of holding inventory (including capital, storage, and obsolescence or spoilage charges) is a fraction h of the variable production cost invested in the inventory. The problem is to find how large a lot Q to schedule for production. A lot of size Q will accommodate demand for Q/D weeks. The setup cost per unit is F/Q. Assuming the simplest possible case, that inventory replenishment takes place instantaneously at the moment in time when stocks have declined to zero, the inventory is Q at time $t = 0 + \delta$ ($\delta \to 0$) and declines linearly to zero at time $t + Q/D$ weeks. Thus, the *average* inventory in any given cycle is $\frac{1}{2} Q(Q/D) = Q^2/2 D$ unit weeks. Dividing through by Q yields the average inventory in unit weeks per unit produced $Q/2D$. With carrying costs of hC per unit stocked per week, average inventory cost per unit produced must be $hCQ/2 D$.

30. Some version of the problem is found in nearly any operations research text. See, e.g., Harvey M. Wagner, *Principles of Operations Research* (Englewood Cliffs: Prentice-Hall, 1969), pp. 803–807.

Average total cost is the sum of average setup, variable production, and inventory costs:

$$(2.15) \qquad ATC = \frac{F}{Q} + C + \frac{hCQ}{2D}.$$

Differentiating with respect to Q, setting the derivative equal to zero, and solving for the minimum-average-cost lot size Q^*, we obtain:

$$(2.16) \qquad Q^* = \sqrt{\frac{2DF}{hC}}.$$

The size of the optimal production lot rises with the square root of demand, that is, less than proportionately. It falls with increases in the cost of holding inventory.

Several more complex lot-size economies also deserve mention. When very long, standardized runs can be achieved, it may be possible to employ a completely different production technique and realize substantial savings. Thus, low- and medium-volume antifriction bearings are generally produced on a job-shop basis. This approach entails heavy setup costs as machines are switched from one type to another and the carrying of large semifinished parts inventories awaiting the next stage of production. However, if a large enough volume of a single bearing type can be sustained, it becomes advantageous to adopt a "straight-line" operation featuring metal cutting and grinding machines assigned full-time to that bearing; automatic work transfer devices to eliminate manual handling of parts and minimize in-process inventories; and specialized labor-saving equipment to check tolerences, match parts of the proper dimensions, and assemble and pack the parts automatically. Manufacturing cost savings as high as 50 percent can be gained by shifting from job-shop methods to such a straight-line operation, assuming that the necessary volume requirements are satisfied. Second, large lots and long runs may permit the realization of "learning by doing" economies, for instance, as workers develop dexterity in carrying out intricate assembly tasks.[31] Similar in principle are certain economies

---

31. See, e.g., Harold Asher, *Cost-Quantity Relationships in the Airframe Industry* (Santa Monica: RAND Corporation R-291, 1956); Armen Alchian, "Costs and Output," in Moses Abramovitz et al., *The Allocation of Economic Resources: Essays in Honor of B. F. Haley* (Stanford: Stanford University Press, 1959), pp. 23–40; Jack Hirshleifer, "The Firm's Cost Function: A Successful Reconstruction?" *Journal of Business*, 35 (July 1962), 235–255; L. E. Preston and E. C. Keachie, "Cost Functions and Progress Functions: An Integration," *American Economic Review*, 54 (March 1964), 100–106; and Leonard Dudley, "Learning and Productivity Change in Metal Products," *American Economic Review*, 62 (September 1972), 662–669.

associated with long steel strip mill and glass bottle machine runs. At early stages in the run there is a good deal of waste until the operators find through trial and error a set of machine adjustments which yields a high ratio of defect-free product. Finally, when long runs can be scheduled, managers and engineers can justify investing much more time and effort developing superior production layouts and methods than they can for short-run products.

It is clear that these product-specific scale economies are important. Even in the steel industry, where the economies associated with operating large-scale capital equipment units are substantial, company representatives stated in interviews that the cost savings potential from getting long runs is at least as great as the variation in cost attributable to differences normally encountered in mill and furnace sizes. By this relative cost variance criterion, product-specific economies are probably more important than plant-specific scale economies in fabric weaving and finishing, shoe making, bottle blowing, and bearing manufacturing, and quite possibly also in some nations' cigarette, paint, and refrigerator industries.[32]

The problems of achieving good-sized production runs are especially acute in small nations like Sweden and Canada, where firms appear to be not much more specialized than their large-nation counterparts and where characteristically higher seller concentration, and hence larger leading-firm shares of a product's total demand, is not sufficient to compensate in the optimal lot size equation for the small overall quantity of demand. Thus, Canadian textile makers claimed that their unit costs on style-sensitive dress goods and decorative fabrics were 20 to 30 percent higher than the costs of comparable U.S. manufacturers, primarily because of the tenfold difference in market size and the attenuated but still substantial differences in lot size. Paint manufacturers operating in both national markets reported that average batch sizes in Canada were one-fifth to one-half those experienced in the United States. Similar average run-length differences were cited by Canadian glass bottle manufacturers. A Canadian cigarette producer observed that it could not achieve enough volume to support the kind of straight-line, rolling-through-packaging setups used for the more popular U.S. brands.

32. For similar views, see the comment of P. J. Verdoorn in E. A. G. Robinson, ed., *Economic Consequences of the Size of Nations* (London: Macmillan, 1960), p. 346; D. J. Daly, B. A. Keys, and E. J. Spence, *Scale and Specialization in Canadian Manufacturing*, Staff Study No. 21, Economic Council of Canada (Ottawa, March 1968), pp. 20–21; Gunnar Ribrant, *Stordriftsfördelar inom Industriproduktionen* (Stockholm: Swedish Finance Department, 1970), pp. 175, 417–420, and 424; and C. F. Pratten, *Economies of Scale in Manufacturing Industry*, pp. 7–11 and 268–280.

Decoupled machines and intermediate in-process inventories were necessary to maintain production balance and good machine utilization. And in 1970 only one type of antifriction bearing was produced by a Canadian firm in sufficient volume to warrant a straight-line, machining-through-assembly operation.

The critical question for present purposes is not whether such market size-correlated run length differences exist, but whether they systematically affect plant size choices and whether large and/or multi-plant firms might be able to achieve longer production runs than smaller enterprises, ceteris paribus.

Lot Sizes, Specialization, and Plant Sizes

The key to any relationship between lot sizes and plant sizes is the ability of managers to cope with complexity. The complexity of a plant manager's task increases with both the size of the work force under his supervision and the number of physically different products assigned to his plant. As complexity increases, control of costs and product quality becomes more difficult and faulty decisions occur with increasing frequency, other things being equal.

If there were a rigid optimum number of products a plant manager could supervise under particular technological conditions, plants in a given industry would gravitate toward equal degrees of specialization even in markets of widely varying size. Then firms enjoying long production runs, for instance, because they serve large markets, would operate larger plants on the average than companies producing the same array of products in smaller quantities.

It seems more plausible, however, that the complexity of the plant management task and hence both salaries for managerial staff and the costs attributable to control loss rise more or less continuously and at an increasing rate with the number of products assigned. This means that the unit cost of management function (encompassing these two quite different kinds of costs) has the general shape illustrated by solid curve CM_1 and the broken curve CM_2 in Figure 2.6.[33] The difference between the two curves shown hinges on the size distribution of product demands served. Plant 2 with curve CM_2 experiences much lower demand per product and hence smaller optimal lot sizes than plant 1 with curve CM_1; therefore plant 2 has to supply more products and run more production lots than its high-demand counterpart to achieve any given total output.

33. See also E. H. Chamberlin, "Proportionality, Divisibility, and Economies of Scale," *Quarterly Journal of Economics*, 62 (February 1948), 229–262, who emphasizes the relationship between managerial costs and overall plant or firm size, with no separate attention to the lot-size distribution problem.

Unit costs of management accordingly rise more rapidly for small-lot plant 2.

Total unit production cost $LRPC_1$ or $LRPC_2$ is the vertical sum of unit cost assuming perfect but costless managerial control, designated by curves $LRPC_1^*$ and $LRPC_2^*$ in Figure 2.6, and the unit cost of manage-

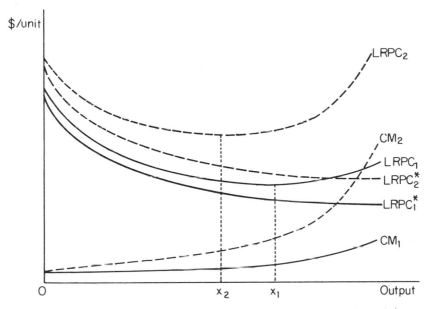

Figure 2.6. Effect of Product Mix and Managerial Costs on the Minimum Optimal Scale.

ment function CM_1 or CM_2.[34] The least total unit cost scale of production is larger for the large-lot plant (OX_1) than for the small-lot plant (OX_2). The small-lot plant makes the best of its plight, but it suffers a triple

34. The links between lot sizes and the slope of LRPC* are complex. We have shown an upward parallel shift for the smaller lot-size plant, assuming the market demand for any particular product to be largely outside the firm's control, so larger plant volumes can be achieved only by assigning more products from a given size distribution and not by varying the volume produced of any assigned product. If on the other hand the number of products is fixed (but larger for plant 2) and only product volume and hence lot sizes are variable, the slope of $LRPC_2^*$ will be steeper at any given total plant output than that of $LRPC_1^*$, since the small-lot plant will for each product be operating at a steeper point on its product-specific unit cost curve. Reality no doubt lies somewhere between these extremes, implying larger optimal total outputs for small-lot plant 2 than Fig. 2.6 suggests. Further complications intrude when a plant's total output can be expanded only by adding products of increasingly small demand and hence encumbered by rising small-lot diseconomies.

penalty: (1) relatively high unit management costs due to the production of more products or, to say the same thing, a lower degree of plant specialization;[35] (2) a smaller overall plant output and hence the realization of fewer plant-specific scale economies owing to the expansion-choking effects of rising managerial costs; and (3) the higher product-specific costs associated with small production lot sizes. Thus, to the extent that firms serving small markets experience weaker individual product demands and hence (by some analog of equation (2.16)) smaller optimal production lots than firms supplying large markets, one should expect from the managerial control cost phenomenon to find smaller overall plant sizes and less product specialization in the more limited markets.

Lot Sizes, Specialization, and Multi-Plant Economies

Within a national (or perhaps multi-national) market of given size, is there any way large and (especially) large multi-plant companies can take fuller advantage of lot-size economies than smaller single-plant companies?

The answer hinges on the bases of the large firm's size. There are three main interesting cases. A large multi-plant company may owe its size to (1) producing essentially the same array of products as smaller firms, each product on the average in larger volume; (2) producing *more* physically distinct products than smaller counterparts, but with individual product demands no larger on the average than those of smaller enterprises; or (3) producing essentially the same array of products with a size distribution of product demands in any given spatial market similar to that of smaller firms, but serving more such spatial markets. Each warrants fuller discussion.

A firm which has somehow managed to secure a larger market share for its products while offering essentially the same product array enjoys advantages directly analogous to plant 1 in Figure 2.6. It will, of course, realize the large-lot production economies associated with its favorable product demand situation. In addition it can, without encountering prohibitive plant management costs, build relatively large plants specialized in a narrower range of products than the plants of rivals experiencing weaker product acceptance. With roughly the same overall product line breadth as rivals but a higher degree of plant specialization, it will tend

35. The number of products is necessarily higher because *total* unit production cost for the small-lot plant is minimized at a steeper LRPC* slope, whose absolute value must at the optimum equal the slope of the CM curve. Barring pathological CM curve shapes, this equality can occur only with more products and hence a more steeply rising CM curve slope.

toward more extensive multi-plant operation. Multi-plant operation in this instance is the manifestation of greater plant specialization and its attendant economies. These in turn are ultimately attributable to whatever set of factors (superior product design, more effective sales promotion, a pricing policy reflecting its lower production costs, or luck) is responsible for the firm's relatively large share of particular product markets.

Next is the case of the large firm whose size is attributable to producing *more* products in quantities no larger on the average than those experienced by smaller rivals. Here the scale economy vs. managerial cost tradeoff will lead our large firm to establish plants of roughly the same size and specialization as those of smaller, more narrowly based counterparts. With similar degrees of plant specialization but a broader array of products, the company will simply operate more plants than its rivals, ceteris paribus. Although such an enterprise might benefit from other multi-plant economies of types to be examined in Chapter 7, there is no reason to believe that it fares any better than smaller rivals in terms of production run-length economies. This conclusion holds a fortiori for firms whose multi-plant posture reflects an adaptation to producing *more* physically distinct items in lots *smaller* on the average than those of narrower specialists.[36]

Perhaps most interesting is the multi-plant firm whose size comes from serving multiple regional (that is, transport cost segregated) markets, in each of which it offers a product size distribution more or less similar to that of regional specialists. One might suppose that its production structure would merely replicate manyfold that of the otherwise comparable regional specialists. But this would be incorrect. If each regional plant of the multi-plant firm autarkically manufactures a full line, the products enjoying high demand will exploit the available lot-size economies more fully than low-volume products. Given diminishing returns in the product-specific scale economy relationship, the slope of the unit production cost function will be steeper for the low-demand than for the high-demand products in the range of single-region production volume. Under these circumstances autarkical regional production is incompatible with minimizing the sum of unit production plus transportation costs. It will pay to ship the low-volume products still experiencing steeply declining unit production costs farther than the high-volume products which have exhausted or nearly exhausted their product-specific scale economies. The production of low-volume items will therefore be concentrated at one or

36. Our company sample included several such firms.

a very few centrally located plants, while high-volume items will be supplied from the full panoply of decentralized plants.

Total costs must be lower under such a strategy, intelligently pursued, than with regionally decentralized production of every item, for centralization of a low-volume item's production will not occur unless the savings in manufacturing cost owing to pooling demands and taking fuller advantage of run-length economies outweigh the increases in shipping cost. To the extent that a multi-region, multi-plant firm can pursue this geographically unbalanced specialization strategy while a single-region specialist cannot, the multi-plant firm secures a cost advantage over the regional specialist actually producing low-volume items. Or if regional specialists drop such low-volume items from their lines, the multi-region firm is likely to accrue supranormal profits supplying those items both because of the lessened actual competition and because the unit cost disadvantage of regional specialists provides a generous ceiling for prices set under a limit-pricing strategy. Either way, the additional degrees of production assignment freedom available to the multi-region, multi-plant enterprise constitute a potentially significant advantage of multi-plant operation.

Whether multi-plant firms are actually able to achieve longer, more economical production runs by capturing larger shares of specific product markets and by centralizing the manufacture of low-demand products, and, if so, how much they can save by doing so, are empirical questions. They will be explored more fully in Chapters 7 and 8.

Uncertainty, Inventories, and Warehouse Location Decisions

An extension of the unbalanced specialization case deserves brief treatment. Just as savings may be realized by pooling all production of certain low-volume products at a geographically centralized plant, so also may economies result from centralizing inventory holdings.

Uncertainty and decision lags interact to create this opportunity. Contrary to the simplifying assumptions accepted for the economic lot-size model of equations (2.15) and (2.16), stocks cannot be replenished instantaneously. There is almost always a lag, which means that new orders must be placed before supplies have dwindled to zero. This alone poses no special problems. But the length of the lag is not always known confidently at the time of ordering. Moreover, product demand fluctuates from week to week so that one cannot be sure how long any given stock on hand will last before running out, causing costly delays in filling orders or even the loss of otherwise profitable sales. A delicate balance must therefore be struck between carrying additional "safety stock" vs. taking one's chances on "stock-outs" and the loss of sales.

There is an enormous literature on various scientific approaches to managing this inventory problem.[37] In such a vast forest, it is easy to lose sight of the single tree which concerns us here. To avoid this fate, a severely oversimplified example will be examined.

Suppose the "lead time" from placing an inventory replenishment order to the availability of newly produced goods for shipment is exactly four weeks. The average rate of demand experienced by a firm for a particular product in some market is 400 units per four-week period, but the flow of orders varies randomly over time, being normally distributed with a standard deviation σ of 120 units per four-week period. If the firm's production planners wait until inventory has fallen to exactly 400 units before issuing a replenishment order, the replenishment will on the average become available just when stocks have dwindled to zero. But there will be a substantial variation in actual outcomes; stock-outs will occur nearly half the time under such a rule. To reduce the incidence of stock-outs, the firm can adopt an ordering procedure providing for some safety stock, defined as inventory in excess of the 400 units expected on the average to be demanded before replenishment occurs. The larger the safety stock, the smaller will be the probability of a stock-out and the fewer will be the sales lost or back-ordered due to stock-outs. But of course, the larger the safety stock, the higher average inventory carrying costs will be.

Let us assume that management resolves this tradeoff arbitrarily, deciding that it will not permit lost sales or back-ordering on more than 2 percent of the units demanded during the average replenishment period. Thus, with average demand of 400 units during the replenishment period, it is willing to sacrifice no more than $0.02 \times 400 = 8$ unit sales. Safety stock must be held to provide protection against various peak demand contingencies except those involving the extreme high-demand tail of the probability distribution of demand, the allowable area of that stock-out tail (the surplus of demand over inventory weighted by the probability of its occurrence) being 8 units per lead time period. Eight units are equivalent to 0.0667 standard deviations, given the four-week standard deviation of 120 units. From tables of the standardized normal loss integral, it can be determined that to have an expected sales loss not

37. See, e.g., Charles C. Holt, Franco Modigliani, J. F. Muth, and Herbert Simon, *Planning Production, Inventories, and Work Force* (Englewood Cliffs: Prentice-Hall, 1960); Fred Hansmann, *Operations Research in Production and Inventory Control* (New York: Wiley, 1962); G. Hadley and T. M. Whitin, *Analysis of Inventory Systems* (Englewood Cliffs: Prentice-Hall, 1963); John F. Magee and David M. Boodman, *Production Planning and Inventory Control*, 2nd ed. (New York: McGraw-Hill, 1967); and Wagner, *Principles of Operations Research*, chap. 19.

exceeding 0.0667 standard deviations, one must hold safety stock equivalent to 1.1 standard deviations above mean demand, or in this case, 1.1 × 120 = 132 units.[38] The firm will therefore adopt an ordering criterion under which replenishment orders are placed when stock on hand falls to 400 + 132 = 532 units: the average lead time demand plus the safety stock. The *size* of the replenishment order placed at that time will depend upon optimal lot-size considerations similar to those embodied in equation (2.16).[39]

Under the conditions assumed, the safety stock is about 33 percent of mean demand during the lead time period. If demand were less variable over time, a smaller safety stock would suffice to satisfy the 2 percent out-of-stock criterion. For instance, if the standard deviation of demand is only sixty units per four-week period, all else equal, the required safety stock declines to forty-five units, or 11 percent of mean demand.

This link between the relative variability of demand and the size of the safety stock gives rise to a possible source of multi-plant scale economies. Consider a company serving multiple geographic markets for which transportation costs are sufficiently important to exert a pull toward decentralized operation. If demand fluctuations in the various regions are statistically independent,[40] the standard deviation of combined demand across all M regions is given by

$$\sigma_M = \sqrt{\sum_{i=1}^{M} \sigma_i^2}.$$

When each region has the same standard deviation, this reduces to

$$\sigma_M = \sqrt{M\sigma^2} = \sqrt{M}\sigma.$$

Thus, the standard deviation of demand rises less than proportionately with the number of regions over which pooling occurs, and, in the special case of identical markets, by the square root of the number of regions. This pooling of regional demands in turn permits a reduction in the proportionate amount of safety stock carried, assuming that the multi-

38. See Wagner, *Principles of Operations Research*, p. 819.

39. However, there is an interaction between the conditions governing the optimal lot size and those determining the optimal safety stock. Taking this interaction into account greatly complicates the analysis relative to our simple example, but the point made here is essentially unaltered. For a detailed example, see Wagner, ibid., pp. 811–821.

40. Statistical independence means that the intertemporal correlation r in demand fluctuations between regions is zero. When $r = 1$, e.g., because demand changes are linked entirely to economywide business cycles, σ_M rises in direct proportion to the number of markets and the safety stock holding economies discussed here vanish.

region firm maintains the same average ratio of stock-outs to total demand for all regions together as do autarkic regionally specialized plants. Figure 2.7 shows how the required safety stock varies in rela-

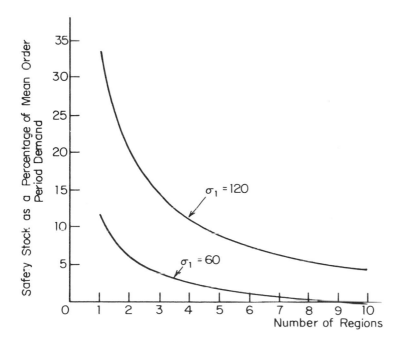

Figure 2.7. The Effect of Regional Demand Pooling on Safety Stock Requirements.

tion to combined average lead time period demand as pooling extends from two to ten markets, each with mean demand of 400 units per four-week period and a standard deviation σ_1 of 60 or 120 units. The more statistically independent regional markets the firm serves, the smaller can be the combined safety stock as a percentage of combined demand, ceteris paribus. Since inventory carrying costs rise roughly linearly with the size of the safety stock, the ability to pool implies an opportunity to realize significant savings.

There are, however, some offsetting costs. Their magnitude depends in part upon the locational adaptations induced by pooling. One conceivable strategy is to decentralize both production and warehousing, letting well-stocked warehouses cross-ship products into the natural markets of sister warehouses caught temporarily in a squeeze between low local safety stocks and high regional demand.[41] Interregional transportation costs are then incurred only for those shipments associated with out-of-stock emergencies. The main constraint on such a pooling strategy is the possibly considerable difficulty of maintaining an inventory control system with sufficiently up-to-date information and rapid response that orders can be matched continuously with dispersed stocks. At the other extreme is a strategy under which inventories are pooled physically as well as administratively, for example, in a common centrally located warehouse. This facilitates recordkeeping and control, but it means that *all* shipments to outlying points—including both routine dispatches and those accommodating peak demands—must travel substantial distances. It seems unlikely that safety stock reduction considerations alone could motivate much centralization of this nature for items whose production (and presumably also warehousing) would otherwise be most profitably decentralized toward end markets. Rather, the safety stock pooling economies are more apt to supplement the pull of production lot-size economies toward centralization of both production *and* warehousing.

If firms manufactured only a single product, the result of these combined pulls would be less multi-plant operation than would occur if the production lot consolidation or inventory pooling motives existed in isolation. In multi-product firms, however, matters become more complicated. We have seen earlier that optimization of production lot sizes vs. shipping costs may dictate a strategy of unbalanced geographic specialization under which high-volume products are manufactured at dispersed plants while low-volume items are produced centrally. If multi-plant operation is already advantageous for this reason, the realization of safety stock pooling economies unavailable to regional specialists adds to those benefits. Safety stock pooling economies exert an incremental pull inducing more centralization of low-volume production than would otherwise be the case.

A more difficult question is whether the advantages of safety stock pooling exert a *differential* pull toward centralization, that is, more strongly for low-volume than for high-volume items.[42] This would be so if the standard deviation of random demand fluctuations were a higher percentage of mean demand for low-volume than for high-volume items,

41. Actually, it may be possible to hold even lower safety stocks under this arrangement than the analysis underlying Fig. 2.7 suggests. As long as production orders are not pending at every plant simultaneously, stock-outs at one plant may be filled from the base-line inventory of another plant, whose replenishment order date will then simply be advanced.

42. See John F. Magee, *Physical Distribution Systems* (New York: McGraw-Hill, 1967), p. 136.

for example, because items demanded in high volume involve the pooling of more independent demand sources, as compared to larger orders from roughly the same number of sources. Then, as Figure 2.7 suggests, the slope of the average safety stock holding cost curve for the low-volume, high σ products will tend to be steeper than the slope of the curve for high-volume products, tipping the inventory cost-transportation cost tradeoff toward relatively farther shipping. Whether such a relationship holds is an empirical question.

Other considerations may also affect the balance. Lower-volume items will be scheduled into production fewer times per year, which, assuming equal production lead times, implies that the period of exposure to stock-out risks owing to inadequate safety stock is less per year than for frequently scheduled high-volume items. Management may therefore accept a relatively high risk of stock-out during the lead time period for low-volume items because the number of orders lost is small in relation to annual demand. The resulting diminution of safety stock requirements must attenuate the pull toward centralized warehousing. On the other hand, it is claimed that a major advantage in centralizing low-volume product inventories is the ability to consolidate numerous different stock items into larger outbound shipments, thereby gaining the lower freight rates associated with carloads, truckloads, or sizeable less-than-truckload consignments.[43] Since shipments are usually dispatched to specific geographic points, however, it is not obvious why similar pooling advantages could not be realized by full-line regional warehouses shipping a shorter distance to the same end delivery points.[44] Clearly, the problem is extremely complex. Inventory pooling economies undoubtedly do exert a *general* pull toward centralization, reinforcing the centripetal influences of lot-size and plant scale economies. But it appears impossible to offer any strong a priori generalizations on whether inventory holding economies alone, untainted by other factors, pull low-volume products more strongly toward centralization than they pull high-volume items.

To the extent that inventory pooling economies are a centripetal force, the effect is likely to be less multi-plant operation, not more, all else equal. At the outset of the research underlying this book it was thought that an opposite linkage might also exist. Specifically, firms serving a national market often maintain a highly dispersed network of warehouses. Might not this decentralization of inventories also draw production toward decentralization? The answer, when cause and effect are properly disentangled, appears to be negative. High outbound transport

43. Magee, *Physical Distribution Systems*, p. 136.
44. An exception may occur when stop-in-transit privileges are attractive.

costs (including the costs associated with delivery delays) induce *both* plant and warehouse decentralization, and it is they, rather than the *resultant* dispersal of warehouses, which cause the observed centrifugal tendencies. Indeed, the dispersal of warehouses in response to prevailing transportation cost structures probably tends marginally to increase the degree to which production is centralized. If plants had to serve as their own warehouses, they would have to make many small shipments to low-volume customers at relatively high freight rates. This encourages decentralization of production. When companies disperse their warehouses more widely than their plants, shipments from plants to warehouses will generally be made in larger average quantities than shipments from warehouses to distributors or end customers. This means that on at least a substantial segment of the shipping radius, unit shipping costs are lower with warehouses serving as intermediaries than with direct shipment. If this were not so, the two-stage shipping strategy would not be adopted. The resulting flattening of the unit transportation cost curve must permit relatively greater exploitation of plant size and lot-size economies through production centralization, all else equal. Thus, it appears improbable on a priori grounds that the dispersion of warehouses, if effected rationally, can in its own right pull production toward a higher degree of multi-plant operation.

Invoking the logic of production plus physical distribution cost minimization, we have identified a number of plausible hypotheses concerning the determinants of plant size and the extent of multi-plant operation. Much of our effort in subsequent chapters will be devoted to extending these hypotheses and shedding empirical light on them. To be sure, other relationships involving such diverse variables as advertising, collusive practices, and economies of large-scale purchasing and finance will also be explored. Yet the grounding in location theory, dynamic plant expansion theory, optimal lot-size theory, and inventory theory is a key feature of this book's thrust into what has previously been terra incognita.

3

The Determinants of Plant Size: A Statistical Analysis

This chapter addresses four main tasks: comparing the average sizes of industrial production units in the twelve industries across the six nations, estimating how far and in what direction the observed average plant sizes deviate from the sizes required to realize all significant production scale economies, investigating the reasons for observed differences between optimal and observed sizes, and examining the rate at which actual plant sizes are converging toward the optimum.

A Comparison of Plant Sizes in the Six Nations

The natural jumping-off point for an international comparison of plant sizes is Joe S. Bain's pioneering study.[1] Bain's technique was to compare average employment in the twenty largest plants for each industry, defined in a standardized way. We have followed the same general procedure, though our approach to industry definition was slightly different. Like Bain, we have used the average size of plants in U.S. industries as our initial bench mark. However, while Bain appears to have applied a fixed U.S. bench mark industry definition as the basis of comparison with every other nation, our bench mark industry definitions here were varied to attain the closest possible match in each case. Thus, some nations report nonintegrated steel rolling plants and steel

1. *International Differences in Industrial Structure* (New Haven: Yale University Press, 1966), chap. 3.

foundries together with basic steel works; others separate them. Similar problems arise for most of the other industries in this sample. Since the U.S. Census of Manufactures four-digit classification is in almost every instance more richly subdivided than the industry data of the other nations, it was possible to combine the U.S. size distributions in varying ways to fit the specific definition used by another nation. By this means quite close matches could be obtained. Variable bench mark dates were also employed. Most of the non-U.S. data related to 1967 (or for France, 1966). In these cases 1967 U.S. Census enumerations were taken as the bench mark. However, for two German and eight British industries employment size distributions were available only for 1961 or 1963, and for the British glass bottle industry it was necessary to revert to 1954. In such situations bench marks were drawn from the 1963 or 1954 U.S. Censuses of Manufactures. Details of the definitions and years can be found in Appendix Tables 3.1 through 3.6. A more complete discussion of data sources and definitions, noting among other things the problems encountered and (at least partly) solved in securing uniform census definitions of a "plant," is provided in Appendix A.

Text Table 3.1 compares the average sizes of the largest twenty plants in each nation's industries with the U.S. bench marks, indexing at 100 the average size of the top twenty U.S. plants in each most closely corresponding industry. When an industry had fewer than twenty plants in total, the average size of all plants is compared to the U.S. twenty-plant bench mark, and the number of plants covered is indicated within subscripted parentheses. From the summary mean and median relative size statistics presented at the bottom of Table 3.1, it would appear that average plant sizes are about the same in Germany as in the United States, slightly smaller in the United Kingdom, and considerably smaller in Sweden, Canada, and France.

Despite substantial differences in coverage, these results parallel very closely the summary statistics reported by Bain, as Table 3.2 shows. Bain's data were largely for 1954 and 1957, ours for 1961 through 1967. His sample is larger and there is direct overlap for only three to seven industries. Yet the national median relative plant size indices are quite similar. Evidently our sample, though smaller, is not grossly unrepresentative.

The comparison for Sweden would be even closer were it not for an error in Bain's procedure. The Swedish industrial plant size distribution series used by Bain and ourselves counts only *arbetare*, or wage earners. It excludes salaried employees, who in 1967 accounted for 26 percent of all employees in Swedish manufacturing and mining industries. Bain relates the *arbetare* averages to U.S. averages including all employees,

Table 3.1. The Average Number of Employees in the Largest Twenty Plants in Twelve Industries and Six Nations, Expressed as a Percentage of Average Employment in the Top Twenty Plants in the Most Closely Comparable U.S. Industries.[a]

Industry	Nation					
	U.S.	Canada	U.K.	Sweden	France	West Germany
Brewing	100	23	100	13	27	61
Tobacco products	100	17	90	11$_{(5)}$	21	31
Cotton and synthetic fabrics	100	22	28	11	21	52
Paints and varnishes	100	40	174	29	58	143
Petroleum refining	100	17	41$_{(19)}$	8$_{(5)}$	39	n.a.
Shoes	100	32	95	15	34	113
Glass bottles	100	54$_{(9)}$	64	24$_{(6)}$	58	80
Cement	100	42	108	57$_{(9)}$	89	136
Steel	100	17	55	17	50	n.a.
Antifriction bearings	100	20$_{(5)}$	68	171$_{(2)}$	31	100
Refrigerators	100	n.a.	n.a.	n.a.	8	n.a.
Storage batteries	100	16	n.a.	n.a.	59	124
Mean of size indices	100	27	82	36	41	93
Median of size indices[b]	100	22	79	16	37	97

[a]When there were fewer than twenty plants, the average is computed for the total number of plants, which is indicated in subscripted parentheses.
[b]When the number of observations is even, the median is calculated as the simple average of the two central values.

Table 3.2. Comparison of Our Industry Sample Size Indices with Bain's, by National Median Indices.[a]

Nation	Number of industries in Bain's sample	Number of industries in our sample	Number of industries in common	Median industry index: Bain's sample	Median industry index: our sample
United States	34	12	7	100	100
United Kingdom	32	10	7	78	79
France	31	12	6	39	37
Canada	14	11	3	28	22
Sweden	27	10	6	13	16

Note: Bain's data were largely for 1954 and 1957, ours for 1961–1967.
[a]The Bain data are from *International Differences in Industrial Structure* (New Haven: Yale University Press, 1966), pp. 36–37.

which biases his relative Swedish plant size estimates downward. To avoid this bias we related the Swedish data to the size distribution of *production workers* for U.S. plants, making a further small upward adjustment in the Swedish estimates to correct for the generally higher fraction of salaried employees in Swedish plants, some of whom correspond to central office staff members not counted in U.S. plant employment data.

The Choice of an Unbiased Measure

The Swedish *arbetare* problem, however, is not the most important bias in Bain's methodology. Consider, for example, the Canadian steel industry. The Dominion Bureau of Statistics census report for 1967 shows forty-one plants assigned to the "Iron and Steel Mills" industry category. But a closer look reveals that there were only four establishments fully integrated from blast furnace operation through primary products rolling. All the others were specialty plants of one sort or another: "mini-mills" based on electric arc furnace technology, specialty rolling or extrusion mills, alloy steel works, and so on. Nearly every industry has its complement of "cats and dogs" plants which exploit special technologies or serve special market segments and which typically fill the small-plant tail of the plant size distribution. The smaller a nation is, the fewer plants in total it is likely to support and the deeper into that "cats and dogs" tail one will penetrate in enumerating the twenty largest plants. For many of the industries in Sweden and Canada, both very small nations in relation to the United States, the bias introduced by such a procedure is serious indeed. As a result, the "Top 20 Plant" criterion is ill-advised if one seeks to compare in a meaningful way the sizes of representative plants in nations of widely varying size.

To escape this bias problem we employ two alternate measures. One, which henceforth will be designated the "Top 50 Percent" size index, is found by moving down the plant size distribution, starting with the largest plants, until enough plants have been included to encompass 50 percent of total industry employment or output.[2] The average size of those plants which account for the top half of the cumulative employment or output size distribution is then calculated. The other, referred to as the "Midpoint Plant" size index, estimates the employment or output of that individual plant which is located at the 50 percent point of the cumulative size distribution.

Each index has advantages. The Top 50 Percent index assesses the

2. To the best of our knowledge, the first to use this measure were W. S. Comanor and T. A. Wilson in "Advertising Market Structure and Performance," *Review of Economics and Statistics*, 49 (November 1967), 423–440.

average size of those plants which constitute an industry's scale economy vanguard, while the Midpoint index provides information on the plant analogous to Alfred Marshall's "representative firm."[3] Estimating these indices from the data normally available is somewhat easier than estimating Bain's Top 20 Plant index for industries with large numbers of plants and somewhat more difficult for industries with relatively few plants. Nevertheless, the estimation accuracy problems which troubled Bain have been minimized,[4] partly by using an effective nonlinear estimation technique[5] and partly because our interviews nearly always provided independent information on the size of the largest plants. Consequently, blind extrapolation was seldom necessary when the largest census size cohort reported included many more than twenty plants or plants with much more than 50 percent of total employment. Though residual interpolation errors remain, they are undoubtedly much less serious than some other inherent errors to be considered shortly.

Tables 3.3 through 3.7 include the detailed size comparisons by nation for all three measures. Table 3.8 summarizes the comparisons. It presents both means and media of the nations' relative size indices. Since the indices bench marked to U.S. = 100 cannot fall below zero but are in principle unbounded upward, the means tend to be strongly influenced by large extreme values. Consequently, the national index media provide a somewhat better indication of central tendencies. Especially for Sweden, Canada, and France—the three smallest nations in our sample—it is clear by either measure that the Top 20 Plant criterion seriously understates the relative size of leading and representative plants. The suggestion that plants in those nations tend to be smaller than their U.S. counterparts remains, but it makes a big difference in scale economy implications whether the central tendency is toward 16 or 22 percent of U.S. size, as

3. *Principles of Economics*, 8th ed. (London: Macmillan, 1920), p. 317.

4. *International Differences in Industrial Structure*, pp. 27–30.

5. Cumulative size distributions were plotted on log normal probability paper, with the cumulative number of plants on the logarithmic axis and the cumulative fraction of output or employment associated with those plants on the normal probability axis. For an illustration, see Fig. 5.1 *infra*. Had the data followed a log normal distribution law strictly, the resulting plot would have been linear. This condition was seldom satisfied exactly, especially in the distribution's small-plant tail, where plant sizes nearly always tapered off more slowly than they would have if the distribution were strictly log normal. Smooth curves were therefore fitted to the plotted points. It was then a simple matter to locate the cumulative 50 percent point and the associated number of plants, or to count up to the largest 20 plants and determine the share of total employment or output contributed by those plants. Midpoint sizes were estimated by interpolation from size distribution tables when the number of plants was fairly large and by unit interpolation on the plotted distribution curve when a very few plants accounted for half of all industry activity.

Table 3.3. Indices of Relative Canadian Plant Sizes, Based on Most Comparable U.S. Industry Bench Mark = 100.[a]

Industry	Employment			Physical capacity or output		
	Top 20 Plants	Top 50 Percent	Midpoint Plant	Top 20 Plants	Top 50 Percent	Midpoint Plant
Brewing	23	$50_{(7)}$	49	n.a.	$32_{(6)}$	32
Tobacco products	17	$25_{(4)}$	38	n.a.	n.a.	n.a.
Cotton and synthetic fabrics	22	$75_{(8)}$	117	n.a.	n.a.	n.a.
Paints and varnishes	40	$103_{(14)}$	122	n.a.	n.a.	n.a.
Petroleum refining	17	$31_{(9)}$	38	23	$39_{(9)}$	58
Shoes	32	$51_{(44)}$	55	n.a.	n.a.	n.a.
Glass bottles	$54_{(9)}$	$94_{(3)}$	135	n.a.	n.a.	n.a.
Cement	42	$68_{(8)}$	80	59	$121_{(7)}$	127
Steel	17	$117_{(2)}$	171	$15_{(18)}$	$75_{(2)}$	89
Antifriction bearings	$20_{(5)}$	$29_{(2)}$	43	n.a.	n.a.	n.a.
Refrigerators	n.a.	n.a.	n.a.	$15_{(12)}$	$12_{(3)}$	16
Storage batteries	16	$34_{(5)}$	48	$17_{(18)}$	$37_{(4)}$	50
Mean relative size	27	61	81	26	57	68
Mean relative size, using physical output whenever possible	28	59	75			

[a]Figures in subscripted parentheses indicate the total number of plants in the Top 20 Plants column and the number of plants included to reach the 50 percent point in the Top 50 Percent column.

indicated for the Swedish Top 20 Plant media comparisons, or upwards of 47 percent with the Top 50 Percent and Midpoint indices. For the two smallest nations, the sizes of Midpoint plants also compare uniformly more favorably than the Top 50 Percent plants, evidently because the very largest plants exert less of a skewing effect than they do in the United States. On the other hand, in England and particularly in Germany, there are indications of even more skewness owing to a few unusually large plants.

Further Measurement Difficulties

Several further measurement problems complicate comparisons of leading or representative plant sizes on the basis of employment. The most serious arises as a result of interplant and international productivity differences. Particularly for the bulk processing industries such as cement, petroleum refining, and brewing, employment can be a meaningless indicator of true plant sizes because output per worker varies tremendously with the technology embodied. For example, the Schlitz

Table 3.4. Indices of Relative United Kingdom Plant Sizes, Based on Most Comparable U.S. Industry Bench Mark = 100.[a]

Industry	Employment			Physical capacity or output		
	Top 20 Plants	Top 50 Percent	Midpoint Plant	Top 20 Plants	Top 50 Percent	Midpoint Plant
Brewing	100	77$_{(38)}$	79	30	30$_{(22)}$	29
Tobacco products	90	81$_{(8)}$	91	n.a.	n.a.	n.a.
Cotton and synthetic fabrics	28	28$_{(124)}$	28	n.a.	n.a.	n.a.
Paints, varnishes, and printing ink	174	340$_{(30)}$	315	n.a.	n.a.	n.a.
Petroleum refining	41$_{(19)}$	150$_{(3)}$	300	44	134$_{(4)}$	208
Shoes	95	97$_{(105)}$	78	n.a.	n.a.	n.a.
Glass bottles	64	86$_{(10)}$	65	n.a.	n.a.	n.a.
Cement	108	157$_{(13)}$	154	n.a.	n.a.	n.a.
Steel	55	65$_{(24)}$	75	33	43$_{(8)}$	52
Antifriction bearings	68	118$_{(5)}$	173	n.a.	n.a.	n.a.
Refrigerators	n.a.	n.a.	n.a.	34$_{(9)}$	21$_{(3)}$	24
Storage batteries	n.a.	n.a.	n.a.	21	110$_{(3)}$	110
Mean relative size	82	120	136	32	71	85
Mean relative size, using physical output whenever possible	66	104	111			

[a]Figures in subscripted parentheses indicate the total number of plants in the Top 20 Plants column and the number of plants included to reach the 50 percent point in the Top 50 Percent column.

Brewing Company's 4.4 million barrel per year brewery at Winston-Salem, North Carolina, completed in 1969, employed a total of 450 to 500 including supporting staff personnel. Roughly the same number of employees was required in 1971 to operate Schlitz' much older Brooklyn brewery, with a capacity of 1.0 million barrels, and some 1700 persons were employed to produce 5 million barrels per year at the company's Milwaukee brewery.

Employment comparisons are also misleading because of differences in product mix and the degree of vertical integration. For instance, in Europe and Canada it is much more common than in the United States to have plants producing washing machines, stoves, and other household appliances under the same roof as refrigerators. Counting total employment in such plants would overstate the size of the refrigerator operations, but detailed employment breakdowns by product within multi-product plants are extremely difficult to obtain. For specialized refrigerator plants product mix problems also intrude, since the typical European

Table 3.5. Indices of Relative Swedish Plant Sizes, Based on Most Comparable U.S. Industry Bench Mark = 100.[a]

	Employment			Physical capacity or output		
Industry	Top 20 Plants	Top 50 Percent	Midpoint Plant	Top 20 Plants	Top 50 Percent	Midpoint Plant
Brewing	13	13$_{(16)}$	17	3	6$_{(7)}$	7
Tobacco products	11$_{(5)}$	10$_{(2)}$	15	n.a.	n.a.	n.a.
Cotton and synthetic fabrics	11	47$_{(8)}$	55	n.a.	n.a.	n.a.
Paints and varnishes	29	121$_{(7)}$	143	n.a.	n.a.	n.a.
Petroleum refining	8$_{(5)}$	28$_{(1)}$	59	21$_{(5)}$	47$_{(2)}$	83
Shoes	15	27$_{(22)}$	23	n.a.	n.a.	n.a.
Glass bottles	24$_{(6)}$	57$_{(2)}$	78	n.a.	n.a.	n.a.
Cement	57$_{(9)}$	129$_{(3)}$	162	60$_{(7)}$	120$_{(3)}$	133
Steel	17	46$_{(6)}$	59	6$_{(15)}$	19$_{(2)}$	25
Antifriction bearings	171$_{(2)}$	209$_{(1)}$	344	n.a.	n.a.	n.a.
Refrigerators	n.a.	n.a.	n.a.	6$_{(20)}$	13$_{(2)}$	20
Storage batteries	n.a.	n.a.	n.a.	17$_{(6)}$	33$_{(2)}$	43
Mean relative size	36	69	96	19	40	52
Mean relative size, using physical output whenever possible	31	59	81			
Same, without bearings	19	46	57			

[a]Figures in subscripted parentheses indicate the total number of plants in the Top 20 Plants column and the number of plants included to reach the 50 percent point in the Top 50 Percent column.

refrigerator was much smaller and less complex than its U.S. counterpart, requiring less labor to assemble. Likewise, German, French, and British refineries transformed roughly 17 percent of their 1967 crude oil feedstocks into gasoline, while U.S. refineries utilized more elaborate (and more labor demanding) cracking, hydrogenation, alkylation, and other processes to achieve a 48 percent gasoline yield. U.S. weaving mills tend to have spinning operations integrated on the site whereas very few British mills are so integrated, and thus employment counts exaggerate the relative size of U.S. *weaving* operations. There is also some tendency for a broader array of blast furnace, steel conversion, and primary product rolling operations to be integrated at a single site in North America than in Europe, leading to higher apparent sizes for American works when employment size distributions are observed.

Many of these problems can be alleviated if not eliminated by using statistics on physical output or capacity rather than employment as the basis of comparison. This substitution proved feasible for every nation

Table 3.6. Indices of Relative French Plant Sizes, Based on Most Comparable U.S. Industry Bench Mark = 100.[a]

Industry	Employment			Physical capacity or output		
	Top 20 Plants	Top 50 Percent	Midpoint Plant	Top 20 Plants	Top 50 Percent	Midpoint Plant
Brewing	27	23(26)	25	17	18(16)	17
Tobacco products	21	15(9)	24	13[b](13)	9[b](5)	16[b]
Cotton and synthetic fabrics	21	27(85)	30	n.a.	n.a.	n.a.
Paints and varnishes	58	94(39)	85	n.a.	n.a.	n.a.
Petroleum refining	39	87(7)	139	46	112(5)	130
Shoes	34	85(76)	55	n.a.	n.a.	n.a.
Glass bottles	58	131(5)	130	n.a.	n.a.	n.a.
Cement	89	95(27)	90	81	116(18)	115
Steel	50	68(14)	111	28	47(6)	56
Antifriction bearings	31	65(4)	65	n.a.	n.a.	n.a.
Refrigerators	8	11(3)	14	35	36(2)	40
Storage batteries	59	112(5)	208	n.a.	n.a.	n.a.
Mean relative size	41	68	81	37	56	62
Mean relative size, using physical output whenever possible	40	71	79			

[a]Figures in subscripted parentheses indicate the total number of plants in the Top 20 Plants column and the number of plants included to reach the 50 percent point in the Top 50 Percent column.
[b]Output of cigarettes only.

with the brewing, petroleum refining, steel, and refrigerator industries and for every nation but the United Kingdom in cement[6]— the industries where employment data have the most serious drawbacks in making size comparisons. The output and capacity data were obtained from trade publications, unpublished trade association materials, individual company annual reports, and interviews. For some steel works it was necessary to estimate plant capacities from data on the physical dimensions of individual processing units, cross-checking the results against the limited information on capacity or output available. Steel plant sizes

6. However, physical output data form the basis of the British cement mill size estimates used in subsequent regression analyses. These were derived by estimating average 1963 output per plant for U.K. and U.S. plants with 50 or more employees (1.71 and 1.92 million barrels, respectively). Since the value added size distributions for the two nations appeared quite similar when plotted, the U.S. Top 50 Percent and Midpoint Plant physical output figures were then multiplied by 1.71/1.92 to obtain U.K. estimates.

Table 3.7. Indices of Relative German Plant Sizes, Based on Most Comparable U.S. Industry Bench Mark = 100.[a]

	Employment			Physical capacity or output		
Industry	Top 20 Plants	Top 50 Percent	Midpoint Plant	Top 20 Plants	Top 50 Percent	Midpoint Plant
Brewing	61	29$_{(95)}$	28	27	13$_{(79)}$	12
Cigarettes	31	24$_{(6)}$	28	n.a.	n.a.	n.a.
Cotton and synthetic fabrics	52	91$_{(57)}$	93	n.a.	n.a.	n.a.
Paints and varnishes	143	162$_{(52)}$	68	n.a.	n.a.	n.a.
Petroleum refining	n.a.	n.a.	n.a.	41	64$_{(10)}$	92
Shoes	113	103$_{(82)}$	72	n.a.	n.a.	n.a.
Hollow glassware	80	114$_{(16)}$	67	n.a.	n.a.	n.a.
Cement	136	171$_{(18)}$	150	71	97$_{(21)}$	100
Steel	n.a.	n.a.	n.a.	52	74$_{(7)}$	75
Antifriction bearings	100	123$_{(7)}$	185	n.a.	n.a.	n.a.
Refrigerators	n.a.	n.a.	n.a.	n.a.	71$_{(2)}$	74
Storage batteries	124	426$_{(3)}$	577	n.a.	n.a.	n.a.
Mean relative size	93	138	141	48	64	71
Mean relative size, using physical output whenever possible	76	114	120			
Same, without batteries	71	85	79			

[a]Figures in subscripted parentheses in the Top 50 Percent column indicate the number of plants included to reach the 50 percent point.

Table 3.8. Comparison of Three Measures of Relative Plant Employment Size for Five Nations, Based on Comparable U.S. Size = 100.

	Mean of national indices			Median of national indices		
Nation	Top 20 Plants	Top 50 Percent	Midpoint Plant	Top 20 Plants	Top 50 Percent	Midpoint Plant
Canada	27	61	81	22	51	55
United Kingdom	82	120	136	79	92	85
Sweden	36	69	96	16	47	59
France	41	68	81	37	77	75
West Germany	93	138	141	100	114	72

were in every case related to *steel ingot* tonnage capacities; rolling mill capacities, integrated or not, were not counted. Also excluded were all steel works whose output consisted mainly of stainless, tool, high-speed, and other special alloy steels. Thus, the physical comparisons focus on capacity for producing ordinary carbon steel ingots. Data for the battery industry were particularly meager, sometimes pertaining to employment, sometimes unit output, and sometimes a combination of the two. When physical output figures were used, it was necessary to convert traction, emergency power, submarine, and other special-purpose industrial batteries to automobile battery equivalents on the basis of employment or value of shipments figures. Because of uncertainties in making this conversion, the battery plant size estimates are susceptible to cspccially large measurement errors.

In all, it was possible to obtain physical output size distributions and to compute the derived plant size indices for from four to six industries out of twelve in the six nations covered by our analysis, as shown in the right-hand columns of Tables 3.3 through 3.7. The most serious barriers to international comparison have consequently been overcome. But substantial international productivity differences also exist for the remaining industries. Where the product mix is heterogeneous and varies widely from country to country, as in refrigerators, antifriction bearings, fabrics, and storage batteries, estimating the magnitude of these productivity differences with acceptable reliability is infeasible. For most of the other industries, a stab at computing output per worker indices assuming a U.S. = 100 base was taken. The results, which in every case relate to the year for which employment size distributions were computed, are presented in Table 3.9. They have many limitations. For instance, the productivity disadvantage of British brewers is overestimated because

Table 3.9. Estimated Output per Worker Indices for Eight Industries, Based on U.S. = 100.

	Nation				
Industry	United Kingdom	Canada	Sweden	France	West Germany
Beer brewing	33	73	27	54	42
Cigarettes	30	61	75	85	51
Paints	23	56	49	31	33
Crude petroleum processing	74	125	137	90	64
Gasoline output	23	95	42	33	22
Shoes	62	95	73	78	n.a.
Glass bottles	47	n.a.	85	56	n.a.
Cement	63	107	96	82	82
Steel	46	95	54	66	76
Mean productivity (excluding gasoline)	47	87	75	68	58

roughly a third of all U.K. brewery workers are engaged in transporting and delivering beer to customers, whereas U.S. plants generally rely upon independent carriers and therefore show little or no distribution labor in their employment figures.[7] Product mix differences had to be ignored. On the whole, the productivity index estimates suggest that output per worker was higher in the United States than in the other nations. The only exceptions are cement and crude oil processing (ignoring gasoline yield differences).[8]

The problem remains: How if at all should these productivity indices be used in comparing plant sizes when physical output data are unavailable? If the main reason for lower output per worker outside the United States were the typically smaller size of plants abroad, applying a productivity correction based on the output and employment of *all* plants might overcompensate for the productivity handicap of the largest plants—those dominating our Top 50 Percent relative size index—which may have progressed relatively far down a productivity-size curve exhibiting diminishing marginal returns. If, on the other hand, output per worker abroad were lower across the board, in large plants and small, because of a bias toward labor-intensive processes induced by relatively low wages, or because of a propensity (uncorrelated with plant size and factor prices) toward the retention of obsolete technology or other forms of pure "X-inefficiency,"[9] adjusting the plant employment size indices to reflect estimated productivity differences would be completely appropriate.

Our interviews provided considerable qualitative evidence that pure X-inefficiency was a significant cause of productivity differentials. A tour through a European cigarette plant, for example, revealed that the machines were essentially the same as those used in other countries, but that "traditional" machine manning standards were much looser. Executives in several British industries admitted that productivity had hovered at low levels because cartel arrangements fostered complacent attitudes. Sharp improvements were achieved in two cases after competition emerged following cartel dissolutions induced by the Restrictive Trade

7. See T. A. J. Cockerill, "Comparative Structure and Scale: A Comparison of Aspects of Structure in the Brewing Industries of Selected Countries" (Cambridge University, 1971), mimeograph.

8. If productivity indices could be computed for antifriction bearings, they would probably be somewhat higher in Germany, France, and possibly Sweden than for the United States.

9. See Harvey Leibenstein, "Allocative Efficiency vs. 'X-Efficiency,'" *American Economic Review*, 56 (June 1966), 392–415.

Practices Act. A well-traveled American paint industry official reported that on his visits to European plants he saw "lots of people hanging around, unneeded," especially in a nation with a history of cartelization among paint makers.

The relationship of factor prices to technology choices will be considered more fully in the next chapter. To anticipate briefly, we found little evidence that the principal production processes differed significantly as a function of wage levels among the nations, all highly industrialized, covered by our study. However, there were numerous indications that less attention was paid to labor-saving techniques in such peripheral areas as paint can filling, bottle packing and inspection, and materials handling. Whether this was attributable to relatively low wages generating less pressure to seek and introduce labor-saving innovations, plain managerial lethargy, or some more subtle set of causes was unclear.

Our quantitative data provide additional insight into the question of size-related productivity differentials. A correlation of Midpoint Plant employment size indices with the productivity ratios of Table 3.9 shows no significant or even interesting associations. This should not be surprising, since low labor productivity inflates the observed size indices, perhaps enough to offset any positive relationships between true size and high productivity. A meaningful analysis is therefore restricted to those industries on which adequate physical capacity or output *and* productivity data were available—notably, brewing, petroleum refining, cement, and steel. For the nineteen cases from these four industries on which both output per worker and Midpoint Plant size in physical terms could be related to a U.S. = 100 base, the simple Pearsonian correlation (r) between the two indices was +0.50. If one outlying observation for the British petroleum refining industry (with Midpoint Plant size 2.08 times the U.S. value, but processing only 74 percent as much crude oil per worker, ignoring gasoline yield differences) is deleted, the correlation coefficient rises to +0.61. When logarithms are taken, the correlation with British petroleum refining deleted is even higher, +0.77, and the elasticity of the productivity indices with respect to plant size is 0.38. Thus, a doubling of the plant size index leads to a rise of approximately 38 percent in the productivity index.

Table 3.10 attempts to squeeze still more out of the data. The ratio of a nation's physical capacity or output plant size index relative to a U.S. base over its employment size index, again relative to the most comparable U.S. bench mark, is a kind of selective productivity index. If the match between the employment and physical capacity or output populations were perfect, the ratio would relate that nation's productivity

Table 3.10.   Comparison of Productivity Estimates Derived from Three Points in the Plant Size Distribution. (U.S. = 1.00)

Nation–Industry		(1) Top 50 Percent physical output relative size index / Top 50 Percent employment relative size index	(2) Midpoint Plant physical output relative size index / Midpoint Plant employment relative size index	(3) Overall industry productivity index
Canada	Brewing	0.645	0.652	0.73
U.K.		.385	.373	.33
Sweden		.429	.425	.27
France		.773	.687	.54
Germany		.442	.421	.42
Canada	Petroleum refining	1.267	1.557	1.25
U.K.		0.891	0.695	0.74
Sweden		1.687	1.413	1.37
France		1.287	0.932	0.90
Canada	Cement	1.784	1.597	1.07
Sweden		0.932	0.824	0.96
France		1.213	1.291	.82
Germany		0.570	0.663	.82
Canada	Steel	.639	.517	.95
U.K.		.670	.688	.46
Sweden		.408	.419	.54
France		.736	.538	.66
Mean (N = 17)		.868	.805	.755

in the specified size category to the productivity of U.S. plants in the same relative size class.[10] For a variety of reasons the match is not

10. The ratio presented in the first line of the first numerical column of Table 3.10 was derived as follows:

$$\frac{\dfrac{\text{Physical output of the Top 50 Percent Canadian breweries}}{\text{Physical output of the Top 50 Percent U.S. breweries}}}{\dfrac{\text{Employment of the Top 50 Percent Canadian breweries}}{\text{Employment of the Top 50 Percent U.S. breweries}}}.$$

A bit of rearranging gives us the new ratio:

$$\frac{\dfrac{\text{Physical output of the Top 50 Percent Canadian breweries}}{\text{Employment of the Top 50 Percent Canadian breweries}}}{\dfrac{\text{Physical output of the Top 50 Percent U.S. breweries}}{\text{Employment of the Top 50 Percent U.S. breweries}}},$$

which is analogous to a productivity index.

perfect—notably because the industry definitions for the physical comparisons have been drawn more tightly than for the employment comparisons, especially in steel, and because the physical output or capacity distributions were frequently for different years than the employment distributions.[11] These imperfections introduce errors, most probably in the direction of overstating productivity abroad, since there is a tendency for relatively more plants to be counted before reaching the 50 percent point of the employment size distributions, and hence for smaller plants to pull down Midpoint Plant and average Top 50 Percent employment figures. Now if the productivity handicap in foreign industries is relatively greater for small plants than for the largest plants owing to diminishing returns in the productivity-scale relationship, relative productivity should be highest for the Top 50 Percent plant groupings, in which the largest plants receive maximum weight, and lowest for the overall industry index, where small plants have considerable weight. The Midpoint Plant indices should fall in between. This is in fact what the data suggest. Moving from Top 50 Percent column (1) to Midpoint Plant column (2), the productivity ratios fall in eleven cases and rise in only six, while the mean ratio (U.S. = 1.00) falls from 0.868 to 0.805. Moving from column (2) to column (3), there are ten ratio declines and seven increases, with the mean ratio decreasing from 0.805 to 0.755. However, there is also a great deal of variance, much more than there is systematic variation. The standard error relevant to testing the difference between column means is 0.093, nearly twice the difference between adjacent column means. Thus, one cannot reject the null hypothesis that the three column means arose by chance through sampling from a population of productivity ratios with a common mean. This plus the possibility of an upward bias in the Top 50 Percent and Midpoint Plant productivity ratios suggests that there is no strong case for believing that the largest and midpoint plants covered by our comparative size analysis are relatively more productive than the population of all plants in their respective industries. Consequently, in the analyses which follow we shall whenever possible apply industry-wide productivity corrections to the indices of Midpoint and Top 50 Percent plant employment. We shall

11. For instance, the petroleum refinery physical capacity data are for January 1, 1969, while the Swedish employment data represent an annual average for 1967. Both distributions show a total of 5 refineries. But during calendar year 1967 a surge of refinery startups raised total Swedish daily crude oil processing capacity from 80,000 barrels to 220,000 barrels. It is not clear how the employment data reflect this midstream change. They could be biased upward to include construction and startup labor or downward if a zero value were included for periods before new plants became operative.

however test the sensitivity of our results to these corrections. We make no attempt to adjust the comparative employment size indices of Tables 3.3 through 3.8, largely because the productivity corrections cannot in any event be applied uniformly for all industries. It must simply be borne in mind that the employment-based indices tend to overstate the size of European and Canadian plants in comparison to the U.S. bench marks, in many cases by a substantial margin.

Minimum Optimal Scales

Our second goal is to determine how far and in what direction the observed plant sizes depart from the scales required for efficient production. To do so, we recall from Chapter 2 the concept of the minimum optimal scale or MOS—the smallest plant capacity or planned output volume at which all relevant economies of scale are achieved and at which unit costs attain their minimum value. Actually estimating MOS values for real-world industries poses numerous conceptual and practical problems.

For one, what costs shall be counted? The precedent-setting empirical work in this area has been done by Bain.[12] Although one can find in his original study casual references to minimizing *production* costs only,[13] his empirical estimates include outshipment and other physical distribution costs where "they have a significant effect on the net advantages of increasing the size of plant."[14] This is an unfortunate convention, since unit transportation costs vary inter alia with the density of customer distribution over geographic space, so no unambiguous MOS can be defined. By Bain's criterion, the minimum optimal scale of a cement plant will be much smaller, say, in central Saskatchewan than in Los Angeles County. Also, the unit transportation cost curve is less steep when for one reason or another a plant commands a large share of the market it serves, since the shipping radius required to sell a given volume is inversely related to market share, ceteris paribus. Bain therefore falls into potentially circular reasoning when he uses his minimum optimal scale estimates, depending in part upon assumed market shares, to determine how large a plant's market share must be to achieve all production and physical distribution scale economies. To avoid these logical pitfalls we define our MOS estimates in terms of long-run production costs only.

---

12. Joe S. Bain, "Economies of Scale, Concentration, and the Condition of Entry in Twenty Manufacturing Industries," *American Economic Review*, 44 (March 1954), 15–39; and *Barriers to New Competition* (Cambridge: Harvard University Press, 1956), esp. chap. 3.

13. Cf. "Economies of Scale," pp. 15 and 20.

14. *Barriers to New Competition*, p. 71.

There are also practical difficulties. Interviews revealed that in certain industries—notably petroleum refining, cement, integrated steel making, and brewing—unit costs were believed to continue falling beyond the size of the largest modern plant with which any significant amount of construction and operating experience had been accumulated. Interviewees in those industries admitted considerable uncertainty as to where the decline in unit costs with increasing scale ceased. Likewise, in the cigarette, refrigerator, and storage battery industries respondents believed that very slight economies might be realized at volumes larger than the scale of current "best practice" plants. One way of dealing with these problems might be to follow T. A. J. Cockerill's approach, defining the MOS as that scale beyond which unit costs are expected to fall by less than two percent with a further doubling of capacity.[15] However, when experience with very large new plants is slight or nonexistent, the estimating uncertainties in applying such a criterion are also great. We have therefore adopted a compromise approach. Where there was considerable experience with plants believed to realize all known scale economies, we have defined the MOS as the smallest scale at which unit costs in 1965-vintage plants attained a perceived minimum or at least came so close that remaining unexploited scale economies were viewed as insignificantly slight. When little or no experience in the highest-volume and still declining reaches of the long-run cost function existed, we defined the MOS as the size of "best current practice" plants in operation during 1965.

This method introduces a certain amount of ambiguity, but ambiguity appears to be inescapable. Its adverse consequences are kept within tolerable bounds because, as will become clear subsequently, other variables are defined in a consistent manner so as to compensate for MOS estimation errors. In particular, one key variable will be the estimated percentage by which unit costs are elevated when plants are built and operated at only one-third of the assumed minimum optimal scale. If the MOS definition for Industry A pushes less fully into the stage of vanishing marginal scale economies than the definition for Industry B, the long-run unit cost curve is likely to be steeper to the left of the assumed MOS for Industry A than for Industry B, and the measurement inconsistency will be reflected by differences in the estimated cost penalties associated with suboptimal scale operation.

Table 3.11 presents the basic MOS estimates for the twelve industries along with estimates of the percentage by which unit production costs

15. "Economies of Scale in the Brewing Industry—A Comparative Study," unpub. diss., University of Leeds, Eng., 1971, chap. I.

Table 3.11. Estimated Values of the Minimum Optimal Scale, circa 1965.

Industry	Minimum optimal scale	Percentage by which unit cost rises building at 1/3 MOS
Beer brewing	4.5 million (31 U.S. gallon) barrels per year capacity	5.0
Cigarettes	36 billion cigarettes per year; 2,275 employees	2.2
Cotton & synthetic broad-woven fabrics	37.5 million square yards per year; 600 employees in modern integrated plants	7.6
Paints	10 million U.S. gallons per year; 450 employees	4.4
Petroleum refining	200,000 (42 U.S. gallon) barrels per day crude oil processing capacity	4.8
Nonrubber shoes	1 million pairs per year; 250 employees on single shift operation	1.5
Glass bottles	133,000 short tons per year; 1,000 employees	11.0
Portland cement	7 million 376-pound barrels per year capacity	26.0
Integrated steel	4 million short tons per year capacity	11.0
Antifriction bearings	800 employees	8.0
Refrigerators	800,000 units per year	6.5
Automobile storage batteries	1 million units per year; 300 employees	4.6

(including the cost of purchased materials) are elevated operating a 1965-vintage plant with one-third the MOS capacity.[16] Where employment figures appear along with physical output estimates, they are bench marked to the productivity of representative United States plants in 1967. The data in Table 3.11 are based upon engineering estimates elicited in our 125-odd company interviews and whenever possible upon similar but presumably independent studies.[17] When there were conflicts

16. A thorough discussion of assumptions underlying the estimates is presented in F. M. Scherer, "The Technological Bases of Plant Scale Economies in Twelve Manufacturing Industries," Preprint I/74-6, International Institute of Management (Berlin, 1974).

17. These include Bain, *Barriers to New Competition*, Appendix B, for cigarettes, petroleum refining, shoes, cement, and steel; Cockerill, "Economies of Scale in the

between our own and others' estimates, those in which we had the greatest confidence—more often than not from our own investigations— were favored.

One conceivable cause of disparity among MOS estimates might be international differences in factor price ratios. However, as we have indicated already, we found little divergence among the views of producers in the six nations with respect to basic process optima, nor did perceived limits on the size of plants which could be managed successfully vary much between nations for a given product mix. There were wide variations in the plant sizes actually chosen, but these were generally attributable to identifiable market, historical, or philosophical characteristics. Interviewees who had thought seriously about the problem exhibited remarkable unanimity in their estimates of the minimum-cost plant size if demand and other constraints were relaxed and it was possible to build afresh embodying mid-1960s' technology.

Much more variance was encountered in estimates of the amount by which unit costs rose for plants built with only one-third the MOS capacity. These deviations were evidently attributable at least in part to systematic international differences in factor costs and especially wages. But simple unfamiliarity with modern plant designs of divergent size or the inability of interviewees mentally or analytically to hold a sufficient number of variables constant while varying plant size was probably a more important source of difficulty. In two cases, glass bottles and antifriction bearings, we were able to obtain only one usable estimate of the cost curve's slope, and the bottle plant penalty estimate may be biased upward because the plant on which it was based was designed with future growth in mind. Our estimates for petroleum refining and cement,

Brewing Industry," for brewing; C. F. Pratten and R. M. Dean, *The Economies of Large-Scale Production in British Industry* (Cambridge, Eng.: Cambridge University Press, 1965), for steel, petroleum refining, and shoes; Gunnar Ribrant, *Stordrifts-fördelar inom Industriproduktionen* (Stockholm: Swedish Finance Department, 1970), for steel, cement, petroleum refining, batteries, refrigerators, and brewing; United Nations Centre for Industrial Development, *Studies in the Economics of Industry*, No. 1 (1963), for cement; R. Sterling Harwell, Jr., "The Effect of Distribution Costs on Plant Size," *Rock Products*, May 1969, pp. 98–103, for cement; several German language monographs on steelmaking processes by Hermann Schenck and associates of the Technischen Hochschule, Aachen; British Iron and Steel Federation, *The Steel Industry* (London, July 1966), pp. 38–45; The Textile Council, *Cotton and Allied Textiles*, vol. I (Manchester, Eng., 1969), pp. 71–72, on weaving and spinning mills; G. D. Quirin, R. M. Sultan, and T. A. Wilson, "The Canadian Appliance Industry" (Toronto: University of Toronto Institute for the Quantitative Analysis of Social and Economic Policy, unpublished study, 1970), for refrigerators; and various older sources referred to in the studies cited.

on the other hand, assume smaller suboptimal scale penalties than those reported in widely cited published studies.[18] This disagreement arises because the published analyses were executed at a time when technical changes had reduced unit costs sharply for large plants but had not yet been adapted to medium-sized plants. Later adaptations lessened the cost advantage enjoyed by the largest plants. In general, the cost elevation estimates presented in Table 3.11 are subject to considerable potential measurement error. The most we can claim is that they reflect our best ujdgment in a situation where perfection is well beyond reach.

Both the rate at which unit costs vary with increasing plant size and the location of the minimum optimal scale may depend, as we saw in Chapter 2, upon the elasticity of labor supplies. Our MOS estimates for shoemaking, weaving, and bearing plants were influenced by nonurban labor supply considerations, but in all three industries, and especially in weaving, the amount of activity a manager could successfully control was also an important constraint. Although the issue was not explored adequately, it appears interviewees assumed that sub-MOS plants would not enjoy still lower wage rates except under special circumstances (for example, when shoe sewing work was dispersed among very small satellite plants). To the extent that this assumption is violated, our cost increase estimates may be biased upward.

Our minimum optimal scale estimates represent a 1965 vintage snapshot of what in certain industries was a rapidly moving target. Particularly in steel and cement, changes in blast furnace, converter, hot strip mill, limestone quarrying, kiln, and grinding mill technology have led to radical increases in the MOS. Bain's estimates for the early 1950s put the MOS of a fully integrated flat-rolled steel products works at 1.0 to 2.5 million ingot tons capacity,[19] a range consistent with the historical information we obtained in interviews. For a cement works, he found the MOS to lie between 2.0 and 2.5 million barrels per year capacity,[20] a moderate underestimate due to the inclusion of outbound freight costs. By 1970, the "best practice" scales had jumped to about 10 million ingot tons and at least 12 million cement barrels respectively, with minor cost savings persisting into still larger capacity ranges. Table 3.11 attempts to "freeze"

18. For a survey of the petroleum refining scale economy literature and a discussion of the basic estimation problem, see Pratten and Dean, *Economies of Large-Scale Production*, esp. pp. 94–95. On cement, see the United Nations report, *Studies in the Economics of Industry*, particularly pp. 22–23, in which the medium-size plants are plainly of inferior design, employing multiple kilns where best-practice works would have only one high-capacity unit.

19. *Barriers to New Competition*, p. 236.

20. Ibid., p. 230.

these developments as of 1965, with some inherent blur. More gradual upward revisions in MOS values occurred in paints, refrigerators, brewing, and battery manufacturing. This trend was visible in all six nations, although its timing varied between countries, again introducing some blur. Meanwhile the minimum optimal scale declined in the bearings, shoe, and (less clearly) weaving industries, partly because wages rose more rapidly than productivity in urban production centers, inducing a flight to smaller towns where labor market monopsony power became a factor constraining plant sizes, and partly because demand changes led to much more complex product mixes, impairing the ability of managers effectively to control operations in very large plants.

Differences in product mix complicate matters. Where it made a significant difference, we have consistently assumed that orthodox product mix requiring the largest MOS. Thus, we focus on a weaving mill producing a narrow range of standard fabrics in very high volume. For fashion-sensitive and other low-to-medium volume fabrics, managerial limitations hold the MOS at one-third to one-half the yardage indicated in Table 3.11, or perhaps even less for fabrics with very volatile demand. Our shoe industry estimates assume a limited range of medium-price items; plants catering to the most fashion-sensitive trade or making shoes with especially high stitching content have a smaller MOS. In paints, a broad line of decorative and/or industrial coatings is assumed; for a plant specializing in a few basic colors the MOS might be considerably smaller. In steel, we assume an integrated works producing wide hot-rolled strip from ordinary carbon steel made in basic oxygen converters using blast furnace pig iron. Much smaller scales are efficient for special alloy steel works or mills making standard bar products from scrap-fed electric arc furnace steel. Rolling mills specializing in bar products, structural members, or heavy plates also sacrifice no economics at scales considerably smaller than the tonnage stipulated in Table 3.11. For petroleum refining we assume a European-type operation with little cracking and other gasoline enrichment capacity. The MOS and cost curve gradients are nevertheless similar in U.S. refineries processing relatively more gasoline. Likewise, the MOS for European refrigerator plants is about the same as for U.S. plants, even though the product mixes are quite different. With a simple European product mix, assembly line specialization and small parts production or procurement economies are largely exhausted at a volume of 800,000 units per year. This is not true in the typical full-line U.S. plant, but the unexploited production line economies associated with still higher annual throughput appear to be offset by the problems of managing a larger, more complex operation.

As the discussion has implied, the amount of complexity a plant manager can handle affects the MOS in many industries. At least at the single-plant level, the U-shaped long-run cost curve is more than a textbook writer's convenient fiction. When a plant exceeds some critical size, its operations become so complex that its manager can no longer cope and unit costs rise. Interviewees in the weaving, glass bottle, and (less consistently) bearing industries reported higher unit costs due to managerial diseconomies at scales not greatly exceeding those indicated in Table 3.11. There was also less compelling evidence of scale dis-economies in shoemaking, although they can evidently be averted in plants several times the specified MOS if the product mix is extremely simple or management is extraordinarily capable.

One further point in the same vein deserves mention. In two industries, paints and automobile batteries, we encountered evidence that the long-run production cost curve has two local minima, as shown in Figure 3.1.

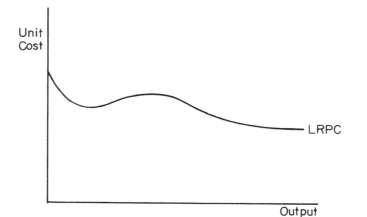

Figure 3.1. Long-run Cost Curve Observed in Paint and Battery Manufacturing.

Very small, limited product mix operations in which a single entre-preneur serves simultaneously as production foreman, chief salesman, and deliveryman were said to experience quite modest unit costs. But as the scale of operations rises beyond approximately 100,000 gallons or 50,000 batteries per year, a one-man show is no longer possible, special-ization becomes necessary, and overhead costs escalate. After a pessimum occurs, economies of scale reappear as still larger volumes are achieved. The high-volume optimum appears to be the optimum optimorum, but in the battery industry the small-scale operator might actually enjoy lower unit production costs than his much larger rivals if he can employ strongly motivated nonunionized help and imputes to himself modest opportunity cost. Proliferation of such plants is inhibited by the scarcity of suitable entrepreneurs. Even when small-scale plants have higher production cost, they may enjoy a production-plus-distribution cost advantage over large plants in serving densely populated local markets. As a result, both small and large paint and battery plants coexisted profitably in nearly all the nations covered by our study, while medium-sized plants realized lower profits and exhibited a long-run tendency to disappear either through shutdown or a great leap forward to larger and more efficient scale.

Plant Size Determinants: A Multiple Regression Model

Tables 3.12 and 3.13 combine the minimum optimal scale estimates of Table 3.11 and the Top 50 Percent and Midpoint Plant size data from Appendix Tables 3.1 through 3.6 to show the relationship between actually observed and minimum optimal scales. Physical output or capacity distributions were used whenever they were available; productivity adjustments were made when possible on the remaining employment-based observations.[21] The percentage relationship of ac-

Table 3.12. Observed Top 50 Percent Plant Sizes as a Percentage of the Estimated Minimum Optimal Scales.

	Nation					
Industry	U.S.	Canada	U.K.	Sweden	France	Germany
Brewing	80_p	26_p	24_p	5_p	14_p	10_p
Cigarettes	206_e	31_a	50_a	16_a	19_p	23_a
Cotton and synthetic fabrics	250_e	187_e	65_e	117_e	68_e	227_e
Paints	55_e	32_a	43_a	33_a	16_a	26_a
Petroleum refining	97_p	38_p	130_p	46_p	108_p	62_p
Shoes	226_e	110_a	136_a	45_a	149_a	221_e
Glass bottles	126_e	118_e	59_a	61_a	93_a	144_e
Cement	69_p	83_p	61_p	82_p	79_p	76_p
Steel	123_p	92_p	53_p	23_p	58_p	90_p
Antifriction bearings	334_e	97_e	264_a	698_e	217_e	411_e
Refrigerators	101_p	13_p	22_p	13_p	36_p	71_p
Storage batteries	170_e	63_p	187_p	56_p	213_e	811_e
Mean of national values	153	74	91	99	89	181
Median of national values	125	73	60	46	74	83

Note: p = measured in terms of physical output or capacity; a = employment index productivity-adjusted; e = measured in terms of unadjusted employment.

21. For the brewing industry, whose Table 3.11 MOS estimate is stated in terms of capacity but for which observed plant sizes were measured in terms of actual output, the MOS figure was multiplied by 0.9.

Table 3.13. Observed Midpoint Plant Sizes as a Percentage of the Estimated Minimum Optimal Scales.

Industry	Nation					
	U.S.	Canada	U.K.	Sweden	France	Germany
Brewing	35$_p$	11$_p$	10$_p$	2$_p$	6$_p$	4$_p$
Cigarettes	105$_e$	24$_a$	29$_a$	11$_a$	17$_p$	15$_a$
Cotton and synthetic fabrics	133$_e$	156$_e$	36$_e$	74$_e$	39$_e$	124$_e$
Paints	28$_e$	19$_a$	20$_a$	20$_a$	7$_a$	6$_a$
Petroleum refining	51$_p$	30$_p$	105$_p$	42$_p$	66$_p$	46$_p$
Shoes	146$_e$	76$_a$	71$_a$	25$_a$	63$_a$	110$_e$
Glass bottles	77$_e$	104$_e$	30$_a$	51$_a$	56$_a$	52$_e$
Cement	47$_p$	60$_p$	42$_p$	63$_p$	54$_p$	53$_p$
Steel	73$_p$	65$_p$	38$_p$	18$_p$	41$_p$	55$_p$
Antifriction bearings	203$_e$	88$_e$	234$_a$	698$_e$	131$_e$	375$_e$
Refrigerators	63$_p$	10$_p$	15$_p$	12$_p$	25$_p$	46$_p$
Storage batteries	91$_e$	45$_p$	100$_p$	39$_p$	180$_e$	500$_e$
Mean of national values	88	57	61	88	57	116
Median of national values	75	53	37	32	48	53

Note: p = measured in terms of physical output or capacity; a = employment index productivity-adjusted; e = measured in terms of unadjusted employment.

tually observed sizes to the MOS was computed directly when industry definitions were appropriately narrow. Otherwise, the ratio of an industry's observed average plant size to the size of plants in the most comparably defined U.S. industry was computed, and that ratio was multiplied by the Observed Plant Size/MOS percentage for the corresponding narrowly defined U.S. industry, that is, by the figure reported in the first numerical column of Table 3.12 or 3.13.

The variation among industry MOS-deflated size indices is considerable, ranging from 2 percent of the MOS for the Midpoint Swedish brewery to 811 percent for employment in the leading German battery plants. In the analyses which follow we shall exclude the German battery and antifriction bearing industry observations because they are subject to especially severe measurement errors.[22] The Swedish bearing

22. The plant employment estimates for leading German battery manufacturer Varta include workers producing automobile equipment other than batteries and hence are seriously biased upward. No satisfactory adjustment was possible, although data on market shares and total industry output suggest that automobile battery production in the Varta plants was in the same volume range as that experienced by General Motors in the United States and Lucas in England. For the German bearing industry we were unable to obtain a usable employment breakdown among the multiple plants operated by Fischer and SKF in Schweinfurt. The figures in Table 3.7 are based upon guesses too rough to warrant much confidence.

industry observations will also be omitted from most analyses because they are extreme "outliers" on several dimensions, overwhelming the values for other industries.[23] Thus, the sample will usually include sixty-nine industries, with plant size values ranging from 2 to 334 percent of the estimated minimum optimal scales.

To determine why plants in some national industries tend to be small in relation to the MOS while others are large, we employ multiple regression analysis.[24] The dependent variables will be the MOS-deflated Top 50 Percent and Midpoint Plant size indices arrayed in Tables 3.12 and 3.13, which we denote as $TOP50_{ij}/MOS_j$ and MID_{ij}/MOS_j respectively, where i refers to the home nation and j to the industry.

Numerous hypotheses can be advanced to explain the variation in MOS-deflated plant size indices. Some invoke the logic of optimal plant size and location choices in geographic space; some emphasize aspects of business behavior in a rivalrous market environment; and some are related to adjustment lags and imperfections in our scale measurements. We consider next how each cluster of hypotheses can be formulated for quantitative testing.

The Location Theoretic Variables

Figure 2.2 of Chapter 2 showed that, as a first approximation, costs are minimized when the (absolute value of the) slope of the long-run unit production cost curve equals the slope of the unit transport cost function. The plant size chosen will be greater, the steeper is the downward slope of the unit production cost curve and the less steep is the upward slope of the unit transport cost curve in the relevant range, ceteris paribus.

Estimates of the long-run production cost function's steepness, or, more precisely, of the percentage by which unit production costs are elevated moving from a plant of minimum optimal scale to a plant

23. In addition to having unusually large plant size values, the industry had a concentration ratio of 100 and exports amounting to 70 percent of production (whereas the next most export-prone industry achieved only 30 percent). Tests assessing the sensitivity of results to this omission will be reported in subsequent sections.

24. Parts of the following analysis appeared in truncated form in F. M. Scherer, "The Determinants of Industrial Plant Sizes in Six Nations," *Review of Economics and Statistics*, 55 (May 1973), 135–145. Because of data corrections made since then, there are minor differences (usually involving the third significant digit) in the results reported here.

The principal precedent for an analysis of this type is H. C. Eastman and Stefan Stykolt, *The Tariff and Competition in Canada* (Toronto: Macmillan, 1967), chap. 3. We imitate Eastman and Stykolt in several details, but there are also fundamental conceptual differences.

one-third the MOS, have been presented for the twelve industries in Table 3.11. We call this variable $COST_j$.

To take outbound shipping costs into account, we recall from Chapter 2 that when a plant with a market share of S serves a circular market area with homogeneous demand density of D units per square mile and a uniform cost T of shipping one unit of output one radial mile, the slope of its unit transport cost curve is given by:[25]

$$(3.1) \qquad \frac{d\ UTC}{dQ} = \frac{T}{3\sqrt{\pi D\ S\ Q}}.$$

This we wish to evaluate at an output Q consistent with the range for which the production cost curve slope term COST is defined. Obviously, Q cannot be scaled in natural production units. Some common denominator is required; one cannot directly compare, say, barrels of beer and assembled ball bearing units. The logical common denominator (used also for the plant size and, as we shall see, market size variables) is the estimated minimum optimal scale. Since the unit production cost curve slope is defined for the range between the MOS and one-third the MOS, one possibility is to define Q at the mid-point of this range; that is, $Q = \frac{2}{3}\ MOS = \frac{2}{3}$ (since the MOS itself has a unit value as common denominator). Then Q simply becomes part of the constant term $1/(3\sqrt{\pi}\,\frac{2}{3} \cong .23$ and $d\ UTC/dQ \cong .23T/\sqrt{DS}$.

However, the problem may be more complicated. Consider the unit transportation cost curve UTC in Figure 3.2, defined for a market of some given geographic expanse and density. As equation (3.1) requires, the larger Q is, the less steep the UTC curve is, ceteris paribus. The relationship between the UTC slope and the average production cost curve depends in a subtle way upon the relationship of the MOS to market size. If the MOS is small in relation to the size of the market, so that the MOS output can be sold within a small radial submarket, the average production cost curve must be related to UTC as with $LRPC_1$ in Figure 3.2. If the MOS is large compared to the market, a relationship like $LRPC_2$ will prevail. Both production cost curves have been constructed to have the same percentage fall between one-third MOS and the full MOS. But for the most plausible UTC curve configurations, an output increment from one-third MOS to the full MOS can be distributed at a smaller increase in unit transportation cost *as a percentage of an MOS plant's unit production cost* when the MOS is small relative to total market demand, as with $LRPC_1$, than when it is relatively large. We may expect therefore an inverse multiplicative relationship through

25. Cf. eq. (2.1) – (2.4).

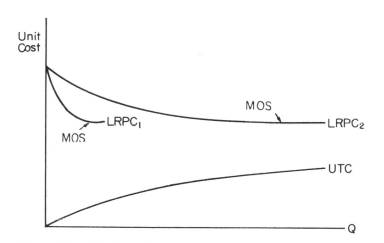

Figure 3.2. Relationship of Production Costs to Transportation Costs for two Market Size/MOS Cases.

Q between overall market size relative to the MOS and the slope of the unit transport cost curve. This point will prove significant in the final choice among regression equation specifications.

The transport cost curve's scaling must also be consistent with that of the unit production cost function, whose ordinate is in value per unit of product terms. The higher production cost is in relation to product weight, the greater is the relative distance between the UTC and LRPC curves, ceteris paribus, and the less rapidly unit transport costs rise in relation to production costs as more output is sold.[26] Data availability considerations lead us to relate unit transport cost to F.O.B. mill product value net of excise taxes, which provides a tolerable first approximation to equilibrium unit production costs. Specifically, our estimate of the variable T in equation (3.1) will be transport cost per hundredweight on a standardized haul as a percentage of product value per hundredweight.

Table 3.14 summarizes the components of the calculation, which is based upon a more extensive set of data collected for Chapter 5.[27] In the table's first numerical column is the cost per hundredweight of shipping in at least 20,000 pound lots representative commodities from Chicago to Cleveland, or over some comparable 350-mile haul. The index for most industries is an average of the prevailing common carrier truck, rail, and private truck commodity rates (assuming the private truck cost to be 90 percent of the common motor carrier rate), with each rate

26. Cf. n. 4, Chap. 2 *supra.*
27. For further methodological details, see Appendix B *infra.*

Table 3.14.   Derivation of the Transportation Cost Index.

Industry	Weighted average freight cost per cwt (dollars)	Wholesale product value per cwt (dollars)	Transport cost per dollar of product value (cents)
Brewing	0.460	5.90	7.8
Cigarettes	.909	138.00	0.7
Broad-woven grey fabrics	.699	100.70	0.7
Paints	.518	23.89	2.2
Petroleum products	.141	1.55	8.9
Shoes	.932	215.00	0.4
Glass bottles	.651	6.60	9.9
Cement	.410	0.90	44.6[a]
Steel mill products	.414	5.50	7.5
Ball and roller bearings	.810	94.00	0.9
Refrigerators	.975	56.00	1.7
Automobile batteries	.614	26.12	2.4

[a]For Canada, 30.4 cents; for Sweden and Germany, 33.2 cents.

weighted by the outbound tonnage share of that medium for the relevant industry in 1963. For cement and steel, estimated water transportation rates were included with appropriate weights; for petroleum refining, transportation in medium-size product pipelines was also assumed.

In the second numerical column are estimates of the wholesale F.O.B. mill value per cwt of a representative U.S. product sample for 1963. These were derived from Census data whenever possible, with supplemental consultation of import and export tabulations, the Sears Roebuck catalogue, and trade sources when Census data proved inadequate.

The final column gives the ratio of the freight cost per cwt and product value per cwt, expressed in cents of transportation cost per dollar of product value. These estimates will be used uniformly for all the nations, except that higher weights are assigned to water transportation of cement for Canada, Sweden, and Germany. Although this uniformity assumption introduces some error, the errors are undoubtedly small in comparison to the variance of the transportation cost per unit value variable, which we shall henceforth call $TRANS_{ij}$.

In the denominator of equation (3.1), one key component is the density of demand per square mile. For consumer goods (but less consistently so for producer goods) demand density depends primarily upon the density of the population distribution and the purchasing power of the population. A problem in computing population densities is the existence of vast, virtually uninhabited areas, especially in Canada and Sweden and to a lesser degree in the United States. To the extent that these areas are served from local production units, the plants are likely to be too small to be included in our dependent variable estimates, which emphasize the top half of the cumulative output or employment distribution. We have therefore recomputed population densities for the six nations, deleting the least densely populated fringe and insular areas until approximately 14 percent of the total population had been excluded. An attempt was made to keep the area retained geographically contiguous, avoiding "islands." The chief exception to this rule was the elimination of most of the U.S. western plains and Rocky Mountain states, including the western three-fourths of Minnesota and Texas, leaving western California, stripped of deserts and high mountains, as a self-contained "island" with some 17.7 million inhabitants. Canada emerges as a narrow band extending from southern British Columbia through southern and central Ontario to Nova Scotia. England was segregated (with no political implications intended) from Northern Ireland, various offshore islands, Scotland, Northumberland, and Cornwall. For Sweden, all the provinces north of Dalarna plus the islands Öland and Gotland were excluded. The French adjustments focused on sixteen Pyrenean and seven Alpine departments. For Germany, insular West Berlin and numerous southeastern, southern, and southwestern counties were eliminated. The preadjustment and postadjustment densities, with all estimates bench marked to 1966, were:

Nation	Total 1966 population (millions)	Inhabitants per square mile		Percentage of population excluded
		Unadjusted	Adjusted	
United States	194.9	66	140	13.9
Canada	20.0	5	37	14.3
United Kingdom	54.7	579	855	14.8
West Germany	59.6	626	676	14.3
France	49.2	240	266	14.5
Sweden	7.8	49	103	14.5

Differences in purchasing power must also be taken into account. The natural candidate is an index of national product per capita. Using exchange rates prevailing during the mid-1960s would exaggerate differences between the United States and the European nations, however. Rather than undertake a major investigation, we have adopted Edward F. Denison's real 1960 national income per capita estimates, assuming U.S. price weights, introducing slight changes to reflect post-1960 developments, and interpolating values for Canada and Sweden.[28] The resulting estimates are crude, but any point approximation is bound to conceal as much as it reveals owing to the divergent trends over time in the six nations. Indexed at U.S. = 1.00, the estimates appear at least to exhibit the right orders of magnitude:

United States	1.00	Sweden	0.86
Canada	0.80	France	0.66
United Kingdom	0.68	West Germany	0.75

Our final estimate of D in equation (3.1) is the product of the adjusted population densities and the indices of real national income per capita. It will be called $DENS_i$.

Because plants must ship farther to sell a given volume when they command a small market share, ceteris paribus, a market share variable appears in the denominator of equation (3.1). It will be represented in the regression analysis by the three-firm concentration ratio $MS3_{ij}$ (generally estimated for 1963–1965 physical output or employment). In most cases MS3 is defined on a national market basis, but more appropriate regional market definitions have been used for the beer, paint, petroleum refining, and cement industries in the United States; for petroleum refining and cement in Canada and France; and for petroleum refining in Germany. The MS3 values are recorded in Appendix Table 3.7.

Market Size, Rivalry, Market Imperfections, and Trade Barriers

There are several reasons beyond the location-theoretic considerations articulated in connection with equation (3.1) why scale economy sacrifices could be greater when national market demand is small in relation to the MOS than when it is large. Here we present only the bare bones of the argument. It will be elaborated in Chapter 4.

For one, some markets may be too small to support even a single plant of minimum optimal scale. And if buyers and government policymakers prefer some diversity of supply sources, two or more independent plants may survive in small markets, each plant too small to enjoy all economies of scale. When transport costs are sufficiently high to segment a national market into relatively insulated geographic submarkets, this fragmentation can occur even in national markets large enough to accommodate several MOS plants.

Dynamics also matter. The smaller the market is for any given (posi-

---

28. E. F. Denison, *Why Growth Rates Differ* (Washington: The Brookings Institution, 1967), p. 22.

tive) growth rate, the more time it takes to accumulate a demand increment sufficient to absorb the capacity of a lumpy new MOS plant. Also, in markets small relative to the minimum optimal scale, oligopoly is likely, and the resulting concern for pricing interdependence and strategic position can aggravate propensities toward investment in inefficiently small plants.[29] Suppose, for example, overall market demand growth creates room for one new MOS plant every two years and the market is supplied by four evenly matched firms. Ideally, each firm ought to build a new plant every eight years on a two-year rotation. But the coordination required to implement such phasing formally is frowned upon by the antitrust authorities of the United States, Canada, England, and (less consistently) Germany. And even when formal cooperation is permitted, oligopolistic rivals may be unwilling to wait long intervals for increments of growth, nor do they trust one another in matters of such strategic importance to forego a share of current growth in the expectation that they will be given their fair turn later. Rather, they are apt to expand more or less continuously to maintain their accustomed share of the market. Each then faces a tradeoff between carrying excess capacity for a protracted period vs. sacrificing scale economies vs. price cutting (with retaliation probable). As the dynamic investment analysis in Chapter 2 showed, the excess capacity-scale economy tradeoff is more likely to be resolved in favor of sub-MOS plants or plant additions, the smaller is the absolute demand growth increment accruing to a firm in any given time period. The size of that increment in turn depends multiplicatively upon the absolute size of the market, the rate of demand growth, and (assuming market share maintenance) each firm's share of the market.

These considerations lead us to expect that average plant sizes will be larger, the larger the market is in relation to the minimum optimal scale, the more rapidly demand is growing, and (still assuming oligopolistic market share maintenance) the higher seller concentration is. However, the concentration relationship should break down if sellers are prone to ignore their interdependence and struggle through price competition to build and absorb the output of large plants.

The market size variable $SIZE_{ij}$ we shall employ will be the ratio of total domestic consumption (domestic production plus imports minus exports), usually measured in physical units for 1967, to the estimated

---

29. An early discussion of this problem was Tibor Scitovsky, *Economic Theory and Western European Integration* (Stanford: Stanford University Press, 1958), esp. pp. 113–130.

Table 3.15. The Number of MOS Plants Compatible with Domestic Consumption in the Six Nations, circa 1967.

Industry	U.S.	Canada	U.K.	Sweden	France	Germany
Brewing	29.0	2.9	10.9	0.7	4.5	16.1
Cigarettes	15.2	1.3	3.3	0.3	1.6	2.8
Fabrics	451.7	17.4	57.0	10.4	56.9	52.1
Paints	69.8	6.3	9.8	2.0	6.6	8.4
Petroleum refining	51.6	6.0	8.6	2.5	7.7	9.9
Shoes	532.0	59.2	164.5	23.0	128.2	196.9
Glass bottles	65.5	7.2	11.1	1.7	6.6	7.9
Cement	59.0	6.6	16.5	3.5	21.7	28.8
Steel	38.9	2.6	6.5	1.5	5.5	10.1
Bearings	72.0	5.9	22.8	3.3	17.0	n.a.
Refrigerators	7.1	0.7	1.2	0.5	1.7	2.8
Storage batteries	53.5	4.6	7.7	1.4	12.8	10.5

MOS.[30] The calculated ratios are arrayed in Table 3.15. They have interest apart from their use in testing the hypotheses formulated here because they provide an indication of the extent to which technological imperatives require high plant concentration for production efficiency. It can be seen that in the United States, plant scale economies compel moderately tight national market oligopoly (for example, with a maximum of seven efficient single-plant sellers) only in the refrigerator industry. But in other smaller nations, and particularly in Sweden and Canada, the conflict between competitive structure and production efficiency is much sharper. Sweden has three natural monopolies (brewing, refrigerators, and cigarettes) and four more natural duopolies. In Canada, production conditions at the plant level are favorable to some degree of atomistic organization only in the shoe and weaving industries.

Under the hypotheses advanced, we would expect an increase in the number of MOS plants an industry can accommodate from 6 to 12 to have a stronger favorable effect on plant size decisions than an increase from, say, 94 to 100. Therefore, we shall transform the SIZE variable logarithmically in all regression runs.

The role of market growth will be tested by a variable $GROWTH_{ij}$ measuring the continuously compounded rate of physical output growth, usually from 1950 through 1967. In a few cases, data limitations made it necessary to use a later initial year, and for British industries on which

30. The Table 3.11 MOS values were multiplied by 0.90 for the brewing, cement, and steel industries to relate actual output to "normal" capacity utilization levels. For petroleum refining, the capacity utilization multiplier was 0.95.

only 1963 plant size distributions were available, that year was taken as the terminus. For the United Kingdom, Sweden, France, and Germany, consistent automobile battery output data series were not available, so initial and terminal year outputs were estimated from statistics on the production and stock of battery-using vehicles, assuming average U.S. battery life expectancies. The growth rates, like other independent variables to be enumerated subsequently, are listed in Appendix Table 3.7.

Seller concentration will be taken into account through the previously defined three-firm regionally adjusted concentration variable MS3, in this instance interacting with the market size variable outside the realm of the transport cost term. Since forty-eight of the sixty-nine main sample industries had MS3 values of forty or more, oligopolistic behavior patterns should play a prominent role.

One limitation of the SIZE variable is that it reflects only domestic national market consumption, ignoring export markets. When producers find themselves able to export in substantial volume, their plant size choices may be less constrained than they would be if domestic market potential alone were tapped. To allow for this possibility we introduce a variable $EXPORT_{ij}$ measuring exports as a percentage of domestic production. Its exact specification poses two problems. First, causality could run in either of two directions. Having an export market in which to work off surplus capacity can facilitate the building of large plants, but building large plants and reaping the related efficiency benefits may enhance an industry's success in penetrating export markets.[31] To increase the likelihood of testing for the first kind of causal link, the export period should antedate the period for which plant sizes are measured. Second, four of the six nations joined the European Community (EC) or the European Free Trade Association (EFTA) during the late 1950s, thereafter widening the export horizons of their industrial enterprises. We should like to capture at least some of the effect these developments had on plant size decisions, although the process is surely a gradual, cumulative one. To compromise these conflicting tugs, we chose 1963, preceding by four years most of our plant size measurements, as the year for which export percentages were computed.[32] It would have been desirable to collect data for additional years and test more sophisticated lag structures, but this was precluded by limitations on both time and the quality of earlier export statistics.

31. See Nicholas Owen, "Intra-EEC Trade and Industrial Structure," mimeographed paper, British Department of Trade and Industry, 1973, for evidence that success in exporting is positively associated with plant size.

32. The main source of data was the O.E.C.D. publication, *Trade by Commodities: Exports*, January–December 1963.

Imports might also affect plant size choices, though the nature of the relationship is less clear on a priori grounds. On one hand, strong import competition could force producers to strive for maximum efficiency, while oligopolists insulated from import competition may become complacent, fail to rationalize existing inefficient plant structures, and accept a division of the market which inhibits large-scale investments. On the other hand, intensive import competition may demoralize domestic producers and discourage aggressive investment. Both tendencies were observed during interviews, the latter with particular strength in certain British and Swedish industries. In testing the $IMPORT_{ij}$ variable, defined as the percentage of 1963 imports to domestic consumption, we therefore postulate a two-tailed hypothesis.

Another means of exploring the import exposure hypothesis is to introduce as an independent variable the average percentage tariff duty (including prorated specific duties) on most-favored-nation imports. In this case a deliberate attempt to antedate the impact of EC and EFTA was made by selecting 1957 tariffs. Adjustments were applied to the U.S. and Canadian data, generally reported on an F.O.B. basis, to harmonize them with European C.I.F. statistics. Analyses using the resulting variable $TARIFF_{ij}$ must omit the brewing and cigarette industries, for which disentangling true import duties from domestic excise levies proved infeasible.

Two additional variables in the same general spirit can be identified. Inefficiently small plants may survive because they supply products differentiated to satisfy consumer demands for variety, distinctiveness, or special service and commanding a price premium sufficiently high to offset production scale economy sacrifices. Such differentiation has at least two distinguishable dimensions—diversity of product design or physical characteristics, and differences in image or other subjective attributes upon which consumer loyalties are built. To characterize these influences we have formulated two variables, $PHYSDIFF_{ij}$ and $LOYALTY_{ij}$, measuring respectively the extent to which the products offered differ in physical and design features and the degree to which customers display loyalty to the brands of particular sellers. These are estimated judgmentally on a scale ranging from zero, implying no product design differences or consumer loyalty, to $+3$, indicating extensive physical differences or strong brand loyalties.

Input market imperfections might also affect plant size decisions. To examine one possible linkage, we employ the variable CAP_{ij}, measuring the amount of capital required to construct and equip ab initio an MOS plant in 1965. We hypothesize that the larger the capital ante is, the more likely firms facing capital rationing are to compromise and build plants of suboptimal scale.[33] The capital entry requirement estimates were pieced together from engineering data, information on actual 1960s investments, and U.S. Census capital asset book value tabulations. Despite generally lower construction and machinery cost levels overseas the U.S.-based estimates will be applied uniformly for all six nations. The sole exception to this simplifying convention will be petroleum refining, for which lower investment figures are used to reflect the less elaborate outfitting of European refineries producing relatively more fuel oil and less gasoline than their North American counterparts.

In somewhat the same spirit is EMP_j, estimating the number of employees staffing an MOS plant of average U.S. mid-1960s productivity. As Chapter 2 brought out, small-town labor markets exert an inhibiting effect on plant sizes, especially in the textile and shoe industries. It is conceivable that this is more generally true, and that the larger the labor force an MOS plant requires, the more establishing a full-size plant is discouraged by rising wage rates. However, firms in industries calling for plants with large numbers of workers might avoid this tradeoff by seeking plant locations with abundant labor supplies, in which case no such association should be evident.

Lag and Productivity Adjustment Variables

Finally, we consider three variables intended to compensate for measurement problems in our dependent variables. In some industries the minimum optimal scale has risen appreciably over the past two decades, while it fell in others. Our MOS estimates caught some of these trends in midstream and some near their apparent culmination. Actual plant sizes, however, can react only slowly to changes in size optima. If the MOS has risen, we should expect a substantial residue of incompletely adapted plants to persist for some time, imparting a downward thrust to the relevant Observed Plant Size/MOS estimates. To take this possible influence into account, we introduce a dummy variable $MOSUP_j$, with a value of one for the paint, cement, steel, refrigerator, brewing, and battery industries and zero otherwise. If there are adaptation lag effects systematically associated with these industries, we expect the variable's regression coefficient to be negative. Likewise, a dummy variable $MOSDOWN_j$ has a value of one for the shoe and bearing industries and zero otherwise, reflecting a fall in the MOS over time for those

33. Eastman and Stykolt found such a variable to be one of the main correlates of sub-MOS plant size incidence in 14 Canadian industries. *The Tariff and Competition in Canada*, pp. 72–79.

fields.[34] For it we predict a positive coefficient. A third dummy variable, ADJ_{ij}, has a value of one for those non-U.S. industries whose plant sizes had to be measured in terms of employment but for which no productivity adjustment could be made.[35] Since the unadjusted employment size indices for such industries tend to be biased upward, we expect a positive regression coefficient.

Summary of Variables

To sum up, we have defined two dependent variables, $TOP50_{ij}/MOS_j$ and MID_{ij}/MOS_j, representing the MOS-deflated size of plants comprising the top half of their industry's size distribution and of the plant at the midpoint in the size distribution respectively. The independent variables are as follows:

$COST_j$	Percentage elevation of the long-run unit production cost curve at one-third MOS.
$TRANS_j$	Transportation cost per dollar of product value on a standardized haul of 350 miles.
$DENS_i$	Adjusted population per square mile times an index of real national income per capita.
$MS3_{ij}$	The three-firm seller concentration ratio, regionally defined when appropriate.
$SIZE_{ij}$	Domestic consumption divided by the MOS.
$GROWTH_{ij}$	Percentage growth of production per annum, 1950–1967.
$EXPORT_{ij}$	1963 exports as a percentage of production.
$IMPORT_{ij}$	1963 imports as a percentage of domestic consumption.
$TARIFF_{ij}$	1957 average ad valorem tariff rate percentage on C.I.F. basis.
$LOYALTY_{ij}$	An index of customer loyalty to particular brands or suppliers.
$PHYSDIFF_{ij}$	An index of the extent of physical product differentiation among suppliers.

34. Weaving has a zero value because it is not certain that the MOS in fact fell, or whether extralarge but no more efficient plants became less efficient with increasingly complex product lines.

35. Because productivity in U.S. bearing plants was said by interviewees to be no higher than in Europe, the French, Canadian, and Swedish bearing ADJ dummies were set at zero despite the absence of a productivity adjustment. The British bearing employment data were adjusted on the basis of Industrial Reorganisation Corporation comparative productivity estimates.

CAP$_{ij}$ The capital cost of an MOS plant, circa 1965 (in millions of dollars).

EMP$_j$ Employment in an MOS plant of average mid-1960s' productivity.

MOSUP$_j$ Dummy variable indicating an upward MOS trend before 1965.

MOSDOWN$_j$ Dummy variable indicating a downward MOS trend before 1965.

ADJ$_{ij}$ Dummy variable indicating plant sizes measured in employment terms and uncorrected for productivity differences.

Model Specification

Economic theory provides only a few indications as to how a multiple regression model incorporating these variables should be specified. The main alternatives are an additive model of the general form:

$$(3.2) \qquad Y_i = a + b_1 X_{1i} + b_2 X_{2i} + \cdots + e_i;$$

and a multiplicative model of the form:

$$(3.3) \qquad Y_i = \alpha X_{1i}{}^{\beta 1} X_{2i}{}^{\beta 2} \cdots \epsilon_i;$$

which can be estimated linearly in the logarithms. Favoring the additive approach are two main a priori considerations: the first-order conditions for cost minimization imply an additive relationship between the unit production and unit transportation cost curve slope variables; and the market growth observations are sometimes negative and therefore incompatible with a multiplicative model. On the other hand, the previous analysis suggested a possible multiplicative interaction among the market size variable SIZE, the concentration variable MS3, and the unit transportation cost variable. If these are to be specified in a form which allows one to decompose their individual effects, the multiplicative approach is superior.

Attention must also be paid to statistical properties. Distortions due to extreme values are more apt to be avoided by taking logarithms, but this will be done in any event to reflect anticipated diminishing returns effects for SIZE and the highly skewed CAP variable. A more important consideration is the distribution of regression residuals, toward which we can only adopt a wait and see attitude.

Since the a priori indications are ambiguous, we shall explore both specification approaches in estimating the core of the model, choosing between or amending them, if a choice must be made, on the basis of the results. For the logarithmic regressions the dependent variable will be scaled in percentage form, as in Tables 3.12 and 3.13. For the additive regressions it will be scaled in ratio form; that is, with the figures of Tables 3.12 and 3.13 divided by 100.

The Results

Ordinary least-squares regressions were computed with the MOS-deflated Top 50 Percent and Midpoint Plant size indices as dependent variables and various clusters of independent variables. In most cases the number of observations covering the six nations and twelve industries totaled sixty-nine; observations on the Swedish and German bearing and German battery industries were excluded. The results were very similar for the Top 50 Percent and Midpoint Plant variables, which are correlated with $r = 0.943$ in the additive version and 0.964 in logarithmic form. To avoid duplication we shall emphasize results obtained with the TOP50/MOS variable.

Tables 3.16 and 3.17 report the zero-order Pearsonian correlations among the principal continuously scaled variables for the additive and logarithmic forms respectively. We note that TOP50/MOS is strongly correlated with the market size and capital requirements variables—a result closely paralleling the findings of H. C. Eastman and Stefan Stykolt in their study of plant sizes in fourteen Canadian industries.[36] In multiplicative form, but not in additive, a significant negative correlation is found between the plant size variable and MOS employment requirements EMP. Among what we shall view as independent variables, numerous relationships of interest appear: for example, the strong negative correlation between seller concentration and MOS-deflated market size, the very high positive correlation between CAP and EMP, and (in Table 3.16) the negative but insignificant correlation between concentration and export performance. More important are the moderate to strong intercorrelations among the production cost curve slope (COST), transportation cost, capital requirements, and physical product differentiation variables. These warn that nature was uncharitable in failing to preserve statistical independence among key theory-motivated variables, with possibly adverse multicollinearity repercussions. We shall in fact find multicollinearity to be moderately problematic. We therefore proceed cautiously, beginning with those few variables enjoying the strongest a priori support and adding refinements only gradually.

---

36. *The Tariff and Competition in Canada*, chap. 3.

Table 3.16. Correlation Matrix: Variables in Additive Form.

Variable	TOP50/MOS	Log SIZE	GROWTH	COST	TRANS/√DENS·MS3	MS3	Log CAP	EMP	PHYSDIFF	IMPORT	EXPORT
TOP50/MOS	1.000	0.641	−0.154	−0.024	−0.133	−0.054	−0.311	−0.199	0.174	0.001	0.062
Log SIZE		1.000	−.373	.035	−.024	−.516	−.413	−.265	.258	−.111	−.153
GROWTH			1.000	.013	.058	.281	.231	.062	−.221	.144	.257
COST				1.000	.806	.261	.315	.042	−.602	−.109	−.044
TRANS/√DENS·MS3					1.000	.256	.295	−.016	−.546	−.170	−.264
MS3						1.000	.342	.051	−.443	.129	−.054
Log CAP							1.000	.809	−.550	.088	.200
EMP								1.000	−.340	.081	.291
PHYSDIFF									1.000	.139	.058
IMPORT										1.000	.392
EXPORT											1.000

Note: $N = 69$.
Five percent significance point = 0.238; one percent significance point = 0.309.

Table 3.17. Correlation Matrix: Variables in Logarithmic Form.

Variable	$\dfrac{TOP50}{MOS}$	SIZE	COST	TRANS	DENS·MS3	MS3	CAP	EMP	PHYSDIFF
TOP50/MOS	1.000	0.674	0.092	−0.171	0.132	0.056	−0.260	−0.320	0.042
SIZE		1.000	−.080	−.185	−.085	−.517	−.413	−.438	.258
COST			1.000	.742	.205	.327	.473	−.024	−.682
TRANS				1.000	.237	.351	.564	.085	−.832
DENS·MS3					1.000	.367	.241	.119	−.280
MS3						1.000	.372	.179	−.483
CAP							1.000	.798	−.550
EMP								1.000	−.167
PHYSDIFF									1.000

Note: N = 69.
Five percent significance point = 0.238; one percent significance point = 0.309.

Core Regression Results

Tables 3.18 and 3.19 summarize the principal results for regressions limited to the key location-theoretic and investment-theoretic variables, with standard errors given in parentheses below the estimated regression coefficients. Coefficients statistically different from zero at the 0.05 level (usually in a one-tail test) are denoted by a single asterisk; those significant at the 0.01 level or higher by double asterisks.

Regressions 3.18.1 and 3.19.1 include only the most basic variables and assume that seller concentration operates solely in a spatial economic context (that is, in the demand density term). All coefficients have the signs predicted by theory, and all are significantly different from zero at the 0.05 level or better. Top 50 Percent plant sizes tend to be larger in relation to the MOS, the larger the market is, the more steeply the long-run unit production cost curve declines,[37] the less steeply unit transportation costs rise, and (discernible only in regression 3.19.1) the denser the demand tapped by the leading three sellers is. The production and transportation cost curve slope estimates illustrate well the classic textbook case of independent variables which exhibit little or no zero-order association with a dependent variable (as inspection of Tables 3.16 and 3.17 shows), but which become highly significant when combined in an appropriate multi-variate framework. By far the most powerful variable in the system is market size. Its removal would cause R^2 to fall to 0.09 in the additive and to 0.16 in the multiplicative version.[38]

37. An alternate variable, relating the change in production costs to *investment* per unit of output in an MOS plant rather than to full cost per unit of output, exhibited performance similar but in most cases inferior to the COST variable.

38. It might be argued that the strong plant size-market size association is spurious because both variables are divided through by the same MOS estimate values. At worst, however, the problem is unlikely to be a serious one. The MOS estimates play a different role in our analyses than they do in most ratio correlations. They serve as a common denominator without which comparisons of plant and market sizes (some scaled in tons per year, some in refrigerators or batteries per year, and some in terms of average employment) would be nonsensical. Spurious ratio correlation can appear then only to the extent that there are errors in measuring the MOS common denominators. Such errors indeed exist, but they are small in relation to the overall variance of the resulting plant size and market size ratios. Thus, it seems unlikely that careful studies based upon similar assumptions would come up with 1965 MOS estimates smaller than half ours or larger than twice ours. This is about the maximum range of disagreement between our estimates and those of Pratten and Dean, Cockerill, and others, who often applied different assumptions. The range of the TOP50/MOS estimates, on the other hand, is from about one-twentieth to 3.5 times (or with Swedish bearings included, 7.7 times) their mean value. With the TOP50/MOS ratio varying by a factor of roughly 100 while measurement errors in the MOS denominators span a maximum factor of four range, it seems improbable that spurious ratio correlation could be responsible for much of the observed association between TOP50/MOS and SIZE.

Table 3.18. Core Results: Additive Regressions.

Regres-sion number	N	Dependent variable; coverage	Independent variables			
			Con-stant	Log SIZE	COST	TRANS / √DENS·MS3
3.18.1	69	PA TOP50/MOS	0.216	0.659** (.096)	0.0319* (.0176)	−0.272** (.104)
3.18.2	69	PA TOP50/MOS	.074	.704** (.103)	.0324* (.0175)	−.278** (.104)
3.18.3	69	PA TOP50/MOS	−.675	.928** (.102)	.0134 (.0157)	
3.18.4	69	PA TOP50/MOS	.354		.0078 (.0157)	
3.18.5	69	PA TOP50/MOS	.131		.065** (.019)	
3.18.6	69	PA TOP50/MOS	−.018		.069** (.018)	
3.18.7	69	PA TOP50/MOS	−1.08	1.015** (.093)	.074** (.019)	
3.18.8	69	PA MID/MOS	0.046	0.388** (0.077)	.0264* (.0131)	−.185** (.078)
3.18.9	69	PA MID/MOS	−.027		.056** (.014)	
3.18.10	69	TOP50/MOS; no productivity adjustment	−.001		.065** (.022)	

Note: PA = productivity adjustment made whenever possible on plant sizes measured in employment terms.
The dependent variables are scaled in ratio form; i.e., observed average plant size divided by the MOS.

The statistical "fit" of the multiplicative model appears generally superior, with higher t-ratios and R^2 values and less tendency toward skewness in the distribution of residuals.

In additive regression 3.18.2, a first look is taken at the role of demand growth. When the variable GROWTH is added, its sign is positive as predicted, but it is statistically insignificant, with a t-ratio of only 1.17.[39]

The specifications adopted thus far embody the location-theoretic assumption that seller concentration affects plant sizes mainly through its impact on demand density and hence transportation costs. Yet, as

39. An absolute growth variable inspired by G in Chap. 2 was also tested. It was formed by dividing the annual average absolute growth in physical output by the appropriate MOS value. As a substitute for SIZE and GROWTH together, its performance was substantially inferior. When used in conjunction with SIZE its coefficient was statistically significant, but SIZE, with which it was collinear ($r = 0.665$), played a much stronger role.

		Independent variables				
$\dfrac{\text{TRANS}}{\sqrt{\text{DENS}}}$	$\sqrt{\text{DENS}}$	GROWTH	TRANS	MS3	Log SIZE·MS3	R²
						0.469
		0.019 (.016)				.398
−0.277** (.103)				1.261** (0.257)		.586
−.208* (.100)					0.916** (.101)	.581
	0.0014 (.0077)		−0.057** (.011)		.955** (.090)	.679
	−.0008 (.0076)	.0254* (.0126)	−.061** (.011)		1.018** (0.093)	.698
	.0021 (.0080)	.0199 (.0132)	−.065** (.011)	1.259** (0.225)		.698
		.0162 (.0123)				.342
	−.0052 (.0058)	.0239** (.0096)	−.043** (.009)		.623** (.071)	.602
	.0167* (.0092)	.0140 (.0153)	−.063** (.014)		.976** (.113)	625

Standard errors are given in parentheses.
*Significant at the 0.05 level (usually in a one-tail test).
**Significant at the 0.01 level or higher.

we have seen, concentration may also interact with market size when small markets are fragmented into output shares too small to support MOS plants and when oligopolists adopt a market share-preserving strategy in expansion decisions. To explore this possibility, regressions 3.18.3 and 3.19.2 remove the MS3 variable from the market density term and estimate its coefficients separately. Relative to most closely comparable regressions 3.18.1 and 3.19.1, there is a striking jump in R^2 of 0.129 for the additive version and 0.186 for the multiplicative version. Both the enhancement of R^2 and the separate MS3 variable's t-ratio are greater in the multiplicative model, which presumably characterizes better the hypothesized three-way interaction among market size, transport costs, and concentration. Multiplicative regression 3.19.2 suggests that most of the transport cost effect resides in transport cost per unit of product value (that is, in TRANS) and not in the geographic density of purchasing power. The density coefficient has a positive sign, as location

Table 3.19. Core Results: Multiplicative Regressions.

Regres-sion	N	Dependent variable; coverage	Con-stant	Independent variables						R²
				SIZE	COST	TRANS	DENS·MS3	DENS	MS3	
3.19.1	69	PA TOP50/MOS	0.863	0.374** (.048)	0.483** (.152)	−0.263** (.085)	0.172* (.072)			0.569
3.19.2	69	PA TOP50/MOS	1.32	.526** (.043)	.351** (.117)	−.286** (.065)		0.038 (.058)	0.817** (.108)	.755
3.19.3	69	PA TOP50/MOS	1.39	.530** (.042)	.350** (.117)	−.282** (.064)			.803** (.106)	.754
3.19.4	69	PA MID/MOS	1.24	.512** (.049)	.476** (.135)	−.351** (.074)		−.023 (.067)	.965** (.124)	.712
3.19.5	69	TOP50/MOS; no productivity adjustment	1.33	.470** (.049)	.247* (.133)	−.298** (.073)		.121* (.066)	.757** (.123)	.674

PA = productivity adjustment made whenever possible on plant sizes measured in employment terms.
The dependent variables are scaled as the base 10 logarithm of observed plant sizes as a percentage of the minimum optimal scale.
Standard errors are given in parentheses.
*Significant at the 0.05 level.
**Significant at the 0.01 level.

theory predicts, but it is exceeded by its standard error. When DENS is deleted from the system, as in multiplicative regression 3.19.3, R^2 drops by only 0.001. This result might be attributed to the unrealism of our initial assumption that demand is distributed uniformly over geographic space or to insensitivity of plant size choices to international demand density differences.

In an attempt to pinpoint whether the apparent interaction between market size and concentration operates mainly in a spatial economic framework or independently, we estimated additive regressions with multiplicative SIZE·MS3 interaction effects both built into the transportation cost curve slope term and separate from it. Regression 3.18.4 shows one simple but extreme form, with MS3 stripped from the transport cost slope term and the role of market size and concentration embodied only through an interaction variable log (SIZE·MS3). The interaction variable performs impressively, leading to an R^2 only 0.017 less than in regression 3.18.3. Evidently, most of the explanatory power of SIZE and MS3 resides in their mutual interaction rather than in their roles separately. When log SIZE and MS3 are alternately added to SIZE·MS3 interaction regressions (not explicitly reported), the interaction term continues to have by far the highest t-ratio. The incremental increase in R^2 owing to the addition of independent log SIZE or MS3 terms is 0.017 and 0.019, respectively, neither statistically significant. When a complex interaction variable TRANS/$\sqrt{}$(DENS·MS3·SIZE) is formed, its zero-order correlation with TOP50/MOS is -0.304, but its coefficient is exceeded by its standard error in a multiple regression containing log (SIZE·MS3) and COST (not explicitly reported). It seems impossible to avoid concluding that the interactive market size-concentration influence on plant size choices is essentially independent of outbound transport cost considerations.

Having come this far toward rejecting a specification based upon equation (3.1), with its assumption of uniform demand density, we now take a further step. In multiplicative regressions 3.19.2 and 3.19.3, we discovered that DENS had no independent explanatory power. We therefore disentangle it from the TRANS variable in additive regression 3.18.5. The outcome is a substantial improvement in the performance of both the TRANS and COST variables, along with a sizeable increase in R^2. As in the disembodied multiplicative version, DENS standing alone is dwarfed by its standard error. Evidently, DENS not only has no explanatory power in its own right, but also interferes with the functioning of the TRANS and COST variables when a ratio specification is adopted. Regression 3.18.6 shows that the market growth variable now comes into its own with the sign predicted by theory and a t-ratio of 2.02.

Additive regression 3.18.7 is identical to 3.18.6 except that separate SIZE and MS3 terms have been substituted for the SIZE · MS3 interaction. The increase in R^2 is perceptible only in the fourth decimal place (not shown), and there is little change in the COST, TRANS, and DENS relationships. We find again that the explanatory power attributable to the market size and seller concentration variables separately is also achieved by a combined SIZE · MS3 interaction term.

To summarize our conclusions up to this point, both the multiplicative and the later version additive regressions reveal that Top 50 Percent plant sizes are larger in relation to the MOS, the larger is the volume of output supplied by leading sellers (associated in turn with both overall market size and the leaders' market shares), the lower unit transport costs are per dollar of product value, the more steeply the unit production cost curve declines between one-third MOS and the full MOS, and the more rapidly industry output has been growing. Market size is the most powerful single explanatory variable, but seller concentration also plays a major part, both when it is included as a separate independent variable or when it interacts multiplicatively with market size.

The additive interaction equation results lead us to believe that the market size-concentration nexus is in fact multiplicative. Whether there are further interactions involving other variables, notably, TRANS, and hence favoring a multiplicative specification over the additive SIZE · MS3 version, is not completely clear. The slightly higher R^2 achieved with multiplicative regression 3.19.2 as contrasted to additive regression 3.18.5 is an inadequate basis for deciding, since R^2 values for dependent variables subjected to different transformations are not directly comparable. Inspection of error term distributions also provides no conclusive guidance. The residuals from these later regressions all conform tolerably well to the normal distribution pattern. The additive residuals show only modest traces of an excessively long positive error tail, while the multiplicative residuals have a slightly elongated negative tail and some tendency toward rectangularity on the positive side. Since the statistical signals are ambiguous, since both specifications can be adapted in forms compatible with the main clues a priori theory supplies, and since each is sensitive in different ways to extreme value problems, we shall carry both specifications into our further analysis. Additive regression 3.18.6 with a multiplicative SIZE · MS3 interaction term and multiplicative regression 3.19.2 will be the core systems upon which the effects of various modifications and new variations will be tested, although for maximum contrast we shall at times also resurrect naïve location-theoretic specification 3.18.1.

Sensitivity to Variable and Sample Coverage Changes

We now examine the sensitivity of our basic results to changes in key variables and sample coverage.

In regressions 3.18.8 and 9 and 3.19.4 we take MOS-deflated Midpoint Plant size as the dependent variable in place of TOP50/MOS. The results are similar to the analogous TOP50/MOS regressions except that some decrease in R^2 is evident. This decline could be attributable to the likelihood that the Midpoint estimates, focusing on a single plant in size distributions with sometimes substantial differences between the sizes of adjacent-ranked plants, are subject to greater measurement error than the multiple-plant Top 50 Percent averages.

In regressions 3.18.10 and 3.19.5 we bring back TOP50/MOS as dependent variable but delete the plant size observations on seventeen industries for which employment size estimates were adjusted by a productivity ratio, replacing them with the unadjusted size data. The industries affected are identified by the subscript a in Table 3.12. There is a moderate drop in the proportion of variance explained, a fall in the multiplicative COST coefficient's t-ratio, and in both versions the DENS variable jumps to statistical significance for the first and only time. Yet no changes of a fundamental character are visible.

The Swedish antifriction bearing industry, with only one domestic supplier and with average Top 50 Percent plant size 6.98 times the MOS, has been excluded because of its tendency to overwhelm less extreme observations. When it is included with a multiplicative specification the impact is quite small, since linearization by taking logarithms compresses large extreme values. For the augmented additive version of regression 3.18.6 (not explicitly shown), which is more strongly influenced by such extreme values, R^2 drops to 0.396. The key SIZE·MS3, TRANS, and COST coefficients nevertheless continue to have the signs predicted by theory, and all are statistically significant at the 0.01 level.

As a further precaution against spurious inferences we deleted observations for the cement industries of all six nations along with Swedish bearings. Cement is an extreme outlier on both the COST and TRANS variables, and it is disproportionately responsible for the high correlation between COST and TRANS—0.900 in additive and 0.742 in multiplicative form. This multicollinearity undoubtedly lies behind some of the COST coefficient's instability in certain specifications. And more importantly, multicollinearity could force one coefficient to have a sign opposite the other's, fulfilling one prediction of the underlying economic theory, although there is no statistical reason why it should cause TRANS and COST to have the *correct* signs and to be statistically significant. Indeed, the most common consequence of severe multicollinearity is to "blow up" standard errors *more than* regression coefficients, making it less likely that significance tests will be passed. When the cement industry observations are deleted, the intercorrelation between TRANS and COST falls to 0.520 in additive and 0.597 in multiplicative form. For regressions (not explicitly reported) without the cement observations but the same specification as 3.18.1, 3.18.5, and 3.19.2, all key variables were statistically significant at the 0.01 level with the signs predicted by theory, and there was visible improvement in the statistical fit, with R^2 increasing by 0.066, 0.008, and 0.035 over the respective full-sample regressions. These results afford reassurance on what otherwise could have been a doubtful point.

Differences Among National Groups

A further test of robustness is executed by partitioning the sample into three national groups consisting of the United States, Canada, and the four European nations. Table 3.20 summarizes the results for three major specification variants. All coefficients have the signs predicted by theory. In twenty-three cases out of thirty they are significantly different from zero at the 0.05 level or better, despite the fact that for the U.S. and Canadian regressions there are only twelve observations and seven or eight residual degrees of freedom. Letting each national group regression assume its own best-fitting coefficients reduces unexplained variance (that is, increases R^2) relative to the directly comparable pooled regression by 0.051 for the multiplicative version, 0.085 for the additive location-theoretic specification (regressions 3.20.4–6), and by 0.014 for the additive version with a SIZE·MS3 interaction term. The associated F-ratios for these variance increments are 1.42 (10,54), 1.36 (8,57), and 0.33 (8,57), respectively, none of which is statistically significant at the 0.05 level. Thus, one must accept the null hypothesis that the observed national group regression coefficient differences could have arisen by chance from a homogeneous population. Certain coefficients do differ sufficiently that they might pass individual heterogeneity tests, but there were no compelling grounds for identifying them ex ante. The most prominent difference is the much lower elasticity of plant size with respect to SIZE in U.S. multiplicative regression 3.20.1, perhaps implying that in markets uniformly quite large, the marginal effect of market size increases on plant sizes is modest.

There is however one respect in which the national groups exhibit a striking dissimilarity. If we delete the seller concentration variable MS3 from multiplicative regressions 3.20.1–3, the coefficient of determination R^2 falls by these amounts: United States, 0.164; Canada, 0.095; Europe,

Table 3.20.   National Group Regressions: Productivity-Adjusted TOP50/MOS as Dependent Variable.

Regres-sion	N	Explanation	Con-stant	Log SIZE	Log(SIZE·MS3)	MS3	$\frac{TRANS}{\sqrt{DENS}\cdot MS3}$	TRANS	COST	R^2
3.20.1	12	U.S. multiplicative	2.25	0.312* (.139)		0.977* (.437)		−0.376** (.110)	0.121 (.215)	0.770
3.20.2	12	Canada multiplicative	1.77	.640** (.117)		.597* (.283)		−.207 (.124)	.421 (.254)	.850
3.20.3	45	Europe multiplicative	1.33	.617** (.061)		.893** (.126)		−.284** (.083)	.400** (.185)	.762
3.20.4	12	U.S. additive	0.496	.525 (.406)			−0.775* (.386)		.103 (.077)	.504
3.20.5	12	Canada additive	−.089	.712** (.151)			−.380** (.102)		.103** (.025)	.823
3.20.6	45	Europe additive	.234	.581** (.129)			−.404* (.184)		.039* (.023)	.415
3.20.7	12	U.S. additive	.027		0.968* (.516)			−.077 (.042)	.089 (.080)	.531
3.20.8	12	Canada additive	.028		.911** (.132)			−.066** (.015)	.082** (.020)	.900
3.20.9	45	Europe additive	.193		1.014** (0.124)			−.048** (.014)	.053* (.023)	.644

Note: Standard errors are given in parentheses.
*Significant at the 0.05 level.
**Significant at the 0.01 level.

0.297. The change for Europe is much larger than for the North American nations—nearly three times the Canadian decline. Likewise, the increases in R^2 moving from additive regressions 3.20.4–6, emphasizing the role of concentration in plants' spatial market demand densities, to regressions 3.20.7–9, which stress the combined effect of concentration and market size on leading sellers' MOS-deflated output volume, are: United States, 0.027; Canada, 0.077; Europe, 0.229. Here again the multiplicative interaction between concentration and market size is vastly more important in Europe than in the New World.

The much stronger role of MS3 in the European regressions might be interpreted as support for the conventional European wisdom that concentration is necessary for the realization of scale economies and hence industrial efficiency. But here caution is in order. Were it not for the relatively low incremental explanatory power of MS3 in Canadian regression 3.20.2, we might infer that concentration facilitates the realization of plant scale economies primarily when national markets are small. Yet the results for comparatively tiny Canada cast doubt on this conjecture. What may be operating in Europe is a set of self-fulfilling expectations: If producers believe they need a large market share to build large plants, concentration will in fact be an important contributor to efficiency. Alternatively, the spirit of oligopolistic interdependence and respect for established market shares may simply be stronger in Europe. In the more individualistic North American business environment, producers may be more inclined to struggle, among other things through price competition, to realize scale economies, and concentration assumes a less important (though not vanishing) role. But here we tread beyond the limits permitted by our quantitative data.

Concentration and Causality

A further, more perplexing aspect of the concentration variable's role must also be explored. Might the suggested causal link from higher concentration to larger average plant sizes be spurious?

One possible argument is that concentration is naturally higher when plants are large and that, if a systematic relationship does exist, the direction of causality runs from plant sizes to concentration. If such a relationship holds in simple form, however, it is not evident in the zero-order correlations between MS3 and TOP50/MOS: $+0.056$ logarithmically and -0.054 additively. Moreover, it is by no means obvious why small plants should necessarily imply low concentration and large plants high concentration, even holding market size constant. Variations in the extent of multi-plant operation are substantial among the industries in our sample, with the mean number of plants per Big Three member ranging from one to thirty. In both small markets and large, high concentration could result just as readily from the operation by leading firms of multiple plants, each small.

Nevertheless, when variations in plant size, market size, and multi-plant operation are taken into account simultaneously, a more serious danger of spurious association arises. From the definition of a concentration ratio follows the identity relationship:

$$\text{Market share of three leading firms} \equiv \frac{\text{average size of leading firms' plants}}{\text{total size of market}} \times \text{number of leading firm plants}$$

where "size" is measured in comparable terms such as MOS plant equivalents. Rearranging to bring plant size to the left-hand side, we obtain:

$$(3.4) \quad \text{Average size of leading firms' plants} \equiv \frac{\text{total size of market}}{\text{number of leading firm plants}} \times \text{market share of three leading firms}$$

Three of the variables analyzed in this chapter correspond to terms in the identity: TOP50/MOS to the left-hand variable, SIZE to the total size of market variable, and MS3 to the market share of the three leading firms. If the correspondence were exact *and* if a fourth variable measuring multi-plant operation were introduced, the identity would be completed and we would have to conclude that the relationship between, say, MS3 and TOP50/MOS was essentially tautological.[40]

No multi-plant operation variable actually does appear in any of the regressions estimated thus far. Also, the correspondence of our variables to those required for an identity is not exact. MS3 measures the average market shares of leading sellers in *regional* markets when appropriate and is therefore not precisely compatible with TOP50/MOS and SIZE, which relate to *national* markets. Moreover, TOP50/MOS concerns

40. One way to avoid the dangers discussed here would be to define the dependent variable differently, e.g., as a ratio of non-U.S. to U.S. plant sizes, or as the percentage of output or employment in plants of at least MOS size or larger. Both possibilities were considered at an early stage in our research and rejected. Taking U.S. plant sizes as a base removes some of the most interesting sources of interindustry variation. Focusing on the percentage of supra-MOS plants throws out considerable information on the nations of greatest relevance in an analysis of scale economy sacrifices. Thus, for Sweden 8 of the 12 industries would have zero dependent variable values, while for Canada 5 industries would have zero values. Also, errors in estimating the MOS threshold can lead to exaggerated measurement errors with such an approach, and productivity corrections are particularly difficult to make when the observations for each industry span a different range of the plant size distribution.

plants in the top half of an industry's size distribution, regardless of whether they are operated by Big Three members or smaller firms. Therefore, none of our regressions satisfies the identity conditions.

It is nonetheless conceivable that the regressions could come close enough to an identity specification that spurious relationships would begin to appear. One way to press the issue is to borrow from Chapter 6 an index of multi-plant operation $MPO3_{ij}$, measuring the average number of plants operated by the three leading firms in our industries as of 1970.[41] We then estimate the quasi identity regression linearly in the logarithms:

(3R.1)
$$\text{Log}\left(\frac{\text{TOP50}}{\text{MOS}}\right) = 1.67 + \underset{(.043)}{.752} \log \text{SIZE} + \underset{(.082)}{.812} \log \text{MS3}$$
$$- \underset{(.072)}{.543} \log \text{MPO3}; \ R^2 = .829, \ N = 69.$$

If an identity were approximately present, each of the regression coefficients should have a unit value. All fall short of this criterion in the estimated equation, confirming the presence of measurement errors. Indeed, the coefficient estimates depart much further from unity than those estimated for similar quasi identity regressions in Chapters 5 and 6.[42] When the MPO3 variable is deleted and TOP50/MOS is regressed multiplicatively on SIZE and MS3 alone, R^2 drops by 0.151 points. This too suggests that the regressions we have been estimating remain some distance away from satisfying the identity specification.

The main unsettling point remaining concerns the behavior of the SIZE coefficient in multiplicative regressions containing MS3. As noted, the asymptotic value of such coefficients in a true identity is 1.0. When TOP50/MOS is regressed logarithmically on SIZE alone, the regression coefficient value is 0.387. As variables are added to approach the quasi identity specification, the SIZE coefficients in multiplicative regressions with TOP50/MOS as dependent variable are:

Independent variables	SIZE coefficient
SIZE, COST, TRANS, DENS	0.376
SIZE, COST, TRANS, DENS, MS3	.526
SIZE, COST, TRANS, DENS, MPO3	.549
SIZE, COST, TRANS, DENS, MS3, MPO3	.708
SIZE, MS3, MPO3	.752

41. To be consistent with the identity specification it must be multiplied by 3, but this is compensated for in the regression constant term with no effect on other coefficient estimates.

42. Cf. regressions (5R.1) and (6R.1-2) *infra.*

At each step where a variable is added or deleted bringing the regression system nearer the identity specification, there is a marked jump in the SIZE coefficient toward its identity value. In the specifications we have emphasized it has moved less than half the distance to the maximum observed value, but the fact that some systematic progression can be seen advises caution in drawing inferences.

We are nonetheless inclined for several reasons to believe that the observed explanatory power of SIZE and MS3 together is more than tautological. One has been pointed out already: regressions containing the SIZE and MS3 variables do not satisfy the conditions expected of an identity system. Second, if an increase in multiplicative SIZE coefficients signified an approaching identity condition, one would expect multiplicative European regression 3.20.3, which experiences by far the sharpest rise in R^2 when MS3 is added, to have a particularly high SIZE coefficient. Yet the European value is less than that observed for Canada, with a much weaker MS3 effect. Third, the performance of additive regressions with SIZE·MS3 terms demonstrates that the two variables interacting multiplicatively do have great power in explaining plant size differences. For our sixty-nine nation-industry cell sample, the log (SIZE·MS3) variable alone "explains" 52.9 percent of the TOP50/MOS variable's variance through bivariate regression—11.9 points more than the unaccompanied log SIZE variable. And it appears improbable that, given the wide but unaccounted for variance in the extent of multi-plant operation, the incremental power contributed by MS3 in this additive relationship is tautological.

Even if this conclusion is accepted, no cross-sectional regression analysis can demonstrate unambiguously that the chain of causation is as we have postulated it: from market size and concentration to plant size, rather than (or as well as) from plant size and (inversely) market size to concentration.[43] The most we can say is that there are plausible behavioral hypotheses consistent with the former set of links.

The Adjustment Lag Variables

Three zero-one dummy variables, MOSUP, MOSDOWN, and ADJ, have been defined to take into account plant size variations associated with lags in adjusting to minimum optimal scale changes and measurement errors owing to our inability to correct certain industries' employment figures for productivity differentials. When the MOS increased

---

43. Or to put the point quantitatively, the partial logarithmic correlation between TOP50/MOS and MS3 given SIZE is +0.641, regardless of whether TOP50/MOS or MS3 is considered the "dependent" variable.

appreciably in the years prior to 1965, we expect the ratio of observed to MOS plant sizes to be relatively small as a result of adjustment lags, imparting a negative sign to the MOSUP coefficient. If there was a fall in the MOS but older, once optimal plants survived at their former sizes, MOSDOWN should have a positive coefficient. The sizes of non-U.S. plants measured in employment terms without productivity adjustment tend to be overstated, and this should be reflected in a positive coefficient for the ADJ dummy variable.

Before considering the results, it is useful to contemplate the meaning of dummy variables in multiplicative as compared to additive regression models.[44] In an additive regression, a zero-one dummy D_i is customarily introduced in the form:

$$(3.5) \qquad Y_i = a + d\, D_i + b_1 X_{1i} + b_2 X_{2i} \cdots + e_i \cdot$$

Here the dummy coefficient d modifies the intercept term a, shifting it up or down by a constant amount regardless of the values of the other independent variables X_{ki}. With a multiplicative regression (estimated in base ten logarithms) dummy variables D_{1i} and D_{2i} enter as:

$$(3.6) \qquad Y_i = \alpha\, X_{1i}^{\beta_1}\, X_{2i}^{\beta_2}\, (10^{\gamma_1 D_{1i} + \gamma_2 D_{2i}})\, \epsilon_i \cdot$$

Here the dummies modify the *slope* term α. This means that when, say, MOS-deflated plant sizes increase with market size, the dummy variable-associated shift will be greater in absolute magnitude, the larger the market is. For the productivity adjustment variable this specification rubs against the grain of common sense. It seems more reasonable to expect productivity differentials to be neutrally or even negatively associated with market size, ceteris paribus. The multiplicative specification also errs in the wrong direction for lags in adjusting to MOS increases. If, for instance, the long-run equilibrium tendency is for plant sizes to equal the MOS in large markets and to be two-thirds of the MOS in small markets, an instantaneous doubling of the MOS will leave average plant sizes 50 percentage points away from their equilibrium level in the large market and 33 points away in the small. The consequent dummy variable adjustment needs to be larger, not smaller, for the small market. On the other hand, similar reasoning suggests that MOSDOWN compensates better for a halving of the MOS in the multiplicative model than in the additive. Some specification error appears therefore to be unavoidable when adjustment dummies are introduced, but the additive

44. See also D. B. Suits, "Use of Dummy Variables in Regression Equations," *Journal of the American Statistical Association*, 52 (December 1957), 548–551.

form is probably better specified because there were MOS decreases in only three industries while there were increases, frequently of considerable magnitude, in six.

Regressions 3.21.1 and 3.22.1 in Tables 3.21 and 3.22 reveal what happens when the three adjustment dummies are added to the two major regression model variants. In five cases out of six the dummy variable coefficients have the predicted signs.[45] The one exception involves MOSDOWN in regression 3.22.1, where the multiplicative specification was actually expected to be superior. In no case, however, are the coefficients statistically significant at the 0.05 level. Introducing the cluster of three dummy variables leads to R^2 increments of 0.015 and 0.007 over the directly comparable nondummy regressions reported in Tables 3.18 and 3.19—changes falling far short of statistical significance in F-ratio tests. Nevertheless, since the dummy variables deal with dependent variable measurement errors known to exist, it is difficult to argue conclusively that they should not be included.

Regressions 3.21.2 and 3.22.2 show the consequence of adding the adjustment dummies when no plant sizes measured in employment terms are adjusted for productivity differentials. Here we might expect the productivity adjustment dummy to perform especially well. It does in both cases, implying that the average size of plants measured without productivity adjustments is overstated by 27 to 30 percent, all else equal.

The International Trade Variables

We anticipated that plant sizes would be positively related to producers' export market penetration and that a correlation might exist between plant sizes and the import inroads made into firms' domestic markets, though its direction was unclear on a priori grounds. Model specification is again problematic. To the extent that exporting expands market boundaries while imports constrict them, a multiplicative interaction with the domestic market size variable SIZE is implied. However, if export markets serve mainly as a special dumping ground to digest large capacity increments while imports aggravate planning uncertainties or stimulate the quest for efficiency, the mathematical form of the relationship is less obvious. We therefore resort again to testing both the multiplicative and additive specifications. For the multiplicative version the market size modifier role will be given explicit shape by defining the export variable as $(1 + \text{EXPORT}/100)$ and the import variable as $(1 - \text{IMPORT}/100)$. In the additive regressions the import and export

45. The ADJ coefficient values imply a size overstatement of 7 to 10 percent relative to the average size of plants in those 9 industries for which productivity adjustments were needed and not made.

Table 3.21. Further Additive Regressions: TOP50/MOS as Dependent

Regression number	N	Description	Constant	Log SIZE·MS3	COST	TRANS	DENS	GROWTH	MOSUP
3.21.1	69	PA	−0.013	0.912** (.113)	0.061** (.020)	−0.051** (.013)	−0.0007 (.0077)	0.0294* (.0130)	−0.038 (.132)
3.21.2	69	NPA	−.120	.921** (.139)	.061** (.023)	−.053** (.015)	.0139 (.0092)	.022 (.016)	−.038 (.164)
3.21.3	69	PA	.101	.979** (.090)	.056** (.020)	−.051** (.012)			
3.21.4	69	PA	.093	.894** (.118)	.053** (.022)	−.045** (.014)	−.0060 (.0087)	.0311* (.0137)	−.088 (.134)
3.21.5	57	PA (brewing, cigarettes excluded)	−.165	1.103** (0.112)	.079** (.022)	−.067** (.014)		.0327* (.0146)	
3.21.6	57	PA (brewing, cigarettes excluded)	−.255	1.123** (0.115)	.071** (.024)	−.061** (.016)		.0312* (.0148)	
3.21.7	69	PA	.196	.860** (.116)	.062** (.023)	−.051** (.014)	.0019 (.0079)		−.087 (.139)
3.21.8	69	PA	.197	.861** (.115)	.065** (.022)	−.053** (.014)	.0020 (.0079)		−.078 (.136)
3.21.9	69	PA	−.036	1.012** (0.096)	.075** (.020)	−.060** (.012)			
3.21.10	69	PA	.181	.873** (.119)	.054** (.025)	−.046** (.014)	.0008 (.0076)		−.089 (.134)

Note: **PA** = productivity-adjusted dependent variables; **NPA** = no productivity adjustment when plant sizes are measured in employment terms.
Standard errors are given in parentheses.

Table 3.22. Further Multiplicative Regressions: TOP50/MOS as Dependent

Regression number	N	Description	Constant	SIZE	COST	TRANS	DENS	MS3	MOSUP
3.22.1	69	PA	1.35	0.508** (.055)	0.321* (.158)	−0.249** (.104)	0.036 (.061)	0.787** (.126)	−0.038 (.073)
3.22.2	69	NPA	1.24	.529** (.056)	.299* (.152)	−.287** (.104)	.086 (.061)	.821** (.130)	.020 (.077)
3.22.3	69	PA	1.51	.593** (.041)	.138 (.114)	−.168** (.063)	−.074 (.058)	.877** (.097)	
3.22.4	69	PA	1.55	.604** (.054)	.149 (.145)	−.182* (.095)	−.094 (.061)	.839** (.111)	−.040 (.064)
3.22.5	69	PA	1.32	.527** (.046)	.350** (.119)	−.286** (.068)	.038 (.059)	.817** (.109)	
3.22.6	69	PA	1.27	.532** (.047)	.354** (.119)	−.287** (.065)	.036 (.059)	.817** (.109)	
3.22.7	69	PA	1.61	.491** (.044)	.254* (.115)	−.396** (.080)	.054 (.056)	.763** (.107)	
3.22.8	69	PA	1.66	.463** (.054)	.145 (.158)	−.333** (.102)	.058 (.059)	.745** (.123)	−.002 (.070)

Note: **PA** = productivity-adjusted dependent variables; **NPA** = no productivity adjustment when plant sizes are measured in employment terms.
Standard errors are given in parentheses.

Variable.

			Independent variables						
MOS-DOWN	ADJ	IMPORT	EXPORT	TARIFF	Log CAP	EMP	PHYS-DIFF	LOY-ALTY	R²
0.222 (.182)	0.095 (.170)								0.713
.146 (.216)	.281* (.149)								.663
		−0.0021 (.0036)	0.0097 (.0072)						.687
.267 (.190)	.137 (.171)	−.0067 (.0040)	.0081 (.0083)						.727
				−0.0014 (.0096)					.694
		−.0023 (.0037)	.0092 (.0083)	.0014 (.0106)					.703
.129 (.206)	.044 (.178)				−0.0126 (.0888)				.688
.116 (.192)	.033 (.177)					−0.013 (.089)			.690
							−0.045 (.068)	0.140 (.087)	.691
.345 (.241)	.198 (.180)						−.184* (.096)	.187* (.091)	.717

*Significant at the 0.05 level.
**Significant at the 0.01 level.

Variable.

			Independent variables					
MOS-DOWN	ADJ	1 − IMPORT	1 + EXPORT	CAP	EMP	PHYS-DIFF	LOY-ALTY	R²
−0.004 (.138)	0.087 (.084)							0.762
−.127 (.138)	.263** (.063)							.755
		0.127 (.176)	3.78** (0.86)					.815
−.103 (.128)	.108 (.074)	.142 (.189)	3.94** (0.87)					.825
				0.0002 (.0430)				.755
					0.018 (.057)			.756
						−0.059 (.046)	−0.090* (.039)	.790
.099 (.133)	.109 (.085)					−.095* (.051)	−.071* (.042)	.799

*Significant at the 0.05 level.
**Significant at the 0.01 level.

percentages are used directly, since a linear transformation would in any event only affect intercept values.

The third and fourth regressions in Tables 3.21 and 3.22 all show plant sizes to be larger, the more export-oriented an industry is and the less imports are as a percentage of domestic consumption. However, none of the import coefficients is significant at the 0.05 level in a two-tail test. The export coefficients are not significant in the additive specification but are highly significant in the multiplicative version, lending support to the market expansion hypothesis. Of special interest are the high multiplicative export elasticities, suggesting that if exports increase from, say, 10 to 20 percent of domestic production, the average observed size of Top 50 Percent plants rises by approximately 35 percent. A more disturbing feature of the multiplicative import-export regressions is the apparent increase in multicollinearity, with a particularly adverse impact on the COST and TRANS coefficients. Yet the substantial increases in R^2 signify that the IMPORT and especially the EXPORT variables make genuine explanatory contributions, and that they do not merely capture power from other variables in the system.

The zero-order correlation between the 1957 ad valorem tariff rate variable TARIFF and TOP50/MOS is $+0.317$, which is significant at the 0.05 level. However, when TARIFF is introduced into additive regressions 3.21.5 and 3.21.6, its coefficients are smaller than their standard errors, and in one case the coefficient sign reverses.[46] Thus, stronger tariff protection did not appear to give rise to significantly larger plant sizes, other relevant variables being held equal.[47]

Capital Rationing, Labor Market Imperfections, and Product Differentiation

In zero-order correlation matrix Tables 3.16 and 3.17, TOP50/MOS is seen to be negatively and significantly correlated with the capital entry requirements variable CAP. The more capital needed to build a plant of minimum optimal scale, the smaller plants tend to be in relation to the MOS. However, this relationship evaporates when CAP is introduced

---

46. The TARIFF variable had positive coefficients in various regressions of the $TRANS/\sqrt{(DENS \cdot MS3)}$ type, but none had a t-ratio exceeding 1.31. Only 57 observations were included in the tariff analysis, it bears repeating, owing to the difficulty of disentangling beer and cigarette excise taxes from true import duties.

47. With our data it is possible to construct a simple model "explaining" imports as a percentage of domestic consumption. The best-fitting regression was:
IMPORT = 15.5 − .678** TRANS + 19.63** MS3 − .647* TARIFF;
        (.210)   (7.98)   (.295)
$R^2 = .220$, $N = 57$.
All the signs have obvious intuitive interpretations. The market size and Top 50 Percent plant size variables had no explanatory power when tested in other regressions.

into multiple regressions, as in regressions 3.21.7 and 3.22.5. With no multivariate specification tested did the CAP coefficient have a t-ratio exceeding 0.64, and the coefficient signs were erratic. Evidently, the simple correlation between TOP50/MOS and CAP stems from more complex associations, some causal and some spurious, between capital requirements, the slopes of production cost functions, concentration, transportation costs, and market size. When those variables are employed directly, they rather than CAP provide the more effective explanation of plant sizes.

A similar fate befalls the MOS plant employment variable EMP. In neither regressions 3.21.8 and 3.22.6 nor other unreported variants does any significant relationship materialize, despite the relatively high negative zero-order correlation.

We also hypothesized that plants may survive at suboptimal scales when their products are differentiated either physically or through image features cementing customer loyalties. The judgmental variables PHYSDIFF and LOYALTY measuring these characteristics are scaled arbitrarily from zero, connoting no significant product differentiation, to +3, implying strong differentiation.

Considering first the LOYALTY variable results, we observe that in additive regressions 3.21.9 and 10 the coefficients are positive, contrary to prediction. Multiplicative regressions 3.22.7 and 8 do exhibit the postulated inverse association, with coefficients presumably significant at the 0.05 level. In view of this divergence, it seems prudent to regard the indications as inconclusive.

The signs of the PHYSDIFF variable are uniformly consistent with expectations, and in the two regressions with dummy variables they are statistically significant. Nevertheless, it is not altogether clear that we have actually captured what we set out to measure. Turning back to Tables 3.16 and 3.17, it is seen that PHYSDIFF is strongly correlated negatively with COST. It is conceivable that this correlation is not merely spurious. The lowest values of PHYSDIFF occur for the cement, steel, and glass bottle industries, all processing more or less standardized products with indivisible, high-capacity equipment. The highest values are for shoes and fabrics, where much of the equipment used has a low capacity in relation to the output of an optimal plant—an important consideration in adapting production to heterogeneous, changing demands. Capital equipment indivisibility is a major source of plant scale economies, and it may well be that product homogeneity, equipment indivisibility, and steeply declining unit production cost curves are more than coincidentally related. If so, the PHYSDIFF variable might be serving as a surrogate scale economies index. That a competitive relationship exists between COST and PHYSDIFF is shown by the marked degradation of the multiplicative regression COST coefficient values when the product differentiation variables are added. We are therefore in doubt as to the exact role of PHYSDIFF. Some effect is evidently present, but whether it reflects the ability of companies to compensate through product differentiation for (characteristically modest) cost penalties owing to small-scale operation, the tendency of PHYSDIFF to supplement or displace the imperfectly measured production cost curve slope term, or some more subtle statistical anomaly is not certain.

To recapitulate, international and interindustry plant size variations in relation to the minimum optimal scale are associated systematically with market size, the degree to which sales are concentrated in the hands of a few leading producers, and a set of variables reflecting the cost minimizing decisions of firms serving spatially dispersed markets. From half to three-fourths of the variance in MOS-deflated plant sizes is accounted for by regressions incorporating those variables. The evidence of a multiplicative interaction between market size and concentration in explaining plant sizes is particularly strong for the European nations, although the relationship persists with attenuated power for Canada and the United States. Whether the differing power of the concentration variable is attributable to the smallness of many European nations, greater respect for oligopolistic interdependence, an unwillingness to struggle for market position and scale economies, or some combination of these and other influences is not altogether clear. Of the location-theoretic variables, transportation cost per unit of product value is the most consistent predictor. International differences in the average density of consumer purchasing power per square mile exhibit no significant influence. There are also indications that plants tend to be larger, the more successful producers were in tapping export markets, the more rapidly markets have been growing, and the less products are differentiated physically, but these relationships are clouded by statistical "noise," specification uncertainties, or doubts concerning true chains of causation.

The Growth of Average Plant Sizes

Our cross-sectional analysis provides a perspective on plant sizes at only one moment in time. Interviews revealed that plant sizes were changing over time, in some cases rapidly, in others slowly. What factors explain the rate at which plants are expanded?

Unfortunately, meaningful statistics on changes in plant size distributions are hard to come by. Employment comparisons can be made for many industries, but they reveal little about true size changes because the observed trends are apt to be dominated by changes in worker productivity. For a valid comparison, physical capacity or output data are needed. Only for the petroleum refining industry were data of sufficient quality and scope available to permit a statistical analysis. Additional qualitative insights on factors affecting the rate at which plant structures adapt in other industries will be presented in the next chapter.

From various annual survey issues of the *Oil and Gas Journal*, data on petroleum refinery capacity size distributions as of 1961, 1966, and 1971 were obtained for each of our six sample nations plus Italy, Belgium, the Netherlands, and Japan.[48] The statistics were sufficient to compute the average size (in stream barrels per day of crude oil processing capacity) of Top 50 Percent refineries and the rate of growth, continuously compounded, of average Top 50 Percent plants' size from 1961 to 1971, 1961 to 1966, and 1966 to 1971. We shall call the average leading plant size variable for the ith nation and the tth year $TOP50_{it}$ and the growth rate from year t to t^* $SIZGR_{i,t-t^*}$. Average plant sizes for 1961 and growth rates from 1961 to 1971 are displayed in the first and second numerical columns of Table 3.23.

Interviews and independent published studies reveal that long-run unit costs in petroleum refining decline at a decreasing rate at least out to refinery capacities of 200,000 barrels per day. Since the cost penalty incurred by a refinery with capacity of 50,000 barrels per day compared to a 200,000 barrel refinery is more than twice as great as that borne by a 100,000 barrel refinery, we expect the strength of the incentive to expand plants to be stronger, the smaller the average initial size of a nation's refineries is. Thus, we hypothesize a negative association between $TOP50_{i,o}$ and $SIZGR_{i,o-t}$, ceteris paribus. Given the tendency toward diminishing returns in the unit cost-scale relationship, we employ a logarithmic transformation of $TOP50$.

One might also expect the rate of increase in refinery sizes to be greater in markets where petroleum products demand is growing rapidly than in slowly growing markets, all else equal. To test this hypothesis, we define another variable $DEMGR_{i,t-t^*}$, measuring the annual growth rate of refined petroleum products consumption (in metric tons) for periods comparable to those spanned by the refinery size growth data. Values for the 1961–1971 interval are printed in the third numerical column of Table 3.23.

Absorbing the output of refineries expanded rapidly should be easier in large markets than in small, all else equal. We therefore introduce

48. The U.S. and Canadian data appeared in the April 3, 1961; March 28, 1966; June 6, 1966; and March 22, 1971, issues. Data for other nations are generally published in the last issue of each calendar year.

Table 3.23. Plant Size and Market Growth in the Petroleum Refining Industries of Ten Nations, 1961–1971.

Nation	Average 1961 capacity of Top 50 Percent refineries (barrels/day)	Annual rate of Top 50 Percent capacity growth, 1961–1971 (percent)	Annual rate of domestic consumption growth, 1961–1971 (percent)	Domestic consumption in 1961 (millions of metric tons per year)
United States	173,493	2.46	3.7	432.3
Canada	64,992	2.61	5.2	41.5
United Kingdom	214,037	1.98	7.1	49.7
Sweden	40,000	10.53	8.2	13.1
France	115,582	5.40	12.1	29.0
West Germany	80,281	5.81	13.4	34.1
Italy	76,198	12.75	13.6	24.3
Belgium	86,977	9.94	12.9	7.8
Netherlands	300,000	3.95	11.0	13.8
Japan	79,662	8.13	17.7	31.4

Sources: Oil and Gas Journal, various issues; and Organisation for Economic Co-operation and Development, *Statistics of Energy*, various years.

variable DEM_{it} measuring the total volume (in metric tons per year) of domestic petroleum products consumption. Values for 1961 are listed in the last column of Table 3.23. Again, we anticipate a diminishing returns effect in very large national markets, so we shall deploy DEM in logarithmic form.

The zero-order correlations between the variables defined for 1961 as base year and 1971 as terminal year are:

	$SIZGR_{61-71}$	Log $TOP50_{61}$	$DEMGR_{61-71}$	Log DEM_{61}
$SIZGR_{61-71}$	1.000	−0.626	0.594	−0.580
log $TOP50_{61}$		1.000	−0.192	0.304
$DEMGR_{61-71}$			1.000	−0.544
log DEM_{61}				1.000

Consistent with expectations, we find a substantial negative correlation between plant size growth rates and average initial plant sizes and a positive correlation between demand growth and plant size growth. The negative correlation between plant size growth and market size is unexpected. It may reflect multicollinearity between the domestic consumption variable and other supposedly independent variables. Specifically, demand growth was significantly less rapid in the larger markets, while (consistent with our earlier cross-sectional results) refineries tended to be larger on the average in the more sizeable markets.

To pin down the separate roles of the three explanatory variables, we estimate the additive multiple regression:

(3R.2) $SIZGR_{61-71} = 25.20 - 6.98^* \log TOP50_{61}$
$$(3.60)$$
$$+ .329\ DEMGR_{61-71} - 1.83 \log DEM_{61};$$
$$(.248) \qquad\qquad (2.35)$$
$$R^2 - .660,\ N = 10.$$

The TOP50 and DEMGR coefficients have the signs predicted, but only the TOP50 coefficient is significantly different from zero at the 0.05 level in a one-tail test. The market size variable DEM continues to have an unexpected sign, but its coefficient is exceeded by its standard error. Collinearity of DEM with the other independent variables also has an adverse impact on their t-ratios, as the following regression with DEM deleted reveals:

(3R.3) $SIZGR_{61-71} = 17.27 - 7.66^* \log TOP50_{61}$
$$(3.39)$$
$$+ .429^*\ DEMGR_{61-71};\ R^2 = .626,\ N = 10.$$
$$(.206)$$

Here both the initial refinery size and market growth relationships are statistically significant. Deletion of DEM from the system caused a reduction in R^2 of only 0.034 points.

Somewhat surprisingly, these relationships do not persist uniformly when the 1961–1971 interval is broken down into two subperiods. For the earlier 1961–1966 period, market growth appears to have by far the more important effect:

(3R.4) $SIZGR_{61-66} = 3.25 - 2.49 \log TOP50_{61}$
              (5.61)
              $+ .655^* DEMGR_{61-66}; R^2 = .472, N = 10.$
              (.270)

In the later period initial refinery size takes over:

(3R.5) $SIZGR_{66-71} = 33.85 - 14.19^* \log TOP50_{66}$
              (5.74)
              $+ .376 DEMGR_{66-71}; R^2 = .512, N = 10.$
              (.463)

One possible rationalization is that the need to keep up with rapidly growing demands was the principal stimulus to refinery expansion in the early 1960s, while the deceleration of demand growth and an increase in competition (associated in part with the reduction of European Community trade barriers) in the late 1960s put special pressure to expand and capture scale economies on national industries with small average refinery sizes. However, our interviews revealed no sharp EC-induced intensification of competition among refiners. Given the smallness of our sample, the change in relative weights over time might also be attributable to more or less random influences. Considering the full 1961–1971 period, the results do provide moderately strong support for the hypothesis that plants are expanded more rapidly, the greater their initial scale economies sacrifice is and the more rapidly the markets they serve are growing.

Epilogue

When the plan for this chapter was first laid out, we contemplated a section comparing the plant size distributions for our seventy-two industries with interview estimates of the extent to which unit production costs are elevated in plants operating at various fractions of the minimum optimal scale. The end product would be an estimate for each nation-industry cell of the percentage by which total industry production costs exceeded the costs which would be incurred if all plants were of minimum optimal scale.

Further reflection convinced us that the enterprise should be abandoned. It would indeed have been possible to generate a set of cost premium estimates with considerable intrinsic interest. But intrinsic interest is no guarantee of validity. And the validity of the estimates we would have been able to make would be dubious on at least three grounds.

For one, most plants are inherited from the past, and many plants were built when the MOS was considerably smaller than it was in 1965. To deal with this problem effectively, we would have needed data on the vintages of all existing plants and on changes in optimal sizes over a considerable time period. We had neither in adequate quantity. Nor were we able to say in hindsight whether firms would have been better off delaying their investments until plants of larger size became optimal. An alternate approach would have been to ask whether observed plants were obsolete in the sense that their continuing *variable* unit costs exceeded the *full* unit costs of best-practice replacements. In more instances than not, our interviews suggested, we would have found existing plants of suboptimal scale not to be inefficient in this sense. But we lacked the information to carry out a comprehensive quantitative analysis.

Second, it is clear that plants of less than the production-cost-minimizing scale are not necessarily inefficient in the broader sense of minimizing production plus physical distribution costs. Our regression analysis shows that high transport costs are associated with scale economy sacrifices. Yet determining what size distribution of plants would be optimal in view of demand densities and transport opportunities in each of the national industries covered by our sample would require collecting data and solving nonlinear programming problems on a scale vastly exceeding the already complex studies to be reported in Chapter 8. To ignore the problem would have guaranteed faulty excess cost estimates, but to solve it was beyond our resources.

Finally, numerous plants specialize in supplying physically differentiated products requiring different production processes or more individualized managerial attention than the product lines assumed in our MOS estimates. For such plants the sacrifice of scale economies may be much smaller than loss estimates based upon a single "best practice" MOS figure would imply. But again, we lack sufficient information on the distribution of MOS values over diverse product types and the incidence of actual plant specialization patterns to tell how large a correction to apply.

As a result we have chosen not to attempt the heroic quantitative leap originally contemplated. Despite these qualifications, nearly all implying that a simple-minded application of 1965-vintage cost functions would overstate the level of excess costs, our general impression is that the excess costs associated with scale economy sacrifices were substantial in many of the non-U.S. industries, and especially in Sweden. We reach this conclusion because we have found significant differences in average plant sizes between nations despite the fact that firms in all six nations could at any given vintage date sample from a similar array of technical possibilities. Also, the transportation cost, market density, and product differentiation variables stressed in our qualifications accounted for much less variance in MOS-deflated plant sizes than the market size and seller concentration variables, shortfalls in which could cause real scale economy sacrifices uncompensated by transportation cost savings or managerial control advantages. Thus, our regression analysis has "explained" the incidence of inefficiently small plants, but it has not shown that no efficiency problem exists.

4

The Determinants of Plant Size: Interview Evidence

Having accounted through multiple regression for well over half the variance in observed MOS-deflated plant sizes, we should perhaps rest on our laurels. To do so, however, would be to leave important qualitative insights from our interviews unexploited. In this chapter we look behind the statistical aggregates to shed further light on why plants of suboptimal scale persist. Given the base of statistical evidence from which we build, we shall not try to be comprehensive, but will focus on several questions begged or resolved incompletely by the regression analysis. We will be particularly concerned with the role of technology and factor prices; the interaction between market size, market structure, and oligopolistic behavior; and the impact of special government policies.

Technology and Factor Prices

In Chapter 3 we asserted with little elaboration that the minimum optimal scale appeared to be similar for any given industry across the six nations studied. This requires further explanation. Shouldn't optimal plant sizes differ among nations because of differential access to the most advanced technology or because of varying factor price relationships?

Differential access to technology was an unimportant determinant of plant size choices for at least three reasons. First, all six nations covered by our study are relatively advanced technologically, enjoying a substantial cohort of persons with the training required to understand and apply the newest techniques. Second, for nearly all the sample industries, major items of capital equipment are supplied by companies which compete on the world market. Hence, any firm which wants to install the most advanced equipment can buy it or, as in the shoe industry, lease it. Third, there is extensive international exchange of information on process and product technology in most of the twelve industries. In addition to supplier brochures, trade journal articles, and industry association technical papers, personal visits to other manufacturers' plants are an important diffusion mechanism. In some respects the international flow of information is richer than intranational diffusion, since companies who will not permit domestic competitors to visit their plants frequently welcome noncompetitive foreign visitors. And even in industries like batteries with a strong propensity toward secrecy, technology flows freely across national borders through licensing agreements. Almost every battery firm we interviewed was licensed to use one or more processes originally developed by foreign companies. For all these reasons, differences in access to technology among the nations in our sample were minimal.

Even when all producers confront the same technology set, their choices might diverge because of varying factor price ratios. Since the principal capital equipment items used in most of our twelve industries were bought and sold on an international market, equipment prices differed from one country to another at most by not much more than the costs of freight and tariffs. Despite imperfections, financial capital markets are also sufficiently international that large deviations in long-term interest rates cannot persist. But labor costs in manufacturing varied widely—from about 60 U.S. cents per hour on the average during 1965 in France, 90 cents in England, $1.03 in Germany, and $1.70 in Sweden to $2.61 in the United States.[1] Differences in capital/labor price ratios were attenuated because domestic labor is embodied in buildings and equipment installations, but this was not sufficient to eliminate substantial international variations in composite factor price ratios.

Nevertheless, production process choices appear to be constrained to the array of alternatives available from specialized suppliers. Especially in the glass bottle, cigarette, beer bottling, shoemaking, and textile weaving fields, relatively few machinery makers compete. Respect for interdependence can induce suppliers to concentrate on equipment with

1. International Labour Office, *Year Book of Labour Statistics: 1971* (Geneva, 1972), pp. 560–567. Exchange rates prevailing at the time were used for the conversion into dollars. Needless to say, the differences have narrowed considerably owing inter alia to the dollar devaluations of the early 1970s.

similar technical characteristics. This tendency is often reinforced by other considerations, even when the number of process suppliers is larger. In capital equipment decisions, the direction of technical progress depends more upon *expected* factor price ratios than upon currently prevailing ratios.[2] And although factor price ratios differed among nations originating the bulk of the demand served by capital goods suppliers, the differences have been narrowing over time, with a uniform tendency for wages to rise relative to the cost of capital.

The result has been a strong incentive for equipment manufacturers to press their innovative efforts in a labor-saving direction. This bias has generally accorded with the desires of equipment buyers, though the cigarette industry provides a partial exception. Cigarette manufacturers with fragmented product lines and small brand volumes expressed displeasure over the race among oligopolistic machine producers toward faster, less flexible "making" machines. Yet none of the dissatisfied buyers considered itself able to develop its own "optimal" making and packaging equipment. This reflects a second constraint. Because of scale economies, machines designed to meet the needs of the largest customer class are likely to be relatively less expensive than equipment produced in small volume for special factor price situations. A manufacturer enjoying low wage levels may therefore find a capital-intensive machine to be the best available bargain despite the fact that alternate machines would become dominant if demand were sufficient to induce their development and/or bring down their production costs and prices.

In principle there is of course no necessary connection between factor proportions and scale economies. Indivisibilities are the primary reason for scale economies. Factor proportion choices are relevant mainly to the extent that relatively high labor/capital price ratios induce the use of more capital-intensive equipment which is simultaneously less divisible. This is possible but, our interviews suggested, not very important. In the process-oriented industries such as steel, petroleum refining, cement, bottle making, and (less clearly) brewing, the minimum optimal scale is dominated by the scales of key equipment units such as blast furnaces, pipe stills, kilns, and a glass furnace with its control apparatus; or by the least common multiple among a few major equipment items. There, as in the development of beer canning machines, technological progress has been such that larger units reduce not only unit labor costs but also unit capital and (in steel, cement, and glassmaking) fuel costs.

2. Cf. William J. Fellner, "Two Propositions in the Theory of Induced Innovations," *Economic Journal*, 71 (June 1961), 305–308; and "Technological Progress and Recent Growth Theories," *American Economic Review*, 57 (December 1967), 73–98.

In the other industries the bases of scale economies are more complex, involving complicated least common multiples among smaller indivisible units (as in shoes, cigarettes, weaving, paints, and bearings), stamping and assembly line indivisibilities (as in refrigerators and batteries), plant management and utilities indivisibilities (especially in brewing, cigarettes, paints, shoes, bearings, and batteries) and advantages from massing reserves of specialized indivisible skills (in cigarettes).

In nearly all such cases the optimal scales of individual units meshing to form a least common multiple, threshold plant overhead requirements, and other indivisible factors appear to be relatively insensitive to differences in factor price ratios across the range encountered among the nations and industries in our sample. Similarly, in industries like weaving, shoes, and bottles, where unit costs might continue falling at larger plant scales were it not for managerial control difficulties, the size of an operation which a manager of normal ability can successfully handle appeared not to vary systematically from nation to nation, despite differences in management education approaches, degrees of work force unionization, and other "cultural" factors. It was largely for these reasons that the MOS estimates elicited in interviews varied so little from nation to nation.

The two industries for which this conclusion is most debatable are batteries and paints. In both, rising wages have directly induced efforts to achieve greater automation, and this in turn has led to rising plant scale optima. In batteries, the principal impact has been on the degree to which assembly operations are automated; and the more automated the line is, the larger its annual volume must be to sustain minimum unit costs. In paints the links are more complex: rising wages have made a greater annual volume desirable in relation to more or less fixed supervisory staff, increased the optimal sizes of individual batches, and induced greater automation of can filling lines. Interviews revealed that producers' estimates of the minimum optimal scale in batteries and paints had been rising more or less steadily during the 1960s, with the judgments of French companies, whose wages were lowest on the average, lagging perceptibly behind those of firms in higher wage countries.

To the extent that such factor price ratio-correlated lags exist, the MOS may differ between nations at a moment in time even though all nations are following the same dynamic trajectory. In formulating our MOS estimates we have nonetheless elected to ignore such differences because some low-wage country producers enjoying market shares or a geographic distribution of demand conducive to large production lots— for example, battery manufacturers Lucas in England and Varta in Germany, plus Imperial Chemical Industries' paint division—had already by 1965 found it advantageous to build plants as large as those believed to confer all significant scale economies in higher-wage nations. In that ceteris non paribus sense the "best-practice" plant size was uniform internationally, even though the MOS for producers comparable except in wage scales may have differed.

Although the MOS estimates varied little from country to country, there was evidence that man/machine relationships did differ, perhaps systematically, between the high-wage North American nations and the lower-wage European lands. When labor is cheap, it may pay to assign fewer looms of a given type per operative, all else equal, since closer attention reduces loom down time and improves capital utilization. Similar considerations may at least partly explain the more generous manning of cigarette-making machines, beer vats, and paint-mixing vats observed in Europe. Likewise, there was perceptibly less compulsion to automate materials handling and outbound product packing activities in the lower-wage European industries. To the extent that this is true, optimal plant *employment* may vary inversely with national wage levels even when the physical output or capacity optima are invariant. Our Chapter 3 analyses have probably not dealt with such differences completely successfully despite emphasis on physical or productivity-adjusted size measures and the use of dummy variables when such measures were unavailable.

A final international difference implies biases in the opposite direction. Especially in the cigarette and weaving industries, multi-shift operation seemed to be much less extensive in Europe than in America. We were unable to determine whether these differences were due to varying labor market conditions manifesting themselves in shift-work premium differentials, social pressures (such as proscribing night shift work by women) of a less conventionally economic character, or other causes.[3] Whatever the mechanism, their existence means that employment counts may show suboptimal scale operation for plants whose physical equipment in fact conforms to MOS standards.

Small Markets and Limited Horizons

Market size and market concentration were the most powerful explanatory variables in our regression analysis of plant size differences. We attempt now to provide deeper insight into the technological and behavioral phenomena which underlie the statistical associations.

3. On the British experience, see Robin Marris et al., *The Economics of Capital Utilisation: A Report on Multiple-Shift Work* (Cambridge, Eng.: Cambridge University Press, 1964), esp. pp. 204–207. Marris finds that market fragmentation (as discussed in subsequent sections of this chapter) leads not only to the construction of smaller plants but also to the underutilization of plants through less intensive shift working.

The Problem of Small National Markets

The existence of small plants cannot be surprising when total national market demand is insufficient to support even a single plant of optimal scale. Sweden and Canada suffered especially from this problem. In four of their industries—Swedish cigarettes, refrigerators, brewing, and Canadian refrigerators—total domestic consumption in 1967 was less than our estimate of an MOS plant's output. In five others—Swedish batteries, ordinary steel, bottles, and paints, and Canadian cigarettes—there was demand sufficient to accommodate two or fewer MOS plants.

Mere paucity of demand is not, however, a sufficient explanation of the plant sizes actually observed. In every case cited, there were more plants of smaller average size than what was needed to squeeze maximum scale economies out of a tight situation. In many of the industries, leading firms operated multiple plants, each smaller than the minimum optimal scale. Why in the nine industries cited and numerous others did plant structures fail to evolve so as to make the best of the demand volume available?

One reason clearly apparent in Canada was that consumers, and particularly industrial buyers, exhibited a strong preference for having at least two alternative supply sources, even if it meant fragmenting what would otherwise be a natural monopoly and causing unit costs (although not necessarily prices) to be higher. Industrial buyers of paints, bottles, cement, steel, and batteries evidently value both the security against total interruption of supplies and the bargaining power conferred by being able to play one producer off against the other. Even when individual buyers' purchases are normally concentrated with a single supplier at any moment in time, there seems to be a self-regulating process under which different firms' choices are dispersed sufficiently to keep two or more contending sources viable. In refrigerators the dispersion mechanism rationale is slightly different. Many of the largest chain and department stores find it profitable to carry two major appliance lines: a private-label line priced at moderate levels and a premium-priced nationally branded line. If the same supplier manufactures both lines, it is difficult to achieve sufficient product differentiation to prevent all sales from gravitating toward the lower-margin items. Furthermore, if one of the leading national chains such as Simpson-Sears adopts one manufacturer's line for its private-label sales, rivals like Eaton's are motivated to seek differentiation by embracing a competing line. The combination of these two differentiation propensities appears to make the survival of three Canadian refrigerator manufacturers probable despite annual consumption only seven-tenths the volume of an MOS plant.

Another important reason for the fragmentation of plant distributions is that small plants were a legacy from earlier periods when smallness was much less disadvantageous. Such legacies are particularly difficult to escape when an industry matured in an earlier technological era, plant and equipment are highly durable, and the market is so small that new units are large in relation to both the total volume of demand and its absolute annual growth.

Steel provides a prime example. From the 1920s through the 1940s, the annual capacity of a good-sized blast furnace ranged from 100,000 to 350,000 tons and open hearth furnaces of 100,000 tons per year output achieved most scale economies. During the 1950s and 1960s there was a rapid increase in optimal blast furnace, converter, slab mill, and hot strip mill sizes. Yet much Swedish, French, British, German, and U.S. capacity had been installed when the least-cost unit sizes were small and the advantages of building a very large plant were outweighed by proximity to ore deposits (in Sweden and the Lorraine) or coal (in northern England and Scotland, the Ruhr, and Pennsylvania). Once these small but durable facilities were in place, it was hard to justify abandoning them (on incremental cost of old vs. full cost of new plant criteria), even after depletion of ore or coal deposits had eroded much of the locational advantage on which their construction was originally premised. The scale handicaps inherent in these legacies are concealed to some extent for the United States and Germany because the excellent raw material access afforded by the Great Lakes and the Rhine River and the existence of huge nearby markets made it possible to build oversized works (consisting of numerous individual furnaces and rolling mills) enjoying at best minor scale economies relative to much smaller plants. U.S. Steel's Gary Works, for example, had twelve blast furnaces in 1968 to do the work which could be done by two or three modern best-practice furnaces. These large aggregations of small processing units did offer one prominent advantage over smaller Swedish, French, and British complexes of comparable vintage: it was easier to replace a battery of old units with a single large modern installation. But even then, plant layouts inherited from ancient investment decisions often imposed severe restrictions on modernization.[4]

4. Thus, in 1974 U.S. Steel completed the construction of a new blast furnace of roughly 2.4 million tons capacity, replacing several old furnaces at its Gary works. It was the largest furnace ever brought on stream in the United States, but it was considerably smaller than new units introduced at the same time in Japan, Russia, Germany, and France. It also lacked best-practice loading facilities, evidently because the site available left no room for the necessary conveyors. The facilities manager of another American interviewee reported that because his firm's largest plant had grown over time "like Topsy," work flows were very complex and a fourth of all on-site processing costs were incurred for materials handling.

Canada and especially Japan have been burdened less by such legacies because the major growth of their steel industries occurred relatively recently. Canada's status as a Johnny-come-lately plus Great Lakes transportation economies did much to offset the drawbacks of a small national market with respect to plant size choices, although individual processing unit size decisions have been constrained appreciably by fear of flooding the market. Japan has been even more fortunate, increasing its national ingot output from 5 million tons in 1950 to 22 million tons in 1960 and 93 million tons in 1968. The growth surge of the 1960s made it possible to achieve a plant structure including a much higher proportion of big, efficient, basic oxygen converters, blast furnaces, and rolling mills in large-scale works than any other major industrial nation.[5] Nearly as significant, Japan's shortage of domestic iron ore and coal forced the location of plants at deep-water ports, where they could take maximum advantage of the best available world market supplies; and the new works were laid out so as to require minimal in-plant transportation of materials between processing units.

Less dramatic examples of ancient legacies impairing the realization of plant scale economies occur in the cement and brewing industries and British textiles. The cotton weaving industry of Lancashire was largely established by 1900 and reached an all-time production peak around 1913. Mills built during the 1890s and early 1900s were well adapted to their time, but technology changed rapidly and they were already obsolescent in size and layout a decade later. Their construction was peculiarly unconducive to modernization, so the industry became locked into a mold from which it has not yet fully escaped. Mere heredity is nevertheless far from a sufficient explanation for British weaving plants' small average size in the 1960s. The textile industry of New England was similarly endowed, but it escaped its heritage through a massive flight to the South and a rebuilding program in the 1920s and later. Evidently there are other variables at work leading some industries to modernize while others vegetate. We shall not have solved our explanation problem until we pin those variables down.

Export Market Orientation

A start can be made by questioning an assumption implicitly accepted thus far: that a national market small in relation to the minimum

5. See Kiyoshi Kawahito, *The Japanese Steel Industry* (New York: Praeger, 1972), pp. 35–60; and Anthony Cockerill in collaboration with Aubrey Silberston, *The Steel Industry: International Comparisons of Industrial Structure and Performance*, Department of Applied Economics Occasional Paper 42 (Cambridge, Eng.: Cambridge University Press, 1974), pp. 38 and 62–66.

optimal scale necessarily constrains plant size decisions. Yet why must that be? Why don't firms unable to support optimal-size operations domestically strive for scale economies by expanding their horizons into export markets?

Tariff barriers are one answer. For at least half the Canadian industries covered by our sample, tariffs charged by the United States—the nearest and most obvious export market—were sufficiently high that they discouraged most attempts to capture scale economies by building export volume. A vicious circle tightened the constraint, since the difficulty of achieving all scale economies within the relatively small Canadian market put Canadian producers at a cost disadvantage compared to firms in the United States, all else equal, and this cost disadvantage made it all the harder to surmount tariff walls and tap the large U.S. market. At the same time, Canadian tariffs, higher on the average than those of the United States, insulated many Canadian industries sufficiently to permit them to adopt a parochial view toward their domestic market.

Tariffs also constricted the horizons of European producers, but their role was secondary, given the fact that all four European nations covered by our sample belonged to a larger free trade bloc. A more important limiting factor appeared to be respect for national spheres of influence. Thus, the amount of steel products crossing national borders among European Free Trade Association and especially the original six European Common Market member nations has been very substantial. But appearances were said by interviewees to be deceiving; considerable respect for spheres of influence in specific product lines reportedly existed. Certain producers made deliberate policy decisions to concentrate their marketing efforts at home and not try to sell more than marginal quantities in other nations of their trade bloc. They reasoned that if they commenced an ambitious cross-border sales effort, their leading rivals abroad were bound to retaliate, while those rivals were expected to continue their relatively unaggressive policy if offered no provocation. Another major steel maker argued that to increase its export market penetration, it would have to undercut its well-disciplined domestic price structure, and this was considered undesirable in view of recipient nation antidumping policy repercussions and possible domestic price feedbacks. For at least two nations, a clear link was drawn during interviews between the unwillingness of manufacturers to penetrate foreign markets aggressively and sacrifices accepted in the scale of new blast furnace, converter, and rolling mill investments.

In steel as well as in petroleum refining, cement making, and glass bottles, where firms eyeing one another across national borders also demonstrated strong respect for national spheres of influence, the products involved were more or less standardized. Product homogeneity is a trait particularly conducive to the recognition of mutual oligopolistic interdependence.[6] In industries with highly differentiated products a more variegated pattern was observed. At one extreme was the experience of SKF, exporting roughly 70 percent of its 1970 Swedish bearing output. In sharp contrast was the late 1960s' experience of firms manufacturing standard refrigerators in Sweden, where consumers had come to demand much larger units than their counterparts in England and on the western European mainland. As a result, the Swedish producers concentrated their marketing efforts on the relatively small national or Scandinavian market, prevented from exporting by the high cost of securing distribution channels for products little demanded abroad and protected from imports by distance, modest tariffs, and the inability of larger Continental firms to achieve a high production volume for the box sizes preferred in Sweden. Follow-up letters in mid-1973 revealed that this situation may have changed as Continental consumers began demanding much larger boxes, simultaneously creating a broader market for the Swedish designs and intensifying import competition as the Continental manufacturers upgraded their product lines. The net impact was evidently a widening of Swedish producers' market horizons, although the full implications were not ascertained.

In summary, tariff barriers, international taste differences, and respect for national spheres of influence have led firms to view their market horizons as predominantly intranational in many of the industries covered by our research. Inward-looking attitudes and plant scale sacrifices were often correlated. Indeed, we could not avoid being struck by the differences in behavior between our interviewees and what many respondents described as the characteristic tactics of Japanese steel, bearing, textile, and appliance manufacturers, who were believed to have mounted aggressive export campaigns with the conscious goal of capturing all attainable scale economies. That there was so much apprehension over Japanese export methods suggests that the rules of the game were not being followed. But when respected, the rules tend to curb the realization of scale economies by firms whose home base is a relatively small nation.

Transport Costs and Other Market-Fragmenting Influences

National boundaries are not the only constraint on firms' output volume horizons. When unit transportation costs are high, national

6. See F. M. Scherer, *Industrial Market Structure and Economic Performance* (Chicago: Rand McNally, 1970) pp. 186–192.

markets may be subdivided into smaller regional markets, each able to hold only a small number of MOS plants. To be sure, plants located in what are normally distinct regional markets may interpenetrate each others' home territories when they have excess capacity which can be utilized at low marginal production cost. Our interviews provided some indication that such intranational, interregional competition was accepted more readily than international cross-shipping—in part because tariffs are absent intranationally, but perhaps also because national borders constitute a kind of focal point around which tacit or explicit bargaining over spheres of influence can coalesce.[7] Still in several industries, transportation costs were sufficiently high that regional markets provided the main framework within which plant scale decisions were made.[8]

Cement is, of course, the most striking example. Every national area among the six covered by our research was subdivided into at least several natural geographic submarkets for portland cement owing to high unit transportation costs, ranging from roughly 8 cents per dollar of F.O.B. mill product value by inland barge to 55 cents by truck on a representative 350-mile haul. Many of the resulting submarkets were too small to accommodate even a single MOS plant. The size of the potential market in relation to the MOS varied widely, however, with the availability or unavailability of water routes, population density, and the type of pricing system employed by producers.

U.S. cement plants comprising the top 50 percent of the cumulative capacity distribution for 1969 had an average annual capacity of 4.8 million barrels, or about 69 percent of the estimated 1965-vintage minimum optimal scale. One reason for this relatively low average size is the dearth of navigable waterways, especially in the southeastern states and in most areas west of the Mississippi River. Also important was the industry's adherence to a multiple basing point system of pricing until it was outlawed in 1948.[9] Under the system as practiced before that time, cement producers quoted only delivered prices assuming shipment by rail—a medium involving freight charges of approximately 30 cents per dollar of product value on a 350-mile haul at 1963 price levels. Moreover, various side conditions adhered to collusively by

7. Scherer, *Industrial Market Structure and Economic Performance*, pp. 179–182; and Thomas C. Schelling, *The Strategy of Conflict* (Cambridge: Harvard University Press, 1960), esp. pp. 54–74.

8. See also Leonard W. Weiss, "The Geographic Size of Markets in Manufacturing," *Review of Economics and Statistics*, 54 (August 1972), 245–257, who estimates from 1963 shipping patterns that the U.S. continental market comprised 6 regional markets in beer brewing, 9 in glass bottles, 24 in cement, 6 in steel, and 6 in storage batteries.

9. *Federal Trade Commission* v. *Cement Institute et al.*, 333 U.S. 683 (1948).

cement companies made it likely that shipment would in fact take place by rail, even though alternate water routes might have provided a lower-cost option.[10] As a result, most cement mills were constructed at geographic locations which struck the best tradeoff between limestone availability and rail access to markets, regardless of water transportation alternatives, and the relatively high cost of the rail shipping media used led to plant size decisions premised on a market radius not exceeding 100 to 150 miles.[11] Once these decisions were taken, it was difficult to escape them, since the principal processing units at a cement plant have useful physical lives of thirty to forty years, and capital costs (sunk once incurred) make up an unusually large fraction of total long-run unit production costs.

In Sweden and Canada, small national market size did not prevent the construction of Top 50 Percent cement plants 20 percent larger on the average than their U.S. counterparts. This appears to be attributable in no small measure to the extensive use of coastal shipping media by the leading Swedish producer and the clustering of much Canadian market demand along the St. Lawrence River and eastern Great Lakes, where several sizeable cement works are located.

The smallest Top 50 Percent cement plants among our six nations were found in Great Britain, at least until the early 1970s, when industry leader Associated Portland Cement Company brought on stream a new 21 million barrel capacity works east of London, large enough to supply one-fifth of total U.K. demand. One reason for the small average size of earlier British cement works was a basing point system under which delivered prices rose by less than the amount of transportation costs as cement was shipped from basing point mills.[12] This discouraged the expansion of plants at basing points and encouraged the construction of small plants at nonbase locations. Contributing factors included the relatively early maturity of the U.K. industry and its slow subsequent growth, the durability of cement-making equipment, and the lack of incentive under a cartel arrangement which maintained prices at levels sufficient to cover the costs of inefficient plants.

In France, prices have traditionally been quoted on a strict and fairly uniform F.O.B. mill basis, with no price shading to expand

10. See Samuel Loescher, *Imperfect Collusion in the Cement Industry* (Cambridge: Harvard University Press, 1959), pp. 102–111; and Scherer, *Industrial Market Structure and Economic Performance*, pp. 262–272.

11. A prominent early exception was the huge Huron Cement Company works at Alpena, Michigan, serving points as far east as Oswego, New York, by lake vessel.

12. See *In re Cement Makers' Federation Agreement*, judgment of the Restrictive Practices Court reported in L.R., 2 R.P. 241 (1961).

market coverage except in the Paris region. Since there are few navigable waterways, this means that the market radius for a plant was determined largely by the high cost of rail or truck delivery. Under the F.O.B. pricing system, a new plant located between two or more existing plants had a decisive sales advantage on orders in its immediate vicinity, so there was an incentive for such plants to be built wherever a sizeable pocket of demand existed. The result was the construction of many relatively small plants, especially outside the densely settled Paris region.

Good water transportation opportunities in much of Germany make it easier to serve large market territories and hence build large cement plants. But plant sizes have also been influenced by institutional considerations. In the south, major producers somehow managed, evidently as a result of intricate joint ownership ties and direct collusion, to maintain substantial distances between rival plant sites while holding prices at comfortably high levels.[13] Relatively large plants were a consequence. In Westphalia (including the Ruhr area), on the other hand, long-standing cartel agreements first encouraged the construction and then permitted the survival of some forty-three cement works with average 1967 output of only 1.3 million barrels apiece, or 20 percent of an MOS plant's volume operating at 90 percent of capacity. Among the devices sheltering inefficient producers were a basing point price structure under which prices rose as cement was shipped westward from the Geseke producing center toward the Rhine valley, where additional plants using inferior limestone deposits operated; an output allocation system which minimized actual shipping costs subject to production quota constraints; and a redistribution of "phantom freight" to subsidize inefficient basing point mills.

In petroleum refining, market localization tendencies are also highly sensitive to the kinds of transportation facilities available. Product shipping costs on a 350-mile haul during the mid-1960s ranged from approximately one cent per dollar of exrefinery product value by 60,000 ton tanker, 2 cents by large-diameter pipeline, 5 cents by inland barge, and 10 cents by small-diameter pipeline to 35 cents by tank truck.[14] Deep-water port refineries and inland refineries with rich pipeline inter-

13. In November 1972, the leading southern German producers were fined for maintaining an illegal output quota cartel. Whether the collusion extended to investment decisions was not made clear. On the structure of joint ownership interests, see Siegfried Mängel, "Technischer Fortschritt, Wachstum und Konzentration in der deutschen Zementindustrie," doctoral diss., Technischen Hochschule, Aachen, 1970, pp. 165–167.

14. These are derived using the methodology described in Appendix B, with further data drawn from Michael Hubbard, "The Comparative Cost of Oil Transport to and within Europe," *Journal of the Institute of Petroleum*, 54 (January 1967), 1–23.

connections can economically serve much larger markets than less advantageously situated inland refineries, and the former tend to be considerably larger than the latter.

The reasons for the predominantly regional or even local orientation of breweries are more complex. Among our twelve sample industries, beer ranked fourth in the height of shipping costs, estimated at 7.8 cents per dollar of product value on a Chicago-Cleveland haul. That alone can explain the regional character of beer markets, but not the much narrower markets, sometimes spanning only a single metropolitan area, still found for many brews. Perhaps more important than shipping costs have been local brand loyalties. This was most vividly the case in Germany. The reasons for enduring local preferences in Germany include differences in brew taste heightened by the typical German imbiber's propensity to drink his beer unchilled; the tendency for local beers to be sold unpasteurized, in contrast to national brands; the control by brewers of popular taverns (Gasthäuser) providing a captive market for their products; brewers' cultivation of loyalties by supporting local sports clubs and public events; and a generous dose of civic pride and tradition in a land where nationalistic sentiments have suffered unusually severe jolts. Whatever the causes, strong brand loyalties permit hundreds of small breweries to survive serving very limited local markets and simultaneously make penetration by regional and national brewers difficult. A relatively large company predicted that it would take ten to twenty years before national brands could make substantial inroads into the market positions of local brewers.

Similar consumer preferences plus explicit territorial spheres of influence agreements kept the Swedish beer market divided into numerous fragments served by tiny local breweries until the mid-1960s. Then, however, the law prohibiting sales of medium-strength beers outside government liquor stores was repealed. New brews appeared and were promoted vigorously by the largest companies, revolutionizing consumption patterns in favor of a few national and regional brands. This in turn paved the way to closure of numerous local breweries and concentration of production at a few larger, more efficient units.

In England the picture is still different. Beer consumption continues to be centered in public houses owned by or otherwise tied to brewing companies.[15] In the past this gave local brewers a limited but assured market for their output. Customer loyalty is nevertheless more strongly linked to the specific pub than to the brand. A few aggressive groups

15. See the Monopolies Commission Report, *Beer* (London: HMSO, 1969).

acquired large numbers of local breweries and with them their "tied houses." They gradually replaced the local brands with their own national and regional brands, in some cases changing the formulas before the brand names. This set the stage for a later consolidation of production.

Finally, in Canada beer prices, advertising, and distribution methods are tightly regulated by provincial laws (or in Ontario, by a cartel). The degrees of marketing freedom permitted are so few that a "brewed at home" image can interact with fierce local pride to make a decisive sales difference. These local preferences, the vast expanse of Canada with its attendant impact on transport costs, and some provinces' policy of imposing higher excise taxes or requiring higher prices on beer "imported" from adjacent provinces, have combined to segment Canadian beer demand into numerous regional markets, most (excluding only the Toronto and Montreal areas) too small to support even one brewery anywhere near the minimum optimal scale.

Thus, for a variety of reasons many brewers' market horizons have been constricted to relatively small local or regional territories. Except when those areas include substantial population concentrations, it has been difficult to tap enough demand to warrant building sizeable breweries. Partly because plant scale economies have been increasing in strength over time and in part because of taste and demand changes, localization forces have been on the wane, but with marked differences in the rate of decline among nations.

From this overview of three industries it should be evident that geographic market segmentation can severely limit producers' sales horizons and inhibit the construction of full-sized plants, but that its effects vary widely and in complex ways from one nation or even one region to another. Crucial variables include the efficiency of available transportation media, the geographic density and configuration of demand in relation to critical raw material sources, subjective buyer preferences toward "made at home" products, and the practices sellers formally or informally adopt to differentiate prices spatially and to make the best of the price structure established.

The Dynamics of Expansion and New Entry Decisions

One reason why plant scale choices are so complex is that high transport costs, national borders, and local buyer preferences can subdivide and segregate markets to the point where oligopoly becomes virtually inevitable. And under oligopoly, how sellers behave in price and investment decisions depends upon how they expect rivals to react to their strategic moves. It is worthwhile to mine our interview data more deeply to see what they say about capacity expansion and new entry decisions under oligopolistic conditions.

Lumping together expansion and new entry decisions as a single oligopoly behavior species is unorthodox, but both embody the essence of the entry decision problem: How large one's addition to the industry's capacity should be depends upon how readily new output will be absorbed in the market, which in turn depends inter alia upon whether existing producers react passively, cooperatively, or combatively to one's inroads.[16]

Expansion Decisions

In laying out the theory of optimal capacity expansion decisions in Chapter 2, we postulated a defensive but passive reaction: oligopolists would permit rivals to capture their accustomed shares of growing markets, but not more. From this assumption follows the inference that capacity increments will be larger, the larger are the relevant market, its growth rate, and the average market shares of the firms involved. Our regression findings are consistent with these hypotheses, although the regression analysis alone could not disentangle the various static and dynamic causal chains leading to particular plant structures. If, contrary to our Chapter 2 assumptions, oligopolists struggle aggressively for market position in a drive for scale economies, we would expect at best a weak statistical association between leading firms' absolute sales volume (the product of market size times market share) and the size of units added in capacity expansion programs.

Our interviews provided insight on this question mainly for those industries in which indivisibilities require relatively large, lumpy capacity expansion increments. Even in such industries, matters are seldom simple. Among our sample members, steel, cement, and petroleum refining display the most prominent equipment indivisibilities. Yet existing blast furnace capacities have been increased by improving the quality of iron ore inputs and by relining the furnaces with improved, thinner refractories. Some cement companies increased the output of older facilities by switching from the wet to the dry process. Petroleum refineries often have process bottlenecks which can be broken at relatively low investment cost to increase overall capacity. Expansion decisions of this sort appeared to be constrained very little by output absorption considerations in markets of widely varying structure. It

16. For a survey of the literature, see Scherer, *Industrial Market Structure and Economic Performance*, pp. 225–231.

was only when all such slack had been taken up and a great leap forward had to be made that the interesting decisions occurred.

In steel the effects of modest market growth potential were most striking. Producers in every sample nation allowing competition showed keen awareness of mutual oligopolistic interdependence. It would be an oversimplification to say that companies expected to capture no more than their historical share of demand increments, since some enjoyed growing market acceptance and others consciously sought an increasing share through the superior quality and service new, modern facilities (and especially rolling mills) could support. But no interviewee (other than firms visited during 1973 in Japan) appeared inclined to engage in aggressive price competition to help absorb the output of a large new capacity increment. All were reluctant to plan on carrying excess capacity for long periods (although in a few cases that outcome resulted when demand growth turned out to be smaller than expected). And in a number of cases where the amount of additional demand a firm could expect to capture over the coming several years was considerably less than the size of an optimal capacity increment, all else (such as equipment retirements) taken into account, producers made deliberate decisions to accept higher unit costs by building sub-MOS blast furnaces, oxygen converters, and rolling mills and by expanding rolling mill capacity through the costly expedient of installing an additional stand every one to three years. Such behavior was most clearly apparent in the small Swedish and Canadian markets, but it also occurred in attenuated form even in the huge United States markets.

Petroleum refiners installed smaller new units in areas where their expected absolute demand growth was small than they did where it was large, all else equal. Again, however, an assumption of steady market share maintenance would be an oversimplification for at least four reasons. First, some refiners were more aggressive than others in expanding their retail gasoline outlet networks, and those adding outlets relatively more rapidly could anticipate market growth greater than a simple projection of existing market shares implied. Second, it is usually possible within certain limits for refiners to buy products from and sell to one another; and this, as the analysis in Chapter 2 brought out, permits less frequent, larger capacity expansions. Refinery throughput shares will then shift among companies over the short run, even if not in the long. Third, the existence of such markets leaves room for preemption. That is, by announcing a major expansion and offering rivals attractive long-term supply contracts, a refiner can discourage competitors from early imitative moves. In the long run, however, the desire for self-sufficiency and maintenance of refinery throughput shares is likely to induce similar preemptive investment by rivals. Miscalculations may then lead to serious excess capacity and price erosion. Finally, interregional investment staging along lines analyzed in Chapter 2 permitted multi-plant refiners to add capacity increments larger than they might have if they optimized expansion decisions taking into account only the expected demand growth in individual autarkic regional markets.

Cement is equally complex. Some plant expansion decisions were inhibited by recognition of adverse price effects from offering too large an output increment, others much less so. The type of freight pricing system adopted and the discipline of producers in adhering to it appeared to be the key variables. Where rigid basing point or non-discriminatory F.O.B. mill pricing systems prevailed, as in England, northern Germany prior to 1967, much of France, and many parts of the United States, cement makers tailored their expansions to what the market could absorb without price disturbances, often accepting scale economy sacrifices in the process. In other areas, however, expansion decisions were more freewheeling. One large, progressive multi-plant company was in 1970 simultaneously installing kilns of 5 million barrels per year capacity in a region where producers vigorously interpenetrated each others' markets and 2 million barrels where strong discipline ruled out such interpenetration.

Unit size choices were also sensitive to the strategies adopted by rivals in classic oligopolistic threat and counterthreat situations. For instance, one interviewee operated the only plant in a moderately important market area, although it experienced competition at the fringes of its natural market, including a major city, from a rival cement maker. At the time of our interview the company had recently completed a program which nearly doubled the capacity of its plant, adding among other things a large new kiln whose output could satisfy at least a decade of future growth. One consideration underlying its expansion decision was the fact that its rival was shading price to dispose of surplus output in the interviewee's market, disrupting the structure of prices. With an overhang of surplus capacity, the interviewee firm believed, it could credibly threaten to retaliate in the rival's home territory if the rival did not cease its price cutting. It did so threaten, the rival stopped its price shading, and the investment was considered a very profitable one even though some older kilns had to be shut down and held as excess capacity for an indefinite period.

Clearly, in the capacity expansion decisions of major suppliers there is considerable variation associated with differences in local market conditions, individual company strategy, and other factors not easily generalized. Amidst this variance however there is a pattern. Although producers can often find ways to build bigger capacity increments than they would if they passively exploited only that fraction of demand growth consistent with their past market shares, the expansion opportunities of firms in small markets or with relatively small shares of oligopolistic markets are simply not as bountiful as those enjoyed by better-situated enterprises. Therefore, the former tend to expand in smaller steps than the latter. And since the size of a plant is the cumulative sum of past expansions, there is also a propensity for firms with large shares of large markets to operate larger plants than do companies enjoying smaller markets, market shares, or both, at least to the extent that geographic decentralization and product specialization patterns are similar.

The Scale of New Market Entry

Decisions to enter a new market, either national or regional, for the first time are logically analogous to capacity expansion decisions, but more dramatic. Since our interviews were predominantly with larger, well-established companies, we were able to explore firsthand only a few cases of completely new entry into a significant national market sufficiently recent for memories to be fresh. In every such case the entering firm showed considerable respect for the competitive impact of its entry. In most cases, however, the entrant found a strategy which helped minimize, even if not to avoid, scale economy sacrifices.

One such case was the entry into steel plate making by the Grängesberg Company of Sweden. When the Swedish government nationalized its principal iron ore mines in Lapland during 1955, Grängesberg sought a new use for the 900 million Swedish kronor ($\cong$ $173 million) it received in compensation.[17] It already produced small quantities of pig iron at an advantageous coastal site linked by company-owned railroad to the central Swedish iron ore mining district. Thus, entry into steelmaking seemed a logical move. There was also one sizeable market, for ship plates and other heavy plates, not yet served adequately by Scandinavian producers. It therefore geared its investment to that specialized market. It constructed a reversible plate rolling mill of some 300,000 tons capacity (later expanded to 650,000 tons), a new 600,000 ton blast furnace, and (because the basic oxygen process had not yet been adapted to high-phosphoric Swedish ores) two special-design Kaldo converters. Each of these decisions, culminating when the new works began operation in 1961, involved some kind of compromise. Thus, its blast furnace was

17. On this phase of Grängesberg's history, see the Institut pour l'Etude des Méthodes de Direction de l'Entreprise case study series, *Grängesberg* (Boston: Intercollegiate Case Clearing House, 1965), ICH 13G 75–80.

about half the best-practice size of the late 1950s. Its plate mill was also smaller than optimal mills of that era.[18] As larger steelmaking units came into use on the European continent during the 1960s and as price competition intensified when steel supplies caught up with demand, Grängesberg's relative scale handicap grew. A locational advantage in serving Scandinavian shipbuilders, superior delivery service, emphasis on higher-priced high-strength plates, and maintaining very tight, efficient operations became increasingly important to its continued viability.

One or more facets of the Grängesberg entry history recur in several other new entry cases turned up by our interview research. Thus, a new entrant to the antifriction bearing industry began on a very small scale in a specialized product line not yet covered adequately by well-established bearing makers. Product differentiation based in part upon technology licensed from a foreign firm compensated for its cost disadvantage until it could grow to MOS size. Firms which moved into new shoe and textile manufacturing lines typically began from some kind of springboard, for example, experience in related boot or fabric production or operation of a shoe retailing chain which provided an already developed outlet for manufactured products.

Three interviewees had entered the refrigerator industry since 1960. In every instance they began with experience in related household appliances. The typical entry strategy was to commence refrigerator production in a plant that already made other major appliances, drawing upon common metal stamping facilities, steel purchasing operations, general plant management and overhead support, and sales forces to minimize the penalties of producing and selling on a small scale. Well-known brand names and established distribution channels helped overcome the obstacles to market penetration. If refrigerator volume then increased sufficiently, production was shifted to a separate plant where the advantages of specialization could be realized more completely.

Three interviewees had within recent memory begun refining petroleum for the first time in one or another of the six nations covered by our sample. Another entered a U.S. region so distant from its home markets that its problems were quite similar to those of new national market entrants. In all four cases the enterprises were already selling petroleum products within the new markets before they invested in refining facilities. In two the entrants already had a well-developed chain of retail gasoline outlets, supplied either with imports from the entrants' refineries in

18. U.S. interviewees estimated the plate mill MOS at 1.0 to 1.2 million tons capacity as of 1970. Some Japanese producers were operating mills with twice that capacity in 1973, although we were unable to investigate the advantages of two as compared to one million ton capacity mills.

another nation or through long-term contract purchases from rival marketers. When a decision to commence domestic refining was taken, the two companies with the most extensive retail distribution networks built by far the largest units. The other two began on a small scale, each acquiring a tiny, technically obsolete refinery turning out special distillates. They made bottleneck-breaking investments to increase gasoline and/or fuel oil output and then, when sales had been developed sufficiently, added in stages new refining units which, though not big enough to achieve all known scale economies, pushed most of the way down the long-run unit cost curve.

In most of the cases discussed thus far, entry took place at less than the minimum optimal scale for both the plant as a whole and individual equipment items, although the scale economy sacrifices accepted by the two petroleum refiners with already established distribution channels were quite modest. This seemed to be common in new entry decisions. The most striking exceptions occurred in the cement industry. Our interviews covered several examples of new entry by interviewees or their rivals, and in a substantial subset, entry occurred at scales reflecting best current practice. Why the experience in cement should be so different from that of other industries is not completely clear. Cement lends itself less to product differentiation (except spatially) than any other product in our sample. The consequence—that even a small delivered price differential will induce a substantial shift in sales toward the low-price supplier—is an important part of the explanation. Also relevant is the characteristically low short-run marginal production cost compared to full unit cost (including capital charges) at less than capacity operation. Compared to steel and petroleum refining, but not the other nine industries, the amount of capital required to build an MOS cement works is also modest. Whether these factors alone are sufficient to explain cement's uniqueness, or whether the cement industry tends to attract or evolve a peculiar entrepreneurial mentality, cannot be established from the interview material we were able to collect. The evidence itself is sufficiently interesting that it bears unusually detailed presentation.

Since the U.S. cement industry's formal basing point system of pricing was outlawed in 1948 there have been significant changes in behavior, precipitated in part by the entry of "maverick" producers. Two mavericks with noteworthy impact and similar strategies were Atlantic Cement, which opened a plant on the Hudson River in 1962, and Dundee Cement, which began serving midwestern customers in 1959. We focus here on Dundee's experience.

Dundee's parent company, Holderbank Financère Glaris Ltd. of Switzerland, is one of the world's largest cement manufacturers. During the early 1950's Holderbank entered the Canadian market by constructing two large plants, one on the St. Lawrence River and one on Lake Ontario. In 1959 production was commenced at Dundee, Michigan (35 miles southwest of Detroit), in a plant with two 3 million barrel capacity kilns—an unprecedented kiln size by the conservative standards generally accepted in the U.S. industry at the time.[19] Dundee's strategy was to take full advantage of scale economies afforded by the latest technology, minimizing the disruptive impact of its large-scale entry on prices by using part of the production cost savings to reach out as far as 400 miles with direct rail carload shipments to bulk customers. This approach proved to be misguided in some respects, largely because cement users preferred more reliable truck delivery to rail when prices were identical, but also because the Michigan economy happened to experience a slump during the late 1950s and early 1960s. However, Dundee solved its delivery problem by establishing a network of terminals (storage silos) supplied by rail. The terminals then served nearby customers by truck. Given this strategy adaptation, Dundee expanded its sales without instigating much price warfare, and the venture proved to be a profitable one.

The question then became, what next? After a survey of market conditions, limestone availability, and technology, Dundee decided to build a second plant astride a huge limestone deposit at Clarksville, Missouri, north of St. Louis on the Mississippi River. In 1968 the plant began operation with a single kiln of 7 million barrels annual capacity, the largest built anywhere in the world, plus supporting facilities geared to future expansion.[20] Its strategy was the same: scale economies would be exploited to the maximum possible degree, while output would be spread over a large market radius to minimize price repercussions. Crucial to this concept was location on a major waterway. From past experience Dundee officials believed that price cutting was an ineffective market penetration strategy, since cuts, however secret, are invariably matched within twenty-four hours. They reasoned too that through high-level personal salesmanship emphasizing excellent delivery service from terminals, they could capture up to 5 percent of any given market without triggering a price war. This penetration strategy necessitated a very wide distribution radius to utilize the capacity of a 7 million barrel plant, and only the central U.S. inland waterway system (including the Mississippi River and connecting channels), on which Dundee's barges could reach all the way to Mobile, Alabama, filled the bill. As events transpired,

19. See "Dundee—Big in Size and Concept," *Pit and Quarry*, 53 (July 1960), 2–17.
20. See "The Really Big One," *Rock Products*, July 1967; and "Dundee Solves a Weighty Problem," *Business Week*, November 25, 1967, pp. 150–154.

Dundee's plan at first turned out to be optimistic. The plant began operation as construction activity (and hence cement demand) was falling. Technical problems characteristic of such "first time" ventures also increased start-up costs. The result was underutilization of potential capacity and a marked drop in Dundee's profits. But the technical problems were worked out, and, with the improved general business conditions of 1972 and 1973, capacity utilization rose and the plant began operating profitably.

In Canada, the Canada Cement Company, Ltd. (CC) held an 80 percent share of the overall Canadian market during 1946.[21] There were only two other cement-making firms: one with a local monopoly of western British Columbia production and an Ontario company which followed CC's price leadership. Neither CC nor its Ontario rival expanded vigorously enough to meet booming postwar demands, so cement was imported from as far away as Europe. This plus generous prices stimulated a wave of new entry during the 1950s. A bench mark against which to judge the scale of entry is Bain's early-1950s MOS estimate of 2.5 million barrels.[22] By that standard, the early entrants included a one-tenth MOS plant in isolated Newfoundland, which had no local supply source; a one-half MOS plant (owned by Ciments Lafarge of France) in the previously monopolized British Columbia market; a plant near Quebec City at 28 percent of the MOS; the first Holderbank plant, also near Quebec City, at 60 percent of the MOS; and the second Holderbank plant, near Toronto, initially 1.4 times the MOS and subsequently expanded to become the second largest cement plant in North America as of 1968. Indeed, all but the Newfoundland and first Quebec City plants subsequently grew to exceed Bain's MOS threshold. In reaction to these intrusions, Canada Cement changed the structure of its basing points to eliminate phantom freight for newcomers, but it avoided more aggressive moves, attempted to defend the *level* of basing point prices, and in effect made room for the entrants. This encouraged still more new entrants, including two at very substantial scales into the Quebec market and one newcomer into Ontario by 1960.

The most dramatic entry, however, was not the largest. In 1966 Independent Cement, Inc., began production at a twin 1.17 million barrel (sub-MOS) kiln works at Joliette, Quebec, northeast of Montreal.

---

21. Substantial portions of this account are drawn from H. C. Eastman and Stefan Stykolt, *The Tariff and Competition in Canada* (Toronto: Macmillan, 1967), pp. 156–168; and D. H. Stonehouse, *Cement: 1969*, Mineral Resources Branch Mineral Review Preprint, Department of Energy, Mines, and Resources (Ottawa, 1969).

22. Joe S. Bain, *Barriers to New Competition* (Cambridge: Harvard University Press, 1956), pp. 230–231.

Its pricing policy was a model of simplicity: $1.00 per barrel off the prevailing list price (of roughly $3.00), cash and carry, no credit, bring your own truck. The strategy was sufficiently successful that in 1970 Independent Cement was planning to double its capacity. Despite this incursion, the prices charged by other cement producers held generally firm and even rose during the late 1960s, although the cumulative effect of entry and a construction industry recession left cement works operating at 55 percent of capacity for Canada as a whole and at 45 percent in Quebec. According to one interviewee, Canada Cement (by then reduced to a 34 percent national market share) threatened Independent Cement with a price war if it continued its dollar-off policy, but Independent in effect thumbed its nose, observing that its own marginal costs were much lower than those at CC's large but antiquated Montreal works and that a price war would hurt CC more than Independent. Nor is it clear that price warfare would have been in CC's interest even if its costs had been lower. CC had a thoroughly modernized, low-cost 5 million barrel plant near Winnipeg when its Manitoba monopoly position was challenged by a 1.86 million barrel entrant in 1965, but CC chose not to cut prices, permitting the intruder to capture a significant share of the market and reduce average Manitoba mill capacity utilization to 41 percent in 1968.

Even in Canada, where the pricing policy of the dominant company made it relatively easy to sell the output of a new plant, more firms entered at sub-MOS scales than at MOS sizes. Particularly great scale economy sacrifices were accepted in entering such markets as Newfoundland, with modest demand and isolated from competitive supply sources by distance and deep water. In other nations sub-MOS entry was also the approach chosen most frequently both by completely new firms and companies extending their geographic reach to markets previously not served. Especially when waterways were absent and strong basing-point or nondiscriminatory F.O.B. mill pricing discipline prevailed, the most common strategy was to find a demand niche from which competing works were relatively distant and to enter at a scale sufficient to win most of the nearby demand without threatening rivals' home markets. Unless the new submarket was densely settled, this generally implied building at less than the minimum optimal scale.

Given the extensive record of new cement plant entry and territorial expansion in several nations, some of our interviewees had devoted considerable thought to how they might best deter further entry. Some considered physical presence important. One executive believed that new entry is likely to occur unless there are as many plants in an area as the annual demand divided by 2 million barrels—a rule which, if followed, would lead to the proliferation of sub-MOS plants.[23] Tangible preemption threats were also considered useful. Thus, one company bought up the best limestone deposit in an area with no plant and constructed a storage silo there, signaling its intention eventually to build a complete plant. Perhaps most crucial, however, is the possession of low marginal cost reserve capacity and the will to use it in a price war. What remained unclear was how one proved one's will except by repeated demonstrations whose cost might well exceed the long-run benefits.

Our final examples of entry involve intranational territorial expansion moves by glass bottle makers already serving in other submarkets. One company entered a small but rapidly growing regional market with a plant whose initial capacity was one-third the least-cost size, but which had built-in potential to permit a doubling of output at modest incremental investment when demand warranted. Another firm built a one-half MOS plant, accepting modest scale economy sacrifices to enter a regional market previously supplied by only one enterprise. Entry was reported to have been facilitated by the desire of bottle buyers to have a second source. Company representatives said an entrant into a market thus monopolized could expect to win 30 percent of the business if it did a poor job of providing customer service and 50 percent if it did an excellent job. Price warfare was considered improbable because cuts could be matched so quickly.

To sum up, several generalizations concerning the scale of entry can be hazarded. Potential entrants are acutely sensitive to the effects of their entry on prices and other market conditions. They devote considerable thought and ingenuity to finding an entry strategy which makes the best compromise between securing scale economies and minimizing price disruptions. In very small national or regional markets, those too small to accommodate even a single MOS plant, entry at suboptimal scales is virtually inevitable. However, for transport-cost-intensive products the size of the market depends upon the shipping media used, which depend in turn upon both natural endowments (such as the existence of a waterway) and the entrant's aggressiveness in exploiting them (for example, by pioneering new water-based distribution systems or building pipelines). All else equal, markets served by a monopolist or tight-knit oligopolistic group anxious to maintain high prices are more apt to attract large-scale entry than those with loosely disciplined supplier groups. On the other hand, certain spatial pricing systems conducive to strong discipline, notably, nondiscriminatory F.O.B. mill and rigid

23. By 1973 he had modified his divisor to 3 million barrels, evidently because of increases in scale economy imperatives.

multiple basing point systems, tend to create market niches luring small-scale entrants. Opportunities for physical differentiation of products have the same effect: new entrants often seek special product line segments, especially those inadequately served by existing sellers, in which they can sustain price premia compensating for the cost penalties of small-scale operation. A frequent concomitant of such niche-filling strategies is building a plant which can be expanded readily once a market beachhead has been secured. The ability of new entrants to build up demand in advance (for instance, by purchasing supplies temporarily from existing manufacturers or importing) facilitates large-scale entry, as does the failure of established sellers to keep pace with growing demand. Finally, the scale at which newcomers enter depends upon such psychological variables as managerial boldness and skill in making credible threats. We know of no way systematically to measure or predict the strength of such traits, but their role is indisputably important.

The Adaptation of Outmoded Plant Structures

We have seen that sub-MOS plants are often a legacy of decisions made in the past, when the optimal scale may have been much smaller, market horizons more restricted, and competition weaker. As time passes, we might expect obsolete technology to disappear and, when the MOS has been rising, average plant sizes to grow. The entry of new firms, the building of new plants by established firms, and the modernization and expansion of existing plants are the means by which this adaptation takes place. In the concluding pages of Chapter 3 we found statistical evidence that increases in the sizes of petroleum refineries were more rapid, the greater the initial scale handicap of a nation's refineries was and the more quickly national demand was growing. Are there further systematic influences leading some plant structures to adapt more rapidly than others?

The Role of Free Trade Agreements

One influence might be the adoption of multi-national free trade pacts, expanding market horizons and increasing competition. In 1957 Germany and France joined four other nations to form the European Economic Community, within which internal tariffs were reduced in stages to zero by 1968. England and Sweden entered the European Free Trade Association in 1960, sharing with six other lands a reduction in mutual industrial goods tariff barriers to the zero level, in most instances by January of 1967. During the first decade of these customs unions' operation there was a rapid expansion of member nations' reciprocal trade. Exports from the six original EC nations to one another increased from $7.5 billion in 1958 to $36.6 billion in 1969, nearly quintupling, while exports by "the Six" to non-EC nations rose by a multiple of 2.5. By 1969, intra-EC exports had increased to roughly 48 percent of the members' total exports, compared to 32 percent in 1958.[24] During the same interval exports among EFTA members trebled to a total of $8.5 billion, or 24 percent of total EFTA nation exports, while exports to non-EFTA nations doubled. On a more limited plane, the United States and Canada reciprocally reduced tariffs on automobiles, trucks, and original equipment auto parts (including batteries and antifriction bearings) to zero in 1965.

We had expected these trade-expanding measures to have a major impact on the adaptation and survival of sub-MOS plants. To some extent our expectations were disappointed. With only a few prominent exceptions, the effect of customs union membership on plant sizes was either so weak or so entangled with other forces that it received little weight as an explanatory variable.[25]

By far the most important exception was the refrigerator industry. There strong effects were observed, especially among EC nations. Beginning in the late 1950s, a few Italian companies began an aggressive export campaign combined with the development of large, highly automated plants enjoying the added advantage of relatively low-wage labor. In sharp contrast to most of the oligopolistic industries covered by our research, they coupled their drive for scale economies with a deliberate policy of cutting prices. They pushed their competitively priced refrigerators into the lines of German, French, and other EC nations' mail order chains and similar low-margin retail outlets, achieving rapid market penetration at the expense of traditional retailers applying a high markup to the already well-padded wholesale prices of more conservative domestic manufacturers. One consequence was an increase in Italian refrigerator production from roughly 500,000 units in 1958 to 2.8 million in 1966, 1.7 million of them exported.[26] By 1966 Italian producers had captured 21 percent of the German market, 29 percent of the French market, and 56 percent of the Benelux market. Success in export markets

24. *Yearbook of International Trade Statistics: 1969* (New York: United Nations Department of Economic and Social Affairs, 1971), p. 24. Belgium and Luxembourg are treated as a single nation in the statistics.

25. Additional effects on the product specialization patterns of plants were observed. The evidence will be examined in Chap. 7.

26. See H. L. von Cube, "Economics and Technology Trends for European Refrigerators and Freezers," *Appliance Engineer*, vol. II, no. 4 (1968), pp. 38–43; and the testimony of H. W. de Jong in the U.S., Senate, Antitrust and Monopoly Subcommittee, *Hearings, Economic Concentration*, Part 7, "Concentration Outside the United States," 90th Cong., 2nd Sess., April 1968, p. 3619.

and the rapid growth of sales at home permitted Italian industry leaders Ignis and Zanussi to achieve production volumes of 600,000 to 1,100,000 units per year, mostly in a narrow range of box sizes so that maximum lot-size economies could be exploited. Other European interviewees viewed the productivity of Ignis and Zanussi plants as the standard against which efficiency should be judged.

As a result of the price competition led by Italian firms, many small- and medium-sized French and German refrigerator makers ceased production. A few did manage to stay in the race, picking up by merger or default part of the business abandoned by industry dropouts and either increasing their volume to levels at which they experienced only minor scale economy handicaps or finding market niches (for example, the larger box sizes) in which the Italian competition was less potent. The most striking transformation occurred in France, where only one firm, Thomson-Brandt, continued to produce standard household refrigerators in 1970. Its 1970 volume was 630,000 units (compared to approximately 200,000 units in 1966), with imports (80 percent from Italy) satisfying the other half of French demand. The ultimate consequence of these developments was a much more efficient, price-competitive European refrigerator industry. Indeed, the growing competitiveness of northern EC rivals plus strikes and rising wage levels at home eroded the Italian manufacturers' cost advantage and, along with approaching market saturation, plunged them into financial crisis.[27]

It is questionable whether all the credit for structural changes in the continental European refrigerator industry can be attributed to the EC-induced fall in tariffs. By 1967 Italian companies had captured 20 percent of the non-EC British market despite tariff barriers. This level of penetration, combined with fears as to what would happen if Great Britain joined the EC, was enough to stimulate structural changes similar to those on the Continent. Some producers dropped out altogether. Others intensified their efforts to bolster production volume. Hotpoint, English Electric, and the General Electric Company merged their appliance groups to form British Domestic Appliances, Ltd., concentrating what had been three separate refrigerator assembly operations at a single plant with an output exceeding 250,000 units in 1970—said to be the largest in the U.K. The upshot was again a significant increase in production volumes and efficiency, though not on as grand a scale as on the Continent.

One might have expected a similar experience in the European steel

27. See "For Appliances, 'La Dolce Vita' Is Just a Memory," *Business Week*, August 28, 1971, p. 32; and "Italy: A Shakeup in the Appliance Industry," *Business Week*, June 10, 1972, p. 33.

industry. In 1953 tariffs on steel and coal were eliminated among the six European Coal and Steel Community (ECSC) nations (who later made up the EC). Steel trade among the six did increase substantially thereafter. Since then there has been extensive modernization of member nation steel works, accompanied by increases in average plant size.[28] Yet the pace of modernization was not noticeably swifter in France and Germany than in nonmember nations such as Canada, Japan, or the United States, and in 1970 many small, outdated plants continued to operate. Unfortunately, our interviews with French and German steelmakers were unable to pin down whether this relatively gentle response to the elimination of tariff barriers was attributable to the greater durability and capital intensity of steel-making equipment, the ECSC High Authority's policy of damping price competition, tacit interfirm agreements not to interpenetrate markets too vigorously, simple concern for oligopolistic interdependence, or some complex combination of these and other influences.

In the petroleum refining industry, the advent of EC and EFTA inspired no major structural changes in part because trade in refined products had previously been relatively free. England and Sweden charged no duty in 1958 on gasoline imported from most-favored nations, for example, and the German tariff was 4 percent. France had the highest tariff, 8 percent ad valorem (which however amounted to an effective rate of 30 to 40 percent on value added). After its entry into the EC, France also continued to protect its refining industry through a system of quotas and import permits which in effect stifled competition from adjoining EC nations.

Free trade played a noteworthy supporting role in stimulating the Swedish Tobacco Company to build a modern cigarette plant at Malmö and close three small older plants. The key precipitating factor was the parliamentary repeal in 1961 of Svenska Tobaks' exclusive control over wholesale distribution of imported cigarettes. Non-Swedish cigarette firms reacted by increasing their promotional efforts and capturing a growing market share with cigarettes imported duty-free from plants in other EFTA nations. To compete effectively with this import threat, Svenska Tobaks' management recognized among other things the need to increase its production efficiency—hence its plant rationalization decision. In the other cigarette industries of Europe, on the other hand, import competition was not cited as a significant stimulus to plant modernization and closure decisions.

The experience of the Swedish brewing industry is in some respects

---

28. Cf. Cockerill and Silberston, *The Steel Industry*, p. 38.

similar to that of cigarettes. As of 1967, the average size of Top 50 Percent breweries was only 5 percent of our minimum optimal scale estimate. However, a series of mergers concentrated control over these small units in the hands of a few sellers. Most prominent was Pripp, which by 1970 had gained a 50 percent market share through mergers involving some forty different breweries. Closure of inefficient plants, expansion and modernization of larger units, and the construction of a relatively large, ultramodern brewery at Stockholm were stimulated by events which created both an opportunity and a challenge. The opportunity came from mid-1960s' legislation changing the alcoholic content classification structure and permitting the 3.6 percent beer types most popular in other parts of Europe to be sold outside state liquor monopoly stores for the first time. This revolutionized consumption patterns and permitted new national brands to take over much of the market from a vast array of low-alcohol-content local brands. Pripp moved especially vigorously to phase out local brands, losing sales at first but regaining them as its national brands took hold. With the number of brands sharply curtailed, closure of small breweries became feasible and advantageous. The change in distribution laws simultaneously opened up the Swedish market to Danish brewers Carlsberg and Tuborg, who imported increasing quantities of beer from their old but large and fairly efficient plants in Copenhagen. To compete successfully with the Danish beers, for which considerable brand preference existed, Pripp was impelled to reduce its production costs through closures and modernization. By permitting duty-free entry of Danish beer, Sweden's membership in EFTA clearly contributed to the stimulus.

Comparable customs union effects were not observed in the German and British beer industries. Imports into Germany were inhibited by strong local brand preferences and by the *Reinheitsgebot* law forbidding the presence of additives used by many foreign brewers. In England the tied-house system offered domestic brewers considerable protection. It is conceivable that growing import competition may eventually have a plant structure impact in France. At the time of our interviews no discernible influence was evident, nor had producers chosen a strategy for digesting multiple mergers consummated during the late 1960s.

All European nations covered by our sample experienced an influx of shoe and textile imports during the 1960s. But in most cases there was no clear connection between joining EC or EFTA and scale economy increasing structural changes. This was so for several reasons. Some of the most severe import threats in the textile industry came not from fellow customs union nations but from outsider countries like Japan, Korea, and Hong Kong. Second, the minimum optimal plant scale in shoe manufacturing was both small and (because of style proliferation) declining. In every country but Sweden most output was produced in good-sized plants before the EC and EFTA tariff reductions began to bite. Third, the cost advantages of low-wage countries were so compelling that in many instances there was no way firms in relatively high wage nations like Sweden, Germany, England, and France could meet the competition directly. One common reaction was to seek refuge in fashion-sensitive lines where costs were less important than closeness to local market trends. This often called for plants of smaller, not larger, size. Another reaction was demoralization and despair. Especially in Sweden, shoe and textile manufacturers simply gave up and closed their plants, large and small. In England, the pressure of low-wage imports on prices and an overhang of underutilized capacity discouraged most textile companies from investing in completely new plants. There and in France a considerable movement of fabric production from the oldest to more modern plants occurred, often increasing the scale of production at the latter. But building completely new facilities was rare.

Demoralization was also the reaction of relatively small Canadian battery and bearing manufacturers to the 1965 auto parts trade pact. Auto manufacturers found they could save money by transferring the production of high lot-size economy original equipment parts to high-volume lines in the United States. The fall of tariff barriers also had little perceptible effect on plant sizes in the European battery and bearing industries, partly because most leading plants were already of considerable size and partly because competitive interpenetration was inhibited by respect for spheres of influence. Little international competition developed in the paint industries either. Only in Sweden did we observe a serious effort to concentrate production in larger plants, and there the principal import competition came from German firms, not from EFTA nations. Finally, trade in the cement and bottle industries was held to nonthreatening levels by high transportation costs and strong respect for spheres of influence.

Thus, the plant-specific scale economy enhancing effects of customs union membership were clearest in the refrigerator industry, with weaker or more complex repercussions evident in Swedish brewing and cigarettes, British and French textiles, and (still less clearly) European steel. A variety of conditions prevented trade from expanding or the growth of trade from stimulating plant structure adaptations in other industries.

Cost-Push Pressures

Import competition is not the only force which can squeeze profit margins and goad producers to seek ways of reducing costs. Exogenous cost-increasing shocks can work in similar fashion. Two examples are sufficiently interesting to warrant elaboration.

As we have observed already, cement kilns and related equipment have long physical lives. Once they are in place, it is difficult to justify replacing them with more modern large-scale units. To be sure, newer kilns have lower capital *plus* operating costs per barrel of output, but the capital cost of existing equipment is already sunk. And the capital cost of a big new kiln is sufficiently high that the *total* (operating plus capital) unit cost of the challenger tends to exceed the *marginal* operating cost of older kilns except when existing equipment becomes so old that it is virtually falling apart.

This fact of economic life discouraged modernization of cement works until concern over air pollution became acute. Once governments began demanding that cement makers eliminate the corrosive dust plume downwind of their mills, however, the economics changed radically. To catch the dust generated in cement manufacturing requires the installation of electrostatic precipitators or similar apparatus, which in turn necessitates a fairly complete rebuilding of kilns and their related smoke dispersion facilities. Once this requirement was imposed, it turned out to be less expensive to install a completely new large-scale kiln than to rebuild several small old kilns. The result was an acceleration of cement plant modernization and small plant closures, particularly in the United States but also abroad.

Pressure to curb pollution from open hearth steelmaking shops similarly accelerated the shift to basic oxygen technology, with a much larger minimum optimal scale. And there is reason to believe that strict enforcement of lead oxide dust and solvent vapor control laws will require investments in equipment for which the scale economies are sufficiently compelling that the viability of numerous very small battery and paint plants will be threatened.

Our other example of cost-push structural shocks comes from the Canadian refrigerator industry. There, as in Eurpoe, a "race toward rationalization" occurred. Import competition, however, played at best only an indirect role. The industry was protected by a 20 percent ad valorem tariff, and imports of standard refrigerators were not only slight, but showed a generally declining trend during the 1960s. Behind this tariff wall some dozen companies divided up the production of 600,000 household refrigerators and freezers in 1967, not enough to fill one plant of optimal scale. The largest producer had an annual output of only 120,000 units.

Competition in the industry intensified perceptibly during the second half of the 1960s, squeezing profit margins. Two clear contributing factors were the proliferation of models and the desire of firms to broaden their lines, reducing average lot sizes and increasing the disadvantages of small-scale operation. Prices meanwhile were kept in check by the threat, even if not the actuality, of increased imports from the United States. Several mergers occurred during the 1960s, leading inter alia to the closure of some plants and expansion of others. Two or three of the smallest sellers also ceased operations. Then, in 1970, three further events shook the industry: the Canadian government seriously considered reducing the tariff to 12 percent or less; the large Franklin plant was shut down for most of the year by a strike; and General Motors announced that manufacturing of refrigerators and other major appliances would be halted at its Frigidaire plant to make room for more profitable automobile parts work. The tariff change threat constituted a danger that already slender profits would be converted to losses unless production efficiency was raised. The availability of Franklin's and Frigidaire's business was seen as an opportunity to increase volume and reduce unit costs. Remaining companies competed strenuously for it on both price and nonprice grounds. Interviewees showed keen awareness that only those who succeeded in building their sales were likely to survive. One company deliberately accepted low to negative profit margins to increase sales and reduce unit costs. Although our field research was completed before the final results of these developments could be assessed, company spokesmen were convinced in late 1970 that the refrigerator industry would evolve to a structure with three firms commanding most of the market while one to three others held on at the fringes.

Mergers and Plant Sizes

Mergers have been mentioned frequently in our analysis of plant structure adaptation histories. A tabulation based partly upon solid data and partly on "guesstimates" reveals that among our 125 interviewees, approximately 36, or 29 percent, were involved between 1958 and 1970 in horizontal mergers which increased their sales or employment in the sampled industry by one-third or more relative to 1958 levels. This estimate is not completely representative, however, since our interview sample included a disproportionate fraction of U.S. firms, whose merger activities were restrained by vigorous enforcement of the Celler-Kefauver Act. Another tabulation compiled for use in Chapter 6 shows that of the seventy-two companies leading their industries in sales as of 1970 for the six nations and twelve industries, twenty-nine, or 40 percent, had between 1958 and 1970 participated in horizontal mergers with firms of roughly equal size or acquired at least as many industry-specific plants as they operated during 1958. It seems clear that mergers have been an important element in the structural development of many industries.

The key question for present purposes is, did such mergers have a significant impact on plant sizes? In particular, did they facilitate the realization of plant-specific scale economies in industries with a legacy of sub-MOS plants?

The conventional wisdom among U.S. economists would suggest a pessimistic answer. As the senior author wrote in an earlier work, "The plants are already built; not much can be done to unbuild them in order to increase their scale."[29] This however oversimplifies the problem. It is possible at least in principle that the output of a sub-MOS plant can be produced at lower long-run marginal cost by transferring it to another expanded plant. This is most apt to be true when two conditions are satisfied: (1) the equipment and layout of the recipient plant are flexible and easily expanded; and (2) among the more or less fixed costs of operating the two plants, sunk costs associated with durable equipment are relatively unimportant compared to the ongoing costs of plant management and supporting services. Industries least likely to satisfy these criteria are those with capital-intensive, lumpy equipment as in cement, petroleum refining, steel melting and primary products rolling, and bottles. More likely candidates include refrigerators, paints, batteries, weaving, shoemaking, and brewing.

The strongest examples of scale increases attributable to post-merger production consolidations were observed in the refrigerator industry. Most involved simultaneous changes in product mix, so that plant-specific and product-specific effects were intertwined. Thus, when GSW, Ltd. acquired Moffats in 1971 to capture the leading position in Canadian refrigerator sales, GSW was producing refrigerators, automatic washing machines, clothes dryers, electric stoves, air conditioners, and water heaters in its London, Ontario, plant. Moffats meanwhile was also manufacturing a broad line of appliances at its main plant. Following the merger GSW specialized its London plant on refrigerators, freezers, washing machines, and dryers, while the production of other appliances previously located at London was reassigned to other plants. Average refrigerator and freezer output per plant, the measure of plant size used in Chapter 3, rose substantially following the consolidation. In this and other mergers involving Hotpoint, English Electric, and General Electric of England; Siemens and Bosch in Germany; and Thomson-Brandt in France, reorganization was facilitated by the fact that production of refrigerators, stoves, dryers, and analogous major appliances requires

29. Scherer, *Industrial Market Structure and Economic Performance*, p. 116.

similar metal cutting, bending, assembly, and finishing equipment. Yet output reallocations unaccompanied by plant closures cannot do much to increase the average *overall* level of in-plant activity, and hence to yield substantial plant-specific scale economies owing, say, to the fuller utilization of indivisible management, custodial, and staff functions. Rather, most of the savings were product-specific, resulting from narrower specialization and longer production runs.

If clear-cut cases of plant-specific economies are to be found, they are more apt to resemble Thomson-Brandt's acquisition and subsequent closure of Claret's refrigerator plant at Romilly, leading to greater production at Thomson-Brandt's own refrigerator plant; or the closing in 1969 of Kelvinator's Canadian appliance facility and transfer of its refrigerator assignments to the Franklin Company's Galt, Ontario, plant. We encountered numerous examples of this sort in the brewing, textile, paint, and battery industries. That such changes were made, usually after careful calculation, suggests that economies were gained thereby. Not all the savings can properly be called long-run scale economies, however. In a substantial subset of the cases—in six of the sixteen sizeable closures we could identify explicitly—the consolidations were a response to declining demand and therefore involved loading up a plant of unchanged capacity more fully rather than expanding the capacity of one plant at the expense of another. In many other instances companies considered closing some plants and expanding others but decided not to, suggesting that there must be a continuous spectrum of payoffs from postmerger consolidation. Unfortunately, our interview research did not pursue this point vigorously enough to estimate the parameters of the payoff size distribution.

It is also possible that mergers which do not lead to immediate plant expansions and closures might nevertheless contribute over the longer run to plant size increases. Two mechanisms are relevant. First, the enterprise with many older plants is likely to have a larger quantity of capacity becoming ripe for replacement at any interval in time than the firm with one or a very few plants. The former is therefore in a better position to build replacement facilities of impressive scale. Second, the company with a large market share, acquired perhaps in part through mergers, can expect to enjoy larger periodic increments of demand growth than smaller rivals *if* respect for mutual interdependence leads to relative stability of market shares over time. And with larger growth increments, more sizeable expansions can be undertaken.

All this begs a set of questions which can no longer be avoided. Why are mergers necessary to increase one's market share and sales at the expense of rivals too small to realize all scale economies? Indeed, why should one pay good money for an old plant one intends to shut down?

One part of the answer is that firms which would have grown even without merger find they can obtain the production facilities they need at lower costs, all else equal, by acquiring a company in trouble than by building from scratch. Thus, an interviewee reported that his staff did numerous projections of the capacity needed to accommodate contemplated growth and how it might best be provided. But then an attractive take-over candidate would appear and force an adjustment in the plan because it was more economical to buy what existed than to build an "optimal" new plant. In many cases, however, small outdated plants are no bargain even at a low take-over price, and this motive for merger was of dominant importance in major post-1958 acquisitions of only three or four interviewees.

In industries with strong product differentiation but slow change in product technology, acquisition of companies with a substantial brand following may be the easiest or even the only feasible means of building sales volume quickly. This factor was highly important in many brewing and refrigerator mergers and to a lesser degree in some paint, shoe, and battery company mergers. Often the acquiring firms considered brand names and access to distribution channels to be more valuable properties than any accompanying physical facilities.

In the British, German, and Swedish brewing industries, opportunities to increase sales by means other than merger were also restricted by special institutions. Best known is the British pub licensing and tied-house system.[30] The bulk of all beer consumption in England continues to take place in public houses, restaurants, and clubs. To sell beer for "on-premises" drinking, such establishments need a license. New licenses have been issued sparingly. Some 86 percent of the on-premises public house licenses outstanding in England and Wales during 1967 (but only 27 percent of those in Scotland) were owned by brewing companies. The quickest and surest way to increase sales within the public house market was to acquire other brewing companies. This was the primary motivation for a merger wave which raised the market share of the leading three U.K. brewing firms from 12 percent in 1958 to 45 percent in 1967. Many of the plants so acquired were small and outdated, lacking among other things the filtering and pasteurization equipment needed to satisfy changing tastes. They were eventually closed down as the acquiring firms expanded their larger and more adaptable breweries to serve the captive demand which was the real acquisition objective. The opportunity to increase market access by extending one's string of

---

30. See the Monopolies Commission report, *Beer*, pp. 27–54.

tied houses was also an inducement to brewing company mergers in Germany, although probably not the most important one. More compellingly, strong local loyalties on the part of German consumers made it difficult to increase sales rapidly without acquiring rival brands. In Sweden a still different set of incentives existed. Most local brewers had agreed formally to respect spheres of influence and not to interpenetrate each others' home markets. To increase their sales without undermining these agreements, expansion-minded companies found it advisable to acquire the local brewers.

Substantial mergers of recent vintage were also undertaken by at least a dozen of the firms in our sample because their management wished to expand, but expansion by internal growth would add so much to supply that prices would almost surely be depressed. This "percentage effect" avoidance motive[31] appeared to be strongest in industries with stagnant or declining demand and weak product differentiation. Closure of outdated plants and expansion of the best-suited facilities, it should be noted, did not in all such instances follow quickly. When the construction of large-scale modern plants was a prime objective *and* demand was growing rapidly, sensitivity to price-depressing effects was much less evident. Steel provides a good example. During the 1950s and 1960s Japanese steel producers carried out a vast program of plant modernization and expansion with almost no mergers of noteworthy size.[32] In the more slowly growing French and (especially) British markets, on the other hand, no entrepreneur appeared willing to accept the risks of building new large-scale works while a considerable overhang of old but serviceable independent capacity persisted. Merger through nationalization was the means ultimately adopted in Great Britain to ensure among other things that expansions did not outstrip obsolete capacity withdrawals. In France the government forced major mergers upon steelmakers de Wendel-Sidelor and Usinor as a condition for granting long-term, low-interest rate loans to support a modernization plan agreed upon in 1966.

Sharp declines in demand or prices were the background for mergers consummated in other industries, particularly the import-riddled European textile industries and the cement industry of Westphalia, Germany. The motives for textile mergers were complex, featuring inter alia the belief that small financially pressed textile firms had valuable salvageable human and physical assets. Also prominent in several cases was the hope that larger textile companies might prevent the retrenchment from turn-

31. Cf. Richard B. Heflebower, "Corporate Mergers: Policy and Economic Analysis," *Quarterly Journal of Economics,* 77 (November 1963), 554. The original concept is from Bain, *Barriers to New Competition,* p. 55.

32. Cockerill and Silberston, *The Steel Industry,* pp. 64–65.

ing into a rout by acquiring plants and shutting the inefficient ones down. Similarly, when the German Federal Cartel Office and then the courts of appeal concluded in 1967 that the Westphalian cement cartel was illegal, a price war broke out. By 1968 prices had fallen 50 percent. Many of the twenty-five firms banded together to buy up and retire excess capacity, but after a million barrels of capacity had been withdrawn during the summer of 1968, the effort ceased for lack of financial backing. Further efforts to form a new cartel which satisfied both the producers and the Cartel Office proved fruitless. The largest supplier, Dyckerhoff, then began constructing a large new works. This move induced several firms to exit voluntarily, and Dyckerhoff took it upon itself to acquire several other competing plants which it planned to shut down when its new works began operating. Our interviews provided too little insight into the evaluations which led Dyckerhoff and merger-prone European textile makers to believe that the acquisition price they paid to distressed rivals whose plants had nothing but nuisance value was justified by favorable price stabilization effects.

We find then many reasons why firms choose the merger route to expansion rather than building internally. Formal governmentally sanctioned restrictive practices such as the tied-house system in British brewing and the erstwhile market division cartel among Swedish brewers made merger the easiest method of expanding. The existence of strong brand preferences has a similar effect. Or businessmen may turn to merger because they fear the price ramifications of internal expansion or because they are simply not willing to accept the rough and tumble of a competitive struggle for market position. Observers of liberal persuasion may regret and even deplore these breakdowns of competition requiring further departures from a competitive structure to increase efficiency. Such artificial restraints as market division cartels and tying contracts appear to have little redeeming social merit, and it ought to be possible to do more about them than deplore. But strong product differentiation and the failure of entrepreneurial nerve may well be facts of life about which government bodies can do little, at least in the short and middle run. To the extent that this is so, mergers may be an important instrument through which firms with small, inefficient plants reach a size at which they can build units of optimal scale. A dilemma is posed for policymakers, particularly when the relevant market is small and slowly growing. We shall return to the problem in our concluding chapter.

Even when mergers take place, there is no guarantee that scale economy enhancing steps will follow quickly. As reported previously, thirty-six of the companies we interviewed participated in horizontal mergers which increased their sales or employment by a third or more compared to 1958 levels. For those thirty-six we attempted to determine whether the mergers were followed by substantial rationalization actions, in the sense that a significant fraction of the acquired plants were modernized and enlarged or closed down to permit expansion of other facilities. The judgments of what was and what was not a "substantial" rationalization were necessarily subjective. Still, for what they are worth, we found that in only about half of the thirty-six cases did substantial rationalization occur.[33] This estimate is biased downward because some mergers had taken place so recently that insufficient time for beginning a modernization program had passed. The bias is more than offset, however, by the omission from our count of some dozen to fifteen companies whose merger activity peaked long before 1958 but which had rationalized their acquired plant structures at an excruciatingly slow pace, if at all.

The crucial remaining question is, why do some mergers lead quickly to rationalization while others do not? One pervasive discouraging factor was durability of equipment combined with high capital intensity of production processes. The only other systematic influence we were able to detect was the presence or absence of pressure. Companies whose profits and even survival were threatened by changes in competitive conditions and/or technology appeared to respond much more vigorously to merger-related scale enhancing opportunities than firms enjoying a comfortable, secure existence.

This generalization, we confess, is more impressionistic than we would like. "Pressure" and "threatened survival" are hard to measure. There were a few cases where the qualitative indications were unmistakable, as in the European and Canadian refrigerator industries and textile manufacturing in Europe. But the less dramatic cases are difficult to categorize. When, for example, a company survives for years at relatively low profit levels without rationalizing an acquired plant structure, one is tempted to draw the possibly unwarranted inference that pressure was lacking. Disentangling the role of pressure from other variables simultaneously at work is also delicate. Thus, one probable reason why the massive German brewery merger wave of the 1960s and early 1970s led to little plant structure change was that the acquiring companies had succeeded at least temporarily in attaining a major goal: damping price competition enough so that the survival of obsolete, high-cost plants was not jeopardized. Yet it is at least arguable (as some firms

33. See also Table 6.4 *infra*, in which we find that "fairly complete" rationalization followed substantial leading firm mergers in only 18 of 47 nation-industry cells.

did argue) that sunk costs, low wages, and brewed-at-home preferences made maintaining numerous small breweries a lower-cost, higher-profit strategy than replacing them with big modern plants. Likewise, it is natural to attribute the extremely slow disappearance of sub-MOS cigarette plants to the previously insulated market positions of the French and Swedish government-owned monopolies and the strong oligopolistic price discipline of producers elsewhere. But the flatness of the long-run production cost curve in cigarette manufacturing cannot be ruled out as an alternative or contributory explanation.[34]

Nevertheless, we found the differences in attitude and behavior between firms which considered themselves to be under pressure and those which did not to be so striking that we are inclined to place heavy weight on a pressure theory of structural adaptation. An important implication is that mergers which increase monopoly power and make it possible to earn profits despite excessive unit costs are apt to counteract and undermine the opportunities for structural rationalization they simultaneously create.

The Effects of Price-Fixing Cartels

If successful, cartels provide a sheltered existence for their members. Our interview sample included sufficiently many firms participating in cartels that their impact on structural adaptation merits separate discussion. To anticipate the conclusion, we encountered little evidence that price-fixing and analogous cartels contributed positively to the emergence of efficient plant structures and a great deal of evidence that they had an inhibiting influence.

The sole exception might be cartels in which producers agree to coordinate their investments, along with prices, with the aim of building larger plants. German steelmakers implemented an investment coordination scheme in 1971, but too little experience had been accumulated at the time this was written to assess its effectiveness.[35] Swedish steel companies negotiated specialization agreements during the 1960s which might have a long-run impact on plant sizes and investment, but at the time they affected mainly the utilization of capacity already in place.[36] Thus, the evidence on positive scale effects is extremely slender.

A much clearer consequence of cartels has been to maintain prices at sufficiently high levels that inefficient plants can operate profitably and hence to minimize pressures which might otherwise have induced

34. Cf. Table 3.11 *supra*.
35. Cf. Herbert W. Köhler, *Das Kontornachfolgekonzept: Vier Rationalisierungsgruppen* (Düsseldorf: Verlag Stahleisen, 1971).
36. A further analysis will be presented in Chap. 7.

the closing down of outmoded units and the expansion of those with modernization potential. This was unmistakably the case in the Westphalian cement cartel. Similar insulation from price competition appears to have retarded modernization in the British cement industry, at least until the 1960s; the U.S. cement industry when the basing point system of pricing was rigidly followed; the British steel industry before nationalization; the Swedish steel reinforcing bar cartel; the British glass bottle cartel;[37] and the various British textile industry cartels, among others. In fact, the role of the cotton yarn spinners' cartel in retarding structural rationalization was stressed as a prime reason for abolition by the British Restrictive Practices Court in its precedent-setting 1959 decision: "So long as the scheme lasts, concentration of the industry will be postponed; it will not be until the excess capacity has been got rid of that the industry can be made into a more compact entity, a reorganisation which we believe will ultimately be beneficial not merely to the nation and the consuming public, but to the industry itself and those employed in it."[38]

Other Variables Affecting the Pace of Adaptation

Finally, certain special institutional variables affecting the speed at which plant structures are rationalized deserve very brief mention. An important role is played in Europe and especially in France by traditions and explicit government policies discouraging plant closures unless workers are either pensioned or alternate jobs in the same geographic area are provided. Inertia also stems from the fact that immobile workers often have highly developed skills which cannot easily be replaced at new or expanded plants. Excise tax rates rising with plant output in the German brewing industry and crude oil import quotas rising less than proportionately with refiners' total domestic throughput in the United States contributed to the survival of sub-MOS installations. And all sorts of ad hoc constraints exist, such as the inability of railroad and highway bridges surrounding a cement maker's plant to accommodate kilns larger than two-thirds the size company engineers considered optimal.

Our objective in this chapter has been to illuminate the statistical results of Chapter 3 with interview evidence on factors contributing to the survival of plants smaller than the minimum optimal scale. It is clear that a host of influences are relevant, and no short summary can do justice to the complexity of the matter. Several generalizations never-

37. Cf. W. P. J. Maunder, "The Glass Container Industry: A Study on the Effect of the 1956 Restrictive Trade Practices Act," *Economics*, 9 (Summer 1972), 207–219
38. *In re Yarn Spinners' Agreement*, L.R., 1 R.P. 118, 196 (1959).

theless appear warranted. First, the fragmentation of markets owing to national borders, tariffs, high transport costs, and local preferences often makes it difficult for even a single MOS plant to find sufficient demand. Second, buyers' desire for a diversity of sources seems to engender a natural tendency for demand to be divided up among several suppliers, fragmenting plant structures further. Third, exporting can expand producers' market horizons and make the construction of good-sized plants feasible even in small national markets, but this potential is often left unexploited, especially when respect for national spheres of influence is strong. Fourth, international factor price differences appear at least for our sample to induce little variation in basic plant capacity optima, although plant-manning practices and the extent of shift-working may vary significantly from one industrialized nation to the next. Fifth, in new entry and plant expansion decisions producers show considerable awareness that building a large unit could depress prices in markets small relative to the output of an optimal plant. This recognition often leads to sub-MOS investments, even though firms exercise ingenuity in devising market penetration strategies which either minimize the need to accept serious scale economy sacrifices or allow eventual growth to an efficient scale of operation. Sixth, a major reason for the survival of sub-MOS plants is the durability of physical facilities, particularly in capital-intensive industries with a history of MOS-raising technological change. Seventh, how rapidly producers adapt their plant structures to technological change depends among other things upon the extent to which there is pressure on their prices and profits. Vigorous import competition accelerates adaptation; cartelization retards it. When market imperfections are unavoidable, mergers may facilitate more rapid adaptation, but this effect can be negated if competitive pressure is simultaneously reduced. And finally, the replacement of sub-MOS plants is sometimes slowed down by government policies discouraging worker layoffs and subsidies which discriminate in favor of smaller producing units.

5

Multi-Plant Operation in the United States

Our focus shifts now from plant size decisions to multi-plant operation. Our approach in this chapter differs significantly from that taken in the other empirical chapters. Whereas most of this volume deals with the twelve industries selected for intensive interview research, here we cast our net more broadly, using census and other data to analyze the patterns of multi-plant operation in a cross section of some 155 United States manufacturing industries.

Measuring the Amount of Multi-Plant Operation

Our initial task is to find a measure of multi-plant operation which is both theoretically acceptable and estimable from existing data sources. Several possibilities exist.

One approach which we reject is the "index of divergence" pioneered by John M. Blair,[1] that is, the absolute percentage point difference between the percentage of industry shipments originated by, for example, the eight largest *companies* and the eight largest *plants*. Such an index validly pinpoints those industries characterized by high company concentration in which multi-plant operation must be high because plant

1. *Economic Concentration: Structure, Behavior, and Public Policy* (New York: Harcourt Brace Jovanovich, 1972), pp. 102–107; and U.S., Senate, Committee on the Judiciary, Subcommittee on Antitrust and Monopoly, *Hearings, Economic Concentration*, Part 6, "New Technologies and Concentration," 90th Cong., 1st Sess., October 1967, pp. 2961–2982.

concentration is low. Thus, Blair found that among U.S. manufacturing industries with four-firm concentration ratios of 50 or more in 1963, nearly 55 percent of the output originated in industries where the *eight-company* concentration ratio exceeded the *eight-plant* ratio by at least 40 percentage points, and 87 percent originated in industries with a divergence index of at least 20 percentage points. However, the Blair index necessarily shows less divergence in industries of lower company concentration but similar degrees of multi-plant operation. For instance, if the eight leading firms in each of two industries operated three plants apiece, all of equal size, the divergence index would be 50 if one of the industries had an eight-firm concentration ratio of 75, while it would be only 14 for the industry with an eight-firm concentration of 20. Because of this bias, the divergence index is not an acceptable measure of multi-plant operation.

A related measure is the "company-plant concentration multiple" used by Bain in his international comparisons study: the ratio of the share of total industry output for the four largest *firms* to the share of output or employment for the four largest *plants*.[2] If the size distribution of plants follows identical distribution laws for both highly concentrated and atomistically structured industries, which appears to be approximately true, this index will not introduce systematic biases like those encountered with Blair's divergence index. However, unless the four leading firms operate without exception the industry's largest plants and either maintain one plant each or multiple plants of identical size, the Bain index necessarily understates the extent of multi-plant operation. The more rapidly plant sizes taper off from largest to smallest, the more the Bain index understates the degree of multi-plant operation.

A more inclusive index in the same spirit as Bain's can be estimated by plotting the size distribution of an industry's plants on log normal probability paper, as illustrated for the U.S. brewing industry in Figure 5.1, with the cumulative number of plants arrayed on the vertical (logarithmic) axis and cumulative value of shipments for included plants as a percentage of total industry sales on the horizontal (normal probability) axis. Census data give only discrete points from this distribution, but a smooth curve can be interpolated to approximate the complete distribution function. Inspection reveals that the function is nearly linear for the largest plants but becomes concave downward in its small-plant tail, implying that plant sizes taper off less rapidly than a log normal distribution law would require. This shape was typical for most

2. *International Differences in Industrial Structure* (New Haven: Yale University Press, 1966), pp. 124–125.

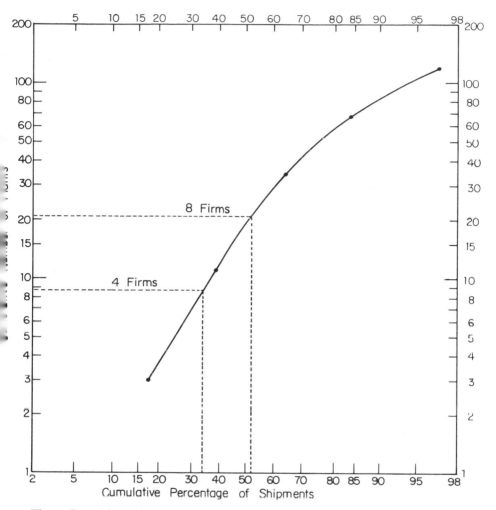

Figure 5.1. Plant Size Distribution: U.S. Brewing Industry, 1963.
Source: U.S. Bureau of the Census, *Census of Manufactures, 1963*, vol. I: *Summary and Subject Statistics* (Washington: USGPO, 1966), p. 2–17.

of the 155 size distribution curves so plotted. To find the minimum level of leading firm multi-plant operation, we need only add data on company sales concentration. To illustrate, the leading four U.S. brewing companies originated 34 percent of total industry shipments by value in 1963. Reading up from 34 percent (dotted line) to the distribution function and then across to the plant count axis, we find that the four leading sellers must together have operated at least 8.7 (and hence 9) plants, or an average of 2.25 each. Reading across from the four-plant value to the distribution curve and then downward to the percentage of shipments axis, it is readily ascertained that the four-*plant* concentration ratio for 1963 was approximately 21. Bain's company-plant concentration multiple is therefore $34/21 = 1.62$. By similar methods, we find that the eight leading brewing companies in 1963, accounting for 52 percent of total industry shipments, operated at least twenty-one plants, or 2.63 each on the average, while Bain's eight-firm company-plant concentration index is $52/32.4 = 1.60$.

It is clear that by determining the number of largest plants required to account for the largest firms' market share we arrive at a higher index of multi-plant operation (which we shall henceforth call the *derived* multi-plant index) than by Bain's technique. However, the derived index still tends to be biased downward. Since the only plants attributed to the leading firms are the industry's largest plants, the derived index will consistently underestimate the true level of multi-plant operation unless each and every leading firm plant is larger than the plants of nonleading firms.[3]

An alternative measurement approach which avoids such downward biases altogether is to count *all* the plants operated by the leading firms, regardless of their size. Normally such data are not available, but for 1963 the U.S. Census Bureau published a special tabulation revealing inter alia the total number of establishments credited to the largest four, eight, twenty, and fifty sellers in each four-digit manufacturing industry.[4] Consulting it, we find a total of twenty-three plants, or 5.75 each on the average, attributed to the largest four brewing companies and thirty-seven plants, or 4.63 apiece, to the eight largest brewers. This implies considerably more multi-plant operation than the corresponding figures of 2.25 and 2.63 plants per firm estimated by the derived method. Evidently, as independent evidence confirms, companies not among the four or eight industry leaders operated breweries larger than the smallest breweries maintained by the largest firms.

It is natural to suppose that a direct count of plants is superior to any multi-plant index estimated subject to systematic downward bias and perhaps unsystematic measurement errors from plant and company concentration data. However, the direct count statistics have their own

3. Another problem arises from the occasional aggregation of so many plants in the Census Bureau's largest plant size category that the first plotted point on the plant size distribution function occurs at a value of shipments share larger than the market share of the leading four companies. In such cases it is necessary to extrapolate the distribution function, with possibly significant estimation errors.

4. U.S., Senate, Committee on the Judiciary, Subcommittee on Antitrust and Monopoly, *Concentration Ratios in Manufacturing Industry: 1963*, Part II, 90th Cong., 1st Sess., 1967, pp. 349–558.

special problems. An enumeration based upon independent sources suggests that the leading four brewing companies operated only twenty or at most twenty-one breweries in 1963, as compared to the twenty-three reported in the Census compilation. Evidently two or three establishments which were not full-fledged breweries crept into the Census count. In this instance the differences attributable to plant classification ambiguities are minor, but for other industries they can be important. For example, a direct enumeration using published data reveals that the four largest steel producers operated in 1963 at most a total of thirty-six installations capable of performing the major refining operations normally associated with a steel works. But the 1963 Census tabulation attributes fifty-seven establishments to the four leading steel companies. The Census count includes numerous specialty melting shops and non-integrated rolling mills much smaller than the typical integrated works and quite different in character. If one is interested in "main-line" plants, the full Census count tends in such cases to overestimate the extent of multi-plant activity.

In view of these ambiguities, we shall consider multi-plant operation as measured by both the direct Census counts and the indirect derivations from plant size distribution and company concentration data. The former index will be called $MPCEN_i$, the latter $MPDER_i$. By analyzing both variables the sensitivity of our results to alternate measurement conventions can be tested.

The total number of industries studied will be 155. These were selected on the basis of two criteria from the population of 430 four-digit manufacturing industries covered by the U.S. Census. First, the industry's value added in 1963 had to be at least $75 million. This size restriction greatly reduced the data collection task while ensuring that the great bulk of all manufacturing activity was included. It may also have imparted some upward bias to the average level of multi-plant operation observed, since for smaller excluded industries extensive multi-plant activity may not have been a viable option. Second, the data for each industry had to be sufficiently complete to permit the estimation of certain transportation cost variables. These, whose derivation will be explained subsequently, were expected to contribute significantly to explaining the extent of multi-plant operation. Values of the multi-plant operation indices and all other variables used in the analyses which follow are presented in Appendix Tables 5.1, 5.2, and 5.3.

Text Table 5.1 summarizes the distribution of multi-plant operation indices for the four leading companies across the 155 industries embraced by our sample. By either measurement technique, single-plant operation appears to be rare and multi-plant operation extensive. Using the

Table 5.1. Incidence of Multi-Plant Operation among the Leading Four Firms, 155 U.S. Manufacturing Industries, 1963.

Total number of plants operated by four leading firms	Number of industries with indicated level of multi-plant operation	
	Census count	Derived estimates
4	2	3
5–8	26	51
9–16	46	60
17–32	47	28
33–80	25	9
Over 80	9	4
Mean number of plants operated by four leading firms	28.3	16.7
Median number of plants operated by four leading firms	18.4	11.2

Sources: U.S., Senate, Committee on the Judiciary, Subcommittee on Antitrust and Monopoly, *Concentration Ratios in Manufacturing Industry: 1963*, Part II, 90th Congress, 1st Sess., 1967; and U.S., Bureau of the Census, *Census of Manufactures, 1963*, vol. I: *Summary and Subject Statistics* (Washington: USGPO, 1966), chap. 2.

direct Census count, the leading four firms are found to operate at least four plants each on the average in more than half the industries. As expected, the estimates derived graphically are a good deal lower, with the mean number of plants per leading firm approximating 4.20 (16.7 $\cdot / \cdot$ 4) and the median 2.80 as compared to 7.1 and 4.6 respectively for the Census counts.

Multi-Plant Operation and Seller Concentration

We turn now to the relationship between multi-plant operation and seller concentration—a domain in which there is a history of prior work. Insight into the principal links will expose prevailing misconceptions and will sharpen our understanding of more complex models seeking to explain the extent of multi-plant activity.

The most important previous study of the connection between concentration and multi-plant operation in the United States was part of a larger work by Ralph L. Nelson.[5] Using special Census Bureau tabulations for 1954, Nelson found the average number of plants operated per Big Four company in eighty-three relatively large four-digit manufactur-

5. *Concentration in the Manufacturing Industries of the United States* (New Haven: Yale University Press, 1963), chap. 4.

ing industries to be distributed as follows among four-firm concentration ratio classes:[6]

Four-firm sales concentration ratio range	Number of industries	Average number of plants per Big Four member
70–100	16	7.2
50–69	24	4.0
30–49	25	5.8
0–29	18	4.3

The implications are less than clear-cut. The highest average level of multi-plant operation occurred in the highest concentration class, but firms in the next highest category operated the smallest average number of plants each. Summarizing these and other tabular analyses, Nelson concluded that his "crude introductory comparisons ... could only suggest that multi-plant operation contributed something to the level of concentration, but did not say anything of its importance."[7]

In an attempt to pin down the relationships further, Nelson partitioned the four-firm seller concentration ratio C4 into two component parts:

$$(5.1) \quad C4 \equiv \frac{\text{Number of leading companies' plants}}{\text{total number of plants in industry}} \times \frac{\text{average sales of leading companies' plants}}{\text{average sales of all plants in industry}}.$$

The product of the two numerators is the total sales of the four largest companies, while the product of the two denominators is total industry sales. Nelson calls the first component of the partitioned expression, giving the proportion of total industry plants operated by the largest companies, LPP (for leading companies' proportion of plants). The second term, giving the ratio of the leaders' average plant size to the average size of all industry plants, is denoted LPI (for leaders' plant size inequality).

With nearly exact measurements of the two right-hand components of equation (5.1) from Census records for eighty-seven industries, Nelson was unable to use orthodox multiple regression techniques to analyze the relative roles of LPP and LPI in explaining C4 because the variables together form a perfect identity. Analyzing simple (zero-order) correlations, he found the correlation between C4 and the large-firm plant proportion variable to be $+0.713$, while the correlation between C4 and

6. Ibid., p. 66.
7. Ibid., p. 67.

the plant size inequality index LPI was -0.366. On the basis of these results and similar ones for industry subsamples, he stated that the findings "on this first general look . . . appear to lend support to the hypothesis . . . that the multiplication of plants by leading companies may be more important than the size of their plants in explaining the level of concentration."[8]

The language Nelson used in less cautious interpretations of his results implies that concentration and multi-plant operation are indeed positively and systematically related. Subsequent interpretations have been even less cautious, so the inference has become conventional wisdom. However, the conclusion does not follow from Nelson's analysis.

The crippling difficulty is that LPP is a totally unsatisfactory measure of multi-plant operation. A high value of the leaders' plant proportion variable may, as Nelson appears at times to believe, reflect the operation of a large number of plants by leading firms. But LPP may also be high simply because an industry includes an unusually small number of plants. To illustrate, in 1963 there were only 22 establishments in S.I.C. industry 3511, steam engines and turbines, 10 of which were operated by the four leading producers. This leads to a relatively high value of 0.45 ($= 10 \cdot / \cdot 22$) for LPP, even though the four largest companies actually operated only 2.5 plants apiece on the average. Conversely, the leading four sellers in S.I.C. industry 3272, concrete products other than concrete blocks and bricks, averaged nearly 30 plants each, but their share of the total number of plants classified to that industry was only $118/3451 = 0.034$. Had they operated 45 percent of the industry's establishments, as did the leading steam engine and turbine manufacturers, each leader would have averaged 392 plants. Thus, LPP can be a wildly misleading measure of the absolute level of multi-plant operation.

A more balanced view of the situation can be obtained using our 1963 data on 155 manufacturing industries. For our sample it was possible to compute the exact analogue of Nelson's LPP index. The simple correlation between it and the four-firm sales concentration ratios is $+0.693$, very close to the 0.713 value obtained by Nelson for his 87-industry 1954 sample. But when our two measures of the number of plants operated by the four leading sellers are correlated with concentration, no evidence of a significant positive relationship is found. The zero-order correlation between the Census plant count variable MPCEN4 and concentration is -0.101; between the derived index MPDER4 and C4 the correlation is $+0.021$. The variable Nelson chose to represent multi-plant activity in fact misrepresented it, becoming

8. *Concentration*, pp. 69–70.

confounded by the fact that leading firms operate a higher percentage of all plants in concentrated than in atomistically structured industries, mainly because there tend to be fewer firms in concentrated industries and hence fewer plants. Indeed, the simple correlation between C4 and the total number of plants per industry for the 155 industries comprising our sample is -0.54.

There exists nevertheless a more complex link between concentration and multi-plant operation which warrants thorough investigation. The relationship is evident from a specification in the same spirit as Nelson's identity equation (5.1). Avoiding the misspecification which confounded his analysis, the identity can be rewritten:

$$(5.2) \qquad C4 \equiv \frac{\text{Number of leading}}{\text{firm plants}} \times \frac{\text{average market share}}{\text{per leading firm plant.}}$$

Since our emphasis will be on explaining the number of plants operated by leading firms, it is more convenient to rearrange the expression to:

$$(5.3) \qquad \frac{\text{Number of leading}}{\text{firm plants}} = \frac{C4}{\text{market share per leading firm plant}}.$$

For the left-hand term we have a completely compatible measure in our Census count variable MPCEN4. Census data also provide values of the concentration ratio C4. From special 1963 Census tabulations the market share per leading firm plant can be calculated, but if this is done, the relationship will be an identity, and analyzing the roles of its component parts becomes impossible. More interesting is the possibility of forming a near-identity by adopting a specification which measures the leading firm plant share term only imperfectly. Our approach, which will prove to have a further and more compelling behavioral rationale, is to introduce a relative plant size variable RPS_i, defined as the average market share of those plants which, when arrayed in descending sales volume order, contribute the top 50 percent of total industry sales. In other words, RPS is the sales of the Top 50 Percent plants divided by the number of plants required to make up the Top 50 Percent cohort, divided further by total industry sales; or more simply, 0.5 divided by the number of plants needed to make up the Top 50 Percent cohort.[9]

It is crucial to recognize that RPS is not an exact measure of leading firms' plant sizes. In industries with four-firm concentration ratios

9. The number of plants needed to make up the Top 50 Percent cohort was determined by means of plant size distribution graphs like Fig. 5.1. We locate the 50 percent point on the horizontal (cumulative percentage of shipments) axis, read to the distribution curve, and then read laterally to the vertical axis scale, ascertaining (for the brewing industry) that the appropriate number of plants is 19.5.

substantially below 50, the plant share cutoff used in deriving RPS exceeds the company concentration ratio. Many of the plants included in calculating RPS must therefore belong to nonleading firms. Though exceptions are possible, these plants would tend to be smaller than those operated by the four largest companies. Thus, RPS probably understates the average size of the leading firms' plants in low concentration industries. The opposite holds true in highly concentrated industries. Then it is far more likely that the plants included in deriving RPS will belong to the four leading firms. (In the extreme case of an industry whose four-firm concentration ratio is 100, all plants must be operated by the largest firms.) Furthermore, these will be the largest of the leading firms' plants. Depending upon the degree of uniformity in leading firm plant sizes, RPS will tend to overstate the average size of leaders' plants.

It follows that if RPS were the only independent variable in a regression equation estimating four-firm multi-plant operation, the estimates would be biased upward in low concentration industries (because leading firm plant sizes are underestimated) and biased downward in industries with four-firm concentration ratios greater than 50. If RPS were used in conjunction with four-firm concentration ratios, a better fit should result, since the concentration variable will assume low values when RPS is overestimating multi-plant activity and higher values when RPS is underestimating. We should therefore expect such a regression to reveal a negative association between RPS and multi-plant operation and a positive relationship between concentration and the multi-plant variable.[10] In and of itself, of course, the regression would be uninteresting since the underlying relationship is definitional. However, awareness of its existence will be helpful in interpreting the results of subsequent regression equations containing these variables.

The more the cohort of Top 50 Percent plants coincides with the cohort of plants operated by the four leading sellers, the less serious these measurement biases will be, but the more closely a multiplicative regression equation will approximate the identity specification of equation (5.3). To the extent that this identity condition is approximated, we again expect a positive association between MPCEN4 and C4 along with a negative association between MPCEN4 and RPS, each relationship with an elasticity (in multiplicative regressions, the absolute value of the regression coefficient) of 1.0.

10. Similar results should hold for a regression based on 8-firm data. The tendency for RPS to overestimate multi-plant operation would be subdued (since there are fewer industries with 8-firm concentration ratios below 50), but the underestimation problem would be more severe.

The multiplicative regression of MPCEN4 on C4 and RPS is:

(5R.1) $\log \text{MPCEN4} = -5.70 + 1.317 \log \text{C4} - 1.044 \log \text{RPS};$
$$(.090) \qquad\qquad (.051)$$
$$R^2 = .735, N = 155,$$

with standard errors given in parentheses beneath the coefficients. The anticipated coefficient sign relationships in fact emerge, and the value of R^2 has jumped by 72 percentage points compared to a logarithmic regression of MPCEN4 on C4 alone or 36 points compared to the zero-order RPS-MPCEN4 correlation. The RPS regression coefficient is insignificantly different from the unity value expected of an identity relationship, while the C4 coefficient does exceed unity significantly, though not by a large amount.

These results warn that, as in Chapter 3, we must be wary of regression specifications which lead to strong but essentially tautological relationships. In particular, it is important to avoid having the concentration and relative plant size variables appear simultaneously on the right-hand side of regressions with multi-plant operation as the dependent variable.[11] When this caveat is observed by restricting the analysis to zero-order correlations, we find no indication of a positive association between concentration and multi-plant operation. A final judgment on the issue must nevertheless await the inclusion of C4 in more complex but non-tautological regressions.

The Behavioral Variables

Armed with these cautionary insights, we inquire now what relationships with deeper behavioral significance might be anticipated.

The theoretical analysis of Chapter 2 provides the most important clues. Assuming that firms adopt plant structures which tend to minimize the sum of unit production and unit transportation costs, we expect multi-plant operation to be more extensive, the less strongly production scale economies at the plant level pull toward centralization and the higher the cost of shipping output to customers is per unit of product value. While heavy outbound freight costs stimulate decentralization, high input transportation costs can exert a force in the opposite direc-

---

11. Surprisingly, an even higher R^2 of 0.830 is obtained when the derived index MPDER4 is regressed logarithmically on C4 and RPS. We had expected a greater departure from the identity conditions because the derived index is an inferior measure of leading firms' multi-plant activity. What actually happened might be due to the greater internal consistency of MPDER and RPS, both derived from the same plant size distributions.

tion when important raw materials are concentrated at one or a very few points in geographic space. We should also expect multi-plant operation by leading enterprises to be greater when firms and the markets they serve are large than when they are small, all else equal. Finally, proliferation of plants specialized by product might be anticipated when the array of products manufactured is particularly broad. An attempt was made to define variables characterizing each of these relationships, although as we shall see, the effort was more successful for some variables than for others.

Plant Scale Economies

One of the more difficult explanatory variable definition problems involved the role of plant scale economies. Ideally, we would like to have something like the COST variable used in Chapter 3. The research required to estimate such a long-run cost function slope term or even to measure the minimum optimal scale for each industry in a sample as large as the one analyzed in this chapter was simply not feasible. We admit defeat then at the outset. An alternative approach has been adopted which, if implemented judiciously, can at least identify those industries whose multi-plant posture is most likely to have been restrained by high plant scale economies. Specifically, we shall employ as our scale economy surrogate the previously defined variable RPS, reflecting the average share of total industry sales accounted for by plants making up the top 50 percent of the industry's plant size distribution. Presumably, the higher the fraction of total industry output individual leading plants supply, the more compelling the centralizing pull of plant scale economies tends to be.

It would of course be better to base the numerator of such a variable on engineering data identifying the least-cost plant size rather than on observations of actually prevailing plant sizes, but again, the former strategy was infeasible. RPS as measured here carries the danger that high values will be observed whenever large, centralized plants are operated, whether or not the agglomeration was inspired by an opportunity to exploit scale economies. That this danger of circularity is not as grave as it might seem is shown by a matching of RPS values with engineering estimates for the industries included in our intensive interview sample.[12] The simple correlation between RPS for 1963 and the ratio of the estimated MOS values to total U.S. production for the twelve industries in 1967 was +0.843, suggesting that if the techno-

12. To ensure maximum comparability with the methods used in computing RPS values for the 155-industry sample, we ignored interview information with which extrapolation errors could have been minimized.

logically based scale optimum is large in relation to the size of the market, actual leading plants will also tend to be relatively large.[13]

The use of RPS in conjunction with our leading firm multi-plant indices also involves mismatching measurement biases and, when a variable reflecting seller concentration is added, near-identity problems discussed in the preceding section. We shall therefore have to exercise caution in interpreting its explanatory role.

It should be noted further that, to the extent actually observed leading plant sizes approximate the minimum optimal scale, RPS corresponds closely to the inverse of the MOS-deflated market size variable SIZE analyzed in Chapter 3. Its role therefore must be quite different from the role of the production cost function gradient variable COST used as a complement to the transportation cost slope term in Chapter 3.

Outbound Transportation Costs

The logic of cost minimization in geographic space implies a positive relationship between the cost of shipping a given dollar volume of output to customers at some specified distance and the number of plants leading firms choose to operate, other things being equal. Nationwide suppliers of cement products will tend to operate more decentralized plants than transistor manufacturers of similar size, since a dollar's worth of cement products costs much more to ship than a dollar's worth of transistors.

The transportation cost relationship can be expressed formally as:

$$(5.4) \qquad \text{Shipping cost per dollar of product value} = \frac{R}{\dfrac{\$1}{W}},$$

where W is the weight of a dollar's worth of the product and R is the freight rate per pound over some specified haul length. If freight rates for all products were identical, equation (5.4) would imply that shipping charges per dollar of product value vary with the reciprocal of the product's value per pound. However, freight rates per unit of weight are not in fact the same. Common carriers structure their rates on a "value of service" basis, levying higher charges on products whose market values are high in relation to their weight. Characterizing the value of service

13. Comanor and Wilson found a similar correlation of +0.89 between their observed average top 50 percent 1954 plant size/industry employment indices for a different sample of 19 industries and the corresponding MOS/total output ratios derived from Bain's 1956 study. See W. S. Comanor and T. A. Wilson, "Advertising Market Structure and Competition," *Review of Economics and Statistics*, 49 (November 1967), 71–73.

rate-setting process by a simple equation of the form $R = \alpha + \beta(\$1/W)$, equation (5.4) can be rewritten:

$$(5.5) \quad \text{Shipping cost per dollar of product value} = \frac{\alpha + \beta(\$1/W)}{\dfrac{\$1}{W}}$$

$$= \alpha W + \beta.$$

If freight rates were directly proportional to value per pound, α would be equal to zero and equation (5.5) would state that transport costs per dollar are identical for equidistant shipments. If, however, both α and β are positive—for example, because shippers consider weight, bulk, perishability, and susceptibility to damage in addition to value in setting rates—shipping costs per dollar for relatively valuable products will be greater in relation to those for low-value items, the higher β is in relation to αW.

Since both value per pound and the per-pound shipping rates set by carriers appear relevant to measuring transport cost per unit of product value, data on both variables were collected. For 101 of the 155 industries in our sample it was possible to estimate F.O.B. plant value per pound using a fairly precise estimation technique explained in Appendix B. For the remaining 54 industries, the information available was too sketchy or product lines were too complex to employ the preferred estimation method. However, approximations were derived using *Census of Transportation* data on four-digit industry outbound freight tonnages for 1963. Since *Census of Transportation* shipping tonnage estimate sampling errors run as high as 50 percent and since industry definitions for the *Census of Manufactures* (from which the product shipment dollar values were obtained) and those for the *Census of Transportation* do not always match perfectly, the value per pound figures for those 54 industries are of less than ideal quality. Their use does have the major benefit of a substantial increase in sample size for certain analyses. The F.O.B. plant product value per pound variable $VALUE_i$ estimated in diverse ways for the 155 industries ranged from approximately one cent for hydraulic cement and assorted industrial gases to $30.40 per pound for semiconductors.

For those 101 industries on which relatively reliable value per pound estimates could be developed, a major effort was undertaken to obtain corresponding data on freight rates, generally for the year 1963. Appendix B describes the methodology. Several different rate sets were compiled: one based upon rail class rates, one on common motor carrier commodity rates, and a third on the average mix of class and (predominantly) commodity rates actually applied to a sample of rail shipments.[14] In every case the rates were standardized for shipments in truckload or carload lots between Chicago and Cleveland or the most closely equivalent observable 350-mile haul.

With these data it was possible among other things to investigate the relationship between freight rate levels (in cents per hundredweight) and product value. The following linear regressions, in each case with 101 observations, were estimated:

(5R.2)   Rail class rate = 92.5 + 0.39 value per pound;
                                     (3.0)   (.05) R^2 = .386.

(5R.3)   Truck commodity rate = 62.5 + 0.35 value per pound;
                                              (3.0)   (.05) R^2 = .336.

(5R.4)   Rail commodity rate = 44.6 + 0.165 value per pound;
                                            (3.3)   (.050) R^2 = .120.

In every case value of service pricing is evident; the value per pound coefficients exceed their standard errors (in parentheses) by from three to eight times. However, considerable variation in rates remains unexplained by differences in product value. As one would expect, unexplained deviations from a strict "value of service" rate structure are considerably greater for the commodity rates, set in response to a host of market considerations, than for the rail class rates. It is important to note also that the intercept values, analogous to α in equation (5.5) above, are all positive and far in excess of their standard errors. This suggests that differences in value per pound should be a significant component of differences in shipping cost per dollar of product value.

The rail class, rail commodity, and truck commodity rates per pound were divided through by the product value per pound estimates to obtain three indices of transportation cost per unit of product value. When freight rates varied for different commodities within an industry, a weighted average index was computed, using the various products' 1963 sales as weights.

A fourth index, which will be called $COMPO_i$, is a composite of the rail and truck commodity freight rates, divided through by product value per pound. The freight rates in this instance are weighted by the relative fractions of total shipment tonnage moving by rail and

14. Motor carrier class rates were also obtained, but they proved to be virtual replicas of the rail class rates. They differed from the rail class rates in only 20 industries, and those differences were extremely small.

truck, as reported in the *Census of Transportation* for 1963.[15] Because it reflects more comprehensively than any single-medium index the actual mix of transportation media employed by manufacturers, COMPO will be emphasized in subsequent analyses of multi-plant operation patterns.

Nevertheless, COMPO could conceivably be subject to subtle biases. The motor commodity rates for the industries in our subsample of 101 are 45 percent higher on the average than the corresponding rates for the shipments upon which our rail commodity rate data are based. This of course raises the value of COMPO for industries whose products are shipped primarily by truck, ceteris paribus. As we shall see, multi-plant operation is more extensive in industries with relatively high values of COMPO. But it does not necessarily follow that higher truck rates have induced firms relying upon motor carriage to decentralize their plants more widely than those of firms stressing rail shipment. On the contrary, it is often more economical for firms with plants oriented toward regional markets to ship their products by truck rather than rail, despite the higher truck rates. It has been estimated that using truck instead of rail saves an initial 48 hours in terminal time plus 8.5 hours for each 100 miles shipped.[16] The shorter (and more reliable) truck transit interval can reduce inventory requirements. Motor freight also eliminates the need to arrange for pickup and delivery. These considerations, which are not taken into account by our transportation cost indices, make motor freight particularly attractive for short hauls, while on longer hauls the advantages may be outweighed by the lower ton-mile commodity rates associated with rail shipment.

All else equal, the average length of haul on outbound shipments declines as the geographical dispersion of a firm's plants (and hence the extent of multi-plant operation) increases. As the length of haul declines, we expect the proportion of shipments carried by truck to increase. And when reliance on motor transport rises, the composite shipping cost index COMPO assumes higher values. We must be wary then of a chain of causation between multi-plant operation and transport costs the reverse of that originally postulated. However, further analysis suggests that the dilemma may be more conjectural than real. The zero-order correlation between the eight-firm Census index of multi-plant operation MPCEN8 and the percentage of ton-miles shipped by

15. U.S., Bureau of the Census, *1963 Census of Transportation* (Washington, 1966), vol. III. Unlike Chap. 3, no attempt was made to include in the composite index the rates and tonnages associated with water, private truck, and pipeline shipment.

16. See Benjamin Chinitz, "The Effect of Transportation Forms on Regional Economic Growth," in G. J. Karaska and D. F. Bramhall, eds., *Locational Analysis for Manufacturing* (Cambridge: M.I.T. Press, 1969), p. 93.

truck for the 101 industries in our subsample was only +0.14. Although some bias undoubtedly exists, it does not appear to be a very strong one.

In certain analyses we shall also introduce a dummy variable PERSH$_i$ with a value of one when an industry's products are perishable and zero otherwise, to reflect another dimension of the feasibility of long distance shipping. Industries with unit values of PERSH are confined to the meat, dairy, bakery products, and frozen foods groups. In all, seven sample industries had unit PERSH values.

Raw Material Shipping Costs and Localization

The cost of shipping raw materials may also affect the number of plants firms operate. If important raw materials are of low value in relation to their weight *and* if their sources are confined to one or a very few regions, geographically dispersed plant operation might entail prohibitively high input transportation costs. No such constraint would exist, however, if the inputs were available throughout the country or if they were of such high unit value that long-distance shipping was economically feasible.

From this brief statement it should be apparent that the problem is extremely complex. Deriving an index to reflect comprehensively the locational pull of raw materials would require an enormous effort to establish for each industry the types and quantities of materials processed, their value per pound, the weight losses or gains during processing, whether their sources are ubiquitous or centralized, the transportation media used, and the appropriate freight rates for each material and medium. The information resulting from such an effort might well prove to "explain" multi-plant operation patterns no better than a much simpler indicator of the extent to which industries are dependent upon geographically clustered resources. Because the cost of developing a sophisticated raw material shipping cost index was expected to outweigh its probable benefits, we have confined our analysis to constructing a series of "coefficients of localization" patterned after those used by P. Sargant Florence in his analyses of U.S. and British industry structure.[17]

Table 5.2 illustrates the calculation procedure, taking S.I.C. industry 2033, canned fruits and vegetables, as an example. The geographic distribution of value added originated by all four-digit U.S. manufacturing industries together in 1963 was derived from Census data for nine major regions. This percentage distribution was then compared

17. *Investment, Location and Size of Plant* (Cambridge, Eng.: Cambridge University Press, 1948), esp. pp. 34–37.

Table 5.2.   Derivation of the Coefficient of Localization for S.I.C. Industry 2033: Canned Fruits and Vegetables, 1963.[a]

| Region | Percentage of value added originating in each census region | | Deviations from all-industry percentages (2) − (1) |
	(1) All manufacturing industry	(2) S.I.C. 2033	
All regions	100.0	100.0	
New England	7.1	2.0	− 5.1
Middle Atlantic	22.7	13.9	− 8.8
East North Central	29.3	17.8	−11.5
West North Central	6.2	3.8	− 2.4
South Atlantic	10.9	12.1	+ 1.2
East South Central	4.9	1.2	− 3.7
West South Central	5.7	4.1	− 1.6
Mountain	1.8	1.1	− 0.7
Pacific	11.5	43.9	+32.4
Total of positive deviations			33.6
Coefficient of localization			33.6

[a]Constructed from data in vol. II, pt. 1, of the *Census of Manufactures, 1963*, p. 20C–8.

with equivalent calculations for each individual industry. For a given industry, the localization coefficient $LOCAL_i$ is the sum of the positive deviations of the industry's geographic shares from those for all manufacturing industries. In principle, the coefficient can range from 0 to 98 (the value for an industry located entirely in the Mountain Region). The actual values run from 5.5, for the corrugated shipping container industry, to 86.5, for typewriter manufacturing. The coefficient of 33.6 for canned fruits and vegetables is slightly above the full-sample mean of 28, reflecting the disproportionate concentration of canning activity in the climate-blessed Pacific region.

Although using coefficients of localization appears to be the only feasible means of taking into account the pull of raw material sources, their introduction poses interpretational problems. While they do pinpoint resource-tied industries, there is a tendency for all industries with low multi-plant operation to exhibit higher than average localization values. If an industry's largest firms each operate only one or two plants, it is likely statistically that these few plants will be less evenly distributed across the country than if the firms were operating large numbers of plants. For example, as noted before, typewriter manufacturing has the highest localization coefficient. There is virtually no multi-plant operation in that highly concentrated industry, presumably because of substantial scale economies at the plant level[18] and the high wholesale value of the product in relation to its weight. Most probably for historical reasons, it happens that most of the industry's plants are located in the Northeast, although there are no raw materials unique to New England essential in typewriter manufacturing. To some extent then, the localization coefficients reflect other determinants of multi-plant activity. We must recognize that including LOCAL as an independent variable in regression analyses will introduce intercorrelation problems and may overstate the true influence of raw material sources on plant operation patterns.

Table 5.3 lists industries with coefficients of localization exceeding 50. Of the sixteen industries, only ten (whose coefficients are starred) appear at all closely tied to centrally located resources, and for one of these—cigarettes—there is reason to believe that labor market considerations are more important than the pull of leaf tobacco supplies.[19]

Table 5.3. Sixteen Industries with Particularly High Localization Coefficient Values.

S.I.C.	Industry description	Coefficient of localization
3572	Typewriters	86.5
2111	Cigarettes	76.0*
2861	Gum and wood chemicals	68.0*
3982	Hard surface floor coverings	65.0
2034	Dehydrated food products	62.0*
2823	Cellulosic man-made fibers	61.5*
2611	Pulp mills	60.0*
2272	Tufted carpets and rugs	58.5
2072	Chocolate products	56.0
2021	Creamery butter	54.0*
2822	Synthetic rubber	52.4*
3331	Primary copper	52.0*
3861	Photographic equipment	52.0
2092	Soybean oil mills	51.2*
2824	Noncellulosic organic fibers	50.0*
3632	Household refrigerators	50.0

Note: Asterisks denote the industries with likely centrally located resource ties.

18. See Joe S. Bain, *Barriers to New Competition* (Cambridge: Harvard University Press, 1956), p. 72.

19. Cf. n. 14, Chap. 2. On the complex locational pulls affecting the noncellulosic organic fibers industry, see Joseph Airov, *The Location of the Synthetic-Fiber Industry* (Cambridge: M.I.T. Press, 1959).

Historical legacies, compelling plant scale economies, and/or very high seller concentration probably explain the high coefficients in chocolate products, tufted carpets, typewriters, refrigerators, photo equipment, and hard surface floor coverings.

Firm Size, Concentration, and Product Specialization

Other things such as unit transportation costs and the size of an MOS plant held equal, we should expect multi-plant operation to be greater in an industry comprised of relatively large leading firms. Such firms are more apt to operate on a nationwide basis and thus find it advantageous to reduce shipping costs by dispersing plants near centers of demand. Also, there is a stronger incentive for sizeable enterprises to decentralize their plant operations because of the enhanced danger that large single plants will experience serious managerial diseconomies of scale.

Leading firm size depends upon two main factors: the volume of output for the whole industry and the share of that output commanded by the largest companies. The industry output measure $VA63_i$ chosen for the subsequent analysis will be value added in 1963. In certain analyses it will be used in conjunction with the four-firm concentration ratio C4. To the extent that it is indeed firm size, rather than industry size and concentration operating separately, which contributes to multi-plant operation, we expect the effect of VA63 and C4 to show up most strongly in a multiplicative specification.

Finally, we must take plant specialization into account. Many of the Census Bureau's four-digit industry classifications are so broad that all the products included would almost certainly not be produced in the same plant. For example, S.I.C. 3842, surgical appliances and supplies, spans such disparate items as bandages and hearing aids. Even when the relevant production processes exhibit more commonality, managerial and labor supply advantages may stem from specializing plants in some narrower segment of the product array, especially for larger manufacturers. A crude index $DIG7_i$ of the potential for realizing economies through multi-plant product specialization is the number of seven-digit product classes encompassed by a four-digit industry. We expect DIG7 to be positively associated with our measures of multi-plant operation.

Summary of Variables

By way of summary, we have formulated four alternative measures of multi-plant operation drawn from two sources: Census leading firm plant counts and derivations from plant size distribution and company concentration data. These dependent variables will be identified in the subsequent regression analyses:

$MPCEN4_i$ Census count of plants operated by the four largest firms.

$MPCEN8_i$ Census count of plants operated by the eight largest firms.

$MPDER4_i$ Derived estimate of minimum four-firm multi-plant operation.

$MPDER8_i$ Derived estimate of minimum eight-firm multi-plant operation.

For a subsample of 101 industries, four variables have been developed to measure the freight cost per dollar of product value on shipments over roughly 350 miles between Illinois and Ohio. The only one which will be reported explicitly is:

$COMPO_i$ Composite index of rail and truck commodity rates per dollar of product value, based on 1963 tonnage divisions.

An important component of the freight cost index to be analyzed separately in some cases is:

$VALUE_i$ Estimated product value per pound in 1963.

Other independent variables will be:

$PERSH_i$ Dummy variable with a value of one for highly perishable products and zero otherwise.

$VA63_i$ Industry value added in 1963.

$C4_i$ The four-firm sales concentration ratio for 1963.

$DIG7_i$ The number of seven-digit commodities included within an industry's four-digit S.I.C. classification.

RPS_i Average sales share of plants comprising the top 50 percent of an industry's plant size distribution.

$LOCAL_i$ Coefficient of industry localization.

The Results

Theory provides little guidance on the specific form of the relationship between our multi-plant operation indices and the various independent variables. The only clue we have is that value added and concentration should interact multiplicatively if leading firm size has a significant explanatory role. Given this ambiguity, we proceed heuristically, testing the quality and sensitivity of our results to alternate additive and multiplicative regression specifications. As the previous discussion has brought out, we must also be wary of interactions between concentration and the RPS variable which could form a near-identity as joint "independent" variables and of certain other intercorrelations which may be more definitional than behaviorally significant. Our strategy will be to begin by estimating regression equations including all potentially relevant independent variables short of a near-identity specification. We then proceed by culling out clearly insignificant and intercorrelated variables to shed as much light as possible on the underlying causal structure.

To keep matters as simple as possible, we shall for the most part emphasize the results for the four-firm multi-plant operation indices. Although the regression results are generally somewhat stronger (at least in terms of R^2 values) for the eight-firm indices, probably because unsystematic variations and measurement errors "wash out" more fully for a larger cohort of leading firms, the four-firm indices are more closely comparable with those to be analyzed for a different sample in the next chapter. As the following simple linear correlation coefficients for all 155 industries reveal, the eight-firm and four-firm indices are closely related:

	MPCEN4	MPCEN8	MPDER4	MPDER8
MPCEN4	1.000	0.986	0.915	0.939
MPCEN8		1.000	.873	.909
MPDER4			1.000	.990
MPDER8				1.000

Tables 5.4 and 5.5 array the zero-order correlations for the principal variables in linear and logarithmic form respectively. Coverage is restricted to the 101 industries for which explicit transportation cost indices were computed. A strong positive correlation is seen between multi-plant operation and both the composite freight cost index and the categorical perishability variable. As expected, RPS and LOCAL vary inversely with multi-plant operation and are themselves moderately collinear. Also of interest is the strong positive correlation between RPS and the concentration variable C4, revealing that concentration tends to be high when individual leading plants are large in relation to the market.

Tables 5.6, 5.7, 5.8, and 5.9 summarize the principal multiple regression results, first for the Census count variable MPCEN as dependent variable in additive and multiplicative specifications and then for the two main derived index MPDER specification alternatives. For maximum comparability, a generally similar sequence is followed in adding, deleting, or substituting variables and observations.

Table 5.4. Correlation Matrix: Variables in Additive Form.

Variable	MPCEN4	MPDER4	COMPO	$\frac{1}{\text{VALUE}}$	VA63	C4	DIG7	RPS	LOCAL	PERSH
MPCEN4	1.000	0.915	0.590	0.467	0.299	−0.124	0.096	−0.343	−0.282	0.485
MPDER4		1.000	.507	.361	.232	.005	.008	−.253	−.264	.449
COMPO			1.000	.966	.111	.005	.034	−.170	−.100	−.012
1/VALUE				1.000	.115	.005	.045	−.161	−.032	−.066
VA63					1.000	−.117	.209	−.192	−.028	.182
C4						1.000	−.230	.675	.360	−.218
DIG7							1.000	−.203	−.145	.144
RPS								1.000	.470	−.213
LOCAL									1.000	−.109
PERSH										1.000

Note: N = 101.

Five percent significance point = 0.196; one percent significance point = 0.255.

Table 5.5. Correlation Matrix: Variables in Logarithmic Form

Variable	MPCEN4	MPDER4	COMPO	VALUE	VA63	C4	DIG7	RPS	LOCAL	PERSH
MPCEN4	1.000	0.900	0.568	−0.533	0.505	−0.180	0.189	−0.679	−0.371	0.428
MPDER4		1.000	.485	−.432	.405	.047	.108	−.561	−.360	.448
COMPO			1.000	−.961	.181	−.056	.084	−.339	−.170	.079
VALUE				1.000	−.180	.054	−.103	.312	.077	−.026
VA63					1.000	−.172	.320	−.373	−.172	.252
C4						1.000	−.219	.757	.394	−.204
DIG7							1.000	−.248	−.142	.144
RPS								1.000	.506	−.424
LOCAL									1.000	−.129
PERSH										1.000

Note: *N* = 101.

Five percent significance point = 0.196; one percent significance point = 0.255.

The first two regressions in each table show the results of regressing the four- and eight-firm multi-plant indices for all 101 industries with estimated transportation cost variables on most of the relevant independent variables except the identity-forming concentration ratio. All variables except DIG7 have the signs anticipated, although in several cases the RPS coefficients are not statistically significant. The strongest explanatory performance is exhibited by the transport cost index COMPO, with t-ratios ranging between 4.51 (in multiplicative regression 5.9.1) to 8.82 (in additive regression 5.6.1). The proportion of variance explained R^2 is higher in the regressions taking eight-firm multi-plant operation indices as dependent variable. Nevertheless, we shall for maximum consistency with Chapter 6 favor the four-firm multi-plant indices as dependent variable in all subsequent regressions.

For the third regression in each table, the sample is expanded to 155 industries and the product value per pound variable VALUE is substituted for the more refined transportation cost index COMPO. Following the logic of equation (5.4), VALUE is specified in reciprocal form in the additive regressions. For all variables but DIG7 the predicted coefficient sign relationships persist, although there is a drop in R^2 of from 5.6 to 13.5 percentage points compared to the 101 observation regressions with COMPO. VALUE is in all cases highly significant statistically.

Referring back to Table 5.1, we recall that nine industries had four-firm multi-plant indices exceeding 80 by the direct count method and 4 by the derived method, even though the median indices were only 18.4 and 11.2 respectively. Analysis of the first three sets of multiple regressions reveals that the extremely high multi-plant industries responsible for this skewness exert a dominant and disproportionate influence on the additive regression coefficients. In particular, industrial gases, with 285 plants operated by the leading four firms according to the Census count and a very low value per pound, and bread, with a MPCEN4 value of 332, virtually guarantee highly significant coefficients for COMPO, VALUE, and PERSH. Owing to the skewness of the multi-plant index distributions, standard errors of estimate (not explicitly reported) in the additive regressions are also as large as, or in some cases even larger than, the dependent variable means.

To ameliorate this extreme value problem, all industries with MPCEN8 values exceeding 150 were deleted from the sample. This reduced the sample size by five, with all casualties belonging to the group of 101 industries for which COMPO estimates had been developed.[20] The

20. No extensive "fishing expeditions" were conducted to find an "optimal" reduction in sample size. It is worth noting, however, that eliminating the 17 industries with MPCEN8 values exceeding 80 yields virtually identical results.

Table 5.6. Additive Regressions: Census Count Index as Dependent Variable.

Regression number	N	Dependent variable	Constant term	COMPO	PERSH	VA63	DIG7	RPS	LOCAL	$\frac{1}{\text{VALUE}}$	C4	R^2
5.6.1	101	MPCEN4	27.1	269.8** (30.6)	79.6** (11.5)	0.781** (.335)	-0.115 (.141)	-70.0 (77.1)	-0.461* (.215)			0.645
5.6.2	101	MPCEN8	41.5	344.0** (40.9)	112.0** (15.4)	1.15** (0.45)	-.050 (.188)	-118.0 (103.0)	-.676 (.287)			.657
5.6.3	155	MPCEN4	25.3		85.1** (11.2)	.804** (.278)	.003 (.118)	-28.4 (55.9)	-.461** (.166)	96.9** (13.7)		.510
5.6.4	96	MPCEN4	21.8	103.8** (25.5)	34.5** (7.7)	.503** (.199)	.100 (.082)	-120.5** (44.3)	-.086 (.126)			.485
5.6.5	150	MPCEN4	20.2		36.1** (6.8)	.504** (.149)	.165* (.063)	-73.8* (29.4)	-.137 (.887)	37.4** (8.2)		.460
5.6.6	96	MPCEN4	16.7	114.8** (27.1)	40.1** (8.1)	.628** (.206)					-0.031 (.075)	.397
5.6.7	96	MPCEN4	20.7	130.4** (27.8)	41.4** (8.5)						VA63·C4 −0.002 (.003)	.335

Note: Standard errors are given in parentheses.
*Significant at the 0.05 level.
**Significant at the 0.01 level.

Table 5.7. Multiplicative Regressions: Census Court Index as Dependent Variable.

Regression number	N	Dependent variable	Constant term	Independent variables								R²
				COMPO	PERSH	VA63	DIG7	RPS	LOCAL	VALUE	C4	
5.7.1	101	MPCEN4	3.21	0.335** (.055)	0.629** (.229)	0.276** (.059)	−0.051 (.063)	−0.281** (.064)	−0.103 (.106)			0.681
5.7.2	101	MPCEN8	3.65	.312** (.045)	.600** (.188)	.260** (.056)	−.042 (.052)	−.285** (.053)	−.131 (.087)			.752
5.7.3	155	MPCEN4	3.43		.876** (.228)	.327** (.054)	.010 (.032)	−.133** (.055)	−.230** (.086)	−0.229** (.034)		.609
5.7.4	96	MPCEN4	2.81	.272** (.058)	.607** (.251)	.291** (.068)	−.033 (.063)	−.261** (.063)	−.058 (.107)			.592
5.7.5	150	MPCEN4	3.26		.801** (.248)	.327** (.052)	−.013 (.031)	−.112* (.053)	−.192* (.084)	−.200** (.033)		.541
5.7.6	96	MPCEN4	2.73	.271** (.057)	.598* (.249)	.281** (.065)		−.258** (.063)	−.053 (.106)			.591
5.7.7	96	MPCEN4	2.72		.636** (.248)	.275** (.065)		−.241** (.062)	−.102 (.106)	−.235** (.048)		.596
5.7.8	96	MPCEN4	−2.31	.186** (0.48)	.342 (.202)	.216** (.054)		−.695** (.076)			0.835** (.120)	.734
5.7.9	96	MPCEN4	3.77	.330** (.063)	.943** (.264)	.359** (.071)					−.046 (.099)	.485
5.7.10	96	MPCEN4	4.37	.320** (.061)	.954** (.253)	.347** (.069)			−.248* (.103)			.515
5.7.11	96	MPCEN4	2.51	.271** (.057)	.580** (.246)	.281** (.065)		−.272** (.056)				.590

Note: Standard errors are given in parentheses.
*Significant at the 0.05 level.
**Significant at the 0.01 level.

Table 5.8. Additive Regressions: Derived Multi-Plant Index as Dependent Variable.

Regression number	N	Dependent variable	Constant term	COMPO	PERSH	VA63	DIG7	RPS	LOCAL	$\frac{1}{VALUE}$	C4	R^2
									Independent variables			
5.8.1	101	MPDER4	19.4	157.5** (23.8)	51.9** (9.0)	0.416* (.260)	−0.176 (.109)	5.9 (60.0)	−0.381* (.167)			0.514
5.8.2	101	MPDER8	31.5	251.9** (37.5)	87.0** (14.2)	.729* (.411)	−.260 (.172)	−6.1 (94.6)	−.555* (.264)			.533
5.8.3	155	MPDER4	17.1		54.8** (8.2)	.412* (.205)	−.085 (.087)	11.3 (41.1)	−.320** (.122)	51.4** (10.1)		.381
5.8.4	96	MPDER4	17.8	28.7* (17.0)	18.9** (5.1)	.259* (.132)	−.038 (.054)	−36.7 (29.4)	−.147* (.084)			.279
5.8.5	150	MPDER4	14.4		19.7** (4.4)	.213* (.095)	.025 (.040)	−22.1 (18.8)	−.114* (.057)	11.1* (5.3)		.264
5.8.6	96	MPDER4	5.9	33.6* (16.9)	22.2** (5.0)	.281* (.128)					0.110* (.047)	.257
5.8.7	96	MPDER4	7.7	40.6* (16.9)	22.8** (5.1)						VA63·C4 0.004* (.002)	.218

Note: Standard errors are given in parentheses.
*Significant at the 0.05 level.
**Significant at the 0.01 level.

Table 5.9. Multiplicative Regressions: Derived Multi-Plant Index as Dependent Variable.

Regression number	N	Dependent variable	Constant term	Independent variables									R²
				COMPO	PERSH	VA63	DIG7	RPS	LOCAL	VALUE	C4	
5.9.1	101	MPDER4	3.48	0.257** (.057)	0.830** (.237)	0.182** (.071)	−0.083 (.065)	−0.138* (.066)	−0.187* (.110)			0.527
5.9.2	101	MPDER8	3.77	.264** (.051)	.766** (.211)	.200** (.063)	−.067 (.058)	−.150** (.059)	−.121 (.098)			.584
5.9.3	155	MPDER4	3.33		1.00** (.22)	.204** (.052)	.014 (.031)	−.038 (.053)	−.247** (.084)	−0.166** (.033)		.471
5.9.4	96	MPDER4	2.98	.170** (.058)	.688** (.250)	.196** (.068)	−.061 (.062)	−.113* (.063)	−.136 (.106)			.381
5.9.5	150	MPDER4	3.12		.809** (.232)	.200** (.049)	.019 (.029)	−.016 (.049)	−.204** (.079)	−.133** (.031)		.367
5.9.6	96	MPDER4	2.84	.170** (.057)	.673** (.249)	.178** (.065)		−.107 (.063)	−.127 (.106)			.375
5.9.7	96	MPDER4	2.83		.698** (.249)	.174** (.065)		−.096 (.063)	−.158 (.106)	−.149** (.048)		.379
5.9.8	96	MPDER4	−4.57	.048 (.032)	.290* (.137)	.084* (.036)		−.745** (.051)			1.191** (0.081)	.813
5.9.9	96	MPDER4	1.94	.201** (.056)	.934** (.235)	.238** (.063)					.249** (.088)	.375
5.9.10	96	MPDER4	3.52	.190** (.057)	.820** (.236)	.205** (.064)			−.208* (.096)			.354
5.9.11	96	MPDER4	2.31	.167** (.058)	.630* (.247)	.176** (.066)		−.141** (.056)				.364

Note: Standard errors are given in parentheses.
*Significant at the 0.05 level.
**Significant at the 0.01 level.

fourth and fifth equations in each table reveal the consequences of this change for specifications otherwise analogous to the first and third regressions. Among the additive regressions, which are most susceptible to extreme value biases, there is a sizeable drop in R^2, especially when MPDER4 is taken as the dependent variable. COMPO, VALUE, and PERSH, like the value added variable, continue to display statistically significant effects, though understandably less strong than in the full-sample regressions. With the multiplicative specification the changes due to deleting outlying observations are less dramatic, since linearization by taking logarithms compresses the large extreme value tail of the multi-plant index distributions. All coefficient signs are the same as in the full-sample regressions, and the magnitudes of the coefficients are little altered.

The coefficient of determination R^2 is consistently higher in the multiplicative regressions than in additive regressions containing the same independent variables. This is not an adequate basis for choosing between the two specifications, however, because of the quite different impact of additive as compared to multiplicative transformations on the dependent variables' distribution properties. More important is the postregression distribution of prediction errors. With the multiplicative specification, a virtually normal distribution results, whether the full sample or a subsample excluding outlying observations is analyzed. With the additive form, there is evidence of marked positive residual distribution skewness even after the most extreme observations are deleted, indicating that the additive regressions tend systematically to underestimate the extent of multi-plant operation in high multi-plant industries. This leads us to prefer the multiplicative specification, although for maximum insight we shall also present selected additional results using the additive model. For unreported additive variants, there was little substantive deviance from the multiplicative results.

Choosing between the Census count and derived multi-plant indices is more difficult. For both dependent variables, the multiplicative regression error term distributions closely approximate normality. The coefficient signs are also essentially the same, but t-ratios and R^2 values are consistently lower for MPDER4 than for MPCEN4. Although this cannot be considered a decisive indication, it suggests tentatively that the Census counts provide a superior, or at least more sensitive, indicator of multi-plant operation differences. The errors of commission that have crept into the Census counts appear, as we had initially anticipated, to be less serious than the aggregation and mismatching errors accepted in deriving multi-plant statistics from plant size distributions. We therefore emphasize the multiplicative MPCEN4 results in subsequent discussions. The derived index results are nevertheless extended in Tables 5.8 and 5.9.

Also noteworthy is the positive and statistically significant DIG7 coefficient in additive MPCEN4 regression 5.6.5, the first and only inkling of a discernible product heterogeneity effect consistent with the hypotheses motivating that variable's inclusion. In neither of the analogous multiplicative regressions, however, is DIG7 significant. In view of this and DIG7's generally erratic performance, we exclude it from subsequent regressions. Multiplicative regressions 5.7.6 and 5.9.6 provide a bench mark with the simplified specification, showing among other things a trifling drop in R^2. Although these results might be interpreted as evidence that product heterogeneity and multi-plant operation are indeed unrelated, it is conceivable that DIG7 is simply an inadequate measure of heterogeneity. Or it may measure heterogeneity less successfully than, say, the industry size variable VA63, with which it is positively and significantly correlated.

Regressions 5.7.7 and 5.9.7 test the hypothesis that differences in freight rates among product groups had no systematic impact on multi-plant operation. This is done by substituting the industry product value per pound variable for the composite transportation cost index. The result is an increase in R^2 of 0.005 or 0.004 relative to otherwise comparable COMPO regressions. From this and the quite satisfactory performance of the hybrid product value variable in the fifth regression of each table, it would appear that differences in product value per pound carry most of the location-theoretic burden in explaining multi-plant operation variations. Differences in freight rates per unit of weight evidently play a much less important role, or else measurement errors have obscured any freight rate effect that does exist. Nevertheless, because the differences in explanatory power between COMPO and VALUE are small and because a priori theory favors taking freight rate differences as well as product value differences into account, we shall retain COMPO as our principal transportation cost variable in remaining regressions.

The next two regressions in each table explore the relationship between seller concentration and multi-plant operation. We have seen earlier that no significant zero-order correlation between MPCEN4 and C4 exists, but that a multiplicative regression of MPCEN4 on C4 and RPS shows a strong effect for each variable because it approximates an identity specification. Regressions 5.7.8 and 5.9.8 provide an upper bound reference point by introducing C4 and RPS multiplicatively together, along with the transportation cost, market size, and product perishability variables. As one would expect, there is a sharp upward jump in R^2. Both C4 and RPS are highly significant, while heavy multi-collinearity leads to some degradation of the COMPO and PERSH effects. In multiplicative regressions 5.7.9 and 5.9.9, the quasiidentities are broken by deleting RPS. In both cases there is a pronounced fall in R^2. In the MPCEN4 regression, the sign of the concentration coefficient reverses, but the coefficient is exceeded by its standard error and provides an incremental contribution to R^2 of only 0.001. Clearly, concentration is of no help in explaining variations in multi-plant operation as measured by the Census count of leading firm plants. With MPDER4 as dependent variable, on the other hand, C4 continues to be positive and statistically significant even after RPS is deleted. The reasons for this difference in performance can only be conjectured. One plausible rationalization is that C4 compensates to some extent for the measurement inadequacies of the derived multi-plant index—a compensation unnecessary with the MPCEN4 index. Thus, when concentration is high, there is a substantial probability that the industry's largest plants will be operated by the leading sellers, and so the derived index will enumerate those firms' plants fairly comprehensively. When concentration is low it is more likely that the largest plants will belong to nonleading firms, and the more true this is, the more MPDER4 will underestimate the number of plants the leaders operate. To the extent that these biases exist, there will tend to be a positive correlation between C4 and the derived multi-plant indices, ceteris paribus, but it is doubtful whether much behavioral significance can be ascribed.

Additive regressions 5.6.7 and 5.8.7 provide a further test of concentration's role, substituting a multiplicative VA63·C4 interaction term for the separate value added and concentration variables used in regressions 5.6.6 and 5.8.6. In the MPCEN4 regression, the interaction term is insignificant and R^2 is 0.061 lower than with an otherwise comparable regression (not explicitly reported) including an unmodified VA63 variable and no C4 variable. Thus, no support is found for the hypothesis that *leading seller* value added explains the Census count of plants better than *total industry* value added. Taking MPDER4 as the dependent variable, R^2 is 0.039 lower with the VA63·C4 interaction term than when separate VA63 *and* C4 variables are deployed, while it is 0.006 *higher* than in a regression (not explicitly reported) including VA63 but not C4. Again we find no substantial support for the existence of a leading firm volume effect, given the existence of a separate statistically significant C4 effect (in regression 5.8.6) from which the interaction term may be borrowing its modest amount of explanatory power.

Finally, we attempt to clarify the influence of the geographic localization variable LOCAL. Our original intent was to account for the shipping cost pull of centralized raw materials, but LOCAL proved in addition to be capturing some effects more directly attributable to concentration and relative plant size. Thus, the simple multiplicative correlation ($n = 101$) between LOCAL and RPS is $+0.506$; between LOCAL and C4 the correlation is $+0.394$. Multiple regressions reveal a definite competitive relationship between LOCAL and RPS. Regressions with both variables included (the fifth equation of each table) exhibit an erratic sign pattern. When either LOCAL or RPS is deleted, as in the last two regressions of Tables 5.7 and 5.9, the other variable is statistically significant. In the regressions with MPCEN4 as dependent variable, exclusion of RPS while retaining LOCAL leads to an R^2 decline of 0.076 relative to regression 5.7.6, while the deletion of LOCAL but not RPS causes R^2 to fall by only 0.001. When MPDER4 is the dependent variable, the R^2 decrease due to removing LOCAL is 0.011; deletion of RPS leads to a 0.021 decline. It seems clear that a definite confounding of effects exists, and that the independent influence of localization is in no instance very strong.

Our statistical analysis discloses unambiguously that multi-plant operation is more extensive in U.S. manufacturing industries, the larger the industry tends to be and the higher outbound transportation costs are in relation to product value. A stronger propensity toward multi-plant operation is also observed for perishable products. Multiplicative regressions incorporating these three variables explain from 48 to 60 percent of the variance in the Census count of plants operated by the leading four firms. Most of the outbound transport cost variable's explanatory power comes from differences in product value per unit of weight rather than freight rate variations on shipments of given weight. Raw material localization and the attendant shipping cost pull appear to have had little systematic impact on multi-plant operation patterns, although measurement uncertainties and intercorrelation problems preclude firm conclusions on this point. The exact influences embodied in the consistently significant industry size variable are also not certain. Plausible interpretations include the fact that larger markets can accommodate more plants, all else equal, and the tendency of industries with higher value added to span a more diverse array of products. An important negative conclusion is that multi-plant operation and seller concentration are at best only weakly associated, except in regressions specified tautologically. There is also no persuasive indication that the multi-plant posture of leading firms is more closely associated with *their own* size, measured in terms of value added, than with the overall size of the industries they occupy. These findings do not necessarily contradict the conventional belief that the size of leading firms in concentrated industries is greater than it need be to permit all single-plant production scale economies. Yet they do suggest that *systematic* associations involving concentration are more apt to be found in the realm of observed plant sizes (as exemplified by the RPS variable in this chapter and the quite different TOP50/MOS variable of Chapter 3) than in the extent of multi-plant operation.

6

Multi-Plant Operation in the Six Nations and Twelve Industries

The strategy adopted in Chapter 5 was to analyze multi-plant operation over the broadest possible cross section of industries, accepting less than the theoretical ideal in variable definitions when this was necessitated by inadequacies in Census and other statistics. Now we pursue a complementary approach, exploiting the rich data provided by our interview research to shed further light on the quantitative contours of multi-plant operation for a much narrower sample of industries.

The Extent of Multi-Plant Operation

The multi-plant operation measure used in this chapter reflects a direct count for mid-1970 of the number of main-line manufacturing plants operated domestically by the three largest firms in each national industry. Table 6.1 summarizes the principal restrictions applied in determining whether plants qualified as "main-line" producers. The criteria are sometimes arbitrary, but they come as close as possible to capturing the essence of multi-plant choices.

In no cases were central offices, research and development laboratories, warehouses, or repair shops counted as plants in their own right, although such activities were often located at the same site as a manufacturing establishment, in which case all the facilities were enumerated together as a single plant. Plants which manufactured raw materials or products appropriately classified to a different industry along with products associated with a sampled industry were counted if the amount of

Table 6.1. Principal Inclusion and Exclusion Criteria in the Multi-Plant Count.

Industry	Criteria
Beer brewing	Excludes malting plants and plants with bottling or kegging lines but no brewing
Cigarettes	Excludes specialized stemming and drying plants; includes plants manufacturing cigarettes along with other tobacco products
Fabric weaving	Cotton, synthetic, and linen fabrics only; excludes specialized spinning or finishing mills with no weaving but includes integrated spinning-weaving-finishing mills
Paints	Excludes plants producing only pigments, resins, or containers
Petroleum refining	Excludes specialty lubricant blending plants and plants producing only asphalt or petrochemical feedstocks
Shoes	Excludes molded rubber and canvas shoe plants and sewing-only plants, but includes separate leather cutting and house slipper plants
Glass bottles	Excludes specialized mold-making, tableware, insulator, and laboratory glassware plants
Cement	Excludes specialized grinding mills with no kilns; includes white cement specialists
Steel	Includes integrated ordinary steel mills and plants specializing in ordinary steel conversion; excludes separate blast furnace works, rolling and extrusion mills, and special alloy steel plants
Antifriction bearings	Includes plants machining major bearing parts for assembly elsewhere as well as integrated machining-assembly plants; excludes bearing steel works
Refrigerators	Includes plants specializing in either refrigerators or freezers as well as both; excludes specialized compressor, condenser, and small parts plants
Storage batteries	Includes industrial battery specialists as well as starter battery plants; excludes specialized case, separator, and lead reclaiming plants

sampled industry production was substantial even if not preponderant.

More difficult problems are posed by manufacturing complexes containing several physical units, sometimes identifiable as distinct production entities, in a particular city or town. We have for the most part in such cases adopted the criterion generally (but not always) applied by the U.S. Census Bureau (and most other nations' census authorities): multiple units were counted as a single plant if their sites are physically contiguous but separately if they are not. The only exception allowed to a strict contiguity rule was for the steel industry, where plants are commonly spread out over vast tracts which may, however, be broken up owing to natural barriers or land acquisition problems. When the distance between plants so separated did not exceed two kilometers (1.24 miles), the units were counted as a single plant. By this criterion the leading German steelmaker Thyssen was found to operate two converting plants in the Duisburg/Ruhr area, although under a strict contiguity rule three plants would be counted, while the whole complex might be viewed as a single plant if one emphasized opportunities for operating the various steel converters (along with nearby but noncontiguous blast furnace installations and rolling mills) as an integrated system. Fortunately, problems of this nature occurred in only a small minority of all cases.

Equally troublesome were partially owned plants and joint ventures. When a plant was owned jointly by two or more firms which otherwise would have been considered substantial competitors, fractional plant shares were allocated in proportion to the ownership interests. When a leading company held less than 100 percent of the equity in a plant or set of plants but had clearly assumed sole control, the plant was counted as a full unit of the controlling firm. Where firms held minority interests in other companies and treated them more as investments than as directly controlled subsidiaries, fractional plant assignments proportional to the ownership share were made. Choices involving one or more of these fractional ownership criteria had to be made for some 20 firms (out of roughly 200 for which plants were tallied), but the resulting plant count was highly sensitive to the convention adopted in only a very few instances.

With only one significant exception, we have attempted to make the count cover plants operated by leading firms on June 30, 1970, when our European interviewing effort had achieved full momentum. Mergers announced at that time but not yet consummated were not considered. A few plant openings and closings were known to have occurred at roughly midyear, but the exact date could not be pinpointed, injecting a moderate degree of measurement inaccuracy.

The sole exception to the mid-1970 rule involved British Steel Corporation (BSC), into which some fourteen previously independent steelmaking concerns were nationalized in 1967. One might plausibly argue that this merger was "unnatural" and that counting the thirty-one ordinary steel converting plants retained by BSC in 1970 overstates what would have been the extent of multi-plant operation under more normal conditions. There were, to be sure, several other firms subjected to "shotgun" mergers at government insistence, for instance, steelmaker de Wendel-Sidelor in France and antifriction bearing producer **RHP** (Ransome Hoffmann Pollard) in England. The only justification for singling out BSC is that its formation was distinctly more unnatural than other mergers and much more recent than other cases of nationalization covered by our sample. We do adopt this position in subsequent analyses, although we hedge by presenting major results for both the prenationalization (1967) and postnationalization (1970) industry structures.

Following these criteria, plant counts were undertaken for each of the three leading firms (when at least three existed) in each of the twelve sample industries for the six sample nations. Data of acceptable quality were secured for all but the French weaving industry, which during 1970 was experiencing mergers and plant shutdowns on so widespread a scale that interviewees were unsure of their own and rival market positions and in one instance even how many weaving plants their own company was currently operating. A rough guess has been made to fill this void, but it is sufficiently unreliable that the industry will be excluded from the regression analyses of subsequent sections.

Table 6.2. Average Number of Plants Operated by the Three Leading Firms in Each Industry, 1970.

Industry	U.S.	Canada	U.K.	Sweden	France	Germany
Brewing	6.3 ↑	11.3	12.7 ↓	8.7 ↓	11.3	13.7 ↑
Cigarettes	2.0	2.0	5.2	2.0$_{(1)}$ ↓	13.0$_{(1)}$ ↓	4.0
Weaving	30.3	5.3	8.7 ↑	2.3 ↓	∼10	4.0
Paints	9.7	3.7	5.3	2.7	2.0	3.3 ↑
Petroleum refining	8.0	8.0	3.7	1.7	3.6	4.0
Shoes	28.3	5.0	12.3	1.8 ↓	4.7	6.8
Bottles	13.0	3.3	5.7	1.7	6.7	4.3
Cement	13.0 ↓	5.0	13.5 ↓	3.5$_{(2)}$	14.2 ↑	9.2
Ordinary steel	9.7	1.3	3.0^a	1.0	6.0	2.2 ↓
Antifriction bearings	7.3	1.0	4.3	2.0$_{(1)}$	5.0 ↑	6.3
Refrigerators	2.3 ↑	1.3	1.0 ↓	1.3	1.0$_{(2)}$ ↓	1.0 ↓
Storage batteries	12.7 ↓	3.0	1.3	2.0 ↓	4.3	2.3
Mean	11.9	4.2	6.4^b	2.6	6.8	5.1
Median	9.7	3.5	5.3^c	2.0	5.5	4.0

Note: When there were fewer than three firms operating, the number of firms covered is given in subscripted parentheses.

Downward pointing arrows indicate a clear downward trend in the extent of multi-plant operation; upward pointing arrows an upward trend.

^{a}11.0 after nationalization, counting leading three firms.

^{b}7.1 after nationalization of steel industry.

^{c}5.5 after nationalization of steel industry.

Table 6.2 summarizes the data, showing the average number of plants operated per Big Three member in each national industry. Although figures are also available for the leading firm in each industry and will be used subsequently, they are not presented in detail to avoid compromising information sometimes obtained in confidence. Some of the industry figures are accompanied by arrows, a downward pointing arrow indicating that the industry had in 1970 recently experienced or was in the process of experiencing a clear downward trend in the extent of multi-plant operation; an upward pointing arrow indicating a trend in the opposite direction. In several other industries more complex trends were evident, for example, toward mergers accompanied by rationalization, but they could not be summarized through a unidirectional indicator.

Multi-plant operation is plainly extensive for our sampled industries. The grand mean is 6.2 plants per leading firm if the British steel industry is evaluated before nationalization and 6.3 postnationalization. The variation among industries is wide, however—five industries average only one plant per leading firm, while two approximate 30 plants per leader. Multi-plant operation is highest on the average in brewing, weaving, shoe manufacturing, and cement. It is by a substantial margin least extensive in the refrigerator industry. Sweden, the smallest nation in our sample, exhibits the lowest mean and median multi-plant operation indices; Canada, the second smallest nation, is next in this respect. The United States, by far the largest nation, has the highest number of plants per industry leader.

These results differ importantly from those Bain reported in his international comparisons study. The differences can be seen most clearly by bringing together in Table 6.3 elements of Table 6.2, the sum-

Table 6.3. Comparison of Multi-Plant Indices from Bain's Study and Ours.

Nation	Median number of plants per Big Three member (Table 6.2)		Bain's median multi-plant index		Median TOP 50/MOS percentages (Table 3.12)
	Raw count	Index U.S. = 100	Raw ratio	U.S. = 100	
U.S.	9.7	100	3.2	100	125
France	5.5	57	3.0	94	74
U.K.	5.3	55	1.9	59	60
Germany	4.0	41	n.a.	n.a.	76
Canada	3.5	36	1.8	56	73
Sweden	2.0	21	1.5	47	46

Source: Joe S. Bain, *International Differences in Industrial Structure* (New Haven: Yale University Press, 1966), pp. 130–131, for the third numerical column.

mary of Bain's findings from Chapter 1, and data on national median Top 50 Percent size/MOS ratios from Table 3.12 of Chapter 3. The ranking of the five nations covered by both studies in terms of median multi-plant operation indices are identical.[1] But Bain's index implies much less divergence in the amount of multi-plant operation between France, Canada, and Sweden versus the United States than ours does. Moreover, for our sample differences in the extent of multi-plant operation by nation and differences in the size of Top 50 Percent plants relative to the MOS are strongly correlated: the simple linear correlation between the second and last numerical columns of Table 6.3 is $+0.903$. The less successful a nation is in achieving economies of scale at the plant level, the fewer plants its producers tend to operate on the average.

Thus, what might be called the strong version of Bain's paradox, that the extent of multi-plant operation does not adjust to international differences in the difficulty of achieving plant scale economies, is not evident in our sample.[2] Only the paradox's weak version shows up: extensive multi-plant operation does coincide, on what appears at least thus far to be an unsystematic basis, with the widespread survival of leading plants too small to realize all production scale economies.

The reasons for the differences between our sample results and Bain's are not altogether clear. One distinct possibility is bias in the selection of our sample. As Chapter 1 brought out, a conscious effort was exerted, with only two exceptions, to load our sample with industries exhibiting moderate to extensive multi-plant operation in the United States. That such a bias exists is suggested by the fact that the average number of plants operated per Big Four member for the median industry among the 155 U.S. manufacturing industries analyzed in Chapter 5 was 4.6. To be sure, the basis on which plant counts were compiled for this broader sample differed in several important respects from the assumptions underlying Table 6.2, but it is a simple matter to derive comparable figures. Using the Census data and assumptions of Chapter 5, the median value of the average number of plants per Big Four member in 1963 for our twelve-industry sample is found to be 9.4. It is clear that we have succeeded in our attempt to draw a sample overrepresenting the multi-plant prone industries.

1. But not in terms of mean indices, under which France ranks ahead of the United States with Bain's data. Compare p. 2 *supra* and Table 6.2.

2. For the statements from which this interpretation of Bain's paradox is drawn, see his *International Differences in Industrial Structure* (New Haven: Yale University Press, 1966), pp. 140–141 and 151. See also p. 2 *supra*.

To the extent that the high incidence of multi-plant operation among the U.S. industries in our sample is the result of systematic basic conditions affecting European and Canadian industries in similar ways, there need be no bias in our comparisons between the United States and other nations. But if some industries crept into our sample because they happened, more or less by chance, to have high multi-plant operation in the United States, international comparisons will be biased, showing a greater proportional deviation between the indices of multi-plant operation for the United States vis-a-vis other nations than would emerge for a representative sample. Although, as we shall see, there are significant systematic influences affecting multi-plant operation across all nations, we cannot rule out the presence of chance-related sampling bias. Therefore, we are unable to generalize with confidence our numerical comparisons to the full population of manufacturing industries.

Although the data in our sample cannot sustain the burden of contradicting Bain's strong paradox generally, a reexamination of Bain's data suggests that the patterns asserting themselves in our sample may characterize the world more accurately than those Bain reported. Of the nations on which our research overlaps, France raises the most important doubts. If Bain's calculations are taken at face value, multi-plant operation appears to be about as extensive there as in the United States. Since both Bain's data and ours show a relatively high incidence of French plants too small to realize all scale economies, such abundant multi-plant operation does seem paradoxical. But Bain's multi-plant estimates are clearly erroneous. Four of the company concentration ratios used to calculate Bain's multi-plant indices for France were transferred inaccurately from the table from which they were supposedly drawn.[3] Also, the method by which Bain estimated company concentration ratios for France (and for Italy and perhaps India, too)—dividing reported sales of the three or four largest *companies* by *industry* sales—has a consistent upward bias if the companies are active in nonsampled industries. Whether for these reasons or others, a recalculation of Bain's French company/plant concentration multiples using the greatly improved 1963 data made available by Jacques Houssiaux leads to very different conclusions.[4] The two sets of estimates are as follows, with ranges given when it was unclear

3. Compare Table 4–4 in his *International Differences*, pp. 92–93, with his Table 5–1, p. 130.

4. See U.S., Senate, Committee on the Judiciary, Subcommittee on Antitrust and Monopoly, *Hearings, Economic Concentration*, Part 7A, "Concentration outside the United States," 90th Cong., 2nd Sess., 1968, pp. 3959–3965.

which of Houssiaux' industry definitions most closely corresponded to Bain's:

Industry	Bain's company/plant concentration multiple	Multiple derived from Houssiaux data
Steel ingots	1.5	1.9
Aircraft	3.2	2.1–2.6
Shipbuilding	3.0	1.05
Flour and meal	16.0	1.2–1.3
Petroleum refining	3.0	1.6–2.0
Cement	6.0	2.8
Canned and preserved fruits	2.3	1.5–1.6
Beer and ale	2.0	1.4
Paper and paperboard	1.4	1.7
Median	3.0	1.70
Mean	4.3	1.76

The median and mean figures drawn from the newer and almost surely more accurate data lie much closer to Bain's U.K. median index of 1.9 than to his U.S. median index of 3.2. And in this respect, Bain's recomputed results for France are consistent with the relationships observed for our biased twelve-industry sample.

We have also recomputed Bain's company/plant concentration multiples for his Canadian and Swedish samples using the new and much better data now available.[5] The median index for our Canadian recalculation agrees well with Bain's, 1.85 vs. Bain's value of 1.80, even though the simple correlation between the two sets of individual industry ratios was only +0.17. For Sweden our recomputed median index was appreciably higher, 1.87 vs. Bain's 1.5, possibly because of significant mergers which occurred between 1959, the date of Bain's company concentration estimates, and 1963. If the tendency for Bain's sample to imply relatively more multi-plant operation in Canada and Sweden than our twelve-industry sample does is to be clarified, the explanation is more apt to involve sample differences or a possible tendency for Bain's (n largest company/n largest plant) concentration ratios for small nations to be higher in relation to the U.S. values than is our plant count index.

5. Dominion of Canada, Department of Consumer and Corporate Affairs, *Concentration in the Manufacturing Industries of Canada* (Ottawa, 1971); and Alf Carling, *Industrins Struktur och Konkurrensförhållanden* (Stockholm: Statens Offentliga Utredningar, 1968), esp. pp. 86–110.

This could occur because the largest firms in small nations tend with greater uniformity to approach the condition under which Bain's index does not understate the extent of multi-plant operation, maintaining a single plant (or a very few of nearly equal size) larger than the plants of nonleader firms. Differences in results due to sampling variations should also not be surprising, since Bain's Canadian multi-plant index sample included only five industries and his Swedish sample only six.

We end up having reconciled a significant part of the difference between Bain's findings and ours, but not all. To fill in the missing pieces, what is needed is a careful comparative study spanning a much larger industry sample than ours. Although the necessary data were not available when Bain carried out his international comparisons study, they are now. We commend the task to an appropriately multilingual scholar.[6]

The Types of Multi-Plant Operation:
An Impressionistic Survey

We return now to the question which will occupy us throughout most of the remainder of this book: what factors explain the fairly substantial amount of multi-plant operation in most of our sampled industries—not only in the United States but also abroad?

Table 6.4 provides a first impressionistic answer. It characterizes the types of multi-plant operation observed among the leading three companies over the seventy-two nation-industry cells in terms of four qualitative categories:

G   Plants are decentralized geographically in order to reduce transportation costs or (in a few cases) to tap small-town labor supplies or secure special tax advantages (other than regional investment stimulus exemptions).

P   Plants are specialized in a limited range of the firm's overall product line.

M   Multi-plant operation is directly and substantially attributable

---

6. For valid results, careful matching of industry definitions between nations is vital. As the breadth of an industry's definition is increased, more plants will be embraced and the average 4-plant concentration ratio must fall. But the 4-*firm* concentration ratio will fall with aggregation much less if the leading firms in the subsectors combined are identical than if they are not. See George Stigler, *Capital and Rates of Return in Manufacturing Industries* (Princeton: Princeton University Press, 1963), pp. 206–211. If there is at least some overlap in the identity of leading firms in aggregated subsectors, there will be more upward bias in company/plant concentration multiple estimates, the greater is the degree of aggregation in a nation's industry classification scheme. And such aggregation differences are probably correlated with nation size.

Table 6.4. Principal Characteristics of Multi-Plant Operation Among the Three Leading Companies in Each Industry, circa 1970.

Industry	U.S.	Canada	U.K.	Sweden	France	Germany
Brewing	G	G,M	M,G,P	M,G	M,G	M,G,P
Cigarettes	P	P,m	M,P,G[c]	P,G[a]	P,G[a]	M,P,G[b]
Weaving	P,m	P,m	P,M	P,m	M,P	P,m
Paints	G,P,M	G,P	M,P	M,P,G	P,M	M,P
Petroleum refining	G	G	G	G,P[b]	G	G
Shoes	P,G[a],m	P,m	P,G[a]	M,P	P,M	P,G[a],m
Bottles	G,M,P	G,P	G,M,P	P,m	G,P,M	G,m,P
Cement	G,m	G	G,M	G,m	G,M	G,M
Steel	m,G,P	G[b]	M,P,G	0	M,P,G	m,P
Antifriction bearings	P	0	M,P	P	P,m	P,m
Refrigerators	P,m	P,M[b]	0	P	0	0
Storage batteries	G,P	G,P	P,m,G	M,P	M,P,G	P,M

Note: G = Geographic decentralization; P = product specialization; M = substantial unrationalized mergers; m = substantial rationalized mergers; 0 = no multi-plant operation among three leading firms.
[a]Influenced by labor market considerations.
[b]Very little multi-plant operation.
[c]Related to tax advantages other than investment subsidies.

    to mergers, usually recent, which have not yet been followed by a thorough plant structure rationalization.

m   Multi-plant operation is the clear legacy of substantial mergers which have been followed by a fairly complete rationalization of geographic and/or product assignments.

An attempt has been made to list the most prominent or important characteristics first. Both the assignment of characteristics and their ranking are the result of subjective judgments and must therefore be taken with the appropriate grain of salt. The merger classifications have an especially large subjective component, requiring decisions on substantiality, historical causality, and the degree to which the opportunities for rationalization had been exploited as of 1970. Still the classifications do provide useful preliminary insight into the bases of multi-plant operation, to be supplemented by the statistical investigations following in this chapter and the qualitative analyses of the next.

Examination of Table 6.4 suggests two main generalizations. First, all three multi-plant operation characteristics appear frequently, with none showing strong dominance over the others. Product specialization is cited as the most prominent single characteristic twenty-five times, geographic decentralization twenty-four times, and the aftereffects of merger eighteen times. Altogether, product specialization is listed in connection with fifty-one of the seventy-two industries, geographic decentralization for forty-one, and merger influences for forty-seven (twenty-nine involving incomplete rationalization).

Second, some of the industries fall rather consistently into either the product specialization or geographic decentralization category. Industries whose multi-plant posture is predominantly of the product specialization type include weaving, shoes, bearings, refrigerators, and (less clearly) cigarettes. Industries characterized by geographically decentralized multi-plant operation are brewing, petroleum refining, cement, and (except in spatially compact southern Sweden) glass bottles. The patterns in paints, steel, and batteries are more complicated for reasons which will be elucidated in the next chapter.

Evidently, any comprehensive attempt to explain the rationale of multi-plant operation must assimilate a fair amount of complexity. With this caveat in mind, we proceed into the statistical analysis.

Multiple Regression Analysis: The Variables

Our approach will be a multiple regression analysis of the extent of multi-plant operation in the six-nation, twelve-industry sample. The principal dependent variable is the average 1970 plant count for the three leading firms (the figures presented in Table 6.2), which we shall call $MPO3_{ij}$, where the subscript i refers to the nation and j to the industry. Owing to measurement uncertainties, the French weaving industry will be excluded. Thus, our sample spans seventy-one nation-industry observation sets. For certain analyses we use as an alternate dependent variable $MPO1_{ij}$, the number of plants operated in 1970 by the leading firm alone.

The theory underlying our choice and specification of independent variables is somewhat more casual than that applied in the statistical analysis of plant sizes, since it is harder to establish rigorous links rooted in the logic of cost minimization or profit maximization to the optimal number of plants a firm should operate. Our hypotheses are best articulated by identifying the variables we will deploy.

The Core Variables

We view four sets of variables as the behavioral core of our model because their relevance is emphasized in the theoretical analysis of Chapter 2.

Two reflect the tradeoff between production scale economies and transportation costs. The steeper the slope of the unit production cost function is, the stronger will be the pull toward centralization of manufacturing activity at one or a very few large plants, ceteris paribus, and hence the less multi-plant operation one would expect. This effect will be taken into account by the variable $COST_j$, estimating the percentage elevation in unit costs from building and operating a 1965-vintage plant with one-third the capacity of a minimum optimal scale plant, as compared to an MOS-size plant. It is identical to the similarly labeled variable employed in Chapter 3.

Working in the opposite direction, the steeper the slope of the unit transport cost function, the more firms will be drawn toward decentralized multi-plant operation, assuming (as is generally plausible at least for industry leaders) that a market of roughly nationwide scope is served. In Chapter 3 it was hypothesized on the basis of cost minimization theory and a uniform average demand density assumption that the unit transport cost curve slope assumes the form $TRANS_j/3\sqrt{(\pi\ DENS_i \cdot MS3_{ij})}$, where $TRANS_j$ is an index of transportation cost per dollar of product value for a standardized haul in the jth industry, $DENS_i$ is the product of population density per square mile in the main contiguous national market area times an index of income per capita, and $MS3_{ij}$ is an index of three-firm seller concentration in appropriately defined (regional when necessary) markets. We introduce this specification again, although we shall feel less committed to it than in Chapter 3 because the total *number* of plants operated per industry leader in cost-minimizing spatial equilibrium seems even more apt to be sensitive to violations of the uniform demand density assumption than variations in the *average* size of *leading* plants. It is worth noting that the TRANS variable used here is based upon the same mid-1960s' data as the composite transport cost index of Chapter 5. The assumptions are slightly different, however, since here we have been able to take into account shipment volume and estimated costs by water, private truck, and pipeline as well as by rail and common carrier truck.

A third behavioral core variable is the volume of industry production $SIZE_{ij}$. We shall measure it here, like Chapter 3 but unlike Chapter 5, in relative terms, that is, as the ratio of domestic production in 1967 to the output of an MOS plant.[7] In this sense SIZE can be considered an index of opportunity to multiply plants. All else (including national market shares) equal, the potential for operating a multitude of plants is

7. In Chap. 3 the numerator measured domestic *consumption*, including imports and netting out production by domestic companies for export. A *production* orientation appears more relevant in determining how many plants manufacturers operate. It should be noted also that our SIZE variable here is analogous to the inverse of RPS in Chap. 5, at least to the extent that the average size of plants originating the top 50 percent of an industry's shipments is a tolerable approximation to the minimum optimal scale.

greater when the market can accommodate many efficient-sized plants than when it can hold very few. Unless a national market concentration variable is also introduced multiplicatively, a positive relationship between MPO3 and SIZE might be taken to imply a kind of quest-for-empire phenomenon: When there is room for many plants, leading firms expand by multiplying their plants to fill the vacuum. However, several other hypotheses are equally plausible. If some natural selection process is at work, the more fit firms will enjoy a less constrained opportunity to expand through plant multiplication in relatively large markets than in small. To achieve a given market share and hence (all else equal) degree of monopolistic control over price, more plants of optimal size are required in a larger market than a small one.[8] When several nations are considered, as in the present analysis, differences in market size may also be associated with differences in geographic expanse and hence in the degree to which optimal spatial adaptation requires multi-plant operation; and with differences in the average volume of individual products, affecting the degree to which product-specialized plants are proliferated.

Discriminating statistically among these alternative hypotheses, all of which suggest a positive association between relative market size and multi-plant operation, will be difficult and perhaps impossible. To the extent that multi-plant operation arises simply because companies large in relation to the MOS can and possibly (for managerial or logistic reasons) must operate more plants than relatively small firms, we should expect the MPO3-SIZE relationship to be stronger when a leading seller concentration variable is included than when it is not. With quest-for-empire or quest-for-market-control motivations, natural selection, and (other things such as transportation cost and population density equal) geographic expanse pulls, we might expect the relationship between MPO3 and SIZE to be approximately linear, although managerial diseconomies of firm scale could introduce systematic nonlinearities of a diminishing returns sort. As the concluding section of Chapter 2 argued, proliferation of specialized plants is encouraged by a high volume of demand, but average plant sizes also rise with individual product volume and lot sizes, and therefore the increase in multi-plant operation associated with greater product specialization in larger markets should exhibit diminishing returns.

8. However, other things are not apt to be equal. In particular, the "percentage effect" on price associated with new optimal-scale entry is greater in a relatively small market, and hence one barrier to entry is inversely correlated with the size of the market. See Joe S. Bain, *Barriers to New Competition* (Cambridge: Harvard University Press, 1956), pp. 53–55; and F. M. Scherer, *Industrial Market Structure and Economic Performance* (Chicago: Rand McNally, 1970), pp. 225–230.

To aid in isolating the role of product specialization, we include a fourth core variable, $PROD3_{ij}$, estimating the average number of physically different products manufactured by the three leading sellers in each nation-industry cell during 1970.[9] Because analyzing raw observations with values running from 4 to 7000 poses statistical problems, and because it seems most unlikely that an increase from 1000 to 1050 products will have the same effect on plant specialization choices as an increase from 10 to 60, we shall in all instances employ a logarithmic transformation of PROD3. We expect that the higher its value is, the more multiplant operation there will be, ceteris paribus.

Identity Variables

Caution is in order against regression model specifications which are tautological. Rearranging equation (3.4) from Chapter 3, we know it is identically true that:

$$(6.1) \qquad \text{Number of leading firm plants} \equiv \frac{\text{total industry output} \times \dfrac{\text{market share of leading firms}}{}}{\text{average size of leading firms' plants}}.$$

This is approximated by:

$$(6.2) \qquad MPO3 \cong \frac{SIZE \cdot CONC}{TOP50/MOS},$$

where $TOP50_{ij}/MOS_j$ is the main plant size variable used in Chapter 3 and $CONC_{ij}$ is a new variable measuring the combined 1970 national market share of an industry's three leading sellers.

The CONC variable has been suggested in the previous section as a possible multiplicative complement to the SIZE variable. It differs in two important respects from the variable MS3 used in Chapter 3 and in the transport cost slope term of this chapter. First, CONC is defined for 1970, whereas MS3 describes 1963–1965 structural conditions. Second, CONC refers to sellers' *nationwide* production shares, whereas MS3 is defined on a regional market plane where this was appropriate

9. Package variations were not regarded as physical differences, although an argument to the contrary could be advanced plausibly, especially for the brewing, cigarette, and paint industries. Differences in cigarette sizes for the same tobacco blend were counted as product differences. Excluded were differences in shoe sizes for the same style and differences in refrigerator and battery colors and labels. In some cases the PROD3 values cannot be dignified as more than rough guesses.

to characterizing plants' cost of penetrating their surrounding markets. The simple linear correlation between CONC and MS3 is 0.817.

Equation (6.2) is not an exact identity because of variable definition date inconsistencies (TOP50/MOS is for 1967 and earlier years) and measurement inaccuracies. Also, TOP50/MOS relates to the Top 50 Percent *plants*, regardless of who owns them, whereas the other variables pertain to the leading three *firms* in each industry. There is no necessary correspondence, although given the tendency for an industry's largest firms to operate plants larger on the average than smaller rivals,[10] the overlap could be considerable. Since (6.2) is not an identity, attempts to estimate its parameters statistically can provide insight into how closely less complete equation systems approach the near-identity state and how significant the measurement inconsistencies and inaccuracies in SIZE, CONC, and TOP50/MOS are.

Other Explanatory Variables

In Table 6.4 we found multi-plant operation to be associated in part with substantial mergers. To include in our analysis a variable measuring the incidence of mergers is clearly desirable. Unfortunately, quantifying the phenomenon is difficult. With the data accessible, the best we could do was to define a dummy variable $MERG_{ij}$ with a value of one if the leading firm as of 1970 had between 1958 and 1970 experienced a major horizontal merger with a company of roughly equal size, *or* if it acquired between 1958 and 1970 at least as many industry-specific plants as it operated during 1958. If neither of these conditions was met, the value of MERG is zero. Out of seventy-one industries, twenty-eight had leading sellers sufficiently active on the merger front to cross the dummy variable threshold. Several industries were nevertheless sufficiently close to the dividing point and the historical evidence was ambiguous enough that some measurement errors undoubtedly intruded. Since the dummy variable summarizes the merger history of only the leading producer in each industry, it is appropriately included only in regressions with MPO1 as the dependent variable.

We must also take into account the influence of small-town, low-wage

10. See Ralph L. Nelson, *Concentration in the Manufacturing Industries of the United States* (New Haven: Yale University Press, 1963), p. 68; and Frederic L. Pryor, "The Size of Production Establishments in Manufacturing," *Economic Journal*, 82 (June 1972), 522–523. A similar pattern is observed for our sample. Thus, for the U.S. industries, the average size (measured in terms of sales or value added) of plants operated in 1963 by the 5th through 20th largest companies was only two-thirds that of plants operated by the 4 leading firms. The range was from 12 percent (for refrigerators) to 110 percent (for cement).

labor supply pulls on firms' multi-plant choices. As Chapter 2 brought out, the characteristically monopsonistic position of plants in small-town labor markets means that it is easier to reduce wage payments through a plant dispersal strategy when the number of employees required in an MOS plant is small than when it is large. This suggests an inverse relationship between the extent of multi-plant operation and EMP_j, measuring the number of employees working in an MOS plant of average U.S. mid-1960s' productivity.

Summary of Variables
   To sum up, the variables we will employ are as follows:

$MPO3_{ij}$	Average number of plants operated per firm in 1970 by the three leading firms.
$MPO1_{ij}$	Number of plants operated by the leading producer in 1970.
$COST_j$	Percentage elevation of the long-run unit production cost curve at one-third MOS.
$TRANS_j$	Transportation cost per dollar of F.O.B. mill product value on a standard haul of 350 miles.
$DENS_i$	Population per square mile times an index of real national income per capita.
$MS3_{ij}$	Three-firm regionally adjusted concentration ratio.
$SIZE_{ij}$	1967 domestic production divided by the MOS.
$PROD3_{ij}$	Average number of physically different products per firm manufactured by the three leading firms.
$CONC_{ij}$	National market three-firm concentration ratio for 1970.
$TOP50_{ij}/MOS_j$	Average size of the Top 50 Percent plants, divided by the MOS.
$MERG_{ij}$	Merger dummy variable for the leading seller.
EMP_j	Employment in an MOS plant of average mid-1960s' productivity.

Values of the independent variable observations new to this analysis, that is, not already considered in Chapter 3, are listed in Appendix Table 3.7.

Regression Model Specification
   In our Chapter 3 plant size analysis, a priori theory provided a fair amount of guidance concerning regression model specification, though the final choice among specifications had to weigh a broader range of considerations. Theory supplies far fewer specification clues on the relationships between multi-plant operation and the independent vari-

ables identified above. It is not even clear, as it was in our plant size analysis, that the unit production cost and unit transportation cost slope terms should be entered additively. We shall therefore adopt an experimental stance, exploring the main two specification alternatives, additive and multiplicative, along with several plausible variants of the principal variable forms. When choices must be made among them, they will be based on intrinsic plausibility, goodness-of-fit, and desirability of statistical properties.

The Statistical Results

Table 6.5 presents a correlation matrix for the main variables in additive form and Table 6.6 in logarithmic form. The number of observations is seventy-one, with the French weaving industry excluded and the British steel industry defined in terms of its prenationalization structure.

We note immediately that the leading-firm and three-firm multi-plant indices are highly correlated; with $r = 0.934$ in additive form and 0.927 (not reported in Table 6.6) when logarithms are taken. As subsequent examples will reveal, the regression results were very similar for either multi-plant measure.

By far the strongest zero-order correlation between MPO3 and the independent variables is with SIZE, r being 0.758 in additive and 0.657 in logarithmic form. It is interesting that multi-plant operation and the three-firm seller concentration ratio CONC are negatively correlated. The observed negativity echoes the results for 155 U.S. manufacturing industries in Chapter 5, but for our multi-national sample the association is even stronger.[11]

Among the independent variables we find a strong negative intercorrelation between COST and the transportation cost terms TRANS or TRANS/$\sqrt{(DENS \cdot MS3)}$, as in Chapter 3, threatening possible multicollinearity problems involving two key components of our behavioral core. Negative collinearity is also evident between the transportation cost terms and PROD3, though no special causal association appears plausible; and between SIZE and CONC, reflecting the well-known propensity for concentration to be lower in relatively large markets. Between PROD3 and TOP50/MOS a somewhat surprising positive correlation is observed.[12]

11. Cf. pp. 178–179 and 201–202 *supra*.

12. Although we failed to consider it when the main Chap. 3 analyses were executed, one might from the reasoning in Chap. 2 expect that a more variegated product line would lead to smaller plants, not larger. When PROD3 was introduced into various Chap. 3 multiple regressions with TOP50/MOS as dependent variable, its coefficient signs were erratic, suggesting collinearity with other independent variables.

Table 6.5. Correlation Matrix: Variables in Additive Form.

Variable	MPO3	MPO1	COST	TRANS	$\dfrac{\text{TRANS}}{\sqrt{\text{DENS}\cdot\text{MS3}}}$	SIZE	Log PROD3	CONC	$\dfrac{\text{TOP50}}{\text{MOS}}$	MERG	EMP
MPO3	1.000	+0.934	+0.120	+0.229	+0.167	+0.758	+0.062	−0.373	+0.035	−0.195	−0.160
MPO1		1.000	+.187	+.315	+.221	+.684	−.009	−.293	+.007	−.116	−.152
COST			1.000	+.898	+.803	−.122	−.213	+.151	−.041	−.092	+.024
TRANS				1.000	+.862	−.111	−.463	+.072	−.171	−.119	−.063
$\dfrac{\text{TRANS}}{\sqrt{\text{DENS}\cdot\text{MS3}}}$					1.000	−.123	−.431	+.035	−.205	−.140	−.018
SIZE						1.000	+.299	−.457	+.224	−.177	−.177
Log PROD3							1.000	−.232	+.360	+.108	+.033
CONC								1.000	+.057	−.064	+.059
TOP50/MOS									1.000	−.068	−.192
MERG										1.000	+.132
EMP											1.000

Note: $N = 71$.

Five percent significance point = 0.234; one percent significance point = 0.304.

Table 6.6. Correlation Matrix: Variables in Logarithmic Form.

Variable	MPO3	COST	TRANS	DENS·MS3	SIZE	PROD3	CONC	TOP50/MOS	EMP
MPO3	1.000	+0.031	+0.169	+0.007	+0.657	+0.052	-0.378	+0.111	-0.250
COST		1.000	+.734	+.208	-.053	-.046	+.307	+.100	-.020
TRANS			1.000	+.188	-.138	-.412	+.235	-.205	+.084
DENS·MS3				1.000	-.009	-.129	+.336	+.217	-.083
SIZE					1.000	+.395	-.666	+.617	-.421
PROD3						1.000	-.255	+.422	-.061
CONC							1.000	-.049	+.264
TOP50/MOS								1.000	-.319
EMP									1.000

Note: $N = 71$.

Five percent significance point = 0.234; one percent significance point = 0.304.

The Identity Relationships

We begin our regression analysis by estimating equation (6.2) which, if all variables were measured consistently and precisely, would be an identity. Linearizing by taking logarithms to the base ten and with both CONC and TOP50/MOS scaled in ratio form, the regression equation is:

(6R.1)   Log MPO3 $= -0.072 + .968$ log CONC $+ .871$ log SIZE
                        (.157)   (.073)

$$-.721 \log \left(\frac{TOP50}{MOS}\right); R^2 = .727, N = 71.$$
     (.086)

(Standard errors for both text and tabular equations are given in parentheses below the regression coefficients.)

If an identity held exactly, R^2 and each regression coefficient would be 1.00. With an R^2 of 0.727, it is clear that the variables do not in fact combine to form an identity. The coefficient for TOP50/MOS, whose measurement is least consistent with the assumptions required for an identity, departs farthest from unity, being significantly different at the 0.01 level.

One source of measurement inaccuracy in TOP50/MOS, though probably not the most important one in terms of meeting the identity conditions, is the fact that the plant sizes for twelve non-U.S. industries are measured in employment terms without adjustment for productivity differences. Since output per worker in the United States tended to be higher than elsewhere, these values of TOP50/MOS are biased upward and hence they force their associated regression coefficient to compensate by shifting toward zero. A crude means of correcting for this bias is to define a dummy variable ADJ_{ij} with a value of unity for industries whose plant size is measured in employment terms without productivity adjustment and zero otherwise,[13] estimating it in the following multiplicative form:

(6.3)   MPO3 $= a \cdot CONC^{\alpha_1} \cdot SIZE^{\alpha_2} \cdot (TOP50/MOS)^{-\alpha_3 + \alpha_4 \cdot ADJ}$.

A positive sign is predicted for α_4 to reduce the absolute value of the complete TOP50/MOS exponent for those industries whose plant sizes have been overestimated. The regression estimated according to this specification is:

(6R.2)   Log MPO3 $= -0.142 + 1.074$ log CONC $+ .936$ log SIZE
                        (.157)   (.075)

---

13. The same variable is used in Tables 3.21 and 3.22. There were nine unit values of the dummy variable in the 71-industry sample.

$$+ (.493 \text{ ADJ} - .841) \log \left(\frac{\text{TOP50}}{\text{MOS}} \right);$$
$$(.197) \qquad (.095)$$
$$R^2 = .751, N = 71.$$

The dummy variable coefficient is in fact positive and significantly different from zero at the 0.01 level, while the general coefficient for TOP50/MOS (corresponding to α_3) has risen to 0.841. Note also the convergence of the SIZE coefficient toward unity and the overshooting by CONC. Except with respect to CONC, taking into account one source of measurement error has brought us closer to satisfying the conditions of the identity specification, although the R^2 value of 0.751 indicates that important measurement inconsistencies remain.

Given this imperfection, it is worthwhile attempting to assess the relative contributions of the variables comprising equation (6R.2). The most useful insights are achieved by identifying the incremental contribution to R^2 of each variable as that variable is deleted to break the near-identity, leaving the other variables in place. The results are:

Variable deleted	ΔR^2	R^2 after deletion
CONC	−0.177	0.574
SIZE	− .585	.165
TOP50/MOS plus ADJ	− .313	.438

In terms of this criterion, by far the most powerful explanatory variable is SIZE. Deletion of CONC has only a moderate impact on R^2, considering that the near-identity specification is broken. This reinforces our conclusions from U.S. data in Chapter 5 and the zero-order correlation analysis of Tables 6.5 and 6.6 that seller concentration and multi-plant operation are not linked in any consistently strong manner.

The Behavioral Core Regressions

We turn now to the nondefinitional regression specifications embodying the relationships suggested by our theoretical analysis. Tables 6.7 and 6.8 summarize the most important specification variants in additive and multiplicative form respectively. Several important findings emerge.

One, of a negative character, is revealed by regressions 6.7.1 and 6.8.1. In no case does the product count variable PROD3 come anywhere near statistical significance, nor are its coefficients consistently positive, as predicted by theory. Its elasticity (measured by the multiplicative regression coefficient) implies a trivially small impact on the extent of multi-plant operation. Although we know from qualitative evidence that multi-plant operation is related to product specialization, these statistical

Table 6.7. Additive Regressions.

Regression number	N	Dependent variable; coverage	Constant term	Independent variables		
				COST	TRANS	$\dfrac{\text{TRANS}}{\sqrt{\text{DENS} \cdot \text{MS3}}}$
6.7.1	71	MPO3	3.54	−0.399* (.163)	0.410** (.109)	
6.7.2	71	MPO3	4.35	−.312* (.135)	.342** (.082)	
6.7.3	71	MPO3	3.19	+.011 (.109)		1.326* (.638)
6.7.4	71	MPO3	2.22	−.379* (.183)	.306** (.111)	
6.7.5	66	MPO3; 5 largest markets deleted	4.57	−.450** (.127)	.395** (.076)	
6.7.6	71	MPO3; British steel nationalized	4.30	−.269* (.140)	.319** (.085)	
6.7.7	71	MPO3	4.45	−.309* (.139)	.340** (.084)	
6.7.8	71	MPO3	4.49	−.282* (.141)	.321** (.087)	
6.7.9	71	MPO1	5.65	−.559** (.218)	.635** (.133)	
6.7.10	71	MPO3	4.25	−.322* (.139)	.349** (.085)	

Note: Standard errors are given in parentheses.
  *Significant at the 0.05 level in a one-tail test.
 **Significant at the 0.01 level in a one-tail test.

results indicate that we have been unsuccessful in characterizing the phenomenon quantitatively. Evidently, it is something more than mere numbers of physically different products which leads to plant specialization in certain cases but not in others.

With only a few noteworthy exceptions, the other three behavioral core variables have coefficient signs consistent with expectations and differ significantly from zero at the 0.05 level or better. Multi-plant operation appears to be more extensive, the greater domestic production is in relation to a single plant's MOS, the higher the costs of increasing a plant's shipping radius are, and the less strongly production scale economies pull toward plant agglomeration. SIZE clearly has the strongest, most consistent effect. The production cost curve slope term, which is highly collinear with the transportation cost variable and which, we observed in Chapter 3, was subject to especially severe measurement

			Independent variables				
SIZE	Log SIZE	PROD3	CONC	$\dfrac{TOP50}{MOS}$	MERG	EMP	R^2
0.0517** (.0049)		0.481 (.504)					0.702
.0533** (.0046)							.698
.0537** (.0050)							.644
	4.86** (0.73)						.449
.0967** (.0185)							.514
.0530** (.0048)							.678
.0531** (.0052)			−0.158 (1.553)				.698
.0542** (.0047)				−0.226 (.296)			.701
.0748** (.0075)					1.15 (1.26)		.660
.0537** (.0047)						0.069 (.166)	.699

problems, has the lowest t-ratios and assumes the wrong coefficient sign in one regression.

Despite its high zero-order correlation of 0.862 with TRANS, and although it comes with impressive credentials from the plant cost minimization conditions derived in Chapter 2, the complex transportation cost slope term $TRANS/\sqrt{(DENS \cdot MS3)}$ performs disappointingly. As a comparison of equations 6.7.2 and 6.7.3 shows, R^2 is lower when the more complex term is employed in place of TRANS, and the COST variable takes on a paradoxical negative sign. Similarly inferior results were obtained when $TRANS/\sqrt{(DENS \cdot MS3)}$ was used in more complex regressions (not presented here). No appreciable change occurred relative to equation 6.7.3 when MS3 was deleted to leave $TRANS/\sqrt{(DENS)}$ as the variable specification, although R^2 fell still further to 0.627. In view of these results, we shall emphasize the simpler shipping cost term TRANS in subsequent analyses.

Table 6.8. Multiplicative Regressions.

Regression number	N	Dependent variable; coverage	Constant term	COST	TRANS	DENS·MS3	SIZE	PROD3	CONC	TOP50/MOS	MERG	EMP	R²
6.8.1	71	MPO3	0.409	−0.271* (.158)	0.260** (.095)		0.389** (.049)	−0.028 (.038)					0.539
6.8.2	71	MPO3	.379	−.319* (.143)	.298** (.079)		.376** (.045)						.535
6.8.3	71	MPO3	.405	−.316* (.145)	.299** (.080)	−0.015 (.067)	.376** (.045)						.535
6.8.4	66	MPO3; 5 largest markets deleted	.431	−.383* (.154)	.327** (.079)		.355** (.055)						.488
6.8.5	71	MPO3; British steel nationalized	.373	−.301* (.145)	.300** (.080)		.375** (.046)						.528
6.8.6	71	MPO3	.020	−.378** (.151)	.309** (.079)		.425** (.062)		0.202 (.174)				.544
6.8.7	71	MPO3	.088	−.091 (.144)	.174* (.079)		.500** (.053)			−0.337** (.090)			.617
6.8.8	71	MPO3	.016	−.144 (.121)	.106 (.067)		.842** (.077)		.919** (.169)	−.656** (.095)			.737
6.8.9	71	MPO1	.454	−.347* (.182)	.355** (.101)		.398** (.058)				0.031 (.080)		.453
6.8.10	71	MPO3	.370	−.319* (.145)	.297** (.080)		.377** (.050)					0.0029 (.0702)	.535

		Independent variables

Note:. Standard errors are given in parentheses.
*Significant at the 0.05 level.
**Significant at the 0.01 level.

The DENS·MS3 term also shows no signs of explanatory power when disembodied and used in multiplicative regressions like equation 6.8.3. Virtually identical results were experienced when DENS alone was substituted for DENS·MS3 (not reported in the table). Since it appears to do neither harm nor good, we shall in most subsequent regressions dispense with DENS·MS3 as excess baggage.

These simplifications make it easier to analyze the important but some-what puzzling role of market size.[14] The coefficients of SIZE in the nonidentity multiplicative regressions are generally on the order of 0.375 to 0.400, implying that multi-plant operation increases much less than proportionately with the number of MOS plants compatible with do-mestic production.[15] But when log SIZE is substituted for SIZE in additive regression 6.7.4 to characterize the sort of diminishing returns relationship suggested by the multiplicative regressions, the explanatory power is greatly inferior, R^2 dropping by nearly 25 percentage points. Introducing higher-order SIZE terms into an additive regression also provides no solution. A regression adding a SIZE^2 term to equation 6.7.2 increased R^2 by only 0.0005 but injected severe multicollinearity. The reason for the apparent linearity of the additive relationship and non-linearity of the multiplicative estimates is brought out by examining the scatter diagram in Figure 6.1. A few extreme values affect the estimates in quite different ways. The bivariate linear least-squares regression function (broken line) is greatly influenced by two outlying observations for the U.S. shoe and weaving industries and by the fact that a fair amount of multi-plant operation occurs even in industries accommodating fewer than ten MOS plants. Yet asymptotically the linear regression, predicting 4.34 plants (with a standard error of 0.47) in a market of zero size, must be wrong. The bivariate logarithmic regression (solid line) avoids this small-market error but underestimates the U.S. shoe and textile values by a wide margin, largely because it puts relatively more weight on downward than upward deviations of the same absolute magnitude.[16] Visual inspection does suggest some diminishing returns effect by any set of standards, but the exact form of the relationship depends critically on how much weight one assigns to a few extreme values.

14. Nation-specific differences in market size appear to be slightly more important in this size relationship than industry-specific differences. See F. M. Scherer, "The Determinants of Multi-Plant Operation in Six Nations and Twelve Industries," *Kyklos*, 27 (1974), no. 1, pp. 40–42.

15. In the simple bivariate regression of log MPO3 on log SIZE, the estimated elasticity is 0.349.

16. E.g., in a logarithmic regression, an error resulting from predicting 15 when the actual value is 30 is the same as an error in predicting 2 when the observed value is one.

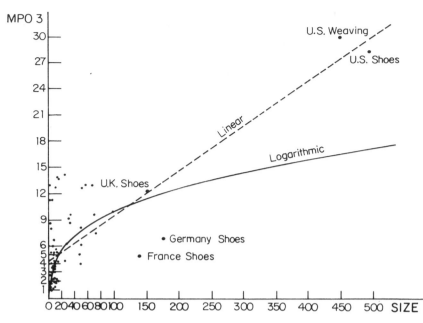

Figure 6.1. Scatter Diagram of Market Size and Multi-Plant Observations.

One possible approach to the weighting problem is to delete altogether the five industries whose production volume was sufficient to accommodate 100 or more MOS plants. The results are shown in regressions 6.7.5 and 6.8.4. In multiplicative regression 6.8.4 we find the elasticity of multi-plant operation with respect to SIZE falling slightly to 0.355. In both truncated sample regressions, the transport cost and (especially) the unit production cost slope relationships are strengthened.

An evaluation of statistical properties also permits no clear-cut choice between alternate specifications. For samples with extreme value problems like ours, comparing R^2 levels between specifications is an unsatisfactory criterion, since the dependent variable's variance characteristics are changed substantially by taking logarithms. Comparisons involving the standard error of estimate, the conventional goodness-of-fit criterion, may also be misleading. When the prediction errors from multiplicative regression 6.8.2 are transformed to an additive basis, the standard error of estimate is found to be 4.14 plants per firm, as contrasted to 3.13 for additive regression 6.7.2. But the average *absolute* (unsquared) deviation with regression 6.8.2 is much closer: 2.54 vs. 2.36 for regression 6.7.2. Compensating in part for the higher average size of its prediction errors, multiplicative regression 6.8.2 has a nearly normal error distribution, while the distribution for additive regression 6.7.2 has an extended positive tail and a truncated, irregular grouping of negative residuals. Thus, each of the specifications has its advantages, depending upon the criterion applied. Our own preference is for the statistical properties of the multiplicative specification, placing relatively more weight on that range of SIZE and MPO3 values most heavily populated by the industries in our sample. Still the best, if not always the simplest, choice is undoubtedly to retain both specifications and test the sensitivity of results to specification differences.

It is worth noting that by far the largest prediction error under any specification tested was for the French cigarette industry. Interviews confirmed that the industry is indeed sui generis. In 1970 the government-owned tobacco monopoly SEITA produced cigarettes in 13 plants, compared to the 4.0 plants predicted by linear regression 6.7.2 or 2.0 by multiplicative regression 6.8.2. This surprisingly large number is chiefly a legacy from the nineteenth century, when factories were dispersed among the various departments as political favors and to solve local unemployment problems. Since then regulations constraining SEITA's ability to discharge or relocate workers have made closures extremely difficult. A company staff study during the early 1960s concluded that the optimal number of plants would be three or four, but the recommendation was rejected as politically infeasible.

The only other industry with one of the six largest errors of underestimation in both regressions 6.7.2 and 6.8.2 is Canadian brewing. Its position is explained in part by the failure of our regression model to take into account adequately the vast geographic expanse of the Canadian market, partly by provincial tax regulations and local consumer preferences encouraging the maintenance of at least one brewery in each province, and partly as a heritage of unrationalized mergers. Two industries, Swedish shoes and U.K. batteries, had overprediction errors among the six largest in regressions 6.7.2 and 6.8.2. There was more multi-plant operation in the Swedish shoe industry during the mid-1960s than in 1970, by which time the former industry leader had closed all but one of its six plants after being driven to the brink of insolvency by a tide of low-priced imports. And for the U.K. storage battery industry, our regressions probably overstate the number of plants because they fail to take into account the compactness of the densely populated English market and the specific advantages of consolidating operations at large plants near automobile production centers located along a 180-mile path between London and Liverpool.

Any prediction error in a quantitative analysis can be rationalized if one has sufficient supplementary information. We confine our discussion of pathology to one more case. Regressions 6.7.6 and 6.8.5 show the effect of substituting the postnationalization values of the British steel industry's MPO3 (and other) variables for the prenationalization values otherwise used. The regression coefficient changes are generally small, suggesting that our estimates are not highly sensitive to how that industry's special plant count problem is handled.

Results for Other Variables

We proceed more quickly now to explore the role of other independent variables, using the behavioral core regressions 6.7.2 and 6.8.2 as a kind of hat rack. Additive regression 6.7.7 and multiplicative regression 6.8.6 show the effect of adding the seller concentration variable CONC to the behavioral core. In regression 6.8.6, which more closely approximates the identity specification, the CONC coefficient is positive and exceeds its standard error, but in neither regression is the coefficient statistically significant at the 0.05 or even the 0.10 level. When a multiplicative SIZE·CONC interaction term was substituted for or included with SIZE in additive regressions, it exhibited slightly more explanatory power than SIZE alone when the observations for all seventy-one industries were analyzed but less power when the five industries with SIZE values exceeding 100 were excluded. These results provide at best only weak support for the hypothesis that multi-plant operation is more closely related to leading *firm* size than to the general pull of large *markets* on firms' ability or desire to expand.

In regressions 6.7.8 and 6.8.7, the TOP50/MOS variable is added to the core. The additive model effect is weakly negative, while a fairly strong negative association between MOS-deflated plant sizes and multi-plant operation is observed in the (more nearly tautological) multiplicative variant, with an accompanying deterioration of the TRANS and (especially) COST coefficients. Regression 6.8.8 goes even further toward approximating an identity specification with the behavioral variables TRANS and COST added. Its purpose is to test the robustness of those variables' effects in a heavily collinear environment. We find that TRANS and COST continue to have the signs predicted by theory, but their elasticities and *t*-ratios are sharply attenuated.

Regressions 6.7.9 and 6.8.9 focus on the role of mergers, using the number of plants operated by the single leading firm MPO1 as dependent variable. The core model variables' performance is very similar to what has been observed with MPO3 as dependent variable, despite a drop in R^2 of about four percentage points in the additive version and eight in the multiplicative version. The merger dummy variable coefficients have the expected positive signs, but they are exceeded by their standard errors under both specifications. Similarly negative results materialized when MERG was added to more complex regressions. Substitution of postnationalization observations for the British steel industry raised the MERG coefficient values and standard errors to $+2.10/(1.46)$ in the additive and $+0.064/(0.083)$ in the multiplicative regressions, but again, the results fall far short of orthodox statistical significance thresholds. As with our product count variable, we are defeated by apparent measurement difficulties, being unable to find statistical verification of a phenomenon which we know from qualitative observation exists.[17]

The final regressions in Tables 6.7 and 6.8 introduce the variable EMP, measuring the number of employees required by an MOS plant of average mid-1960s' U.S. productivity. The hypothesized inverse relationship between it and multi-plant proliferation fails to materialize, and both coefficients are dwarfed by their standard errors. Similarly counterintuitive but weak results were obtained when a variable EMP/TRANS was analyzed, taking into account the possibility that multiplant operation is more apt to be inhibited when MOS plant employment is substantial *and* transport costs are low.[18]

National Group Regressions

Table 6.9 presents regression equations estimated after the sample was partitioned into three potentially more homogeneous national groups: the United States, Canada, and the four European nations. For the most part the results are consistent with those from the combined six-nation regressions. However, in three cases—all from the U.S. subsample, with its extremely wide spread of values, and all statistically insignificant— the coefficient signs are the opposite of those predicted by theory. Of the fifteen coefficients whose signs are consistent with a priori expectations, twelve are significantly different from zero at the 0.05 level or better and fourteen at the 0.10 level or better.

Comparison suggests some qualitative differences among the groups. In the United States, market size is all-important, while the production cost function slope term and (in contrast to the Chapter 5 results) transportation cost variable perform poorly. In geographically vast and sparsely populated Canada, the production and transportation cost variables appear to play a stronger role than sheer market size. Europe exhibits greater balance, with all three variables significant in both the additive and multiplicative regressions.

Despite these ostensible differences, a variance analysis forces us to

17. An alternate explanation could be that leading firms with an extensive post-1958 merger experience were merely catching up to firms in the same industries elsewhere which had previously developed a multi-plant structure through merger or internal growth. Our interviews provide a small amount of support for this conjecture, but it was quite clearly not the case generally.

18. See the discussion of labor inputs in Chap. 2.

Table 6.9. National Group Regressions: MPO3 as Dependent Variable.

Regression	Explanation	N	Constant	SIZE	COST	TRANS	R^2
6.9.1	U.S. additive	12	3.13	0.0526** (.0053)	+0.384 (.331)	−0.049 (.175)	0.926
6.9.2	Canada additive	12	6.00	.0144 (.0595)	−.713* (.271)	.588* (.205)	.518
6.9.3	Europe additive	47	4.92	.0295* (.0126)	−.413** (.171)	.407** (.103)	.393
6.9.4	U.S. multiplicative	12	−0.408	.694** (.066)	+.096 (.146)	.143 (.081)	.935
6.9.5	Canada multiplicative	12	.541	.364* (.158)	−.595 (.326)	.444* (.180)	.596
6.9.6	Europe multiplicative	47	.449	.310** (.065)	−.355* (.191)	.313** (.106)	.390

Note: Standard errors are given in parentheses.
*Significant at the 0.05 level in a one-tail test.
**Significant at the 0.01 level in a one-tail test.

accept the hypothesis that the differences in regression coefficient values could have arisen by chance from a homogeneous population. Relative to pooled regressions 6.7.2 and 6.8.2, letting each national group assume its own best-fitting coefficients reduces unexplained variance (that is, increases R^2) by 0.053 in the additive case and 0.061 for the multiplicative variant. The *F*-ratios associated with these variance reductions are 1.57 and 1.11 respectively, well below 2.10, the five percent significance point.

Conclusions

We conclude by bringing together the findings from our statistical analyses of multi-plant operation for two quite different samples—the Chapter 5 sample embracing 96 to 155 four-digit U.S. manufacturing industries and the six-nation, 12-industry matrix covered in this chapter.

For both samples, one of the most consistent and powerful explanatory variables has been market size. In Chapter 5, multi-plant operation was found to be strongly correlated positively with industry value added and negatively with the share of total industry activity accounted for by an average leading plant. In the present chapter we found a strong positive association between multi-plant operation and a variable combining these two dimensions of size: the number of MOS plants compatible with domestic production volume. For both samples there is reason to believe that multi-plant operation rises less than proportionately with market size, although the strong influence exerted by a few extreme and not necessarily representative observation values makes it difficult to be certain.

The U.S. analysis indicates that multi-plant proliferation is more closely linked to overall market size than to the size of leading firms, while results for the six-nation analysis are equivocal. A possible reconciliation is that firm size is more important for companies operating an unusually large number of plants in vast markets, while market size has greater relevance in smaller markets. The statistical analyses could not, however, determine whether the observed relationships mean that firms seeking power or blessed with especially favorable operating conditions expand commensurately with available opportunities, that there are cost-saving or other advantages of multi-plant size which can be exploited more fully through plant multiplication in larger markets, or that some combination of these and perhaps other motive forces prevails.

Another strong theme features the location-theoretic variables. With both samples, multi-plant operation was found to be more extensive, the higher outbound transportation costs were in relation to product value. There was less consistent evidence for the six-nation sample that multi-plant operation is restrained by the centripetal pull of powerful plant scale economies. These findings in combination with the market size results suggest that leading firms expand to take advantage of their market frontiers, adopting that plant size and location pattern which secures the best tradeoff between production scale economies and shipping cost.

A third common result was our inability to discern consistent non-tautological positive relationships between the market shares of leading firms and the extent of their multi-plant operation. This is a telling blow to the conventional wisdom which, we have shown, has been based upon faulty interpretations.

Somewhat more disconcerting is the failure of the analyses in both chapters to find significant support for the expected positive association between product line breadth and multi-plant operation. Similar disappointment attends the insignificant correlation between the number of leading firm plants and an index of past merger activity among six-nation sample members. Qualitative evidence suggests the presence of fire, but our statistical investigations have been unable to find much smoke.

Although the conclusions summarized here appear to hold with a high degree of consistency for different specifications and samples, some deviations from the general pattern do appear for national subsamples, and a fair amount of variance remains unexplained. It is hard to compare our success in this respect with the results of the Chapter 3 plant size analysis because the six-nation multi-plant analysis suffers more severely from extreme value problems. The additive multi-plant model "explains" a higher fraction of its dependent variable's variance than does the multiplicative model largely because outlying multi-plant observations for the U.S. shoe manufacturing and weaving industries are closely associated with market size. Extreme value biases of this sort tend to be less severe with a multiplicative specification. A multiplicative analysis using four independent variables explained three-fourths of the plant size variable's variance, whereas the most closely comparable regressions from this chapter achieved R^2 values in the neighborhood of 0.54, and the R^2 in a four-variable multiplicative analysis of the ninety-six U.S. industry sample in Chapter 5 was 0.59. Given the difficulties of comparison, this cannot be considered proof, but our impression is that multi-plant operation tends to exhibit somewhat more unsystematic variation than plant size choices.

7

The Economies of
Multi-Plant Operation:
Interview Evidence

Chapters 5 and 6 reveal that multi-plant operation is associated systematically with high outbound transportation costs, suggesting a cost-minimizing spatial adaptation by firms serving a nationwide clientele, and, in a less systematic way, with product specialization. The question remains, do nationwide multi-plant, multi-product firms realize advantages not open to companies maintaining only a single plant, appropriately specialized by geographic region and product segment? That is, are there "system effects" from operating a network of spatially decentralized and/or product-specialized plants interdependently rather than independently?

It is also clear that much multi-plant operation, especially in Europe, is the heritage of past mergers, many of which have not been fully rationalized through the replacement of inefficiently small units by facilities of optimal scale. Do the companies with these incompletely rationalized plant structures enjoy significant economies which would not have been available to their once-independent constituent parts?

These are the questions we tackle in this chapter, drawing primarily upon our interviews with some 125 firms in six nations. The reader is warned not to expect precise, all-encompassing answers, for none exist. What one finds is an extraordinarily complex amalgam of technological opportunities, institutional constraints, and behavioral adaptations. The most we can accomplish is to delineate the dimensions of that complexity, to give it logical order, and to hazard rough generalizations about the importance of the main observed multi-plant economies.

Real vs. Pecuniary Economies

An elementary but essential distinction must be made between *real* and *pecuniary* economies. A real economy is secured when the quantity of resources employed in supplying some bundle of outputs is reduced. Building a big, modern cement plant provides an illustration. With it, a ton of cement can be produced using less labor, fuel, *and* capital than with plants of considerably smaller scale and less advanced technology. Pecuniary economies are achieved when the firm is able, by exerting some kind of market power, to obtain a given set of inputs at lower monetary cost without any essential change in the physical processes of production. A simple example is the company which extracts raw materials price concessions from oligopolistic suppliers by threatening to begin producing its requirements internally unless they accede. Unfortunately, these distinctions frequently become muddied in the real world; for example, because price concessions are granted partly to placate powerful buyers but also because suppliers can effect real production and distribution cost savings in filling the large buyer's orders; or because plants which have migrated to small towns in search of low-wage labor sacrifice some real economies of scale to avoid bidding too hard for the labor supply.

Economists generally consider real economies to be almost unambiguously desirable because they free resources for use in satisfying otherwise unfilled wants. The social desirability of a purely pecuniary economy is more ambiguous, since such economies characteristically reflect income redistributions benefiting their recipients but reducing the welfare of agents whose supply price has been beaten down. If the pecuniary concession comes at the expense of a big, powerful oligopolistic supplier and if it leads the recipient to reduce prices to the general consuming public, most onlookers of a liberal stripe applaud. But if the pecuniary gains are merely trapped as additional profits by monopolistic corporations, doubts intrude; and if the burden is ultimately borne by workers or moderate-income small businessmen, the social consensus may well be disapproving.

Another distinction is between economies which are strictly private, accruing exclusively to the instigating organization, and those which are diffused to the benefit of the general consuming public—e.g., when real economies lead to product price reductions. Pecuniary input cost savings not passed along to consumers are a prominent example of strictly private economies. The concept can also be stretched to include price-setting advantages. Increased size might confer nothing more than the monopolistic power to raise prices and profits, benefiting its possessor but reducing social welfare in well-known ways. Or the large enterprise may secure pecuniary and real advertising and sales promotional advantages which enhance its profits, but which do not necessarily lead to lower prices and other societywide benefits. More complex mixed cases arise when, for instance, the realization of scale economies frees resources to satisfy additional wants but simultaneously confers sufficient monopoly power to thwart a fall in prices.

Economists have made some progress toward dealing analytically, at least in a static framework, with situations in which real economies and monopoly power emerge jointly.[1] Our concern in this chapter is a different one: not to find the best tradeoff but to estimate some key components of the tradeoff. Many of the distinctions between real vs. pecuniary and private vs. diffused economies are in any event value-laden, and at least in the present state of the art, one cannot state unequivocally that one type of scale advantage is praiseworthy and another contemptible. Nevertheless, there is among economists a fairly widely accepted hierarchy of values, with real diffused economies leading the parade in terms of perceived desirability, the monopoly pricing advantages of size running a poor last, and purely private pecuniary economies straggling near the rear.

Consistent with this implied consensus, our interviews placed more stress on identifying and attempting to quantify the real economies associated with multi-plant operation than on the pecuniary and monopolistic advantages. Still, a good deal was learned about each. We begin therefore in the grey areas of promotional and pecuniary economics and end with a thorough investigation of investment, physical distribution, production, and technological research economies.

Selling and Promotional Advantages

There are several linkages through which firms may be drawn toward multi-plant operation because of advantages in large-scale sales promotion and product differentiation. First, through advertising, word-of-mouth, population diffusion, and other mechanisms which may or may not be under the firm's direct control, it is often possible to gain a nationwide "image" or reputation which creates or reinforces consumer

1. See especially Oliver E. Williamson, "Economies as an Antitrust Defense: The Welfare Tradeoffs," *American Economic Review*, 58 (March 1968), 18–34; with comments and rejoinder in the *American Economic Review*, 59 (December 1969), 947–959; and Charles K. Rowley, *Antitrust and Economic Efficiency* (London: Macmillan, 1973).

preferences for one's products. A favorable nationwide image can be an important asset whose full value is realized only by serving the entire national market. If this is done, the firm's production structure must be organized accordingly, and if transport costs are substantial in relation to product value, a geographically dispersed multi-plant structure is likely to prove optimal, especially in nations as vast as the United States and Canada. Second, there may be economies of scale in utilizing the principal media of image creation and product differentiation—most prominently, advertising—which persist into the range of multi-plant production. Third, offering a broad line of products may provide certain advantages in fielding a sales force and securing market outlets. Commitment to a broad-line strategy in turn may imply a production structure with multiple plants specialized by product. Fourth, when product differentiation requires periodic design changes, the multi-plant producer might achieve savings spreading the costs of design, tooling, testing, and retooling over a larger volume than the company with only a single efficient-sized plant. The importance of the first three potential advantages of size in our twelve industries will be explored in this section; the fourth is better considered in a later section.

A further complication must be noted. Economies of scale in sales promotion, unlike most other advantages of size, can affect both costs and demand. The large-scale advertiser might enjoy a lower per-unit cost of promoting its product, or it may be able to charge a price premium relative to smaller sellers for a given expenditure per unit on advertising, or it may experience some combination of cost savings and price premia. Sales promotional advantages might also interact with production scale economies by permitting a producer to sell more at a given price and hence to advance farther down its long-run unit cost curve. Our analysis must take into account these interacting dimensions.

Image Advantages

Table 7.1 summarizes the influence of brand image and reputation, however derived, on consumer acceptance and pricing latitude under U.S. market conditions as of 1970. It also indicates whether sellers must be of a size and geographic scope calling for multi-plant operation to achieve the maximum image advantage with an efficient plant structure. We note immediately a marked difference between the consumer goods industries (the first seven or eight) and producer goods. Image advantages are of moderate to substantial importance in the majority of consumer goods fields, while they tend to be of little to no importance in the producer goods industries.

The weaving industry lies at the borderline. Design and price are

Table 7.1. Importance of Brand Image in the Twelve Industries, 1970.

Industry	How important is image differentiation?	Wholesale price advantage associated with a favorable brand image (percent)	To what extent is multi-plant size essential?
Beer brewing	Substantial	8–40	Strongly
Cigarettes	Substantial	10–50	Little or none
Trade paints	Moderate	0–20	Moderately
Gasoline	Moderate	8–20	Little
Shoes	Slight	0–20	Little to moderately
Refrigerators	Moderate	1–8	Little
Auto batteries	Slight	10–30	Considerably
Fabric weaving	Slight to moderate	0–15	Considerably
Glass bottles	Negligible	None	Negligibly
Cement	Negligible	None	Not at all
Steel	Negligible	None	Very little
Bearings	Slight	0–5	Moderately

overwhelmingly stressed in the cotton and synthetic cloth purchase decisions of clothing and furnishings manufacturers, although weavers may be able to command a price premium for certain nationally advertised dress fabrics and for such items as sheets and blankets sold directly to consumers. In the industries more uniformly preoccupied with producer goods, buyers may hold slight preferences for one supplier over another, but these are almost never sufficient to sustain a lasting price differential, other things such as quality and speed of delivery being held equal.

Beer occupies the opposite end of the spectrum, at least in the United States. Yet the relationships between company size and image are complex. The nationwide premium image patiently cultivated by Budweiser, Schlitz, Miller, and Pabst since the repeal of Prohibition in 1933 became an extremely important asset, especially during the 1960s, when increasingly affluent consumers began "trading up" to what they considered more prestigious products. Consistent with the Chamberlinian product differentiation model, this image advantage imparts a significant negative slope to the demand curve of its possessor, prices of other brands being held constant. How it is exploited then becomes a strategy question. By contenting themselves with market shares in the range of 2 to 6 percent, Budweiser and Schlitz could command price premia relative to regional "popular" brands of 15 to 30 percent, depending upon specific market conditions. By squeezing the differential they can make much heavier inroads. The experience of Pabst in this regard is particularly informative. During the late 1950s Pabst had fallen upon adversity owing to declining brand acceptance. In 1962 it sought a way out by eliminating completely the traditional price differential between the Pabst Blue Ribbon brand and popular price beers in the state of Michigan, supporting this strategy change with a vigorous promotional campaign. Its share of the Michigan market rose from roughly 2 to 30 percent. However, as the price reduction policy was extended to other territories, it proved to have distinct costs. Although image conditions pricing policy, pricing policy reciprocally affects a beer's image. With its price premium eliminated in many areas, Pabst's brand image weakened. The pricing latitude it once possessed had been narrowed considerably, quite possibly permanently.

Whether multi-plant operation is necessary to sustain a premium image in the U.S. beer market is difficult to state conclusively. Certain regional and specialty beers brewed at a single location have enjoyed success selling at premium prices in limited markets. The most spectacularly successful is Coors, which by 1969 had captured 30 percent of all sales in the eleven-state, western U.S. market while maintaining a solid premium price. Yet Coors' single-plant production approach was by orthodox criteria decidedly nonoptimal, with enormous quantities of chilled beer being transported some 1200 miles in insulated unit train cars or refrigerated trucks from Golden, Colorado, to Los Angeles or San Francisco.[2] Were it not for the pull of Coors' much acclaimed (but, competitive brewers insist, chemically irrelevant) "pure Rocky Mountain spring water," the company would almost surely have profited from building at least one West Coast brewery. So if multi-plant operation is not a mandatory condition for *achieving* image differentiation, success in the quest for nationwide (or nearly nationwide) image nevertheless draws brewing companies toward spatially decentralized operation.

This conclusion holds only for the United States and to some extent (limited by regional taste differences) Canada. In the four European nations covered by our study, national markets were sufficiently compact that transport costs exerted a much weaker pull toward multi-plant operation. The main spurs to decentralized brewing were rather regional taste differences and "made at home" preferences, the antithesis of a nationwide image.

2. *Railway Age*, December 22–29, 1969, p. 74. See also "The Brewery That Breaks All the Rules," *Business Week*, August 22, 1970, pp. 60–64; and Charles G. Burck, "While the Big Brewers Quaff, the Little Ones Thirst," *Fortune*, 86 (November 1972), 105.

Brand image is clearly very important in cigarette marketing. But its links to multi-plant operation are tenuous. What matters is the brand, not the company, and nearly all major sellers in the six nations have offered a broad array of brands during the past decade. Also, in all six countries the output of an MOS cigarette plant is larger than the volume needed to sustain strong image differentiation for any single brand.

Paint sales are customarily classified into two main market categories —industrial, accounting for 45 percent of 1969 U.S. volume, and "trade" or decorative sales. The latter market has two further subdivisions: sales to commercial painting contractors and to the general public through retail outlets. On sales to industrial buyers and commercial contractors the advantages of national image are negligible, and no image advantage not associated with real quality differences will support a price differential. For sales through retail outlets, store coverage, shelf position, and dealer recommendations are said to be much more important than image. Nationally known brands such as "Lucite" and "Kem-Tone" do enjoy substantial consumer preference when other conditions are held equal; they can retain a sizeable share of the market at price premia up to 20 percent. The problem is, other things are seldom equal. So many viable trade paint marketing strategies exist that even producers with well-accepted national brands considered their image advantage to be of only moderate importance.

"Major" brands of gasoline sold at retail price premia of 2 to 4 cents per gallon in 1970, or from 16 to 40 percent of the average pretax, exrefinery wholesale price, relative to "unbranded" gasolines.[3] Some of this margin was absorbed at the retailer and wholesaler level. Estimating the premium retained by the refiner on branded gasoline is difficult because of the complex distribution channels. It probably averaged between 12 and 20 percent, dipping lower during price wars. Regional producers, it must be stressed, often enjoy premium images comparable to those of the nationals. And since numerous premium brands are available in any given territory, station location and the reputation of the dealer were said to influence sales much more significantly than marginal brand image differences. For sales of gasoline to industrial customers, image differences are completely unimportant, and on sales of heating oil, the second largest-volume refinery product in North America and the largest in Western Europe, they tend to be slight.

Shoe manufacturing presents an even more complicated picture. The variety of product offerings is enormous, and marketing strategies

---

3. See, e.g., "The Oil Giants Fight the Independents," *Business Week*, May 13, 1972, pp. 135–144.

run the gamut from selling unbranded items to which independent retailers affix their own labels to pushing one's own nationally advertised brands through company-owned outlets. In both Europe and America, style, the balance between price and quality, and store location count for much more than image in the vast majority of sales. However, in certain segments of the market, particularly medium price casual lines and infant's shoes, it is possible to build a brand image which enhances access to independent retail outlets and which may support wholesale price premia as high as 20 percent, ceteris paribus.

In refrigerators, national brand acceptance is essential to achieving substantial sales volume through conventional marketing channels, though private-label sales to mail-order, chain, and department stores are a possible alternative. A single plant of minimum optimal scale (producing at least 400,000 units per year and preferably 800,000) has more than enough volume to sustain a national brand image in all the countries we studied. Indeed, the overriding problem is getting sufficient market acceptance to support efficient production. The image derived from selling washing machines, stoves, and other household appliances is transferable to refrigerators, and in this sense multi-plant production of different products can bolster or reinforce one's refrigerator brand acceptance, especially for firms with modest refrigerator sales. Market research by a leading U.S. producer suggests that a branded refrigerator price premium of $10 to $12 relative to similar private label brands can be sustained before consumer acceptance falls off sharply. In sales to U.S. apartment builders, a well-known national brand confers only a very small advantage, commanding a price premium not exceeding $1 per unit.

Original equipment automobile battery sales are highly price competitive in the absence of vertical ownership relations, and national brands cannot gain a price premium unrelated to substantive quality differences. Replacement battery purchases are usually precipitated by a failure, which makes shopping around difficult. Some consumers turn for help to outlets which offer only nationally branded batteries; on such sales the manufacturer may realize a price premium as high as 30 percent. However, especially in Canada and the United States, a large and growing share of all purchases involves private-label batteries, on which the manufacturer's image advantage is negligible. Battery makers in both Europe and North America stated that consumers will seldom pay a price premium for a nationally advertised battery when offered a choice of products with comparable guarantees. Consumers are also not strongly disposed toward duplicating their original equipment brand. If a nationally advertised brand approach is to be successful in the replacement market, it must therefore be accompanied by extensive access to retail outlets stocking one's batteries exclusively, or at least, not carrying low-price competitors. Except in Germany and to a lesser degree Sweden, this has been difficult to accomplish because of the trend toward private branding by gasoline chains and vigorous competition for independent outlets from small battery manufacturers. As a result, most of the battery manufacturers to whom we spoke considered the image advantages of nationwide operation to be quite modest.

Advertising, Firm Size, and Multi-Plant Operation

We find then that a favorable nationwide brand image provides substantially to moderately important price and market penetration advantages on a broad plane in four industries and in much narrower segments of three others. We ask next, are there systematic relationships between firm size and ability to build and sustain a strong image?

It should be apparent already that image creation is not the kind of process readily reduced to a mathematical formula. Much depends upon having done the right kinds of things for a long time. Obviously, a record of supplying a good product and good service is important, except in pathological cases largely absent from our sample. Mystique also plays a role. Or at least, we find it hard to offer an alternate explanation for the Coors phenomenon, since any of several dozen competing brewers could imitate closely the Coors chemical formulation if they set their minds to it. What remains after these imponderables are dismissed is the main systematic tool of image differentiation: advertising.

Multi-plant size could conceivably favor an advertiser in several ways. First, the media might offer discounts to companies buying space or time in large quantities—a basically pecuniary economy. There is a substantial literature on the question of whether large television advertisers have benefited from such discounts in the United States.[4] The weight of the evidence indicates that they have not, or at least, that preferential discounts have played a small and transitory role in the overall structure of television rates. Second, large-scale advertisers can use media such as network television and full-page

4. See Harlan Blake and Jack A. Blum, "Network Television Rate Practices: A Case Study in the Failure of Social Control of Price Discrimination," *Yale Law Journal*, 74 (July 1965), 1339–1401; David M. Blank, "Television Advertising: The Great Discount Illusion, or Tonypandy Revisited," *Journal of Business*, 41 (January 1968), 10–38; the comment by William Leonard with rejoinder by Blank in *idem*, 42 (January 1969), 93–112; John L. Peterman, "The Clorox Case and Television Rate Structures," *Journal of Law and Economics*, 11 (October 1968), 321–422; and Peter C. Riesz, "Size versus Price, or Another Vote for Tonypandy," *Journal of Business*, 46 (July 1973), 396–403.

national magazine insertions not economically practical for regional specialists and other small firms. Third, creating or sustaining an image or communicating to the public some claim requires a fair number of messages before something approximating widespread audience awareness is achieved. For the high-volume seller this threshold may be reached at an expenditure smaller in proportion to sales than for the low-volume seller, unless the smaller firm can exercise greater selectivity in targeting messages toward its audience. Finally, there may be certain fixed costs in preparing an advertising campaign; for the large-scale advertiser they can be spread over a larger volume of messages and sales than for the small firm. How important these potential advantages are must be ascertained empirically.

Table 7.2 shows the ratio of advertising expenditures to sales (net of excise taxes) during the mid-1960s for the closest approximations to our twelve industries on which reliable U.S. data were available. In the producer goods fields, advertising outlays are uniformly modest—well below one percent of sales. (The glass products figure overstates bottle advertising, since it includes household glassware and window

Table 7.2. Advertising Outlays as a Percentage of Sales (excluding Excise Taxes), circa 1965-66.

Industry		Advertising percentage
Beer		9.2
Tobacco products		6.9
All paints, varnishes, and lacquers		1.6
Trade paints	c. 2.3	
Industrial paints	c. 0.5	
Petroleum refining		
Based on gasoline sales alone		1.2
Based on all products sold		0.6
Footwear, excluding rubber shoes		1.5
Household appliances		2.8
Storage batteries		less than 1.0
Cotton and synthetic fabrics		0.5
Glass products		0.9
Cement		0.3
Steel		0.3
Bearings		less than 0.5

Sources: U.S., Internal Revenue Service, *Source Book, Statistics of Income, 1965,* "Corporation Income Tax Returns," undated computer printout; National Paint, Varnish and Lacquer Association, *Operating Cost Survey: 1969* (Washington, 1970); and interview data.

glass, with stronger orientation toward the ultimate consumer.) Interviews with steel, bearings, bottle, and cement producers confirmed that advertising is an unimportant dimension of their business strategies and that firms large enough to operate only a single efficient plant suffered no advertising disadvantages.

As an intermediate good sold primarily to knowledgeable, price-conscious converters, but with a lesser made-up consumer products subsegment, textiles are more complex. Advertising was said to be ineffective and unimportant on sales to converters, but it can have a significant impact in certain consumer goods lines, and there the largest firms evidently enjoy some promotional advantage. Burlington Industries in particular, the U.S. industry sales leader, captured a strong position in the sheet and pillowcase market despite a relatively late start, building its sales through network television advertisements run back-to-back with commercials for other Burlington consumer products such as hosiery and carpeting. There was general agreement among smaller textile firms that they could not hope to match the Burlington television "specials," and as a result they suffered a brand recognition handicap in the bed linens market.[5] Among textile firms outside the United States, the prevailing view was that moderate size was not a serious handicap in advertising one's products.

In the U.S. brewing industry, as Table 7.2 implies, advertising is a major dimension of rivalry. Yet interviews with companies revealed that the advantages of advertising on a nationwide plane are in most respects not very great. The leading nationwide brewers do advertise in selected national magazines, a strategy denied regional specialists. But a wide selection of effective media remains open to single-plant companies. Television is the most prominent. How it is used varies from firm to firm and also over time, suggesting no clear-cut advantage for a network approach over local coverage. Officials of one major national company said that they buy relatively little network time, even though they are fully capable of doing so. Instead, they buy spot commercial time in some 125 different submarkets defined by local TV station coverage, in this way tailoring the intensity of their campaigns to specific market conditions. Although this was considered a more rational approach than blunderbuss network advertising, regional brewers were said to offer "very tough" competition playing the same game. The main benefits of a nationwide approach were said to lie in utilizing a common theme, common preparation and filming costs, somewhat greater flex-

5. However, in 1972 Burlington reduced its advertising budget and moved away from special programs toward spot advertising. See "Critics Look at Burlington Industries," *New York Times*, June 12, 1972, p. 56.

ibility in the choice of media, and very modest savings in printing point-of-sale display advertisements. No quantitative estimates were hazarded by interviewees, but the cost savings attributable to advertising on a nationwide scale could hardly amount to more than one percent of pre-excise unit sales revenues, other things held equal.

There is, however, another more subtle promotional advantage of multi-plant operation involving an interaction with image effects. The nationally oriented St. Louis and Milwaukee brewers developed their premium image during the 1930s and 1940s by charging prices sufficient to cover heavy transport costs, supporting their sales with moderate amounts of advertising touting their premium quality, and leaving most of the market to lower-price regional and local brands. But they then began acquiring or building regional breweries. This reduced transportation costs and, with the modern large-scale breweries constructed during the late 1960s, production costs. The marginal cost of delivering "premium" beer to what had previously been remote markets fell sharply. Prices meanwhile remained more or less constant, governed at least as a first approximation by local market conditions. Thus, for the national companies the ratio of price to marginal cost rose, and, by a well-known theorem of Robert Dorfman and Peter O. Steiner, one would expect the optimal amount of advertising in away-from-home markets to rise, ceteris paribus.[6]

Pabst, the first national premium producer to adopt a multi-plant strategy, appears to have led the sharp escalation of advertising expenditures during the late 1940s.[7] By 1948 it had breweries in Milwaukee, Peoria, Newark, and Los Angeles. Schlitz acquired its second production site (Brooklyn) in 1949. Its measured media advertising outlays jumped from 37 cents per barrel in 1952 to $1.35 per barrel in 1954, when it added a third plant at Van Nuys, California. Anheuser-Busch expanded to Newark in 1951 and opened a third plant at Los Angeles in early 1954, while its advertising expenditures increased from 45 cents per barrel in 1953 to $1.17 in 1954.

The combination of intensified advertising by multi-plant producers and the desire of affluent consumers to "trade up" led to increasing

6. "Optimal Advertising and Optimal Quality," *American Economic Review*, 44 (December 1954), 834–835.

7. See Douglas F. Greer, "Product Differentiation and Concentration in the Brewing Industry," *Journal of Industrial Economics*, 19 (July 1971), 214. Greer emphasizes the advent of television as a stimulant to the advertising escalation of the early 1950s, although he also notes a possible link to increasing multi-plant operation. Actually, the major brewers began putting heavy weight on television in their media mix only in the early 1960s. See Burck, "While the Big Brewers Quaff," p. 107.

market shares for the leading national premium brewers. With greatly reduced marginal delivered costs, they also found it advantageous to squeeze the traditional premium-popular price differential. This too contributed to the erosion of regional brewers' market shares except in the special case of Coors. In sum, a combination of accumulated image advantages, changes in consumer income levels, the cost implications of a shift toward efficiently decentralized multi-plant operation, and the ensuing advertising and pricing responses made Anheuser-Busch, Schlitz, and Pabst a potent marketing force, permitting them to increase their combined share of national beer production from 16.4 percent in 1950 to 43.8 percent in 1972.

No such phenomenon was observed within the Western European nations, where the trend is away from inefficiently small local breweries toward centralized production. There was also much less advertising than in the United States, in part because of government restrictions and partly owing to the slow pace at which strong local preferences could be overcome. As a result, the advantages of nationwide advertising appeared to be much smaller in Europe than in the United States, although they may grow in the future as strategies more like those of American producers are adopted.

Until a legal ban took effect in January 1971, roughly 75 percent of all U.S. cigarette advertising expenditures flowed into television, much of it nationwide. By a 1970 industry rule of thumb, expenditures of approximately $10 million were required to launch a new brand; $20 million would be "overkill," said one executive. To justify such outlays, marketing planners had to anticipate that a brand would gain one percent of the national market, or sales of about 5 billion cigarettes per year; 2 percent was said to be "plenty." This represents between one-eighth and one-fourth the output of an MOS plant. The main advantage of larger volume was the ability to spread more fully the risks of unsuccessful campaigns, but firms in the 40–80 billion volume range considered themselves to suffer little or no launching handicap relative to the U.S. industry leader, Reynolds, with sales of 165 billion cigarettes per year. In Canada the cost of launching a new brand through nationwide television was estimated at $2.5 million, one-fourth the U.S. sum to reach one-tenth the population. This implies promotional economies associated with the absolute size of the market and perhaps with geographic compactness.

Once a brand is launched, it can generally be sustained with annual advertising outlays lower than the original launching cost, at least until a very substantial sales volume is approached. There is reason to believe that sustaining advertising costs rise less than proportionately with brand sales volume. Thus, average annual measured media outlays per billion cigarettes sold during 1969 and 1970 for fourteen of the sixteen best-selling U.S. brands, by sales rank group, were:[8]

Sales rank	Thousands of advertising dollars per billion cigarettes	Average annual unit sales (billions)
Leading 4 brands	381	58.0
Next 4 brands	453	28.8
Brands 9 through 14	570	12.5

Since the leading four brands each enjoyed annual sales exceeding 36 billion units, the estimated output of an MOS plant, some advantage for multi-plant firms is implied. The indicated average advertising outlay difference between the leading four brands and the next four (whose production volume could be accommodated by a single MOS plant) was 7.2 cents per thousand cigarettes, or about one percent of average 1969–70 sales revenue net of excise taxes.

How the ban on television advertising will affect scale economies in the U.S. cigarette market remained conjectural at the time of our interviews. It seemed likely that overall advertising expenditures would fall, as in fact they did.[9] With access to the most powerful medium barred, it will be more difficult to introduce new brands on a scale sufficient to make a major market impact and perhaps even to achieve good rolling and packaging machine utilization. Smaller firms may find it harder to challenge the industry leaders through aggressive promotion. A smaller European producer reported suffering some disadvantage relative to its larger rivals in billboard advertising, a medium which saw greatly increased use in the United States following the television ad-

8. Calculated from data in *Advertising Age*, 41 (August 24, 1970), and 42 (August 31, 1971); and *World Tobacco*, 9 (June 1971), 54–55. Data for the Kent and Lucky Strike brands were incomplete, so those brands had to be omitted from the analysis. It should be noted that all the brands included were well established, and most enjoyed fairly stable market shares during the period covered. If anything, taking into account differences in advertising strategies leading to rising market shares (e.g., for Marlboro) or falling shares (for Camel, Raleigh, and Chesterfield) would increase slightly the indicated unit advertising cost handicap of the lower-volume brands. For additional 1951 and 1967 data suggesting scale economies in advertising at the companywide level, see Henry G. Grabowski and Dennis C. Mueller, "Imitative Advertising in the Cigarette Industry," *Antitrust Bulletin*, 16 (Summer 1971), 268. See also "Why Philip Morris Thrives," *Business Week*, January 27, 1973, pp. 50–51.

9. See "Cigarette Makers Do Great without TV," *Business Week*, May 29, 1971, pp. 56–57; and "Where Cigarette Makers Spend Ad Dollars Now," *Business Week*, December 25, 1971, pp. 56–57.

vertising ban. The number of displays that firms in the European inter-viewee's market maintained was roughly proportional to their sales volume. When a new brand was introduced, the larger companies could therefore mobilize a more intensive saturation attack. Yet it is also possible that sustaining the market positions of leading brands will become more difficult, in which case one might anticipate a gradual trend toward equalization of brand shares and perhaps market shares.

Gasoline brands with a strong national position such as Texaco and Gulf can and do use network television advertising. That they choose to do so suggests that they consider it superior to the alter-natives. New Jersey Standard Oil's decision in 1972 to abandon (at least in the United States) its Esso, Enco, and Humble brands and adopt a completely new brand and company name, "Exxon," implies that considerable value was imputed to having a uniform nationwide image.[10] Nevertheless, our interviews revealed mixed views about the value of nationwide advertising. Only one interview was with an American petro-leum company employing network television. The executive interviewed said that a network approach definitely involved lower total costs than an equivalent campaign using spot TV. However, given the greater targeting precision possible with spot advertisements, he was uncertain whether the net benefits of the network strategy were great. At most, he said, the effect was marginal. Representatives of two companies with regional brands said they had no difficulty holding their own against nationally advertised gasolines in their home markets. Lack of a nation-ally advertised image was more a barrier to entry into new markets than a handicap in supplying familiar markets.

Paint advertising also presents a complicated picture. A few brands have achieved a strong nationwide image through television advertising. But none of the paint companies we visited in the United States or abroad believed that such a strategy was necessary; many other profitable marketing strategy options exist. One of the largest U.S. paint producers reported that it spent only enough on network television to support a claim that its products were in fact nationally advertised. Most of its resources were devoted to local spot and newspaper advertising pin-pointed in markets where its share was large enough to justify the effort.[11] When asked why it didn't rationalize its complex brand structure and focus national advertising on a single line, the sales vice-president of another large company pursuing a similar strategy replied that it could

10. See "Advertising: Esso To Be Exxon," *New York Times*, May 10, 1972, p. 75; and "Jersey Standard To Become Exxon," *New York Times*, June 22, 1972, p. 2.

11. In England, it is worth noting, network television advertising is infeasible, since the commercial TV stations operate on a regional basis.

achieve deeper market penetration with a diversity of more narrowly advertised brands, each appealing to different segments of the market. Representatives of both nationwide producers stated that aggressive regional firms with one to three plants could use spot television and other media to secure strong brand acceptance and that they represented extremely tough competition. What seems to matter then in all but special cases is not multi-plant operation, but having or being disposed to struggle for a sufficiently strong position in some identifiable submarket to justify product differentiation through advertising.

The shoe industry is similar to paints in the complexity of its marketing strategies but different because transport costs are low enough in relation to product value to permit serving the whole U.S. market from one location. For shoes which lend themselves to image differentiation, a sharply focused nationwide television advertising campaign can be mounted profitably by a firm with 3 to 6 million pairs per year sales potential, or the output of three to six MOS plants. But per-unit advertising costs are likely to run from 6 to 8 percent of the selling price, which must therefore incorporate a significant image premium. *If* production could then be doubled while maintaining product line focus, substantial unit advertising cost savings might be realized. This is apparently difficult or impossible, however, in most segments of the shoe trade. As a result, shoe producers seldom strive to secure strong image differentiation through intensive nationwide advertising. One of the largest national sellers reported that it did almost no nationwide advertising, even for its best-known brand, preferring to focus its spot television, radio, and newspaper advertising in particular local markets. Even then, there are advantages in supplying a sufficiently broad product assortment to secure appreciable shares of submarkets, and this usually implies the operation of several efficient-size plants. So there appear to be modest advertising economies of multi-plant operation, although many shoe manufacturers operate profitably doing virtually no brand advertising at all in market segments where style or price is the key to the consumer's purse.

Our interviews in the refrigerator industry provided no conclusive evidence on the size which must be reached before scale economies in advertising cease. Clearly, a favorable national brand image carries price and market penetration advantages in that segment of the trade where consumers buy appliances directly rather than through builders or landlords. Equally clearly, there are scale economies in advertising to build and maintain such an image—at least up to a point. We were nevertheless unable to identify in our six sample nations any refrigerator producer which lacked a well-established brand image but met the volume requirements for loading an MOS plant to capacity, that is, at roughly 800,000 units per year. Once that threshold is crossed there *may* be modest advertising economies associated with still higher refrigerator sales volume or with a promotional program spanning the efficient production of several major appliances, but we obtained no indication of their magnitude.

The data on battery advertising scale economies are also meager, mainly because most interviewees viewed brand differentiation through advertising as an unimportant strategy option. It seems unlikely that the advantages of nationwide advertising could be any greater than in the paint industry, which experiences a similar pull toward regional production, comparably weak brand loyalties, and complex distribution channels.

Access to Customers and Distribution Channels

Sales promotion in most industries involves much more than commissioning some advertisements and waiting for the orders to roll in. There is usually a substantial effort by field salesmen meeting customers and cultivating channels of distribution. For instance, trade (end-consumer oriented) paints had the fourth highest emphasis on advertising among the industries in our sample, with 1969 outlays averaging 2.4 percent of sales in forty-two representative companies. Those same companies devoted 8.0 percent of their sales dollar to the compensation and travel expenses of salesmen and sales executives.[12]

Are there advantages connected with multi-plant operation in this aspect of marketing? A multi-plant production structure optimally adapted to supplying a broad geographic market or a broad product line could conceivably afford cheaper or easier access to customers and distributors in several ways.

For one, when brief sales calls must be made upon a large number of actual or potential customers, salesmen for the firm with a broad product line or a large share of some product market segment may be able to achieve higher average sales in the same time per call as their more narrowly constrained peers, or they may spend more time on each call and relatively less time on unproductive travel between calls, or they may specialize and gain greater expertise in some narrow segment of the product line, or some combination of these three.

It is important to distinguish between size associated with a large share of some narrowly defined product market and size gained from having a broad assortment of products. With a large product market share, it is

---

12. National Paint, Varnish, and Lacquer Association, *Operating Cost Survey for the Year 1969* (Washington, 1970), p. 22.

often possible to deploy salesmen more effectively in a given territory. However, multi-plant operation is not a prerequisite, especially if transport costs impel geographic decentralization of production. Suppliers of paint, cement, gasoline, and beer can hold substantial shares of some market corresponding to a salesman's call territory without operating more than one MOS plant. So can steel and bottle manufacturers, although in this case the economies of sales route scheduling cannot in any event be great because the number of customers contacted is relatively small and the order volume per customer large.

The only industry among our twelve in which market share, multi-plant operation, and efficient salesman deployment were closely linked was cigarettes. Reynolds, with an output at its Winston-Salem production complex equivalent to that of four MOS plants, was said to be able to field a larger sales force with salesmen covering smaller geographic territories, at least in the less densely populated areas of the United States. Some travel expense economies definitely result; their magnitude was not estimated directly. Perhaps equally important, Reynolds and the dominant cigarette sellers in other nations are able to reach smaller retail outlets more economically and to call more frequently upon the larger outlets. This ability was said by smaller companies in two different countries to be the most significant single advantage of size in cigarette marketing. It can be counteracted to the extent that successful advertising by the smaller cigarette companies "pulls" their brands onto the retailer's shelf without salesman "push." Also, smaller firms sometimes compensate for less intensive field sales coverage by buying shelf space from the less frequently visited retail outlets.[13]

For companies with complex product lines, having salesmen specialize and assigning them a full line may be alternative or even inconsistent strategies. In most of the industries we studied, specialization was favored unless there were powerful extenuating circumstances. There were four main reasons. First, physical constraints may force a fair amount of specialization. The shoe salesman calling upon independent retail outlets can carry only a small number of items in his sample case. He has little choice but to emphasize them. Second, the amount of time

13. When television advertising of cigarettes was banned in 1971, the leading U.S. firms evidently began paying supermarket chains for prime shelf space. Philip Morris also doubled the size of its field sales force. See "Why Philip Morris Thrives," *Business Week*, January 27, 1973, pp. 48–49. Employing independent "detailing" service firms may also minimize the relative disadvantage of smaller manufacturers. See "Making Sure the Goods Get on the Shelves," *Business Week*, July 22, 1972, p. 46. This possibility was mentioned by none of our interviewees, perhaps because it was so new at the time.

buyers are willing to spend with salesmen is usually quite limited, and this compels the salesman to focus his efforts on one or a very few products if he is to be effective. Third, selling technically complex products demands a considerable amount of specialized knowledge, and, except when highly qualified (and expensive) salesmen can be employed, this is most readily achieved through sales force specialization. Finally, there is the human factor. A salesman may get along famously with one customer but experience personality clashes with another. The company which can dispatch two or more salesmen to a potential customer, each with his special line or gimmick, may win more sales than the firm with a monolithic approach.

Largely for these reasons, multi-plant firms often deploy multiple sales forces. The large shoe companies have different field sales groups for the various brands in their lines, and within a brand line there may be further specialization by shoe types, especially in the more densely populated markets. Some tobacco companies specialize their salesmen between cigarettes vs. smoking tobacco and cigars, and there may be further specialization by brands within the cigarette line. Both large and medium-sized textile companies typically have numerous sales units dealing with distinguishable customer classes, quality lines, and so on. The president of a textile firm with more sales groups than plants noted that he had often considered integrating his selling organization to achieve less duplication of contacts, lower travel expense, and better utilization of field office space. But these benefits were outweighed by the advantages of specialization and decentralization: a greater diversity of business contacts and more flexibility in reacting to demand changes. Paint companies likewise maintained multiple and overlapping sales forces for their various brand lines on the assumption that diversity permitted them to penetrate more retail outlets in any given area. And extensive distribution was said to be a key to high volume, given the ultimate trade paint consumer's propensity to buy paint from neighborhood stores.

To the extent that multi-plant production is paralleled by multi-unit sales organizations, significant savings due to integrated selling are unlikely. With only a few notable exceptions, multi-plant companies in our twelve-industry sample appeared to enjoy at best only very minor sales force deployment economies compared to small producers with sales staffs well adapted to their production volume. One exception, as we have seen, is cigarettes. Antifriction bearings might also be an exception. Broad-line manufacturers claimed some advantage because their field sales engineers were able to satisfy the full spectrum of machinery makers' needs and they therefore had a higher probability of making a sale, particularly on visits to small potential customers. Two broad-line manufacturers which had consummated significant mergers stated that they had realized appreciable cost savings by streamlining their consolidated sales engineering organizations. Nevertheless, the ability of salesmen to sell a broad line is constrained by the need for focus. It appears sufficient to offer a full line within one of the three main categories—ball, roller, or tapered bearings—and even then, a partial-line producer did not consider itself to be seriously handicapped in its sales representation function. Finally, steel producers asserted that operating more than one (typically small) specialty (stainless or tool) steel plant permits distinct economies in maintaining a sales force in export markets. Similar statements were made by textile manufacturers. No such advantages were claimed for the home markets.

To sum up, the field sales representation advantages of multi-plant size appear to be fairly significant in the cigarette industry; of modest importance in antifriction bearings, shoes, and some export activities; and characteristically negligible in the other industries.

The multi-plant operator may also benefit because customers prefer dealing with broad-line suppliers or firms serving the whole national market. Our interviews revealed that such preferences were of some importance in the refrigerator, shoe, fabric, auto battery, and bearing industries. There were three main reasons. For one, many dealers find it either more convenient or more conducive to maintaining a strong image to carry a full line of one or more manufacturers' products. This phenomenon is encountered among refrigerator, auto battery, and (at least within coherent product line bounds) shoe retailers and general-line bearing wholesalers. Second, appliance makers can better afford to maintain repair centers in most sizeable cities if they offer a broad line (including white goods other than refrigerators), and the existence of such centers enhances access to retail outlets unable or unwilling to provide their own service. Third, more homebuilder sales can be won when refrigerator makers coordinate the designs of several kitchen appliances, and textile manufacturers found it advantageous to offer design-coordinated decorative fabric lines ranging from pillowcases and curtains through rugs. Still there are ways by which narrow-line firms can escape such preferences—for example, by seeking out that subset of dealers without broad-line preferences, by offering price discounts sufficient to induce middlemen to do their own coordination or repair, and by filling out their lines through purchases from other producers or selling their narrow line for labeling by large chain buyers. With any of these escapes firms may achieve viability, but usually they sacrifice either expansion potential or profit margin compared to broad-line suppliers.

Finally, a word must be said about the relationship between vertical integration, multi-plant operation and access to distribution channels. In the petroleum refining, paint, and shoe industries, there is a substantial to moderate amount of vertical integration by manufacturers into retailing; in refrigerators there are small amounts. In cement, some manufacturers have integrated downstream into ready-mix and concrete products applications; and certain weavers have integrated into converting (end-product manufacturing). This integration typically has some tendency to foreclose channels of distribution to independent producers. Integrated gasoline, paint, and ready-mix outlets exhibit strong biases toward their upstream affiliates' output; textile converters and shoe stores modest preferences. But with few prominent exceptions, such integration has not prevented nonintegrated firms from finding independent distribution outlets. And when for either defensive or offensive reasons downstream integration into distribution has appeared desirable, efficient single-plant cement makers, paint firms, and refiners have suffered no noteworthy handicaps playing the game against much larger multi-plant enterprises. Indeed, small regional paint producers have been among the most vigorous retail chain operators; and regional gasoline marketers like Hess, Marathon, and Clark have more than held their own in opening up new stations. Vertical integration by the automobile manufacturers into the production and distribution of bearings (by General Motors and Renault) and batteries is quite another matter. It appears next to impossible for an independent to sell General Motors a standard original equipment battery in the United States, and it is hard to sell replacement batteries through GM's franchised dealer network.[14] General Motors evidently buys at least some special types of bearings from outside suppliers, but overcoming the preference for the company's own New Departure-Hyatt products was said to be difficult. To crack those markets, multi-plant operation spanning automobile manufacturing may be necessary. But these are pathological cases which we must either dismiss as such or remand to the antitrust authorities.

In sum, multi-plant size confers important distribution channel access advantages in the refrigerator and antifriction bearing industries and

14. For an excellent analysis of the automobile companies' incentives to integrate into parts production, see Robert Crandall, "Vertical Integration into the Market for Repair Parts in the United States Automobile Industry," *Journal of Industrial Economics*, 16 (July 1968), 212–234.

modest advantages in fabrics, shoes, and (ignoring the original auto parts equipment market) batteries. In the other seven industries, specialists either compete for outlets with nationwide manufacturers on evenly matched terms, or the requirements of the market are sufficiently heterogeneous to give single-plant producers an array of distribution strategies as attractive or nearly as attractive as those open to multi-plant operators.

It would be pleasant if we could conclude by enunciating precise unequivocal estimates of the promotional cost savings and price differentials attributable to varying degrees of multi-plant operation in our twelve industries. That, however, is not in the cards. The world is too complicated. The essence of product differentiation is imparting some slope to one's demand curve so that a choice can be made between selling small quantities at a relatively high price or larger quantities at lower prices. Thus, point estimates of product differentiation advantages are impossible. Moreover, tastes and market conditions are sufficiently diverse that many different product differentiation strategies prove viable, each in its particular niche. Every firm has its gimmick, whether it be Pure Rocky Mountain Spring Water or owning the New York Mets or buying up pubs or having the biggest tent and the largest oompah band at Oktoberfest, and many of them work. Consequently, the relationship between multi-plant size and promotional advantages exudes statistical "noise," and except in strong cases it can be described only crudely and impressionistically.

Table 7.3 presents our summary assessment. Perhaps its most prominent feature is the relative scarcity of industries in which large multi-plant operators are found to enjoy major promotional advantages. To be sure, product differentiation was very important in many of our industries. In six—brewing, cigarettes, textiles, petroleum refining, refrigerators, and shoes—an overwhelming majority of our North American interviewees agreed that marketing was a much more important dimension of business strategy than production. If promotional and product image efforts go astray, efficient production would not be sufficient to save the day. Yet firms with only a single MOS plant are by no means barred from success in the product differentiation arena. In several cases they can promote their products on virtually equal terms, realizing most or all promotional scale economies; in others they can find sizeable market segments in which to operate profitably despite a promotional handicap. Only in brewing, cigarettes, refrigerators, bearings, shoes, and perhaps petroleum refining and broad-woven fabrics do single-plant enterprises face more than slight promotional handicaps, and for five of these our judgments span a range of uncertainty because marketing strategies exist

Table 7.3. Summary of the Promotional Advantages Associated with Multi-Plant Size.

Industry	How seriously disadvantaged are efficient single-plant producers?	Main sources of multi-plant promotional advantages	How many MOS plants needed to achieve all significant promotional advantages in U.S. market?	Percentage of U.S. market required, circa 1967
Beer brewing	Slightly to severely	National brand image, choice of media.	Possibly one, but as many as five	3-17
Cigarettes	Slightly to moderately	Sales force deployment, advertising economies.	Two for advertising; up to four for sales force deployment	12-27
Fabric weaving	Slightly to moderately	Broad-line preferences, advertising economies.	As many as twenty	Up to 6
Paints (trade)	Slightly	National brand image, choice of media.	Three or four	4-6
Petroleum refining	Slightly to moderately	National brand image, choice of media. Broad-line preferences,	One to four	2-8
Shoes	Moderately	sales force deployment, national brand image, advertising economies.	Four to eight	1-2
Glass bottles	Negligibly	None.	One	1.5
Cement	Negligibly	None.	One	1.7
Ordinary steel	Negligibly	Nationwide customer ties.	Four	2.5-10
Bearings	Moderately	Broad-line preferences, sales force deployment.	Four to eight	6-11
Refrigerators	Slightly to severely	National brand image, broad-line preferences, service networks.	As many as twelve, including other appliances	c. 30
Automobile batteries	Slightly	Broad-line, national supply preferences.	Five	10

by which the relatively small but efficient producer can thrive. However, in refrigerators and (less confidently) bearings the promotional and distribution channel access advantages of size appear sufficently compelling that they enable multi-plant firms to dominate all but small market segments, at least in the very large U.S. market.

That multi-plant enterprises realize promotional economies owing to their size does not necessarily mean that society gains. Some of the benefits flowing from size—for example, the price premium on nationally branded paint or the high markups prevailing on replacement auto bearings—are strictly private and pecuniary, reflecting a transfer of income from the consuming public to particular sellers. Some, such as the salesman's travel cost savings realized by multi-plant shoe companies, are real and, given the competitive structure of the shoe industry, they may well be passed along to the consumer in the form of lower average prices. Many and perhaps most lie in that grey area where difficult value judgments intrude. Does John Q. Consumer get 2 cents worth of satisfaction drinking a bottle of Budweiser rather than the local brewery's product? Is his wife better off having paid $10 more to be sure her refrigerator is Westinghouse instead of the private-label model made by the same plant? Is society's welfare enhanced because the Reynolds man comes in twice a week to spruce up the supermarket's Winston display rack, while the Lorillard man makes a visit only every other week? Economists are inclined to think not, but economists are strange creatures, so we shall not attempt to impose our values.

Economies from Multi-Plant Procurement

Size may also confer advantages in the procurement of raw materials and parts. This is a sensitive issue for some firms because of Robinson-Patman Act prosecution fears and the desire not to let rivals know about secret concessions. We were inclined not to jeopardize other interview objectives to press hard for purchasing-savings data. The interviews nevertheless yielded a considerable amount of information on some of the industries.

Economies of large-scale purchasing are very important in the paint industry. They were said by several U.S. sources to be the most significant advantage large producers have over small. One large company estimated its total procurement concessions as roughly 5 percent of sales. However, not all these savings can be credited to multi-plant operation. A company with one MOS plant can do about as well as much larger firms playing off one seller against the others in procuring solvents, resins, and (to a lesser degree) containers. Pigments, whose costs averaged 9.5 percent of the U.S. paint manufacturers' sales in 1967, are probably the main exception. In the United States and Canada (but not in Western Europe) the pricing discipline of pigment producers was reported to be very firm, so it was difficult to extract discounts on more than truckload quantities, which even moderate-sized paint manufacturers can afford.[15] As a result the larger paint companies have integrated backward into pigment production, realizing significant savings on the high-volume items, although the profitability of manufacturing low-volume pigments at inefficiently small scales was said to be dubious. Only the multi-plant paint companies have found it feasible to produce their own pigments, so the savings must be credited to size beyond the single-plant threshold. Making one's own paint cans was reported also to confer savings beyond those realized accepting the best prices can makers would offer. To do so economically evidently requires a volume approaching 20 to 30 million gallons per year.

Our interviews indicated that large multi-plant weaving firms enjoyed some raw material cost savings not accessible to their smaller rivals. These took two forms. First, owing to the excess capacity with which they were burdened during the 1960s, American synthetic fiber manufacturers were granting price concessions to large buyers but apparently not to small. Also, sundry bargains are available if one is able to shop around in the world fiber markets, but a company with only one or two weaving mills cannot afford to invest the manpower and money to seek them out. The savings associated with these two advantages of large-scale buying appear to be modest.

For the shoe industry the evidence is mixed. Multi-plant firms evidently realize modest material and parts savings relative to single-plant companies located away from the main shoe manufacturing centers. However, experienced entrepreneurs running single-plant firms in such leather-goods industry centers as St. Louis and Boston were said "to turn all sorts of deals" that the purchasing staff of larger corporations simply wouldn't find. A different but apparently effective approach was taken by the numerous small firms around the German shoemaking center Pirmasens; they organized a collective agency to procure their supplies. Also, many small independent shoemakers are apparently able to purchase leather with minor defects and keep their production operations sufficiently flexible to cut around the defects—a feat the large organizations can seldom manage. When these skills and the external economies of being in a leather-goods center coincide, single-plant firms may bear no materials purchasing cost penalty at all.

15. A one million gallon per year producer uses roughly one 15 ton truckload of pigments per week.

Significant pecuniary and real purchasing economies are observed in refrigerator manufacturing. A European firm producing 50,000 units per year estimated its materials cost disadvantage to be 2 or 3 percent compared to a competitor with twice that volume. Another firm making 250,000 units believed that it saved 1–2 percent by purchasing steel, plasticizers, and other materials on a pooled basis with its other appliances rather than separately. Materials cost savings evidently persist all the way out to plant volumes of one million units per year, although at that scale the main economies appear to stem more from producing one's own small parts internally rather than buying them, with resultant transportation, breakage, and order cost savings. It is not clear whether such economies would survive in a multi-plant framework if interplant shipping of parts were required.

In brewing and batteries there are economies of larger scale procurement up to the volume of an MOS plant, but beyond that scale they are probably negligible. Our interviews yielded little evidence on procurement relationships in the cigarette, cement, petroleum refining, bottle, steel, and bearing industries. For none of the six was there reason to believe that significant procurement economies of the orthodox variety are realized beyond the scale of a single MOS plant. However, possible exceptions concerning access to crude oil, iron ore, and coal supplies will be noted in the next section.

Thus, although economies of large-scale materials procurement are important in several industries, most can be realized by a single MOS plant. Only in the paint, fabrics, and shoe industries do advantages of any significance persist into the range of multi-plant operation. Most of the economies gained in the multi-plant size bracket appear to be largely pecuniary in nature. That large U.S. paint companies save by producing their own pigments is the result of oligopolistic pricing in the pigment industry, not real savings, and social costs may actually be increased by the decisions of paint makers to produce their own specialty pigments in suboptimal quantities. We are unable to say whether or to what extent the savings associated with large-scale materials procurement are passed along to consumers in the form of lower product prices.

Vertical Integration and the Least Common Multiple

When the advantages of vertical integration into component or material production are compelling, and when the integrated activity's minimum optimal scale exceeds the scale of an optimal main-line plant, the minimum optimal size of an integrated firm—that is, of a firm encompassing the "least common multiple" combination of plants at the various vertical stages—may be considerably larger than the size of a firm operating a single MOS main-line plant. In this section we explore the extent to which pressures toward vertical integration push firm size beyond the scale of an MOS plant. We also consider the reasons for these pressures, for example, whether they reflect real or pecuniary integration economies, and why the same result cannot be achieved through arm's length transactions in the market.

The petroleum refining industry exhibits a high degree of integration from crude oil extraction through pipeline and tanker ownership to the operation of retail gasoline stations. In the United States, but less so in Western Europe, regional cartelization and the special income tax treatment accorded both domestic and foreign crude extraction have created incentives to be integrated backward into crude operations. The tax structure makes it advantageous to record as much of one's profit as possible at the crude stage, and the fully integrated major oil firms who exercise price leadership in the U.S. crude market were said, at least before the dramatic changes of the early 1970s, to be content to run their refinery and distribution operations on a break-even basis in order to generate volume supporting the profits reported on crude production.[16] This can make life difficult for nonintegrated refiners. When crude supplies were abundant relative to demand at quasi-collusive posted prices, the nimble nonintegrated refiner could bargain for special deals and sustain a profitable existence. But when the crude market is tight, the nonintegrated firm runs a risk of being squeezed between high crude prices and sticky refined products prices, or it may have trouble getting enough crude oil to keep its refining units operating.[17]

To protect themselves against such a squeeze refiners have an incentive to integrate backward. This, however, is not easy. Oil wildcatting can be done at small scales, but to engage in crude exploration and extraction on a scale sufficient to supply the better part of a good-sized refinery's requirements demands, at least under recent U.S. domestic reserve conditions, an investment about as large as the investment in a refinery.[18]

16. See the testimony of Alfred E. Kahn in the U.S., Senate, Subcommittee on Antitrust and Monopoly, *Hearings, Governmental Intervention in the Market Mechanism: The Petroleum Industry*, Part 1, "Economists' Views," 91st Cong., 1st Sess., March 1969, pp. 132–142. For an updated analysis, see the Federal Trade Commission staff report in U.S., Senate, Government Operations Committee, Permanent Subcommittee on Investigations, *Investigation of the Petroleum Industry*, 93rd Cong., 1st Sess., July 1973, pp. 20–21.

17. Cf. "A Gas Pinch Hurts the Independents," *Business Week*, November 18, 1972, p. 21.

18. See, e.g., "Offshore Total-Project Approach Is Best," *Oil and Gas Journal* (September 15, 1969), pp. 89–93; "Independents Search for Entry Offshore," *Oil and Gas Journal* (November 6, 1967), pp. 57–58; "Costs Soar as Drillers Tackle Deeper Waters," *Oil and Gas Journal* (June 20, 1966), pp. 162–167; "Wildcatters Face 11 Year Payout," *Oil and Gas Journal* (April 20, 1964), pp. 74–75; and "Offshore Oil Reshaping Industry," *New York Times*, February 12, 1967, pp. 1ff.

Although it is possible for a regional specialist operating only one refinery approaching minimum optimal scale to make the jump backwards into crude, such firms suffer some pecuniary disadvantage relative to large, integrated multi-plant companies owing to inferior ability to pool risks on the large (and generally highest-yield) off-shore exploration projects and because they are likely to face more severe credit rationing and pay higher capital costs. Joint ventures with other companies can provide a partial escape, but even so, many regional refiners have not found themselves able to integrate backward successfully, and they suffer a more perilous existence then their larger integrated rivals. The least common refining-crude exploration multiple in terms of risk minimization probably involves several efficient-sized refineries. This economy of scale, it must be reiterated, stems directly from market failure.

Integration by refiners into petrochemical production, in part to utilize refinery by-products more effectively, is also widespread. Transportation of feedstocks from one optimally located refinery to another to balance supplies with requirements internally is prohibitively costly under normal conditions, and so active regional feedstock markets exist. These were said to function competitively, so that multi-refinery operation conferred no advantages in utilizing by-products as petrochemical feedstocks. Thus, vertical integration into petrochemicals did not appear, at least under pre-1972 conditions, to render multi-refinery operation more attractive.

Our estimates of an MOS steel works have assumed integration from coke production through blast furnaces, converters, and hot rolling of basic shapes. Experience in the badly balanced French and British steel industries suggests that failure to integrate the later rolling mill stages, while seldom more costly in terms of reheating, does impose significant cross-shipping and coordination costs.

Integration into iron ore and coal mining is more problematic. For Europe, a sufficiently diverse set of iron ore supply sources exists so that steel producers felt no compulsion to integrate backward. Integration into domestic coal mining was considered a hindrance because of the generally high cost and/or poor quality of Continental and British coking coal.

In the United States, most of the better domestic iron ore has since 1900 been controlled by the largest steel companies and by mining firms with intricate financial ties to the leading steelmakers.[19] As in petroleum,

19. See Richard B. Mancke, "Iron Ore and Steel: A Case Study of the Economic Causes and Consequences of Vertical Integration," *Journal of Industrial Economics*, 20 (July 1972), 220–229; and Daniel R. Fusfeld, "Joint Subsidiaries in the Iron and Steel Industry," *American Economic Review*, 48 (May 1958), 578–587.

depletion tax provisions encourage taking one's profits at the ore mining stage if possible, and the oligopolistic structure of the mining industry gave ore sellers considerable pricing power. Pressure therefore existed to integrate backward to avoid an ore price squeeze. Exploiting the rich ore deposits of Labrador, Brazil, Australia, and West Africa has called for investments of hundreds of millions of dollars in railroads, ports, and new towns as well as on-site mining facilities. To be economical, such projects appear to require an ore output sufficient to satisfy at least two 4 million ton steel works. A project of this size exceeds both the needs and financial capacity of most single-plant steelmakers. However, drawing upon Southern Hemisphere ores fails to satisfy the needs of most existing U.S. steel mills, typically located so far away from deepwater ports that overseas ore cannot be supplied at acceptable transportation cost.

Following World War II, recognition of this constraint and the approaching exhaustion of high-grade domestic ore reserves induced advances in concentrating and pelletizing technology, permitting the economical exploitation of low-grade but abundant taconite deposits. Since ownership of those deposits has not been as highly concentrated as ownership of the earlier high-grade ore sources and since access to them is not foreclosed, the danger of a serious squeeze on nonintegrated steelmakers has diminished. Nevertheless, as a conditioned response to past difficulties or because of fears that history would repeat itself, most steelmakers felt compelled to integrate backward to secure their ore supplies. Accessible Minnesota, northern Michigan, and other North American taconite deposits can apparently be worked at acceptable cost on a scale not larger than the requirements of a 2 million ton, basic oxygen furnace-oriented steel works. This implied a mining and pelletizing investment on the order of $50 to $80 million at late 1960s' price levels, although modest scale economies may persist up to ore outputs consistent with steel production of ten million tons annually.[20] A venture at the lower end of this range can definitely be accommodated by an ordinary steelmaker operating one plant achieving all scale economies by mid-1960s' standards. Many companies have nonetheless chosen to enter ore mining through joint ventures, with a possible concomitant diminution of rivalrous attitudes.

Integration into coal mining is also considered advantageous by

20. See "Minnesota Votes Taconite Tax Lid: New Plants Set," *Wall Street Journal*, November 5, 1964, p. 4; "New Life for the Old Mesabi," *Magazine of Wall Street*, November 26, 1966, pp. 250ff.; and (for a list of pelletizing operations in North America along with joint venture details) "Iron Ore Pelletmakers Squeezed for Capacity," *Steel*, September 22, 1969, pp. 28–30.

American steel producers as a hedge against price fluctuations and to assure uninterrupted high-quality supplies. However, the minimum optimal scale of a coal mine is well below the scale of an efficient 1965-vintage steel works, and control of coal reserves has not been so concentrated as to preclude backward integration by smaller mills. Consequently, multi-plant steelmakers appear to have no special integration advantage.

Vertical integration of weaving mills with spinning and finishing (bleaching, dyeing, printing, flocking) activities is widespread, though its extent varies from nation to nation. Rough estimates by the British Textile Council of the percentage of cotton and synthetic fabric looms controlled during the late 1960s by integrated spinning/weaving companies are:[21]

Nation	Percent
United States	85
Canada	100
United Kingdom	36
France	50
West Germany	65
Sweden	"very large"

Despite a wave of vertical mergers during the early 1960s, England continued to trail in the extent of integration between spinning and weaving. Its position in textile finishing was similar. Our interviews with large British companies disclosed strong views that the lack of vertical integration was a significant cause of England's decline in world textile markets and that "verticalization" was the key to future success. Vertical integration does indeed offer real advantages, but the original British problem also had special characteristics. Notably, the various stages were strongly cartelized before the Restrictive Practices Court intervened in 1959, and as a result a classic case of pyramided monopolistic price distortions existed. Economic theory shows that vertical integration can eliminate such distortions, although a healthy dose of competition could have the same effect.[22] The cartels also had more subtle efficiency effects not discussed in theory textbooks. For example, the finishing cartels set prices on the assumption of single-shift operation, and since entry and investment were premised on that assumption, sufficient excess capacity

21. The Textile Council, *Cotton and Allied Textiles: A Report on Present Performance and Future Prospects*, vol. I (Manchester, Eng., 1969), p. 159.

22. See Joseph J. Spengler, "Vertical Integration and Antitrust Policy," *Journal of Political Economy*, 58 (August 1950), 347–352; and F. M. Scherer, *Industrial Market Structure and Economic Performance* (Chicago: Rand McNally, 1970), pp. 242–251.

developed to render it valid. The weaving firms which later acquired finishing plants closed many of them down and achieved much higher levels of capacity utilization in those remaining. Also, the rigidity of the price system made it difficult for weavers and converters to establish any rational system of finishing shop scheduling priorities, so rush orders frequently were processed on the same basis as routine jobs. This problem too could be corrected by direct managerial intervention in a vertically integrated production structure.

Our interviews in other nations yielded considerable evidence on textile cases much less pathological than that of Britain. Nowhere else did we encounter comparable enthusiasm over the virtues of vertical integration, but nowhere else was the initial situation as badly distorted as in Britain. Every interview nonetheless provided evidence that the vertical integration of spinning, weaving, and finishing affords real planning and coordination benefits.

A benefit stressed by nearly every respondent was the control vertical integration gave over quality. Minute differences in the raw material, twist, or the like can apparently have large repercussions on the finished cloth. Coordinating such production stage interrelationships and controlling overall quality were said to be easier in an integrated operation, though most interviewees observed that arm's-length relations could also be made to work under favorable conditions. Integration was considered particularly advantageous when outside suppliers were also competitors at another stage and when customers placed a premium on product uniformity, for instance, in dyeing, over time.

It is clear, however, that integration has costs in the form of inflexibility, and these increase with the tightness of interstage ties. For example, the optimal balance of equipment in a spinning shed is extremely sensitive to the "count" of the yarn spun. A thin yarn (high count) requires much more spindle capacity in relation to carding capacity than a thick yarn; heavy cloth needs more carding capacity in relation to loom capacity than light cloth. If demand variations compel significant changes over time in the cloth weaving mix, it becomes very difficult to maintain balance in integrated spinning-weaving mills—the more so, the more intensively one tries to use one's equipment, since working extra shifts on bottleneck operations is a standard remedy for mill imbalances. When many different counts and types of yarn are to be woven in a single shed or when yarn count requirements are expected to be unstable over time, it may be better to locate spinning in separate mills in the hope that the fluctuating yarn demands of several weaving sheds will tend to average out over several spinning mills. When the demand mix is expected to be moderately stable, many producers consider the best approach to be integrating the bulk of yarn production physically with weaving, having a specialty yarn mill or two serving low-volume requirements of the various weaving sheds, and/or "rounding off the edges" by buying some yarn from independent spinners and selling to other weavers yarn made with excess capacity.

All this has much to do with our ultimate concern: the least common multiple for a vertically integrated weaving firm. One optimal spinning mill produces about the right amount of yarn to feed a single optimal weaving mill, but balance is the big problem. Under the law of large numbers, a firm is likely to approach internal balance more closely in the face of randomly changing demands if it has numerous products and mills making them. This suggests that optimal balance may involve a very large least common multiple. But all the producers to whom we spoke argued that one could not expect to come anywhere close to perfect internal balance, and attempts to do so were apt to cause more problems than they solved. The largest firms in particular appear to be no more successful in eliminating imbalances than companies with only a few weaving mills of efficient size. Furthermore, market transactions were reported to be fairly effective in rounding off the edges, despite the difficulties of arm's-length coordination and the risk that yarns for which one has excess capacity are apt to be in excess supply everywhere. As a result, our interviews strongly suggested, firms with only three to five MOS weaving mills generally suffer no perceptible spinning/weaving balance disadvantages compared to much larger companies.

Integration between weaving and finishing is not greatly dissimilar, though it is complicated by the tremendous diversity of finishing processes and the large scale of certain processes. Given random fluctuations in the demand for various types of finishing, one might expect internal balance to be better when numerous weaving mills are feeding their output into a number of finishing mills. But actually executing such a balancing operation was said to be very difficult, especially in the decentralized organizational structure needed to keep a large textile firm responsive to market changes. When demand is strong, small firms often find it possible to round out the edges of their finishing operations by accepting small commission jobs. When business is bad generally, the largest producers evidently experience about as much difficulty as the small finding jobs to maintain balance. Thus, resort at the margin to competitively functioning finishing markets equalizes what might otherwise be an advantage of multi-plant operation, and this holds the least common multiple at a scale somewhere on the order of three to eight weaving mills served by one-third to one-half as many integrated finishing plants. Much smaller weavers can also maintain balance under special circumstances, notably, when they specialize in style-sensitive fabrics for which flexible access to a diversity of commission finishing sources is more important than getting the lowest possible price at any moment in time.

How well markets are working also affects vertical integration incentives in the refrigerator industry. The main problem area is the compressor, the most costly single component, representing from 32 to 40 percent of total manufacturing costs for small, stripped-down European refrigerators but a smaller fraction for the larger North American models. The minimum optimal scale for compressor production entails an output of two or three million units per year, not necessarily of the same design— well above the needs of a single MOS refrigerator assembly plant and indeed more than the total national demand of all but the very large U.S. market. Modest scale economy sacrifices are experienced in plants with only one production line making roughly one million units per year of a single basic size. At still smaller scales, unit costs rise rapidly. We learned of no refrigerator assemblers with volumes below 200,000 units per year who were producing their own compressors in 1970, and those in the half million unit range with integrated compressor production were said to labor under distinct cost disadvantages relative to firms buying at favorable prices from independent compressor makers. However, buying outside was considered a fragile advantage. The number of independent compressor suppliers is very small; the nonintegrated firms to whom we talked typically faced only two or three real alternatives. Some were deeply concerned over the trend toward mergers among European refrigerator and compressor makers during the late 1960s. They feared that further mergers could leave them with only a single independent source, undermining their bargaining power, or force them to buy from competing refrigerator assemblers. In either case a price squeeze could result. Should the market fail in this way, the minimum optimal scale for refrigerator assembly would be raised to at least one million units and (if a broad range of sizes is to be offered) perhaps even two million units per year.

As we have seen earlier, a similar MOS-increasing propensity can be traced to the scale relationships between pigments and paints, at least in the U.S. market, where price competition among pigment suppliers has been languid. The filling of aerosol spray paint cans also involves scale economies well beyond the requirements of broad-line paint producers with one MOS plant or even several. In this case, however, paint companies reported no serious qualms about shipping their paint in bulk to independent aerosol fillers or even to direct competitors for filling and reshipping. It was unclear whether this arrangement was satisfactory because competition among the few aerosol can fillers was sufficiently vigorous or because the aerosol lines were too small to have any strategic importance in the struggle for overall market position, so that a squeeze would be fruitless.

In shoe manufacturing there are a few operations with scales larger than the output of an MOS shoe assembly plant. These include certain injection molding activities and the automatic cutting of soles, insoles, and other parts from synthetic materials meeting uniform size and quality specifications. Such operations are often located at specialist plants. Interviewees reported that there were slight scheduling and coordination advantages in securing such services from one's own plants as opposed to the market. Still, the impact of integrating these activities on the least common multiple is not great. The fastest automatic cutting machine of which we learned provided stock for some 8000 pairs of shoes per day, or the approximate output of two optimal plants. In the other activities ancillary to shoe manufacturing such as tanning, special chemicals production, and metal parts fabrication, integration was said to be neither necessary nor important. The relevant supply industries function competitively.[23] In fact, they yielded lower returns on capital during the 1960s than the cutoff one large shoe manufacturer imposed in its own investment decisions.

In none of the other industries did vertical integration imperatives significantly affect the least common multiple, either because high scale economy inputs could be fitted into the operations of a single MOS plant or because critical component or material supplies were available in the market on satisfactory terms.

We see then that the workability of competition in component and material supply markets is a crucial variable determining whether the least common efficient plant multiple is pushed upward by the need to integrate vertically. When markets function competitively, vertical integration is unnecessary even when the scale of certain activities exceeds by a considerable margin the scale of a main-line production plant. Purchases in the open market bridge the gap. But when there is market failure owing to scale economies necessitating monopoly or tight oligopoly, governmental intervention (as in crude oil), or any other cause, companies may be driven to multi-plant operation to achieve vertical balance; or they may suffer a cost and profit disadvantage relative to

23. Because supply conditions in the Soviet Union are much less reliable, there are much stronger incentives for shoemaking enterprises to integrate backward, and this increases the advantages of multi-plant operation. See Alice C. Gorlin, "Soviet Firms and the Rationalization of the Shoe Industry of the USSR," unpub. diss., University of Michigan, 1972.

rivals big, farsighted, and/or lucky enough to control the supply of an important input. In the United States, less secure or more costly access to significant inputs has imposed handicaps on nonintegrated single-plant firms in the petroleum refining, steel, paint, and possibly the refrigerator industries. Difficulties of coordinating multi-stage production relationships through arm's-length market transactions have also induced vertical integration and increases in the least common multiple, particularly in textile manufacturing. Still, the existence of workably competitive interstage textile markets has made it unnecessary to seek perfect vertical balance internally, thereby preventing the least common multiple from exploding to high levels of multi-plant operation.

Multi-Plant Transportation Cost Economies

Under certain circumstances transportation costs can be reduced through multi-plant operation. There are two main possibilities. First, multi-plant firms may be able to operate their own transport fleets and schedule them more efficiently by taking into account interactions between plants. Second, the shipments of multiple plants might be pooled to achieve larger average loads and hence lower rates.

Petroleum companies have extensive integrated water transportation and pipeline facilities, the latter typically on a joint venture basis, and many steelmakers operate ore ships linking mines with blast furnace works. Unfortunately, our interviews provided almost no information on the implications of multi-plant operation for such activities. A cement manufacturer forced into barge ownership by the lack of suitable independently owned equipment said it was able to schedule its barges more intensively by having them serve several plants, but that common carriers might achieve even better utilization if they had the necessary equipment and deployed it to serve all water-based cement companies.

The integration of manufacturers into private trucking is attributable in no small measure to market failure. The value-of-service pricing approach of common motor freight carriers, the rigidity of the U.S. rate regulation system, and the regulatory restrictions placed on common carrier operating routes have created incentives for shippers to develop their own trucking fleets, even though common carriers might be able to carry the freight at lower cost than private trucks in a less constrained competitive regime owing to their ability to tap diverse sources of traffic and secure fuller backhaul loads.[24] Despite these problems, the amount of integration into private trucking has for a number of reasons been quite

24. See Walter Y. Oi and Arthur P. Hurter, *Economics of Private Truck Transportation* (Dubuque: Brown, 1965), esp. chaps. 2 and 5.

small in several of our sample industries, notably, cigarettes, steel, refrigerators, bearings, and cement.

Among industries with more substantial amounts of integrated shipment, the extent to which multi-plant size affords cost advantages varies from case to case. In paints, brewing, and batteries, integrated fleets tended to be assigned to and operated autarkically by individual plants, suggesting minimal advantages of multi-plant control. A medium-sized textile company reported, on the other hand, that it had saved 30 percent relative to common carrier shipping costs by owning its own trucks and carefully scheduling them to take full advantage of interplant materials flows, so that almost every truck moved fully loaded. Likewise, an MOS shoe plant completes only about three to five tons of shoes per day. The output of several such plants must be pooled to load trucks efficiently for regular runs to key forwarding gateways such as Chicago, St. Louis, and Newark. Still, a shoe manufacturer with a particularly impressive integrated trucking system stated that it could schedule its fleet as efficiently at a volume of five or six million pairs per year as at twenty-five million pairs. It appears that, in at least a few cases, scheduling an integrated transport fleet to meet the needs of a multi-plant production network yields savings beyond those realizable in a single-plant framework, but the extent of multi-plant operation required is often modest and the integrated approach may be only a second-best solution reflecting the absence of competitive common carriage.

The multi-plant firm may also benefit by consolidating the output of its plants and amassing larger shipments, thereby spreading over a larger volume the costs of pickup, delivery, and administration. Such costs vary little with volume, at least on relatively small shipments, and are priced accordingly in common carriers' less-than-truckload rate structures.

The shoe industry provides by far the most important illustration. Most shoe companies serve hundreds of retail outlets. The typical multi-plant manufacturer consolidates all its shoes of some general class (for example, men's vs. women's) in a single warehouse to achieve maximum inventory control and dispatches combined truckloads from its warehouses to gateway terminals, where they are broken down for final shipment and delivery to customers. It is at the final shipment stage that the principal advantages of consolidation arise, though, as noted above, there are also gains from sending fully loaded trucks to the gateways. A well-located family shoe store sells approximately 100 pairs of men's shoes and 300 pairs of women's shoes per week on the average. Frequent replacement of stock is important if sales are not to be lost. If weekly replacement is attempted, as was the objective of two interviewees with strong ties to their retail outlets, the average shipment from a men's shoe warehouse will be about 250 pounds (100 pairs times 2½ pounds per pair) if the manufacturer supplies its outlets' total requirements but only 83 pounds if it covers a third of its customers' men's shoe needs. To span all or most of customers' needs calls for a broad line which, given specialization imperatives to be analyzed later, almost always implies the operation of five or more plants. On a 500-mile shipment in 1970 of medium-price men's shoes from St. Louis to retail stores in Detroit, freight charges averaged roughly 1.9 percent of wholesale value in 100-pair lots but 3.35 percent on an order of 33 pairs. This difference of approximately 1.5 percent on product value defines a rough upper limit on the penalties of producing and shipping less than a broad line, since less frequent shipment is an alternative means of saving freight costs (penalized, to be sure, by the loss of sales owing to out-of-stock situations) and since orders much smaller than 33 pairs can often be shipped more economically by parcel post or express.

Extending the logic, one might expect shoe manufacturers to centralize their inventories of *all* shoe types to achieve maximum shipment pooling. This was done by the smallest firms we interviewed, with from one to six MOS plants. Larger companies did not do so for at least four reasons. First, truck freight rate structures are graduated so that there is little or no advantage in pooling between shipment weights of 150 to 700 pounds. Second, different price, style, and sex lines are often purchased by different retail outlets and therefore are not always susceptible to shipment pooling. Third, retailers were said not to like very large shipments because they often lack storage space and are not always able to unpack the cartons quickly. Fourth, there may be diseconomies in maintaining a very large warehouse: physical movements become excessively long and items are more apt to get lost. Consequently, the shipment pooling advantages of multi-plant operation appear to taper off in the neighborhood of five to eight efficient-sized shoe plants.

We had expected to discover similar multi-plant economies in the cigarette industry,[25] but the evidence indicates otherwise. The U.S. cigarette manufacturers ship most of their output to some fifty or more bonded warehouses which then reship them to wholesalers and retailers. Each plant ships directly to the warehouses; unlike shoes, there is no preliminary consolidation and therefore no opportunity to pool the shipments of multiple plants. Pooling economies do exist at the individual plant level; with a large volume, a plant has a better chance of dispatching full carloads or truckloads. This is one factor pushing the

25. See Joe S. Bain, *Barriers to New Competition* (Cambridge: Harvard University Press, 1956), pp. 243–244 and 256.

estimated minimum optimal scale to a capacity of 40 billion cigarettes per year, although the manufacturers' transportation costs total only about one percent of pre-excise wholesale revenues. Very slight pooling economies continue out to single-plant volumes as high as that of Reynolds' Winston-Salem complex.

A special kind of pooling economy is realized when several different types of home appliances are produced at a single plant or cluster of plants. With several appliances shipped from a common warehouse it is possible to serve more customers in full carload quantities. Also, the U.S. railroads offer lower rates per hundredweight for mixed shipments of refrigerators and smaller appliances because the smaller units can be stacked on top of the refrigerators, using otherwise wasted headroom. A third advantage is the opportunity to utilize warehouse space more fully, since the seasonal peaks for refrigerators and air conditioners fall in the summertime while dishwasher demand peaks before Christmas.

Among the other industries covered by our sample, a paint producer reported slight savings from stacking paint cans atop bags of pigments in mixed shipments. A bearing manufacturer said that modest transport cost and warehousing economies were realized when two different automobile replacement bearing lines at diverse plants were pooled. In the remaining industries the advantages of multi-plant shipment pooling appeared to be either negligible or nonexistent.[26] Thus, only in shoes, refrigerators, bearings, and paints were multi-plant nonintegrated shipment pooling economies discernible, and in the last two industries the savings were evidently quite small in relation to total production and distribution costs.

The Economies of Massed Reserves

Another potential advantage of multi-plant firms is the ability to realize "economies of massed reserves,"[27] averaging out random or periodic demand fluctuations and production deviations and hence holding smaller reserves against them. There are numerous variants: hedging against random demand fluctuations and unexpected production breakdowns, balancing disparate seasonal variations and scheduled main-

26. For an analysis of the savings due to shipping gasoline to exclusive as compared to nonexclusive retail stations, see the U.K. Monopolies Commission, *Petrol: A Report on the Supply of Petrol to Retailers in the United Kingdom* (London: HMSO, 1965), pp. 90–92, 117–120, and 137–141. Here again there is no essential connection to multi-plant operation.

27. The concept was originally developed and named by E. A. G. Robinson in his classic treatise, *The Structure of Competitive Industry*, rev. ed. (Chicago: University of Chicago Press, 1958), pp. 26–27.

tenance shutdowns, protecting one's sales position against strikes and fires, pooling repair staffs to even out their workload, imparting greater flexibility to short-run production responses, and averaging out the risks of localized price wars or erroneous marketing decisions.

Demand and Production Fluctuations

Although one cannot by definition predict when random demand peaks or production failures will occur, the experienced producer knows that they will happen and usually has some notion of their frequency distribution. The problem is, how to make the best of them? One way is to engage in flexible peak-load pricing, but this was rare in the industries we studied. Alternatives include building reserve capacity and holding hedge inventories. Tradeoffs can be made among the alternatives; for example, by carrying somewhat more inventory a firm can satisfy the same quantity of demand under given prices with less reserve capacity. If, however, it operates several plants, and if the peaks or shutdowns are more or less randomly distributed over time, another alternative exists, for there is a good chance statistically that some plants will be under-taxed just when others are unable to fill all their orders, and those in the first category can help out those in the second, perhaps (in a geograph-ically decentralized production structure) at some additional transporta-tion cost. What exists then is a potential multiple-way tradeoff among order sacrifices, inventory carrying costs, excess capacity costs, trans-portation costs, and possible specialization losses. The firm with multiple plants has more degrees of freedom in this tradeoff than the single-plant firm, and if random deviations can be averaged out, it ought to benefit— for instance, by being able to maintain a lower margin of reserve capacity or smaller inventories, ceteris paribus. If demand at the several plants has predictable but disparate seasonal patterns, similar peak-spreading should be possible. Likewise, a multi-plant posture may permit smaller inventory buildups against planned plant maintenance shutdowns.

Transportation costs are one component of this tradeoff, and it is useful to distinguish between commodities with low shipping costs in relation to product value and those at the opposite pole. Cement occupies one extreme. Most cement industry interviewees indicated that the ad-vantages of multi-plant peak-spreading were very minor, primarily because transportation costs are too high to permit interterritorial shipping except in the most pressing situations. Peak-spreading inter-actions did occur at the fringes of certain plants' territories, but they usually were confined to pairs or trios straddling some important market. The availability of good water transportation and unusually close spacing of affiliated plants tended to increase the amount of peak-spreading, but even in the most extreme case identified, only 4 percent of a firm's output crossed natural territorial boundaries in an average year. Factors other than high shipping costs limiting the amount of multi-plant interaction included the uniformity of seasonal patterns within major European nations, the preference of some cement users for a particular mill's output because there are small interplant variations in chemical properties and color, and the possibility of buying cement in bulk from nearby rivals (albeit at prices higher than the marginal cost of a plant operating below capacity) to cover unexpected kiln shutdowns.

Glass bottles also have high transport costs in relation to product value. Again, those costs were found to constrain severely the opportunities for interplant peak-spreading. The long time required to duplicate molds, differences in production know-how which lead to cost variations as high as 25 percent for a given bottle between two plants, customer preferences for the quality assured by a particular plant, and a tendency for peak demands to coincide at all plants were other limiting influences. Most of the companies interviewed said they did only a small amount of territorial job reallocation to spread peaks and cover glass tank shutdowns, almost always between pairs or trios of plants clustered in an important market area.

Only slight variations on this theme were encountered in the brewing industry. Seasonal patterns are quite uniform in the Western European nations, so all plants and companies tend to be simultaneously affected by demand changes. In the United States the regular seasonal peaks are coincident though not of uniform magnitude between north and south. This combined with the high cost of shipping and relatively low cost of holding inventories inhibits interplant peak-spreading. Heat wave peaks come so suddenly and unexpectedly that they must be met from inventories, although replenishment was said to be somewhat more flexible in a multi-plant framework, and one large multi-plant brewer claimed it was therefore able to maintain slightly lower capacity reserves.

In petroleum refining, the impression we gained was one of surprisingly modest massed reserve economies. According to one of the largest refiners, the territories served by a single refinery are often sufficiently large that most truly random demand fluctuations damp out internally; not much unsystematic residual variation remains between natural plant markets. Multi-plant nationwide operation does afford some advantages in dealing with seasonal variations *if* the various refineries have sufficiently flexible equipment. But the multi-plant refiners to whom we talked indicated that their short-run flexibility in making such shifts was quite limited, especially when they are running at a high rate of capacity utilization. Purchases on the spot market were widely used to fill the gap created by unexpected refinery shutdowns, though this can prove difficult if the shutdown coincides with a demand peak. In the United States it is common to cover *planned* maintenance shutdowns through swap arrangements; for example, one refinery processes an adjacent competitor's products during the shutdown period in the expectation that reciprocity will be extended when its own maintenance time comes. European refiners were said to be less cooperative in such matters, in which case more inventory building or spot market purchases were accepted to cover an anticipated supply gap.

Interplant cooperation in the steel industry is limited owing to plant specialization, high transportation costs, and the tendency for demand peaks in major product lines to coincide. Moreover, the sharpest peak of all for U.S. producers—before an expected industrywide strike—hit all companies and products uniformly, so the ability to spread lesser peaks permitted no significant reserve capacity shaving.

In batteries and paints, with somewhat lower transport costs per unit of product value, the picture was similar. Even though the seasonal automobile battery demand peak falls during winter in the northern United States and summer in the south, transport costs are too high to justify much interregional shipping. Holding reserve capacity, which is not particularly expensive in battery making, was said to be a better solution. In paints, the best approach to seasonal fluctuations was said to be adding counterseasonal lines at a given plant; for instance, interior and exterior paints have different seasonal patterns and are therefore combined successfully. Interplant cooperation to spread peaks is limited by regional brand label differences in some multi-plant companies, small differences in formulations between plants, and the ubiquitous burden of shipping costs.

For the industries in which transportation costs are of major moment, then, we end up with a rather uniform conclusion. There is some peak-spreading and shutdown hedging between affiliated plants in most industries, but it is kept at very modest levels for a number of reasons, among which shipping costs and congruence of regional demand movements are the most prominent. When fluctuation-damping cooperation does take place, it is usually between geographically clustered plants, so the massed reserve advantages of a multi-plant posture seldom extend beyond the operation of two to four neighboring plants. Frequently, the ability to cover random and planned imbalances through spot market transactions, swaps, and price rationing also provides an effective alternative to intracompany hedging, especially for physically homogeneous products.

When transportation costs are low in relation to product value, a different mix of constraints appears. The main feature is product specialization by plants. Short-run inflexibility of specialized processes makes it difficult to shift product assignments between plants in cigarettes, bearings, refrigerators, and weaving. The main possible exception occurs in shoemaking. The demand for many shoe styles is mercurial. Coordinated multi-plant scheduling can average what might otherwise be significant plant workload fluctuations. Most shoemaking machinery is fairly flexible, although production transfers are inhibited somewhat by worker skill specialization and the need to relocate lasts. Still, larger shoe firms agreed that 15 percent or so of their plants' base load production volume could be reallocated to secure better balance without impairing efficiency. This helps stabilize employment for skilled workers and keeps capacity utilization high. Single-plant producers have more difficulty achieving production stability unless they specialize in style-insensitive items on which inventory carrying risks are small, enter into low-margin long-term supply contracts, or are nimble enough to "turn on a dime" and meet the volatile demands of the fashion shoe market. Companies with three to five plants producing a moderate assortment of types and styles appear to be about as successful in averaging out fluctuations as much larger multi-plant firms.

All in all, the peak-spreading and production balancing advantages of multi-plant operation tend to be negligible in refrigerators, bearings, and cigarettes; of moderate importance in shoes; and slight in the other eight industries. This qualitative generalization is as far as we can go. When advantages were identified, interviewees were typically unable to estimate their magnitude quantitatively, partly because their realization depends upon a complex set of side conditions and partly because it was so difficult conceptually to collapse them to a single dimension such as the annual cost of reserve capacity avoided.

Catastrophic Shutdowns

Major strikes, fires, explosions, and the like differ from the contingencies examined thus far mainly in their magnitude. They are more likely to be catastrophic, driving a total and perhaps protracted wedge between what a plant can supply and its normal demand. To many respondents this implied a difference in kind. Some viewed the hedge multiple plants afford against such disasters as one of the most important benefits of multi-plant operation.

This belief was manifested most strongly in the cigarette and brewing industries. In each, building and preserving customer brand loyalty is a crucial dimension of marketing strategy. Product purchases are made often and repetitively. Loss of production for a period long enough to deplete inventories can force customers to switch to competing brands, and a significant fraction may never return. What is at stake is not the short-run profit on marginal sales or the additional costs of seasonal inventory buildups, as in hedging against routine fluctuations, but the risk of substantial long-run profit sacrifices. The desire to protect themselves against this risk was one of the main reasons why medium-sized cigarette producers in both the United States and abroad maintained more than one plant, accepting unit production cost penalties of one or 2 percent as a consequence. Nearly all the brewing companies we interviewed had several plants and considered themselves adequately hedged, but some European producers who were closing down inefficient breweries and concentrating production were reluctant to go all the way to a single unit, despite the lure of scale economies, because of the risk. A large U.S. brewer also accepted modest packaging cost penalties in duplicating production assignments for a low-volume specialty product so that the product's market position would not be endangered by local issues strikes.

Concern over the danger of fire or explosion and a desire to protect brand loyalties led several petroleum refiners and paint manufacturers to maintain multiple plants of suboptimal scale. In the automobile battery business, consumer brand loyalties are weak, but the wish of original equipment and private-label customers to be assured of an uninterrupted supply makes multi-plant hedging important. Firms with only a single plant, for instance, because scale economy sacrifices would otherwise be prohibitive, were penalized by lessened bargaining power in dealing with unions and the decision of some prime customers to split their orders between two competing sources. An assured source of supply is also important to glass bottle buyers, and therefore multi-plant operation, especially if accompanied by staggered union contract expiration dates, was considered to be advantageous.

Less significance was attached to the risk-reducing benefits of multi-plant operation in the remaining industries. The reasons are diverse. In the American steel industry a common nationwide union contract expiration date precludes supply maintenance from unstruck plants. Equipment like blast furnaces subject to catastrophic failure is usually duplicated and triplicated in individual plants, and in the rare event of multiple failures, ingot or slab supplies can usually be obtained at acceptable prices from rivals. Cement buyers are fickle, and the cost of winning them back after an extended supply interruption is evidently less than the cost of supplying them from distant mills. Plant specialization limits the ability of textile firms and (to a lesser degree) shoemakers to maintain priority deliveries when subjected to local strikes.

The same is true of multi-plant refrigerator producers. Plant specialization also appears to be a significant constraint in bearing manufacturing, although one European producer noted that certain original equipment automobile bearing orders could be obtained on an exclusive basis only if the bearing supplier was capable of producing in at least two plants.

Central Troubleshooting Staffs

Another economy of massed reserves can come from maintaining a central troubleshooting staff to deal with nonroutine equipment repairs and maintenance. If breakdowns occur randomly and infrequently, it may be feasible to utilize such a staff more intensively if its services are spread over several plants. This advantage appeared to be appreciable only in the cigarette and glass bottle industries. Cigarette making and packaging machines are complex, and at least in recent years the best designs have been offered by European manufacturers who do not maintain extensive field troubleshooting staffs. Therefore the cigarette companies must retain their own. Some multi-plant producers concentrate their best machine repair technicians at their main or home plant, dispatching them to other plants when problems arise which the branch maintenance staffs cannot handle. Minor reserves massing economies of this genre may continue into the volume range of two MOS plants, or 72 billion cigarettes per year. Similar practices are observed in the glass bottle industry, where a firm with three or four MOS plants can afford to have a better central troubleshooting staff and utilize it more efficiently than smaller companies. Pooling over a larger number of plants was said to add little or no benefit. In none of the other industries did such practices appear to be important, usually because most repair problems are routine and individual plants are large enough to support their own staffs, because machinery suppliers provide good maintenance service, or because it is more economical to hire special repair services on the market.

Cost Function Flexibility

Microeconomic theory suggests a further flexibility advantage of multi-plant firms.[28] The usual requisite is that the short-run average variable production cost curve be U-shaped, as assumed in most introductory theory textbooks. Under these conditions, multi-plant firms

28. The pioneering treatment is Don Patinkin, "Multi-Plant Firms, Cartels, and Imperfect Competition," *Quarterly Journal of Economics*, 61 (February 1947), 173–205; with a comment by Wassily Leontief and reply by Patinkin, *Quarterly Journal of Economics*, 61 (August 1947), 650–657.

will tend to shut down some plants during a recession, thereby incurring lower unit costs than a set of independent single-plant operators, each of which keeps its plant going and cuts back on its output in proportion to the demand decline. The more tightly U-shaped the average variable plant cost curve is and the more such plants a producer controls, the more adjustment flexibility that firm has.

Matters become more complicated if the average variable cost function slopes upward continuously or is roughly ⌐-shaped. If all plants have identical cost functions and react to identical price or marginal revenue signals, multi-plant control confers no adjustment advantages. The same is true if some plants have lower variable costs than others at any given output on their upward sloping cost curves and all attempt to maximize short-run profits in response to identical price signals. But if some plants have lower costs than others and if the high-cost plants continue production for strategic reasons when price falls below their minimum average variable cost, or if the several plants perceive themselves to face different prices or marginal revenue functions (as in a monopolistically competitive market), multi-plant operators may still be able to adjust to changing demand conditions in more economical ways.

The shape of the cost function therefore is important though not decisive in assessing this potential advantage of multi-plant firms. We did not attempt a systematic verification of short-run cost curve shapes. The weight of evidence from numerous published econometric and other studies suggests that the variable cost curve is either ⌐-shaped, especially in the process industries like brewing, cement, and petroleum refining; or flat at low and intermediate output levels before beginning a gradual ascent as capacity operation is approached through the addition of third and overtime shifts and as older reserve equipment is brought into use.[29]

We were sensitive in our interviews to assertions that multi-plant firms possessed cost advantages in adjusting to demand changes, and when they were made we attempted to explore their bases. Only a few were encountered. Certain cement manufacturers claimed an advantage in being able to run their most efficient works at full capacity and let the burden of demand adjustment fall upon high-cost works. A single cement plant with several kilns of varying efficiency has the same opportunity, and a works with nothing but best-practice processes is better off in terms of unit costs averaged over boom and slump. But

29. For surveys of the literature, see J. Johnston, *Statistical Cost Analysis* (New York: McGraw-Hill, 1960), chaps. 4 and 5; and A. A. Walters, "Production and Cost Functions: An Econometric Survey," *Econometrica*, 31 (January-April 1963), 39–51.

aggregate real costs during a demand slump are almost surely lower when high-cost mills are under the control of a multi-mill firm than with independent operators anxious to retain their accustomed share of the market. A brewing company claimed similar advantages, stating that having several plants made it easier to make marginal adjustments to seasonal or general demand reductions by cutting back more sharply at its high-cost plants. Again, it seems probable that this multi-plant strategy saved resources compared to a situation in which independent high-cost plants struggle to keep going. But in none of these cases were the savings from multi-plant adjustment said to be very substantial. Usually, transportation costs prevented large shifts, overpowering the production cost savings if the low-cost plants tried to ship very far into the home territories of high-cost installations.

Small textile firms also considered themselves to labor at a production adjustment disadvantage. One such company noted that smaller weavers find themselves saddled with inflexible processes and few ways of "shaking loose" without serious convulsions when demand shifts, whereas large multi-plant companies are able to close down whole plants or transfer them to another field with something approaching equanimity. The president of a firm with two weaving sheds observed that "if you're a Burlington Industries, you can chop out the least efficient parts of your system without feeling much pain, since they're small and the system has enough flexibility to provide the needed inputs from elsewhere." In his company adjustments were much more constrained, he said. For instance, the best way to react to a slump might at first glance seem to be closing down an entire plant for a week or two, which among other things allows the workers to receive unemployment compensation. But the need to keep supplies of some items flowing instead forces the firm to move to four-day weeks and other inferior solutions.

These were the only convincing assertions of greater multi-plant cost flexibility turned up by our interviews. It is conceivable that interviewees were unaware of what has to be a complex advantage of multi-plant operation. It appears more likely, however, that the advantages are simply not very great because transportation costs and specialization inhibit workload reallocations, because cost functions are relatively homogeneous and ⌐-shaped, and because top management lacks the comprehensive control over decentralized operations needed to "fine tune" them continuously. That all four constraints existed in the twelve industries we analyzed was quite clear.

Ability To Absorb Shocks and Mistakes
Finally, large multi-plant companies are better able to take in stride mistakes in some segment of their operation or adverse developments

like a price war or the loss of a major customer in one market or product line. Inability to do so on equal terms was considered by several of the smaller firms we interviewed to be one of their most serious handicaps, particularly in the textile, petroleum refining, glass bottle, bearing, and cement industries. Indeed, ability to spread the risks of price disturbances was the *only* benefit of multi-plant operation for companies with cement mills so far apart that they had no real logistic interactions, said an executive who had previously worked for such a firm.

The extent to which the risk-spreading advantages of geographic and product line diversification accrue to a company's work force, as distinguished from its stockholders, may nevertheless be correlated *inversely* with the degree of multi-plant operation. A well-diversified U.S. bearing producer observed that its plants were mostly specialized, so stability was achieved mainly at the overall corporate level and not at individual plants, which might suffer sharp fluctuations. On the other hand, SKF has nearly all of its Swedish bearing machining and assembly operations centralized at a single complex in Gothenburg. A substantial geographic concentration of activity also exists at SKF's Schweinfurt, Germany, plants and at the neighboring Fischer bearing production complex. Workers in those installations were said to enjoy more stable employment owing to the averaging out of demand fluctuations.

To sum up, multi-plant operation confers massed reserve economies of varying magnitude in several categories. Often such benefits are strictly private and pecuniary rather than being diffused beyond a narrow interest group. Thus, it makes a great deal of difference to the stockholders and officers of a company whether customers normally served by a fire-impacted plant are supplied by another of that firm's facilities or whether the business goes to rivals; but from a broader societywide perspective the interests largely cancel out. The same is true of a corporate umbrella under which the sales and profit variations of twelve plants are averaged out, as compared to averaging among the same twelve plants separately owned. Were it not for transactions costs, investors would be equally secure and well off buying shares of stock in the twelve single-plant enterprises or in the twelve-plant corporation, all else equal. And to the workers of a multi-plant company, a layoff is not sweetened by the fact that somewhere else far away the firm is hiring. On the other hand, if multi-plant corporations feel less compulsion to build and replicate plants of suboptimal scale because they have reserves elsewhere, if they can plan for smaller average capacity reserves or hold thinner inventories because affiliated plants will cover one another in emergencies, if larger production lots are achieved because the supply assurance a multi-plant firm offers induces major buyers not to split orders, and if central production schedulers cut back at high-cost plants more sharply than at low-cost units during a slump, real resource savings result. What we find is a mixture of these variants. The interview evidence suggests that the mixture is richer in purely private risk-spreading benefits than real economies, but both surely exist.

Capital Raising and Dynamic Investment Advantages

It is well established from others' research that sizeable corporations can obtain new capital on more favorable terms and in bigger chunks than relatively small enterprises. Two main factors, risk and transactions costs, are responsible. Primarily because of the risk-pooling opportunities described in the previous section, large multi-plant companies experience less variability of sales and earnings over time than small single-plant firms, ceteris paribus, and the actuarial risk of default therefore tends to be lower. Also, the securities of larger firms are usually better known and are more apt to be traded on major exchanges, making it easier for investors to liquidate their holdings when necessary. The higher risks of default and being caught with illiquid, thinly traded securities lead investors to buy small-firm securities only when a risk premium is embodied in the price. Because there are market absorption and managerial constraints on rapid growth, a new capital issue of given (but substantial) size is also considered less risky for a large enterprise than for a small one, all else equal. Consequently, smaller companies must generally raise their capital in smaller increments. And since many of the legal, negotiation, promotional, and servicing costs of floating a new securities issue or administering a loan are more or less fixed, flotation and servicing charges per dollar raised tend to be higher, the smaller the enterprise is and hence the smaller is its capital issue.

Quantitative Evidence

Since there is a substantial literature on the links between firm size and capital cost and since the phenomenon is an important one, we digress from our interview evidence to put the size-cost relationship into quantitative perspective. It is convenient to focus separately on three different modes of financing: stock issues, publicly held debt, and bank credit.

For most very small firms, a public issue of common stock is virtually impossible because underwriters are disinterested or would be interested only at prohibitively high commissions. Average common stock flotation costs for a cross section of manufacturing corporation issues during the early 1950s ranged from 20 percent of the funds raised for issues totaling less than $500,000 through 10 percent for issues in the $2–5 million bracket to 5.5 percent for issues between $20 million and 50 million.[30]

Measuring the relationship between common stock cost and firm size is more difficult, since the yields anticipated by investors (determining what price they will pay) depend upon growth expectations, and small firms whose shares are listed on major exchanges are more apt to be those with above-average expected growth. Statistical analyses which attempted to take into account differences in earnings potential, risk, and other variables show a negative relationship between earnings/price ratios or similar measures of equity capital cost and firm size.[31]

On long-term corporate bonds, including those placed directly with large investment holdings as well as those offered publicly, there is evidence of a negative correlation between interest rates paid and issuing firm size.[32] That the higher interest rates prevailing on smaller firms' debt reflects genuine subjective aversion by investors to the risks or other attributes of smallness rather than an actuarial adjustment to the objectively higher risks of small-firm default is strongly suggested by W. B. Hickman's monumental study.[33] He tracked a large sample of corporate bonds over the period from 1900 to 1943 and found that relatively small firms did default on their bonds more frequently than large corporations. However, after adjusting yields for default losses, the inverse relation between actually realized yields and company size persisted. For corporations with assets of less than $5 million at the time of bond issue, the average long-term default-adjusted yield was 6.6 percent; for firms in the $5–99 million asset range it was 5.7 percent, and it dropped to 5.3 percent for firms with assets of $200 million and over.

Bonds have the advantage over common stocks of lower flotation costs, all else equal. However, there is still a negative correlation between issue size and cost. Thus, on public bond issues in the early

30. Glenn R. Miller, "Long-Term Small Business Financing from the Underwriter's Point of View," *Journal of Finance*, 16 (May 1961), 280–291. See also S. H. Archer and L. G. Faerber, "Firm Size and the Cost of Externally Secured Capital," *Journal of Finance*, 21 (March 1966), 69–83.

31. See, e.g., Myron J. Gordon, *The Investment, Financing, and Valuation of the Corporation* (Homewood: Irwin, 1962), pp. 163–166; and Martin J. Gruber, *The Determinants of Common Stock Prices* (University Park: Pennsylvania State University Office of Business Research, 1971), pp. 57–76.

32. On directly placed issues, see Saul B. Klaman, "Life Insurance Companies," in Federal Reserve Board, *Financing Small Business* (Washington, 1958), p. 519; and Avery Cohan, *Yields on Corporate Debt Directly Placed* (New York: Columbia University Press, 1967).

33. *Corporate Bond Quality and Investor Experience* (Princeton: Princeton University Press, 1958), esp. pp. 499–510.

1950s, average flotation costs were 11.5 percent of issue value on issues totaling between $500,000 and $1 million, compared to 21.8 percent for common stock issues of similar size. For issues in the $20–50 million range, the flotation cost was 1.3 percent for bonds and 5.4 percent for common stocks.[34]

On bank loans small borrowers also pay higher average interest rates, in part because of the higher perceived risk and partly because small firms borrow smaller sums, so that roughly fixed negotiation and servicing costs are higher per dollar borrowed. A Federal Reserve study revealed that average interest rates paid to banks on business loans in 1957 were 5.1 percent by borrowers with assets of from $1–5 million, 4.7 percent for firms in the $5–25 million bracket, 4.3 percent for firms with assets of from $25–100 million, and 4.1 percent for the largest borrowers.[35]

A method of financing on which the smaller borrower's disadvantage appears to be modest is mortgage loans, presumably because the security afforded by tangible property minimizes size-correlated risks. Saul B. Klaman found that between loans in the $0.25–1.0 million and over $10 million size ranges, the spread of interest rates on general business and industrial bonds purchased by life insurance companies was 0.91 percentage points in 1953 and 0.68 in 1956. But between mortgages in the same two size ranges, the spread was only 0.18 and 0.20 percentage points respectively.[36]

Since the capital cost penalty borne by relatively small firms varies with the financing method adopted, we undertook a further statistical analysis of capital structure and average interest costs for all manufacturing corporations covered by the U.S. Internal Revenue Service's fiscal year 1964 and 1967 surveys.[37] The first year was one of more or less "normal" prosperity, the second a boom accompanied by accelerating inflation and rising interest rates. Significant results included the following:

a) Manufacturing corporations with assets exceeding $250 million

34. Cf. Miller, "Long-Term Small Business Financing," pp. 280–291. The comparison is for securities of all types of corporations and not merely manufacturing corporations, as in the earlier citation.

35. Leonard Laudadio, "Size of Bank, Size of Borrower, and the Rate of Interest," *Journal of Finance*, 18 (March 1963), 20–28.

36. Klaman, "Life Insurance Companies," p. 519.

37. U.S., Internal Revenue Service, *Source Book of Statistics of Income* (Washington, special computer print-out, annually). The research was done by James M. Kennedy. A much fuller analysis of the results is contained in the long version of this chapter. See n. 24, Chap. 1 *supra*.

appeared to rely somewhat more heavily upon equity financing than smaller firms. However, this relationship fades to insignificance and perhaps even reverses when equity-asset size patterns are analyzed on an industry-by-industry basis. If size-correlated biases toward equity as compared to debt financing do exist, they are apparently not very strong.

b) There was a marked propensity for larger corporations to have a bigger fraction of their debt in obligations maturing in one year or more. Greater reliance on short-term financing leaves small firms exposed to more severe refinancing risks, especially in a time of generally rising interest rates like the mid- and late 1960s.

c) Increased size confers debt cost advantages all the way out to the billion-dollar asset group. When the average interest cost incurred by manufacturing corporations in diverse size classes is regressed on the logarithm of average assets, the results for each year separately and for the two years pooled were:[38]

Variable	1964	1967	Pooled
Intercept term[39]	6.08	6.41	6.21
Regression coefficient	−0.434	0.522	−0.463
Standard error	(.067)	(.075)	(.057)
R^2	.936	.952	.835

Since the 1964 and 1967 slope coefficients differ from one another by a statistically insignificant amount, the pooled estimate serves best as an indicator of the size-correlated interest cost differential.[40] It suggests that, relative to a firm with assets of $5 million, a $200 million corporation enjoyed an interest cost advantage of 0.74 percentage points. For a firm with assets of $1 billion the advantage was 1.08 percentage points.

Summing up, we find that there are economies of scale in capital-raising all the way out to very substantial firm size levels. The unit cost handicap borne by single-plant firms as a result of these economies depends primarily upon two factors: the capital intensity of production processes and the relative size of multi-plant as compared to single-plant operators. The more capital-intensive the industry tends to be and the

38. In multiple regressions, variables measuring the fraction of debt with maturities of one year or more and the debt/equity ratio had statistically insignificant coefficients. Similar results were obtained in regression analyses of corporations in various size classes for 10 of our 12 sample industries, with each industry-size class taken as a separate observation.

39. I.e., since the assets data were scaled in millions of dollars and the logarithm of one is zero, the average interest cost of a firm with assets of $1 million.

40. However, the intercepts are significantly different between years.

greater the disparity between the size of leading multi-plant firms and companies operating only one MOS plant, the larger the single-plant firm's unit capital cost disadvantage will be. The size disparities relevant in this sense may stem not only from plant proliferation in a given national market but also from overseas expansion or conglomerate diversification. Relative to the size of an undiversified firm with the U.S. industry leader's 1970 market share or a conglomerate enterprise with assets of $2 billion—whichever more closely approximated actual U.S. market conditions—the industry in our sample for which a single MOS plant firm would labor under the largest unit cost handicap owing to foregone capital-raising economies was cement. If the interest cost differential pattern observed in our regression analysis of all manufacturing corporations held for all types of capital (including equity), the unit cost penalty borne by such a single-MOS-plant cement firm would be roughly one percentage point. If, as seems plausible, size-correlated differentials are larger for equity capital than for debt, this estimate is probably biased on the low side. The next largest unit cost penalties are attributable to single-plant firms in the antifriction bearing and battery industries, in both of which very large conglomerate firms play a dominant role. The smallest penalties (in the range of 0.14 to 0.22 percentage points) are found for the brewing and cigarette industries, in which production processes are only moderately capital-intensive and (more importantly) the leading firms as of 1970 were neither highly conglomerate nor very many times larger than the size of a single MOS plant.

The extent to which capital-raising economies of scale are real as contrasted to pecuniary is arguable. Certainly, many of the flotation and servicing cost savings associated with large loans and stock issues are real, backed by tangible legal, administrative, and informational economies. Risk premia exceeding the actuarial default cost of small-company securities pose harder questions.[41] It is true that the individual investor faces default and liquidity risks, and to him they represent a real subjective cost which must be compensated. But for society as a whole or even for investors as a general class such risks are greatly attenuated under the law of large numbers. Indeed, if securities markets could

41. For a stimulating discussion of the issues and survey of the literature, see William J. Baumol, "On the Discount Rate for Public Projects," and Jack Hirshleifer and David L. Shapiro, "The Treatment of Risk and Uncertainty," in the Joint Economic Committee compendium, *The Analysis and Evaluation of Public Expenditures: The PPB System*, vol. I, 91st Cong., 1st Sess., 1969, esp. pp. 497–498, 511–517, and 521–527; and the several comments on a paper by Kenneth J. Arrow and Robert C. Lind in the *American Economic Review*, 62 (March 1972), 161–174.

somehow be organized so as to pool the risks of many independent ventures without raising transactions and informational costs prohibitively—a feat mutual funds accomplish only imperfectly—the rationale for pure size-correlated risk premia would virtually disappear. Yet such premia do exist, condemned to a classificational limbo between the real and pecuniary cost category extremes.

Impact on Investment Decisions

Whatever we call them, capital cost differentials associated with firm size can have repercussions on investment of a decidedly real character. When a new MOS plant is large in relation to the absolute growth of demand, a tradeoff often has to be made between carrying excess capacity for a considerable period vs. building in sub-MOS increments and accepting higher unit costs throughout the life of the investment. As Chapter 2 brought out, the choice depends upon the firm's discount rate, which in turn varies with its cost of capital. The higher the discount rate is, the less weight long-run savings will receive and the more scale economies will be sacrificed to avoid early excess capacity costs. Similar behavior might be expected when smaller firms are subjected to more severe capital rationing than large companies, either because they simply cannot raise the capital required for a fully efficient new plant or because the opportunity cost of capital is higher to them, implying a higher discount rate.

Our interviews provided a fair amount of evidence that small firms have in fact accepted scale economy sacrifices owing to high capital costs and/or capital rationing. It was confined, however, almost entirely to the petroleum refining, steel, and cement industries, where the amount of capital required for an efficient capacity increment is large and the processes are relatively indivisible, making step-by-step movement toward an eventually efficient operation difficult or impossible. Interpretation of the evidence is complicated because in almost every case capital constraints were accompanied by market absorption constraints for large output increments, and firms' decisions were influenced jointly by the two. Interviewees tended to place somewhat greater emphasis on the market absorption restraints, but in several cases capital rationing or the high cost of capital played a clearly identifiable role in decisions to expand in sub-MOS steps.

In industries other than steel, petroleum, and cement, the modest investment required for an MOS plant and/or the possibility of moving toward an efficient operation in stages made serious scale economy sacrifices due to capital constraints unnecessary, at least among all but the smallest firms we interviewed. Some felt restrained in other ways, however. For example, three relatively small textile companies believed they were unable to respond to major demand shifts as quickly as their larger rivals because capital for new equipment was difficult to marshal. And for the two smallest firms in our sample, each operating a single plant much smaller than the MOS, capital rationing imposed very distinct sacrifices. Each managed to "get by" by cutting corners, picking up bargains on the used equipment market, or simply accepting the cost sacrifices associated with units of suboptimal size. Major investment decisions precipitated by technological change or legal mandates (such as for pollution control equipment) had a traumatic quality. On several occasions the company owners had seriously considered shutting down operations or accepting a gradual process of decline rather than trying to finance what to them was a huge leap forward.

Multi-Plant Investment Staging

Staging investment decisions in a multi-plant framework to achieve the optimal tradeoff among scale economies, transportation costs, and excess capacity costs is another possible advantage of size. The theory, pioneered by Alan S. Manne and associates,[42] has been summarized in Chapter 2. To recapitulate briefly, capacity additions are whipsawed back and forth among the various nodes in a geographically decentralized production network. Investments at some nodes are deferred as long as possible, reducing the burden of excess capacity, while part of the output from newly expanded plants is transported to satisfy growing demands in the natural market territories of the deferred-investment plants. When a capacity increment is added, it tends to be larger than could have been justified if the plant affected always served only the customers in its own territory. Higher transportation costs are incurred, but if conditions are favorable, they are more than compensated by the fuller realization of scale economies and the reduction of excess capacity. In his studies of capacity expansion decisions for the Indian economy, Manne found that an optimally coordinated multi-plant investment staging strategy could reduce the discounted present value of costs by as much as 17 percent (for caustic soda) compared to a strategy under which each plant satisfied capacity expansion needs in its home territory autarkically.[43]

This is an impressive saving, dwarfing any estimates reported in the industrial organization literature on the benefits of multi-plant operation. Whether similar economies are attainable in the more highly

42. Alan S. Manne, ed., *Investments for Capacity Expansion* (Cambridge: M.I.T. Press, 1967).
43. Ibid., pp. 77–85 and 229–235.

industrialized nations covered by our sample is therefore an important question. We pushed hard in our interviews to learn whether companies pursued Manne-type investment strategies and to ascertain the savings they realized by doing so. In fact, numerous clear-cut examples were discovered in the petroleum refining, steel, cement, brewing, and glass bottle industries.

Manne-type investment staging was most prevalent in the U.S. petroleum refining industry and (on an international plane) among Western European refiners. It played an insignificant role in the operations of only two interviewees. One of the exceptions was for Germany, where limited pipeline facilities and water routes isolated the southern market, while quota restrictions on refined product shipments into France (despite the Common Market) inhibited what would otherwise be a natural coordination between French and German refineries. The other exception was Canada. In the West the refineries were too far apart and (until 1970) product pipeline interconnections too meager to permit much interaction. In the East an import quota system discouraged southwest shipment beyond the Ottawa River of products refined in Quebec from imported crude oil, drawing an artificial boundary between Ontario and Quebec refineries and preventing the coordination of their capacity changes.

For the petroleum refiners who did coordinate their investments on a multi-plant scale, how great were the savings? No interviewee was able to provide an explicit answer, since multi-plant phasing was the obvious way to proceed, and the costs of an uncoordinated alternative had not even been considered seriously. There is, however, more to the benefit estimation problem than mere failure to cost out dominated alternatives. The existence of a further alternative, resort to the market, complicates matters. Manne's original multi-plant analysis focused on more or less benevolent state monopolies attempting to minimize costs while satisfying rigid demand requirements autarkically, or at most with some occasional help from imports. But the petroleum companies we interviewed seldom possessed anything approaching a monopoly position. Always there were rivals operating in the same territory, and their presence implied the possibility of alleviating capacity imbalances through market transactions: buying or selling on spot markets, concluding a processing agreement under which a nearby competitor with surplus capacity refines one's own crude or vice versa, and/or entering into a swap arrangement under which products are obtained from a nearby competitor with surplus capacity, who in turn takes products from one's sister refinery in a market where the imbalance is reversed. Our interviews revealed that such market transactions played at least as important a role in helping absorb large new capacity increments as interterritorial shipping did. Given this, a correct estimate of savings achieved using the Manne approach must take as its base of comparison not the costs under an assumption of plant expansion decisions made autarkically within the confines of a particular firm, but the costs under a system in which plants interact *within the market* in the most favorable manner possible. To this we add the slight qualification that multi-plant firms may have more favorable options playing the market than single-plant operators because only the former are able to enter interterritorial swap arrangements.

If the market functioned perfectly one would expect Manne-type staging strategies to confer little or no net benefit, since cross-shipping products is more costly than equating supply and demand locally unless there is no residual slack in the local market. In a perfectly functioning market there would also be no tendency for two or more firms simultaneously to build refineries of less than optimal size, though this happens with some frequency. There are several reasons why coordination in the market is imperfect and total reliance on market transactions is eschewed.

For one, market imperfections might prevent prices from falling to the level of marginal refining plus transportation cost from an affiliated refinery operating below capacity. But in general, markets for petroleum products appeared to function fairly competitively. Interviewees reported that on longer-term contracts in particular it was possible to secure "very satisfactory" prices both buying and selling. Second and more important, most refiners were reluctant to become highly dependent upon competitors as outlets or sources of supply. There was too much danger of being left in the lurch at a critical moment. As a result of these fears, refiners generally try to phase capacity expansions so as not to be dependent upon competitors for much more than a third or at most a half of their supply or demand. If within this general framework they can absorb bigger capacity increments by playing the Manne game on a multi-plant plane, scale economies will be realized more fully than they would be if each plant operated independently. Finally, "perfect" coordination of investments among rival firms can mean no competition at all or unhealthy respect for spheres of influence when the market is large enough to accommodate only a few MOS plants.

Thus, securing all potentially attainable scale economies through market transactions linked to investment decisions may be both impractical and socially unpalatable. To the extent that this is so, multi-plant investment staging à la Manne can be an important second-best solution yielding real economies. The magnitude of the benefits is difficult to ascertain, but their existence in petroleum refining was undeniable.

Similarly complex benefit assessment problems are encountered in the steel industry. Our interviews turned up several prominent examples of multi-plant staging for major investments. However, representatives of both the multi-plant companies involved and smaller single-plant rivals believed that the multi-plant firms enjoyed no really significant cost advantages therefrom. This was so partly because many steel markets are so large that even very sizeable capacity increments can be absorbed fairly quickly and partly because regional specialists, especially the smaller single-plant companies, are inclined to fill their order books through sub rosa price shading when they are burdened with excess capacity following a significant expansion. In this sense the Manne approach again emerges as a second-best strategy—more conducive to optimal-size plant investments than rigid-price oligopolistic rivalry among single-plant regional specialists, even if not necessarily superior to markets operating with considerable price flexibility.

In cement only a modest amount of Manne-type investment staging was observed. Its incidence was inversely correlated with unit transportation costs. U.S. companies whose plants were predominantly land-locked and/or widely dispersed did almost none. Postinvestment territorial reallocations were observed most frequently in England, where distances between markets are fairly short and good water routes connect Thames estuary mills with Liverpool, Scotland (which has almost no usable limestone), and Northern Ireland.

Because beer is physically differentiated, brewers almost never buy from and sell to competitors to smooth investment transitions. There were pronounced territorial reallocations following the opening of new breweries by several of the multi-plant companies we interviewed, and this made it easier to absorb output jumps. In Europe the adjustments commonly took the form of closing down small, obsolete breweries. The investments of rapidly growing U.S. brewing companies corresponded more closely to the Manne model. Officials of one firm observed that they would have found it difficult to construct new units as large as they did if they had been unable to diffuse the output absorption repercussions over several plants. Another brewer, however, failed to follow the logic of the Manne staging approach to its full scale economy consequences. A programming analysis of alternative investment strategies indicated that very large capacity increments with substantial distribution territory reassignments yielded the lowest discounted cost stream. But the analysis was rejected and smaller, more frequent steps were taken because the large increment approach would have caused unacceptably wide employment swings at a centrally located brewery and because less ambitious investment projects were expected to precipitate milder shocks (and drive costs up less) in local construction labor markets.

Finally, territorial reallocations were effected to help integrate some new or expanded glass bottle plants into multi-plant networks. But this appeared to influence scale economy choices less than in the industries discussed previously because the output of new bottle plants can be expanded in steps at no serious long-run cost penalty, because demand was growing rapidly during the 1960s in relation to the size of an MOS plant as a result of the trend toward no-return bottles, and because bottle producers have not been averse to using price and delivery time quotation variations to choke off orders when capacity is inadequate and to capture them when it is excessive.

We conclude then that there is evidence of Manne-type investment staging strategies in roughly half the industries studied. Their use contributed significantly to the realization of scale economies and reduction of excess capacity in a smaller subset. It is difficult however to quantify the resulting long-run cost savings, partly because respondents themselves had not attempted to make such estimates and partly because resort to market transactions could at least under favorable conditions permit similar plant structure choices.

Obsolete Capacity and New Investment

That investment in new plants displaced obsolete plants in some industries has already been noted. Having numerous plants ready for replacement certainly makes it easier to absorb large new capacity increments, especially in slowly growing markets. The ability to shut down some dozen small old plants was, for example, a key contributing factor in the British Associated Portland Cement Company's decision to construct a new 21 million barrel per year plant at Northfleet on Thames east of London. Smaller rivals of APC said they saw no feasible way of building an equivalent works or even one half the size (which would yield nearly all the scale economies attained at Northfleet). And in this respect they suffered a unit cost disadvantage relative to APC which they expected to persist into the indefinite future. Less grandiose multi-plant displacement opportunities facilitated the realization of new plant scale economies by other cement companies in all six of the nations covered by our research; by brewing firms, especially in England and Sweden; in the U.S. automobile battery industry; in the U.S. and Canadian petroleum refining industries; and in the steel industries of several nations. Nevertheless, single-plant producers proved able to pursue the same approach, albeit on a more limited scale. For instance, a small steel producer shut down its least efficient blast furnace when a large new unit went on stream. It then held the older furnace in reserve to handle peak demands and to fill future capacity gaps before demand growth warranted still another new full-size unit. Compared to single-plant firms, the main investment absorption advantages enjoyed by multi-plant operators lie in the greater array of capacity displacement options available and the larger absolute quantities of capacity falling due for replacement during any given period. In industries requiring very large-scale, lumpy equipment, these advantages are not inconsiderable.

Product Specialization in a Multi-Plant Framework

The economies of product specialization in a multi-plant framework will now be explored with special thoroughness. Our objective is to determine whether and to what extent there are product-specific scale economies open to multi-plant firms which cannot be realized by single-plant companies. Before confronting the issues directly, however, it is useful to review briefly the logic of specialization and to survey with some care the kinds of product specialization observed in our sample of twelve industries.

Three broad types of plant specialization can be identified: geographic, product, and composite. Geographic specialization entails concentration by plants on serving specific narrowly drawn geographic markets, for instance, New England as opposed to the whole United States. Its driving force is the desire to reduce outbound transportation costs. Product specialization exists when plants produce for a broad geographic market some narrow segment of the product line normally encompassed within an industry's definition—heavy steel plates rather than all carbon steel products, or women's dress shoes with cemented soles out of the myriad types offered by shoemakers. Composite specialization involves a blend of the two types, such as producing steel plates for some geographic submarket. We shall see that it takes on particularly interesting characteristics in a multi-plant framework.

There are several reasons why plants engage in product specialization. For one, equipment may be better suited to producing some items than others, or its applications may be rigidly determined by technological constraints. A 130-inch Sulzer automatic loom is more suitable for long-run sheetings than for style-sensitive dress cloths; a reversing mill cannot produce steel strip of adequate surface quality for exterior automobile body stamping applications. Second, worker productivity and product quality tend to increase owing to the development of proficiency when a limited range of products can be manufactured in long runs. As the British Textile Council observed: "When staff at all levels can concentrate on the production of a very limited number of products the smallest details can receive attention and be brought to near perfection. Production planning becomes relatively easy. Time and effort which would be wildly uneconomic in normal circumstances can be justified if the volume of production is sufficiently great."[44] From a study of nine comparable rayon weaving sheds, the Council reported that output per worker increased by 167 percent and loom efficiency (the fraction of time when an attended loom is actually weaving cloth) rose from 67.5 to 88.5 percent when the average run length increased from 3,800 yards to 31,000 yards.[45] Third, specialization which increases run lengths reduces average machine setup time per unit produced—an important consideration in fabric printing, bearing manufacturing, cigarette making, and many other processes. And although there may be other ways of achieving the same result, economies are realized by concentrating special raw materials stocks and finished goods inventories in one place so that random variations in the level of consumption are averaged out under the law of large numbers over the largest possible base.

Of course, equipment specialization, maximization of run lengths, and inventory centralization are at least in principle consistent with concentrating all one's production under a single roof or at a single site. But even when outbound transportation costs per unit of product value are modest, there are forces checking the indefinite expansion of individual plants and hence, given run-length economies and equipment specialization, leading plants to specialize. As we have argued in Chapter 2, the difficulty of managing a large multi-product manufacturing complex significantly limits plant sizes. This is especially evident in the textile, shoe, glass bottle, and (less clearly) antifriction bearing industries. Monopsonistic limits on hiring low-wage or high-productivity labor in smaller towns have led textile, shoe, and bearing makers to disperse relatively small, specialized plants among numerous labor supply areas. All sorts of special considerations also intrude. For example, weaving disparate yarn colors and types in a single shed is undesirable because airborne lint can cross-contaminate and streak the woven fabrics. Automotive and industrial battery production is commonly separated to prevent the slow work pace prevailing in industrial unit assembly shops

44. *Cotton and Allied Textiles*, p. 72.
45. Ibid., p. 73.

from spreading to the mechanized automobile battery lines. High- and medium-price shoe production operations are kept apart so that quality standards on the former do not regress.

For these and other ad hoc reasons there are incentives for plants to specialize. The specialization pattern emerging in any given industry reflects a complex set of tradeoffs taking into account transportation costs, plant-specific scale economies, lot-size and work simplification economies, managerial diseconomies of scale, and labor market constraints, among others.

Assigning industries to pigeonholes involves a certain amount of arbitrariness. Specialization patterns differ inter alia from nation to nation, depending upon the size of the relevant market. For the United States a first approximation would put the cement, petroleum refining, brewing, bottle, and automobile battery industries in the geographic specialization category. Examples of relatively pure product specialization include antifriction bearings, shoes, broad-woven fabrics, cigarettes, and refrigerators. Composite specialization is strongly evident in paints and steel; several other industries exhibit traces. We begin our more detailed analysis with the purest product specialization cases and then take up more complex mixed cases.

Product Specialization Cases

Antifriction bearings provide a classic example of product specialization. Transportation costs are low in relation to product value, seldom averaging more than 3 percent for intranational shipments of good size. Plant specialization occurs along three dimensions: by product type (ball vs. roller vs. tapered roller vs. needle), by size range (miniature precision vs. standard vs. oversize), and by volume range. Multi-plant company representatives stated that producing the same bearing at two different affiliated plants in the same nation is almost unheard of. This is so because there are compelling lot-size and machinery specialization economies. Setting up an automatic screw machine to perform the main metal-cutting operations on a standard bearing cone or cup takes about eight hours. Once ready, the machine produces from 80 to 140 parts per hour. To split the machining of, say, 10,000 identical bearing cones between two plants (or even between two screw machines) raises setup time from approximately 10 percent of running time to 20 percent. The rise in unit machining costs is even greater, since machine setup is a labor-intensive job performed by especially skilled, highly paid operatives while a less skilled worker may attend several screw machines once they are running smoothly. Similar setup cost economies exist for grinding and honing machine preparation, cage tooling and stamping, and assembly operation preparation. Further economies can be secured by establishing straight-line production operations with specialized machines and automated work piece transfer for bearings demanded in sufficiently high volume (at least one million assembled bearings per year) to sustain an unaltered flow week after week. The manager of a highly automated Japanese plant estimated that output per worker with a straight-line setup is roughly twice as high as with job-shop production of medium-volume bearings. Capital costs are higher with automation, but since wage costs were expected to rise much more rapidly than machine costs, he believed *total* in-plant unit cost savings were also likely over the long run to approximate 50 percent. Because automated bearing assembly requires less skilled workers than manual methods and because the plant layouts are quite different, multi-plant companies have tended in recent years to establish separate plants to house their high-volume production lines.

The lot-size economies in bearing production are so compelling that product specialization on a multi-national plane can yield substantial net benefits even after shipping costs are deducted. The formation of the European Common Market and European Free Trade Association created especially attractive opportunities for cost saving through international multi-plant specialization. A spokesman for one company with extensive European operations gave 10 percent as his best-guess estimate of the production economies attainable by moving to a fully specialized multi-national strategy, though the savings might be as little as 3 percent under adverse circumstances. In view of the opportunities, we were surprised to find during our 1970 interviews that relatively little progress toward increasing international specialization had occurred. European and American interviewees cited several barriers to rapid adaptation. Despite international dimensional standardization (except for tapered bearings),[46] many bearing design details vary with specific national applications. Getting users to accept completely standardized designs is difficult. Second, the national divisions of certain multi-national bearing manufacturers, most notably SKF, enjoyed considerable organizational autonomy, and they resisted specialization measures which would reduce their sales without a suitable quid pro quo. Also, fear of supply interruptions due to war or less violent trade breakdowns sometimes leads major bearing buyers to insist that the bulk of their requirements be produced domestically. This attitude appeared to be crumbling in the early 1970s, however, as many bearing users found they could achieve

46. See "When a Standard Doesn't Measure Up," *Business Week*, July 24, 1971, pp. 54–55.

important savings placing substantial orders with a price-competitive foreign manufacturer (often Japanese) while ordering enough from domestic firms to ensure a backup supply.

The movement toward international specialization accelerated markedly during the early 1970s. The actions of SKF, by a considerable margin the largest Western European bearing manufacturer, are of special interest. At the time of our interviews in 1970, SKF's main response to the European Community's formation had consisted of building a new plant in France to supply threaded bearings for the entire Common Market and concentrating the production of needle bearings at a single EC plant. But after experiencing falling profits owing in part to increasing competition from both European and Japanese rivals, SKF announced an ambitious international rationalization program. Under it, according to the company's 1972 annual report: "Each factory taking part in the coordination will radically reduce its previous range of bearing types and substantially increase its manufacturing volume for each bearing type. As a result, over a five year period, parallel manufacture of the same bearing type in the five [major SKF European] companies will in principle cease. Over the same period, two thirds of the Group's European production volume will be manufactured on completely automated plant."

Apparently to assuage buyers' fears of international trade breakdowns, the plan also provided that "coordinated bearing production can . . . be separated and resumed in all factories at short notice if necessary." To coordinate and expedite the program, among other things ensuring that workloads would be evenly redistributed among the principal SKF national companies in Germany, France, England, Italy, and Sweden, a special new supranational office with staff drawn from the various national companies was established in Brussels. A concurrent reorganization placed the previously autonomous SKF Canadian branch under the control of the U.S. branch, facilitating production assignment reallocations to take advantage of the 1965 trade pact eliminating tariffs between Canada and the United States on original equipment automobile parts (including bearings). A similar action had been taken much earlier by the Timken Company, which reorganized its product assignments to concentrate all North American production of certain bearings in its St. Thomas, Ontario, plant, removing other items from that plant for specialized production in U.S. installations.

Textile manufacturing is technically similar to bearings. There are modest costs in resetting looms for new weaves and, as pointed out earlier, significant "learning by doing" economies from achieving long runs on a given bank of looms. Once the bugs have been worked out, an operative may be able to double the number of looms she attends without experiencing significantly higher loom inactivity time. Setup costs in certain finishing processes are also high in relation to subsequent processing costs for short and medium-length runs.[47] Multi-plant operators consequently enforce the maximum possible amount of product specialization within plants. Producing the same fabric simultaneously in different plants is rare; it occurs only when demand is very strong (as for blue denim during the late 1960s) or there are unusual peak load pressures. When the volume of orders is sufficient, companies try to load their weaving mills continuously with a single fabric or at most a few very similar fabrics. When this is impossible, they tend to concentrate high-volume runs in certain plants and isolate the troublesome low-volume jobs in special plants with augmented management. A modest amount of multi-plant, multi-national specialization has also begun to appear. For instance, certain British companies have acquired plants in Hong Kong, Portugal, and Spain employing low-wage labor to produce grey goods which are then shipped to England for specialized finishing. In some countries there is also a fair amount of international specialization through market transactions between spinners, weavers, and finishers of diverse national origin.

The machinery used in most shoemaking processes is very flexible, and setup costs in changing from one shoe design to another within a broad construction class are generally not large. But "learning by doing" economies are very important. According to Pratten and Dean, savings amounting to roughly 10 to 15 percent of labor and overhead costs can be realized by increasing average production run lengths from 200 pairs to between 1,000 and 6,000 pairs.[48] Even larger savings were reported or conjectured by some of our interviewees. A work methods engineer for one company estimated that output per worker could be doubled if the product mix of a Canadian plant assembling 4,000 pairs per day were simplified from the 40 different designs actually assigned to one design of a given size. A three-plant, 12,000-pair per day company which actually succeeded in pruning its product line from a very complex assortment of men's, women's, and children's shoes to 120 men's styles, mostly similar, saw its output per direct worker rise by 200 percent between 1961 and 1971. Most of this increase, the firm's head insisted, was directly attributable to larger lots and increased specialization.

These lot-size economies strongly encourage specialization of shoe production assignments. So also do the expenses of duplicating lasts.

47. Cf. p. 49 *supra*.
48. C. Pratten and R. M. Dean, *The Economics of Large-Scale Production in British Industry* (Cambridge, Eng.: Cambridge University Press, 1965), p. 57.

A shoe company with three relatively small plants reported that it never duplicated assignments between plants. High-volume items were specialized in two plants and "cats and dogs" were concentrated in a third. A company with six plants and another with fifteen produced certain very high volume shoes in two different plants simultaneously. A still larger firm reported assigning sales leaders to as many as three plants. Low-volume makes were in all cases produced by no more than one plant. In none of the companies we interviewed was an attempt made to have plants devote their entire capacity to a single design, although such extreme specialization was said to be practiced in some small firms. The more typical specialization pattern among large multi-plant concerns was for a given plant to have half its volume provided by a single design, with the balance filled out by ten or twenty different makes. This approach was said to provide the best tradeoff between specialization economies and flexibility in adjusting to fluctuations in the demand for any given design.

Cigarette production presents a rather different picture. Rolling and packaging machines are quite inflexible. It takes at least sixteen hours of work plus a sizeable quantity of parts to convert a rolling machine from one size configuration to a slightly different one, although tobacco blend changes or simple brand name imprint changes can be made more quickly. A single 1960s' vintage machine can make about a half billion cigarettes per year on continuous two-shift operation. Newer machines are twice as fast. Brand sales fluctuate widely over time. The need to schedule machines fully but flexibly so as to minimize setup costs, along with economies of large batches in the blending departments, lead to concentration of at least the low-volume brands (those selling less than a billion units per year) at a single plant. Short-run demand fluctuations are then accommodated by running machines more or less intensively and by shifting workers from a central labor pool back and forth between machines. This practice was followed by every producer we interviewed except for the French tobacco monopoly, which had two of its thirteen cigarette plants specializing in low-volume items, with no overlap. Centralization of low-volume production also has the advantage of massing machine rebuilding staff reserves against the inevitable reassignments dictated by shifting demand.

High-volume cigarette assignments, on the other hand, are often given to more than one plant. In the United States, where nearly all production takes place in the Louisville-Richmond-Winston Salem triangle, this is done largely to ensure security of supply. In Europe, where smaller and more numerous plants are more widely dispersed geographically, transportation cost savings were cited as an additional benefit. Unlike the United States, the European pattern suggests a composite type of specialization, but there is reason to believe it is merely an optimal adaptation to a suboptimal plant location inheritance. Costs would probably be slightly lower if production were concentrated in fewer plants of considerably greater scale.

Plant-specific scale economies exert pressure toward concentration of refrigerator production in a single plant for all but the largest suppliers. There are also modest changeover costs in switching from one model to another on assembly lines and significant "learning by doing" effects leading to lower costs and fewer assembly errors as production runs are lengthened. These plus the high costs of box stamping press tooling (which can support an output exceeding 200,000 boxes of a given size per year) call for specialization when a firm is large enough to operate more than one plant. This is in fact the pattern adopted by the only multi-plant U.S. refrigerator makers. During the 1950s and early 1960s there was some duplication of box sizes between General Electric's Chicago (Hotpoint) and Louisville plants. But in the late 1960s, GE began moving toward greater specialization between Chicago and Louisville. A new plant at Bloomington, Indiana, specialized in the largest side-by-side models. Whirlpool, the second largest U.S. producer in 1970, had three refrigerator plants, one specializing in chest freezers, one in side-by-side units and upright freezers, and the largest in standard models. All of the General Electric and Whirlpool plants were large enough to realize most, if not all, plant-specific scale economies.

Lot Sizes, Transportation Cost, and Composite Specialization

The paint industry affords the clearest illustration of geographically unbalanced composite specialization, at least in the territorially vast U.S. and Canadian markets. Larger companies offer thousands of different products, if variations in chemical formulation, color, and package size are all counted. The "80-20" rule holds approximately; that is, the best selling 20 percent of a firm's stock items by number account for roughly 80 percent of sales volume.[49] Shipping costs are sufficiently high in relation to product value to exert a pull toward geographic decentralization. But lot-size economies tug centripetally. Certain skilled jobs such as color-matching take as much time for a big batch as for a small, and setup costs on a packaging line are substantial. One company reported that the average mixing labor plus overhead cost per gallon for five standard paints fell from 43 cents on 200 gallon

49. See John F. Magee, *Physical Distribution Systems* (New York: McGraw-Hill, 1967), p. 38.

batches to 14 cents on 2500 gallon batches. Over the same batch size range, filling line labor costs declined from 13.5 cents to 5.0 cents. For low-volume paints these batch size economies overwhelm the centrifugal pull of transportation costs, leading to an unbalanced specialization pattern in multi-plant companies. High-volume paints well down the lot-size cost curve are decentralized among regional plants, while every effort is made to centralize the production of low-volume products.

Further specialization emerges because of interregional demand variations. For instance, industrial paints tend to be highly specialized to a particular customer's needs, and many customers operate only in a single plant's market territory. The result is a high degree of plant specialization on low-volume items and special industrial paints, combined with multi-plant duplication of standard decorative paint mixing. As Adam Smith anticipated, the extent of specialization is related to the size of the market. The British Columbia plant of a leading producer depended upon broader-line sister plants in Ontario and Quebec for about 30 percent of its market's requirements by volume, whereas the same firm's U.S. West Coast plants drew less than 10 percent of their needs from other company units.[50] There is almost no planned cross-shipping of low-volume items between Canada and the United States, however; tariffs are prohibitive. In Europe, it should be noted, a quite different pattern is found. Multi-plant firms there practice almost no geographic specialization at all within their compact national markets. Except where mergers have not yet been rationalized, plants specialize by products.

One might expect the pattern in storage batteries to be similar. It is not, at least in the United States and Canada, where specialization is preponderantly of the geographic variety. Average transport costs per unit of product value are close to those for paints. The typical full-line North American starter battery producer manufactures somewhere between 50 and 150 physically different types, with the best-selling 20 percent by number accounting for 80 to 95 percent of volume. In these respects paints and batteries are similar. But there is an important difference in production processes. Three main assembly approaches are found: automated high-volume, straight-line processes with throughputs up to one million units per year; flexible semiautomatic lines with capacities up to 250,000 units per year; and low-volume, labor-intensive batch processing methods. Even the higher-volume automated lines are fairly flexible, requiring only one to two hours for retooling to accom-

---

50. The total population of British Columbia and Alberta in 1966 was 3.3 million, compared to 18.7 million in California.

modate a new but similar type. The lower-volume processes are very flexible, and "learning by doing" economies following a change in types are said to be minimal. As a result, the unit cost-lot size relationship is quite flat; there are significant unit cost decreases only when a battery's volume increases sufficiently to warrant a shift from one processing mode to another. U.S. and Canadian producers have not found the batch size economies sufficiently compelling to attempt much centralization of low-volume types. One of the largest manufacturers reported that only one percent of its output was produced centrally for all distribution territories; all other standard types were produced at every general-line plant. The experience of three other U.S. and Canadian multi-plant firms was similar, although one company was beginning in 1970 to keep low-volume types out of its most automated plants, assigning their production to another plant in the same geographic region.

The glass bottle industry has characteristics strongly resembling those of paints, but much higher unit transportation costs and certain special features cause it to be classified as geographically rather than compositely specialized. A broad-line manufacturer is apt to produce as many as 2,000 different designs, with most of its volume concentrated in a much smaller number of types, notably, the leading beer, liquor, soft drink, and (in Europe) wine bottles. Like paints and unlike batteries, lot-size economies are pronounced on the smaller jobs. A significant investment in molds is required for each design. It takes from two to three hours to set up a bottle-blowing machine for a new job, and several more hours of low-yield production usually follow before all the bugs are worked out. On the average, five hours of production are lost with each new setup. The average run of a U.S. manufacturer tends to be on the order of 10,000 gross, although the variance is wide; for a Canadian producer the average is nearer 5,000 gross. Run speeds depend upon bottle size and machine design, but speeds of one gross per minute are not uncommon for standard bottles on modern multi-stage machines. Thus, a 1,000 gross run involves setup time amounting to roughly 30 percent of running time, a 5,000 gross run 6 percent, and a 10,000 gross run 3 percent. These lot-size economies pull low-volume orders strongly toward specialized production. But high transportation costs exert a countervailing pull. Equally important, the low-volume orders often come from some customer taking delivery at only one point, so production is drawn into the nearest plant and there is little or no need to ship into other plants' natural territories. Conversely, bottles demanded on a nationwide plane are usually consumed in such large quantities that the incremental lot-size economies achieved through centralization are not sufficient to offset transportation costs, so production is duplicated on a decentralized basis.

There are only three noteworthy exceptions to this geographic decentralization pattern. First, small items such as medicine and perfume bottles are sometimes produced centrally and distributed nationwide because shipping costs are much lower in relation to product value. Second (and in part related), the largest producers often designate a single plant to specialize in costly, low-volume fancy bottles which can bear longer shipment. It is usually located in a traditional glass center where there are many highly skilled workers able to cope with special designs and frequent startups. Third, when a company is large enough to have two or more plants serving a single region, a pattern of product specialization is likely to develop. One may specialize in high-volume items such as beer bottles and another in low-volume orders. Or when the plants are too small to have three molten glass tanks each, they will specialize by color, one, say, in flint (clear) plus amber, the other in flint plus green. Or in one case encountered, moderately distant plants adhered to a color rotation schedule so that routine orders could be processed for inventory in the nearest plant, minimizing transport costs, while rush orders were fitted into the plant which had the desired glass color running.

The desire to ship what is mostly water as little as possible pulls breweries toward geographic specialization. However, packaging complicates matters. The packaging preferences of American (but not yet European) consumers are highly diverse. Some like cans, some bottles; some small containers, and some large. There are economies of scale and specialization in packaging. The highest-speed canning machines operating in 1970 processed approximately 1.2 million barrels per year on three-shift operation; the fastest bottling machines 750,000 barrels. Slower machines exist, but they have significantly higher unit labor and capital costs. Setup costs for minor label changes are small, but for package size changes they are substantial. For low-volume packages, brewers face a Hobson's choice among small machines, poorly utilized special machines, high setup costs, less frequent processing and hence higher inventories (with attendant physical deterioration), or foregoing the sales that the special packages permit. Multi-plant companies have an additional degree of freedom: they can centralize the production of low-volume packages, trading higher transport cost for production cost savings. Large multi-plant brewers in the United States and Canada believed that shipping costs were too high to warrant regular centralization on a nationwide scale. But they engaged in considerable regional specialization, assigning cans exclusively to one brewery and bottles to an adjacent one, or concentrating the production of special sizes at one brewery to supplement the high-volume packages of one to three neighboring plants. And in this limited sense a pattern of unbalanced composite specialization existed.

Finally, there is the extremely complex case of the steel industry. Transportation costs are high enough in relation to product value to mandate regional specialization on most ordinary steel items, at least in a market as large as the United States. Rolling mills are specialized over limited ranges of products—some, such as continuous hot strip mills, much more narrowly than others, like bar and structural mills. The scale imperatives for efficient production differ widely from product to product. For most products the match between scale requisites and market size is such that rolling mills can be kept busy supplying a relatively small geographic radius, so geographic specialization has been possible.[51] But this is not always true. Thus, in 1970 there were only two plants, both located in the East, supplying 36-inch flange I-beams to the entire U.S. market. Historically, product specialization has been prominent in every major nation's steel industry, some plants specializing in flat-rolled products, some in bar products, some in structural shapes, and so on. But recently polarization has begun to develop. Increases in the optimal scale of blast furnaces, converters, and primary mills have made it desirable to build very large works. The need to utilize these large agglomerations of hot metal capacity fully, among other things balancing out product class demand fluctuations, has exerted a pull toward consolidating more diverse types of rolling mills at a single integrated works. Simultaneously, "mini-mills" specializing in rolling such simple bar products as concrete reinforcing rods from steel made out of scrap in relatively small electric arc furnaces have become increasingly viable. The result has been a complex combination of regional, product, and composite specialization within multi-plant firms. No single strategy appeared to be dominant.

There are also lot-size economies of a sufficiently complicated nature that interviewees were uncertain about the importance of their links to multi-plant operation. In strip production, the time required to readjust

51. We were surprised to find that in Japan, plants 350 to 400 miles apart specialized geographically rather than by specific product. Thus, a 2-plant firm often rolled the same plate, strip, and structural products at both of its plants, each serving the geographic area in which it had a production plus delivery cost advantage. Since the plants in question delivered most of their production by low-cost water media, this pattern suggests that unexploited product-specific scale economies could not have been very important despite the duplication of production assignments.

rollers for a different width or gauge is small. But usually a period of trial-and-error fine-tuning follows, during which some of the rolled product will prove defective. The longer the run, the lower will be the rejected product ratio. Also, different orders may require small differences in the steel's chemical composition, and a short special-composition run is apt to use less metal than the output of a single efficient basic oxygen converter heat. This implies expensively small heats or slab stockpiling. Furthermore, jobs must be rolled in a rigid sequence, from widest strips to narrowest, because the mill rollers score at the edge of the strip being rolled. With short runs of widely varying widths, roller life is likely to be lower, causing higher roller regrinding costs. Similar problems are encountered in rolling structural steel products. Sequencing is particularly important. Structural mills follow a systematic rolling cycle to minimize the number of roller changes required in shifting from one product to another, for example, from small angles to large angles to large I-beams to small I-beams. Small lots are not intrinsically costly, but if a mill has many short bursts of small lots its changeover costs will be increased significantly.

Except for certain highly standardized products, most steel products rolling is done on a to-order basis.[52] Problems often crop up in filling an order; for instance, a coil of steel strip may be found at the cold-rolling stage to be excessively pitted, or structural members may be bent or otherwise damaged. The U.S. producers we interviewed believed that it is prohibitively costly to hedge against such problems by rolling more than the quantity ordered. Therefore, when problems are discovered, a replacement order must be worked into the rolling schedule. On rush orders this can cause scheduling crises, especially for structural products, since the mill cycle may have progressed to a different product size or shape before the problem is discovered, and to break into the cycle would entail high setup costs. There are no easy solutions, but multi-mill companies appear to have a potential advantage in coping with such problems. They schedule their rolling mills to have oppositely phased cycles so that the time between replications of a given shape somewhere in the system is halved with two mills, cut to a third for three, and so on. Nevertheless, single-plant producers were said to be almost equally successful in getting good rolling mill utilization—some,

---

52. Production to order is more prevalent for strip and plate products than for bar and structural products. There is reason to believe that Japanese steelmakers produce relatively more of their structural steel for inventory than U.S. firms, evidently because a higher fraction of Japanese output is sold through warehouses which among other things cut standard shapes to the specific lengths desired by both small and large customers.

like Inland Steel, by having two oppositely phased rolling mills of a given type at a single location; other smaller firms by cutting prices to land the orders needed to fill out their rolling schedules.

The Cost Savings from Product Specialization

It is no easy task to extract generalizations from this extraordinarily complex mosaic. Many multi-plant producers realize cost savings from the product and composite specialization strategies they have adopted. A point of departure for estimating the magnitude of those savings in the crudest impressionistic way can be had by invoking the 80-20 rule. On that 80 percent or so by number of broad-line firms' products which make up the small-lot tail of the product size distribution and account for approximately 20 percent of total volume, the potential savings from optimal specialization might run somewhere between 20 and 50 percent of in-plant processing costs, or 10 to 25 percent of an industry's sales revenue from such low-volume products. This implies a savings potential on the order of 2 to 5 percent of *total* sales revenues. Only the antifriction bearing, textile, paint, and shoe industries come anywhere close to enjoying a potential of this magnitude through product specialization strategies linked to multi-plant operation. For steel, brewing, bottles, batteries, cigarettes, and refrigerators the specialization potential of multi-plant operation appears to be more modest. For cement and petroleum refining, it is negligible.

This first approximation begs a question of the utmost importance: Why is multi-plant operation necessary at all to secure optimal product and composite specialization? Is it possible to achieve the same result through a collection of independent single-plant specialists? For instance, in the textile industry, is there any reason why one firm cannot crank out cotton blend sheetings by the mile, another dacron print cloth, another pile fabrics? Or in the more complex case of the paint industry, might high-volume trade paints be supplied by geographically dispersed independents while other firms serve a nationwide market for specialty paints from central locations?

It is clear that many independent specialists do coexist side by side with geographically, product, and compositely specialized multi-plant firms. To the extent that such firms realize the principal product-specific economies of scale and their products are perfectly substitutable for those of multi-plant operators, the incremental benefits attributable to specialization in a multi-plant context are zero. The multi-plant enterprises must specialize merely to enter the market on a par with their single-plant rivals. If real economic benefits are to be credited to multi-plant specialization, there must be a strong interaction between the other advantages of multi-plant operation and the specialization economies. In particular, if there exist markets or submarkets in which multi-plant firms could survive the competition of optimally specialized single-plant rivals, *whether or not* the multi-plant concerns themselves specialized optimally, then whatever economies the multi-plant firms achieve through specialization beyond that survival threshold must be counted as incremental real benefits.

It is so difficult to determine whether and to what extent this condition is satisfied in actual industrial markets that the benefit measurement problem must probably be regarded as insoluble. The most we can hope to accomplish is to identify cases in which the interaction effect between specialization economies and other multi-plant advantages is particularly strong, and in which therefore a reasonable argument exists for considering multi-plant specialization to yield real benefits.

One case occurs when buyers prefer to deal with a broad-line supplier, and when supplying a broad line efficiently implies multi-plant operation. Likely candidates identified earlier include the preference of many shoe retailers for obtaining at least a sizeable fraction of their line from one manufacturer, the desire of home builders and retail chains selling under their own labels to offer compatibly designed complementary kitchen appliances (in which case multi-industry, multi-plant operation may be implied), the market for coordinated home furnishings fabrics, and the full-line preferences of replacement bearing wholesalers. Yet the mere existence of such preferences is not enough; their strength counts too. If Marshall Field's would do its own fabric coordination at any price premium exceeding 2 percent of the average price quoted by competitive independent specialist weavers, multi-plant textile firms could not survive carrying a cost penalty owing to incomplete specialization exceeding that magnitude, and only the incremental savings from specialization inside that threshold can be counted as real economic benefits.

More compelling are certain joint cost features of the physical distribution process. Once a paint company has cultivated a dealer relationship and has its wares on the dealer's shelves, the marginal cost of adding another low-volume specialty item may be slight. The economics here are not simple; one must consider not only incremental production and physical distribution costs but also the relationship between the additional item and sales of other products. For instance, the extra item may or may not displace the offering of a competitive firm. It may complement the manufacturer's other products and make consumers more likely to buy them, or it may compete with them. Generally, however, the net balance in adding specialty paint products appears to be favorable. A leading U.S. trade paint manufacturer indicated that a study showed the marginal profit from adding items to fill out its product line to be "shockingly high," given that distribution channels were already established. For a firm producing a limited line of specialty paints for the national market, on the other hand, the cost of securing similar access to retail outlets is apt to be prohibitive. To the extent that this is so, the savings realized by a multi-plant paint manufacturer through geographically unbalanced composite specialization can have a significant real component. It seems probable that similar specialization economies interacting with low marginal distribution costs exist for automobile replacement bearing manufacturers, refrigerator producers, and shoemakers broadening their product lines.

Even here, however, we must raise doubts. Why must a paint manufacturer serving the national market produce low-volume specialties in its own plants? Might it not do as well buying the products from independent specialists and distributing them through its own channels? Or even better, since the specialist may be able to supply several such manufacturers and put together even larger production lots? The answer is by no means clear. If the market for the specialty item were competitive, we should expect the manufacturer to be roughly indifferent between making its own and buying from specialists. However, because the essence of the low-volume product problem is paucity of demand in relation to product-specific scale economy imperatives, competition is likely to break down. The independent specialist, though small, enjoys pricing discretion consistent with its ability to take fuller advantage of run-length economies than less specialized rivals and potential entrants. It may choose to exercise that discretion by setting prices exceeding its own unit costs and the unit costs a large multi-plant firm can sustain internally through composite specialization. If it does, or if potential customers merely fear such pricing, market failure will induce the multi-plant firm to produce its own requirements, though it enjoys no real cost advantage, or even suffers a disadvantage, relative to independent specialists. To the extent that distribution of independent specialists' output *is* a viable alternative for broad-line firms with well-established marketing channels, the incremental real benefits of specialized internal production by multi-plant firms shrink toward zero. But if market failure is unavoidable and price-setting practices encourage internal production, real benefits accrue from specialization measures which reduce the multi-plant enterprise's unit costs below the buy-vs.-make indifference threshold.

The image advantages of nationwide firms can interact with multi-plant specialization in similar ways. A specialty item offered under the du Pont or Sherwin-Williams banner is apt to command a higher price than the same item supplied by a small unknown independent. So will a specialty package with the Budweiser trademark or a marginal addition to the Stride-Rite or Florsheim shoe line. Given their price premium, such specialty products can survive profitably even if produced at unit costs elevated owing to inadequate specialization. Multi-plant specialization measures which reduce unit costs below the survival threshold confer real economies, *if* in addition the multi-plant firm cannot buy the specialty products (for example, as "stencil brands") from independent specialists at prices as low as its internal unit costs, or if outside procurement would jeopardize the products' image advantage.

Product specialization in the multi-plant context can also yield real economies owing to market failure of a more pervasive character.[53] Suppose that, because of respect for oligopolistic interdependence or strong product differentiation, prices are set at levels yielding supranormal profits. Unless entry barriers are substantial, outsiders are likely to enter. Even if they do not, insiders will try to expand by broadening their product spectrum coverage. Especially if demand is growing slowly, the result is apt to be an equilibrium in which each firm supplies numerous products in quantities too small to realize all run-length economies. The tendency for this equilibrium to emerge will be heightened in slowly growing industries by the fact that as new entry or internal product line broadening occurs, each producer finds its sales of existing products eroded and searches for additional complementary products to fill out capacity voids. Unless they are willing to break pricing discipline in a quest for added volume on existing products or (when feasible) innovate technologically, small broad-line firms will find themselves squeezed by rising unit costs to a position in which they realize only normal profits. But assuming that their size has not been achieved merely by producing proportionately more items than single-plant rivals in comparably inefficient lots, larger multi-plant operators may fare better. If they can develop a higher degree of specialization among their multiple plants, they will enjoy real run-length economies.

Multi-plant specialization in this instance affords efficiency gains of a second-best type. That is, *if* the market were working competitively, the incentives for product segment overcrowding and consequently inefficient run lengths would have been absent. Or even if such over-

---

53. This analysis is similar in spirit but different in substance from the rationalization analysis by Donald Dewey in *The Theory of Imperfect Competition: A Radical Reconstruction* (New York: Columbia University Press, 1969) esp. chap. 4. It is similar in substance to M. Howe, "Competition and the Multiplication of Products," *Yorkshire Bulletin of Economic and Social Research*, 12 (November 1960), 57–72, of which we became aware only as our manuscript was in the final revision stages.

crowding had materialized, it could have been alleviated by vigorous price competition among firms seeking to win more sales in selected product segments and hence to enlarge their production lot sizes. But given strong respect for oligopolistic interdependence or other market failures inhibiting competition, specialization in the multi-plant context reduces costs compared to what they would be in a market populated by broad-line single-plant producers.

Mergers between firms with overlapping product lines are one means by which production efficiency can be increased through enhanced multi-plant specialization. Among the mergers covered by our research, this was most strikingly the case in the consolidation of three British antifriction bearing firms to form RHP (Ransome Hoffmann Pollard), Ltd. in 1969.[54] In promoting and organizing the merger, the British government's Industrial Reorganisation Corporation was motivated by the desire to create a strong British-owned bearing manufacturer and by its realization that the U.K. bearing industry's productivity was extremely low compared to other major nations, in part owing to inadequate specialization.

The three merger partners, and especially Ransome & Marles and Hoffmann, offered extensively overlapping product lines, no segment of which was produced on an automated straight-line basis. A significant reason for the failure of specialization to develop was the languid price competition among bearing manufacturers up to the late 1960s. Even when cartel agreements were outlawed under the Restrictive Trade Practices Act of 1956, industry traditions and respect for mutual interdependence inhibited most bearing manufacturers from cutting prices to secure longer production runs on standard bearings. Indeed, companies were willing to add new low-volume items to fill out their product lines and keep their plants busy. The principal exception was Pollard, which had cut prices to capture a 60 percent share of the water pump bearing market, a strategy which, representatives of other firms claimed, had been carried to the point of jeopardizing Pollard's long-run profitability.[55]

54. For a summary of conditions leading to the merger, see the *Antitrust Bulletin*, 15 (Winter 1970), 846–857, reproducing reports of the Industrial Reorganisation Corporation. More extensive information on the merger and events of the subsequent three years is contained in the Harvard Business School case studies, Ransome & Marles Bearing Company, Ltd. and Ransome Hoffmann Pollard, Ltd., nos. 4-374-040 through 4-374-043, 1973.

55. In 1968, the last calendar year prior to the merger, Pollard earned 5 percent before taxes on stockholders' equity, compared to 10–15 percent in the mid-1960s. In acquiring Pollard, Ransome & Marles offered a 60 percent premium over the value of common stock prices prevailing on the last trading day prior to the first takeover offer announcement.

Immediately following the merger, production assignments were completely revamped to eliminate duplication and lengthen runs. Within three years, output per employee had been increased by roughly 40 percent, partly as a direct result of the increase in plant specialization and partly through simple belt-tightening. Substantial further productivity gains were expected from the introduction, beginning in the fall of 1973, of six automated lines for high-volume standard bearings. Given the failure of efficient product specialization to emerge in most segments of the U.K. bearing market, the RHP merger afforded a second-best solution with real efficiency benefits.

Product line specialization cartels offer a route short of full merger toward the same end. A prime example is the Japanese antifriction bearing industry. High-volume items are manufactured by all or most of the five major bearing firms, often on straight-line setups the equal of any in the world. Medium-volume bearings are typically produced by two or three companies, and, with almost no exception as of 1971, only one firm engaged in the production of any given low-volume type. It seems indisputable that this system permitted the exploitation of run-length economies more fully than the sluggish oligopolistic pricing mechanisms prevailing in the bearing industries of the six nations on which our interview research was primarily focused. It was also clear that the cost advantages of Japanese bearing producers (related to low wages as well as lot-size economies) were being manifested in export prices some 30 to 40 percent below U.S. price levels, allowing Japanese firms to capture substantial and rapidly growing shares of the U.S., Canadian, and European bearing markets before the impacted nations imposed import restrictions in the early 1970s.

A question left unanswered by our six-nation interview program was how the Japanese bearing specialization cartel affected *domestic* prices and how domestic bearing users, who in other nations attached considerable value to having competing potential suppliers, viewed their dependence upon a single source for low-volume bearings. A trip to Japan by the senior author in 1973 provided an opportunity to explore this issue with executives of a bearing firm and diverse Japanese academicians. Several institutional and attitudinal differences relative to U.S. and European industry were identified. For one, Japanese labor relations have been such that prolonged strikes occur very rarely, reducing therefore one of the risks against which buyers hedge by having dual sources. Second, there appears to be great stress on harmonious relationships and trust in Japanese business. One simply doesn't expect one's suppliers to let him down, and when disputes arise, there is a strong social convention in favor of resolving them amicably. Third, the powerful Japanese Ministry of International Trade and Industry has actively intervened in past bearing price-setting decisions, and it was considered likely that MITI would intervene again if serious disputes over prices could not be resolved through buyer-seller negotiations. Fourth, a company executive observed that any low-volume bearing assigned to only a single firm under the specialization agreements by definition involved only a small volume of sales, so an occasional supply interruption or price problem would as a rule be only a minor annoyance to major buyers. He noted, however, that very small specialized users might be seriously disadvantaged by such problems and that MITI was much less likely to intervene on their behalf than it would for the large companies with well-established ties to government. For these "forgotten men" of Japanese business, he acknowledged, the cartel might well have significant adverse effects.

Specialization agreements of a similar character existed in the Swedish steel industry.[56] We focus here on only a single facet. In the Swedish market there has scarcely been room for one wide hot strip mill and one heavy plate mill of efficient size. Beginning in 1957, the Grängesberg Company constructed a heavy plate mill. Meanwhile the Stora Kopparberg Company was developing capacity to roll both hot strip and plates. If Stora Kopparberg were to produce plates in sizeable quantities, it would take away sufficient business to prevent Grängesberg from using its plate mill efficiently. Grängesberg's equipment was incapable of rolling sheets and strip, but through additional investment the capacity to do so could be acquired. To ward off a situation in which each firm would be producing both classes of products in uneconomically small quantities, the two companies negotiated an agreement limiting Stora Kopparberg's plate production and preventing Grängesberg from entering the strip and sheet markets. Recognizing the scale imperatives of the situation and the impossibility of achieving more than duopolistic competition, at least among domestic producers, even the most zealous American competition advocate must concede that this agreement made considerable sense. It almost surely increased the efficiency of steel plate production, though it simultaneously eliminated an element of business rivalry from the Swedish market.

Merger through nationalization was the remedy chosen in 1967 to deal with the structural ailments of the British steel industry. Among other things, the degree of specialization by plants was far from optimal and lot sizes were often inefficiently small. Cartel and (later) Iron and Steel Board established prices were rigid and (until the years immediately

---

56. On German steel industry specialization agreements too recent to be explored in our interviews, see Herbert W. Köhler, *Das Kontornachfolgekonzept: Vier Rationalisierungsgruppen* (Düsseldorf: Verlag Stahleisen, 1971).

preceding nationalization) too far removed from minimum possible costs to encourage specialization or drive out the least efficient producers. There was often excess capacity, and each producer scrambled to win orders which would keep its mills busy, even though others might be able to produce at lower cost if they could achieve longer runs. Following nationalization, a program of rationalization was put into effect. It began with such simple measures as reducing the number of plants producing reinforcing rods (an operation with one of the smallest optimal scales in ordinary steelmaking) from twenty-six to sixteen. In the early 1970s product assignments in other lines such as structural sections were reallocated, increasing specialization and in some cases doubling mill outputs.[57] Progress during the early years after nationalization was retarded by inherited work rule rigidities, social obstacles to plant closure, and the sheer managerial difficulty of sorting out and reorganizing operations at more than 100 geographically scattered works turning out finished steel products. Only in 1972 was government approval given for an ambitious program of plant closures and expansions which would among other things exploit fully the opportunities for specialization.[58] Whether these changes would have taken place as rapidly or completely under prenationalization behavioral patterns is arguable. From what we have been able to observe, we are inclined to believe that nationalization, though not the only conceivable solution, provided a much more conducive climate for rationalization and modernization than the failure-ridden market institutions previously existing.

The United States steel industry is also burdened inter alia with run-length problems, albeit much less severe than those in England and Sweden, resulting from the tendency of major steel buyers to divide up their orders between suppliers. Buyers are given no incentive to do otherwise under a fairly rigid price structure reflecting considerable respect for oligopolistic interdependence. Special discounts on large homogeneous orders might be one way of alleviating the problem, but for reasons which were not adequately explored in our interviews, the price structure has simply not developed in such a manner. Specialization within the existing multi-plant structures of U.S. steel companies has not permitted consolidation of orders and longer mill runs because of high intermarket transportation costs and difficulties in scheduling a very complex multi-plant job-shop production operation. Mergers on a modest scale appear unlikely to improve matters, since they would only strengthen oligopolistic coordination and dry up altogether any

57. *British Steel* (October 1971), pp. 21–25.
58. Department of Trade and Industry, *Steel—British Steel Corporation: Ten Year Development Strategy* (London: HMSO, February 1973).

residual incentives steel buyers have to concentrate orders. Evidently, the problem of achieving optimal specialization is an extremely stubborn one in industries with few sellers and strong traditions of pricing interdependence.

Except in the antifriction bearing industry, in which considerable duplication of small-scale production for low-volume items persists, comparably strong examples from other United States industries covered by our research are scarce. Serious failures of specialization to develop have been avoided for the most part because competition has worked tolerably well in encouraging smaller firms to specialize and because product and composite specialization has been practiced by multi-plant enterprises.

To recapitulate, we emerge thus far from our attempt to assess multi-plant specialization benefits with not much more than a will-o'-the-wisp. It is clear that specialization in a multi-plant framework confers savings, sometimes of impressive magnitude. The "with or without" principle of benefit/cost analysis has been invoked implicitly (and now explicitly) to identify cases in which those savings represent real economies attributable incrementally to multi-plant operation. We know that such cases exist. But confident statements about the frequency of their incidence are hard to make. The strongest cases appear almost uniformly to have materialized where a breakdown of competition prevented specialization from emerging through market processes. In at least a significant subset of those cases, most prominently in the bearings and steel industries, multi-plant specialization has increased efficiency. Yet this is a second-best solution. Before we can credit multi-plant operation with un-ambiguous benefits, we must know whether market failure was inevitable or whether it might have been avoided through some alternate set of institutions and policies. And that knowledge all too frequently lies beyond our grasp.

Firm Size, Lot Sizes, and Product Standardization

We move on now to a closely related dimension of the product-specific scale economies issue. Is it possible, especially in industries where products are highly diverse and run-length economies are important, that large firms *systematically* achieve larger average lot sizes than small firms as a direct consequence of their size? Besides those already advanced in the previous section, several hypotheses come to mind. First, in any industry there exists some frequency distribution of individual product demands. It is often characterized at the company level by the 80-20 rule. If all industry members sample more or less randomly from this distribution in proportion to their total sales volume, one would expect firms with the largest shares of the market to have higher sales of any given product than smaller concerns. This follows in the most straightforward way for industries in which product specialization is the dominant mode of multi-plant operation and smaller firms nevertheless offer broad lines. The sequitur is subtler for firms decentralizing their production in response to high transportation costs. Then firm size may merely reflect having more plants producing the same products in different territories. But in such cases the larger firm enjoys greater freedom to practice composite specialization, centralizing the production of low-volume items. Second, it is conceivable that companies which are both large and integrated vertically downstream into final product manufacturing and retailing can exercise greater control over product specifications and order patterns and by so doing secure longer production runs in upstream operations. Finally, there is the Galbraithian assertion that larger corporations are better able to "manage their demand," enforcing product standardization so that the less popular types can be consolidated into larger uniform production lots.[59]

The industry in which large firms most clearly realized important product-specific scale economies by capturing larger shares of the demand for individual products was refrigerators, at least in the United States. Lot-size economies are substantial, and compulsions toward full-line supply are sufficiently strong that the medium-sized U.S. refrigerator makers such as Westinghouse, Frigidaire, Philco, Admiral, and Amana offered nearly as broad a line as industry leaders General Electric and Whirlpool. In Europe, the range of sizes, styles, and colors offered has been much narrower and the medium-sized firms have tended to specialize, quite possibly experiencing production runs comparable to those of the largest manufacturers as long as they avoided the most popular three to five cubic foot box sizes.

In the antifriction bearings industry, broad-line multi-plant firms appeared to enjoy some advantage in accumulating a larger volume of general-line bearing orders which they then combined into larger lots through at least some stages of the production process. Single-plant companies showed greater willingness to accept small-lot jobs. But there was no perceptible correlation between overall sales volume and lot sizes among the broad-line firms; product type and the size of the relevant market were much more important lot-size determinants than firm size. In nearly every nation small companies proved capable of

59. John Kenneth Galbraith, *The New Industrial State* (Boston: Houghton Mifflin, 1967), chaps. XVIII and XIX.

doing well in special market segments amenable to high-volume runs. Thus, the picture is far from uniform, though our overall impression was that the broad-line firms enjoy a run-length advantage on the average.

Among shoemakers there was a strong consensus that multi-plant size beyond a modest threshold conferred no significant advantage in winning larger production lots. The largest companies owed their size primarily to producing a very broad assortment of types and styles, not to greater average volume in particular lines. The main requisite for matching the lot-size distribution of the leading general-line suppliers is an adequate field sales force, which in the United States can be supported without difficulty by a firm with three to five MOS plants producing for a well-defined segment of the market. Smaller firms can also achieve very long production runs by accepting private-label contract work, though they are likely to suffer more intense pressure on prices from powerful buyers. Long runs are also possible for single-plant firms in high-demand specialty lines such as work shoes.

Textiles are similar. There is considerable specialization by both small and large firms. A given product's volume depends mainly upon the nature of the product, strategy choices (such as emphasizing standard shirtings vs. fancy dress goods), and the accidents of history. What correlation between firm size and run length one might observe is mostly spurious, reflecting the fact that the biggest concerns have tended to shun the most fashion-sensitive, inherently short-run fabric lines because they lack the managerial flexibility to succeed in them. The principal exception may be end consumer product lines like sheets and pillowcases, where large companies like Burlington Industries have built strong positions through nationwide advertising campaigns that smaller producers could not afford.[60]

The main lot-size economies in brewing occur at the packaging stage. Small- and medium-sized brewers offer at least as wide an array of packages as the U.S. industry leaders. Since transport costs discourage extensive centralization of low-volume packaging by the multi-plant firms, single-plant brewers with a strong regional market position can achieve packaging runs nearly as long on the average as those of multi-plant brewers. Small firms with weak market positions, on the other hand, experience serious run-length handicaps.

In none of the other seven industries did multi-plant firms enjoy systematic, economically significant run-length advantages as a consequence of their overall size, at least under U.S. market conditions.

60. See p. 247 *supra*.

In cement and petroleum refining this was so because lot-size economies are simply unimportant. Small paint manufacturers have been quite successful specializing on the higher-volume types, where they do as well as the industry leaders. The same was true of smaller U.S. and Canadian bottle makers during the sellers' market of the 1960s, although in Europe there was evidence that the smaller firms were saddled with a disproportionate share of the low-volume business. In the United States and the United Kingdom (but not in Canada and Germany) the largest cigarette sellers have achieved deeper market penetration across their full spectrum of brands than smaller rivals. The economic implications of this difference were slight in the United States, however, since less than 2 percent of total demand was for brands manufactured in quantities insufficient to keep at least one 1960s' vintage making and packaging line busy. There is a tendency toward full-line supply among both small and large automobile battery makers. Because European industry leaders Varta, Chloride, and Lucas are very much larger than their rivals this may imply some significant product-specific cost advantages. But in the United States size per se conferred at best slight advantages for the largest firms because the main noncaptive producers were all of similar size and because the cost savings associated with increased lot sizes were small over the range of volume variation distinguishing single-near-MOS-plant regional specialists from the regionally oriented plants of multi-plant manufacturers. Finally, in the steel industry there was a strong consensus that firm size and average lot sizes are essentially uncorrelated, and that the largest companies owe their size to obtaining *more* physically differentiated orders, not more of any given order.

There were seven industries in which vertical integration downstream coincided on an appreciable scale with potential opportunities for cost reduction through lot-size enhancement. In most, the benefits clearly assignable to integration were either slight or uncertain. U.S. auto makers' integration into battery and bearing production definitely permitted very long production runs, but the same effect was achieved without integration by European auto makers who contracted out all of their requirements for some type to a single supplier. The lot-size implications of Ford's, SKF's, and Timken's integration from auto and bearing manufacturing into steelmaking were inadequately explored. There is reason to believe that Ford's steel works may benefit from unusually long runs. Little attention was paid either to the package run-length implications of British and German brewers' integration into pub ownership. In all probability, the impact has been slight, assuming that comparable quantities of kegged beer would continue to be sold even if pubs were untied. Paint manufacturers with their own retail chains appeared to be no more successful at achieving large average batch sizes than nonintegrated firms, other things such as the degree of trade paint orientation being held equal. Downstream integration by shoe manufacturers conferred no clear lot-size advantages because success in retailing demands that even captive stores seek out the most fashion-responsive and price-competitive supply sources, regardless of ownership affiliation. This competitive pressure leads to equivalent degrees of specialization by integrated and nonintegrated manufacturers, other things such as national market size being held equal. No interviewee outside England placed any stress on vertical integration of spinning, weaving, and textile finishing as an important contributor to lot-size economies, though many other benefits from integration (for instance, in the realm of coordination) were cited.[61]

We found only three industries in which multi-plant firms enjoyed any perceptible advantage in enforcing product standardization. The leading U.S. brewers experienced some success in curbing the proliferation of package types during the late 1960s, in part by eliminating off sizes and partly by raising the prices of low-volume packages in relation to others. Smaller regional brewers with waning brand acceptance were unable to do the same, and some felt compelled to fight sales losses by actually increasing their package offerings. That image strength rather than size per se was the more important factor is suggested by Canadian experience, where the largest brewer, Carling, was the first to break away from an industrywide bottle standardization agreement following a decline in its market share from approximately 60 percent in 1956 to 30 percent in 1970. Antifriction bearing manufacturers mounted a campaign to discourage customers from ordering special designs, typically by announcing large increases in low-volume bearing prices or discontinuing production altogether. Although we observed one small producer pursuing a similar policy with fair success, there was reason to believe that larger, more powerful firms had an easier time at it. In automobile batteries some of the largest producers led the way to run-length increasing standardization—General Motors through its vertically integrated control of vehicle and battery designs in the United States and British market leaders Lucas and Chloride by raising the price differential for low-volume types.

In the other industries with complex product lines, consumer or user demands for variety and special features proved too strong for large and small manufacturers alike. Thus, certain large European

---

61. For the orthodox British view, see *Cotton and Allied Textiles*, pp. 112 and 125.

shoemakers attempted to force standardized designs through their company-owned retail outlets, but the effort was rebuffed by style-conscious consumers and the firms were forced to offer increasingly diverse lines. And even General Electric, the largest U.S. refrigerator maker, was forced to embark upon a "crash" retooling program when it underestimated the rate at which large side-by-side models came into vogue.

To sum up, being large enough to operate multiple MOS plants appears to confer significant advantages in putting together larger production lots and longer runs in the refrigerator and possibly the bearing industries; moderate advantages in subsegments of the textile and brewing industries and (up to the operation of three to five plants) in shoemaking; uncertain or small advantages in the automobile battery and cigarette industries; and no discernible advantage in steel, bottles, paints, petroleum refining, and cement. The benefits tend to be highest in those fields where the product line is variegated, offering a broad line is important to successful marketing, and the gradient of product-specific unit cost functions is steep. It is lowest when competition is working well to encourage specialization, when buyers are relatively few in number and well informed, and when transportation costs curb what might otherwise be attractive opportunities for geographically unbalanced composite specialization. Vertical integration downstream has been found to yield probable lot-size economies in the battery, bearing, and steel industries, although other means of achieving the same end are found to work in some nations. Multi-plant firms may also enjoy an advantage in encouraging standardization of low-volume products, though the pattern is erratic, and producers' power to override consumer preferences for variety appears to be weak.

The Economies of Central Staff Spreading

It is conceivable that multi-plant firms realize scale economies in central administration and staff functions. Four hypotheses are relevant. First, certain administrative and service activities may require a staff of roughly fixed and indivisible size over a broad range of production levels. If so, the unit cost of such functions will decline as they complement a larger volume of corporate output. Second, there are economies of massed reserves if the need for a staff service fluctuates randomly over time. The multi-plant firm can average out such fluctuations more fully, securing better staff utilization and carrying smaller reserves against its relatively flat demand peaks. Third, large companies can sustain a richer division of labor, employing specialists in such fields as linear programming, arbitration law, quantitative market research, and the like where smaller firms must do without or make do with less intensively trained personnel. Fourth, the greater volume of business over which the talents of a top manager or central staff specialist will be applied in a large multi-plant corporation may warrant paying a higher salary to attract superior talent.

Of course, size also has drawbacks. To manage a multi-plant enterprise, it is usually necessary to establish additional layers of control and coordination staff. Decisions are often removed farther from the locus at which they will be executed. This plus the greater complexity of the decision-making apparatus can lead to more frequent delays and mistakes. These characteristics in turn may discourage the most able and energetic individuals from seeking or retaining staff jobs in large corporations, despite the lure of high salaries. And smaller firms may be able to sidestep their talent specialization and massed reserves handicaps by hiring outside specialized services only when they are needed, though coordination problems may make resort to the market a less than perfect alternative to inside staffing. What we have then in assessing the net central staff advantage of multi-plant firms is a balancing job.

The only industry among our twelve for which we were able to obtain systematic administrative staff cost data was paints. For four paint company size groups, the median percentages of office, administration, and general expenditures (excluding selling and research expenses, among others) in relation to 1969 sales were:[62]

Company sales in 1969	Number of companies reporting	Office & administration expenses as a percent of sales: median values
Less than $1 million	28	10.0
$1–3 million	25	8.3
$3–10 million	21	8.6
Over $10 million	18	6.3

To the extent that they are representative—and on this point some doubts can be entertained but not settled[63]—the data suggest a significant

62. Source: National Paint, Varnish, and Lacquer Association, *Operating Cost Survey for the Year 1969* (Washington, 1970), pp. 14–21. For 1973, the corresponding percentage had risen to 10.9 for companies with sales of less than $1 million and fallen to 5.7 for paint makers with sales of $10 million or more. *Operating Cost Survey for the Year 1973*, pp. 20–26.

63. The smaller companies reporting represented only a fraction of all paint companies in their size classes. It is conceivable that respondents tended to be firms with relatively large accounting and administrative staffs able to handle the necessary paperwork. It is also possible that the denominator of the cost/sales ratio is biased downward for the smaller firms, who suffer from weaker brand recognition and receive lower prices per gallon for trade paints than large producers.

unit staff cost advantage for paint manufacturers with sales exceeding $10 million. This is not a particularly large threshold. A single MOS plant (producing 10 million gallons per year) would have sustained sales of more than $30 million at 1969 price levels. It seems reasonable to suppose that the unit administration cost savings from surpassing the efficient single-plant threshold are considerably smaller than those realized approaching the threshold. Supporting evidence came from an interview with a firm which had jumped to a sales level equivalent to two MOS plants through a merger between two paint companies of roughly equal size. Executives of the surviving organization said that they were able to prune many central staff functions following the merger, realizing cost savings totaling 0.6 percent of combined sales.

There has been considerable research on the relationships between organizational size and administrative staff levels. Unfortunately, the results are inconclusive and often conflicting, largely because of deficiencies in the data and analytic techniques used. Following an extensive literature survey and his own reanalysis of the most promising data collected by others, W. H. Starbuck concluded that the ratio of administrative employees to production workers is largely independent of organizational size for companies with 100 employees or more.[64] In a more recent examination of 1960 Population Census data for forty-five diversely defined U.S. manufacturing industries, L. R. Pondy found with one multiple regression specification no significant relationship between "administrative intensity" (the ratio of administrative to production employees) and the average size of an industry's *plants*.[65] However, when a variable measuring the ratio of owner-managers to total managers was added to his regressions, a statistically significant negative relation between administrative intensity and average plant size emerged. Since the owner-manager variable was probably serving as a proxy for ease of entry and other market structure features, and since it in turn was highly collinear with the plant size variable, it is difficult to be sure which of Pondy's regressions better estimates the relationship between administrative intensity and organization size. The issue remains unsettled, awaiting analyses of much better data.

In our interviews the firm size-unit staff cost question was accorded low priority. The limited amount of evidence and opinion we obtained presents an unclear picture. That central staff costs are not fixed as firms move from single-plant to multi-plant status was unmistakable.

64. "Organizational Growth and Development," in James G. March, ed., *Handbook of Organizations* (Chicago: Rand McNally, 1965), esp. pp. 495–520.

65. "Effects of Size, Complexity, and Ownership on Administrative Intensity," *Administrative Science Quarterly*, 14 (March 1969), 47–61.

We identified a few cases in which the rise in costs was believed to be less than proportional to output, but the preponderance of evidence suggested that the largest firms bore a higher unit administrative cost burden than small- and medium-sized rivals. The cost disadvantage of industry leaders appeared especially marked in the steel, glass bottle, petroleum refining, textile, battery, and refrigerator industries.

Generalizations on the quality of managerial and administrative staff personnel are even harder to reach. Our interviews included companies with sales ranging from $150,000 to billions of dollars per year. Of the 125 interviews, 23 were with firms or divisions of firms recording sales of $1 billion or more in 1970. Although there were discernible patterns associated with particular countries and industries, we perceived no obvious association between firm size and such attributes of managerial quality as dynamism, intelligence, awareness, and skill in interpersonal relations. Larger companies did display the expected tendency to maintain a richer array of staff specialists, but the size-correlated differences on this dimension were modest, partly because staff personnel in smaller companies had learned to wear several hats well and partly because small firms exercised considerable ingenuity in tapping outside sources of expertise. And to repeat, whatever systematic relationship there was between quality and size at the top levels was drowned in statistical "noise."

It is clear that the organizational climate of a company alters in largely unfavorable ways with increased size. There was virtual unanimity among interviewees, in large companies and small, that decision-making in the large multi-plant firm is slower and that top executives are farther removed from the personalities and problems of operating levels, with a possible (but less certain) degradation in the quality of decisions. As veteran staff members at a very large corporation observed, no one quite knew how the system held together. "We barely seem to cope," said one.

The standard remedy for problems of corporate size is to decentralize decision-making authority. Yet to gain the advantages of product specialization (especially of the composite variety) and multi-plant massed reserves, extensive central office intervention in production planning is essential. Inability to manage this task effectively was one of the main reasons why numerous companies failed to realize the full economic potential of their multi-plant networks. One firm with a complex product line and the opportunity to save substantial sums through composite specialization lacked detailed central knowledge of items being produced at its diverse plants because it had granted the plants virtual operating autonomy. Another had an order allocation system which took into account capacity constraints at its plants and outbound transportation costs, but not the prospective production costs under alternative allocation plans. A paint company noted that its ability to develop a rational system of unbalanced composite specialization was inhibited by information voids: its central staff could tell where low-volume items were being produced and in what quantities, but not where they were ultimately delivered.

Problems of this genre are potentially amenable to solution through the imaginative application of large-scale computerized order processing, job assignment, production scheduling, and delivery routing systems. Some of the companies we interviewed had already advanced an impressive distance in this direction, achieving better integration of the production and logistic interrelationships among their plants as a result. Leaders included certain petroleum refining, brewing, and cement companies—all with simple product lines and a heavy transportation cost burden. In such industries as steel, shoes, bearings, textiles, and paints progress has been slower, largely because product lines are so much more complex, compounding the data collection and manipulation problem. Yet in each of these industries the problem was receiving attention, and there is reason to expect that significant advances will occur in the future. If they do, multi-plant producers are apt to take fuller advantage of cost-saving opportunities presently left unexploited because of managerial shortfalls.

All things considered, it seems unwarranted to credit much of a net administrative cost-cum-quality advantage to multi-plant size, and in more cases than not the balance appears to be unfavorable, at least with respect to the very largest enterprises. The relative disadvantage of multi-plant firms is probably smaller or the relative advantage larger when product lines are simple, as in brewing, petroleum refining, and cement, than when they are complex, as in shoes, fabrics, steel, and antifriction bearings. More we cannot conclude without overstepping the bounds of our data.

Research, Development, Innovation, and Technical Services

In some industries technical research and development of new products and processes are significant dimensions of business strategy. Do multi-plant firms enjoy advantages in undertaking such activities not readily accessible to companies operating only a single MOS plant?

Economists have made more progress toward pinning down the conceptual ramifications of this question and answering it than on most of the issues with which we have been concerned in this chapter.[66] The a priori arguments are well known. Large firms are said to have an

---

66. For a survey of the literature, see Scherer, *Industrial Market Structure and Economic Performance*, pp. 352–363.

advantage in mustering financial support for costly, risky research and development (R&D) projects; they may realize scale economies due to indivisibilities in research skills and equipment; and they may be able to spread the costs of a given research project over a larger existing or anticipated sales volume. Conversely, the cumbersome decision-making processes of large organizations may impede innovation and drive out the creative individuals most apt to make significant new technical contributions.

Before we examine the evidence on these opposing propensities, a bias in our twelve-industry sample should be recalled. Industries with dramatically changing product or process technologies were deliberately shunned in order to maximize the probability of obtaining consistent historical data and estimating static production cost-volume relationships with some precision. Therefore, our sample yields little insight into the links between size and technical progressiveness for especially dynamic areas of technology.

It is also important to recognize that there are economies of specialization in activities that advance knowledge, as well as in routine production.[67] Certain industries such as electronics and chemicals with roots in a rich scientific base enjoy comparative advantage in developing new materials and equipment to be used by a host of other industries. And even when the science base is not particularly fecund, some companies (such as the machinery makers) find it advantageous to specialize in developing and supplying capital goods for other industries. Because these specialization patterns exist, it is often possible for progress in an industry's technology to be rapid even though the industry itself performs little formal research and development. We shall encounter numerous examples in our survey.

The paint industry is really two distinguishable industries in terms of research and new product development. In trade or decorative paints, expenditures on R&D approximate one percent of sales. In the industrial coatings field, where products are custom-developed for specific applications, the expenditure ratio is nearer 7 percent. Very little research of a fundamental nature is carried out in either area; most laboratory work focuses on the solution of detailed application problems. Firms selling from 20 to 30 million gallons annually (the equivalent of two to three MOS plants) were said to be about as vigorous in conducting the more fundamental kinds of research as the largest companies. Smaller firms seldom do any. Breakthrough-oriented research was gen-

---

67. This phenomenon was recognized by Adam Smith in the first chapter of *Wealth of Nations*. For a modern analysis, see Jacob Schmookler, *Invention and Economic Growth* (Cambridge: Harvard University Press, 1966), pp. 165–178.

erally considered to be of little strategic importance. Most of the key advances in paint technology have originated not with the paint makers but with raw material suppliers (chemicals and petrochemicals companies) or in the case of electrodeposition, a user (the Ford Motor Company). The raw material suppliers have an incentive to encourage widespread utilization of their products, so nearly all advances have been available to any paint maker willing to carry out the final formulation development work.

The combination of these circumstances has meant that trade paint specialists too small to support more than routine formulation and quality control research have experienced no significant technology handicap compared to larger firms with more ambitious R&D programs. In industrial coatings, the custom-engineering work of large companies is decentralized to the plant producing coatings for a particular customer application, suggesting the absence of important multi-plant economies, although there are know-how spillovers between work on related applications. Some of the most progressive industrial coatings suppliers were said to be those with total output in the 7–15 million gallon range. However, a few applications, notably, automotive finishes and steel or aluminum coil coating, evidently require a level of technical effort beyond the reach of smaller paint formulators. Here larger multi-plant firms have enjoyed an R&D and sales advantage. It is probably exhausted when a total volume (including related coatings) equivalent to the output of two or three MOS plants is attained.

In antifriction bearings it is also possible to serve most market segments without doing fundamental research. Suitable metals and lubricants technology is in the public domain and/or available from materials suppliers. Detailed applications engineering cannot be avoided, but it requires few special skills or equipment inaccessible to a single-plant enterprise. Nevertheless, there is some sales advantage in maintaining a central research laboratory working on such topics as metallurgy, surface finish, and lubricant technology, particularly for special design bearings operating in hostile environments. The agenda of research possibilities is fairly well bounded, and so the largest firms do not find it necessary to support central research staffs proportionately larger than those of medium-sized companies. For an increase in size from three to six MOS plant equivalents, the savings in central research costs probably amount to less than one-half percent of company sales. Our evidence was insufficient for judging whether the largest firms enjoy any advantage in the quality of research performed.

Only the largest glass bottle companies, with from ten to twenty plants, find it worthwhile to support anything like a comprehensive program of research on glass properties and to undertake the development of complete new bottle-blowing machines. However, the bottle-making art is an ancient one. There have been few recent technical advances of importance and nearly all key patents have expired. Since the legal dissolution during the 1940s of the U.S. bottle machinery cartel, blowing machines have been available from independent specialists on seemingly competitive terms. As a result, medium-sized companies believed they labored under only very slight technological handicaps relative to larger rivals. An American producer noted that if a significant breakthrough did occur, it would probably be made available under license because major bottle customers insisted upon second sources of supply. First-rate bottle design, customer technical service, and production process troubleshooting staffs were said to be much more important to commercial success than fundamental R&D. For an interviewee with four plants, this staff totaled about 7 percent of the company work force. Single-plant producers evidently experience serious disadvantages maintaining such a staff. Beyond the operation of three or four plants, few further technical staff economies can be gained; the staff must be expanded more or less proportionately to handle the increased workload.

Research and development expenditures for U.S. petroleum refiners during the 1960s averaged about 1.0 percent of sales or 5 percent of value added at the refining stage. Firms with capacities of 100,000 barrels per day or less support very little R&D. The medium-sized refiners are about as vigorous in proportion to their size as the largest companies. More than a fourth of all petroleum R&D is devoted to petrochemical applications, which in a strict sense fall outside the scope of our inquiry. Much of the balance is process research and development. Small refiners unable to support their own R&D programs suffer no perceptible process technology handicaps because there are no crucial patents or trade secrets. Detailed variants of the main refining processes can be licensed from either the large research-oriented refiners or from independent refinery engineering specialists such as the Universal Oil Products Company. According to Bain, the royalties charged "hardly cover the allocated development costs"—a point on which our research provided no insights.[68] An executive of a small refining company believed his firm actually enjoyed an advantage relative to refiners developing their own processes because it does not suffer from the "not invented here" syndrome, that is, the tendency to favor one's own inventions over superior outside technology.

68. *Barriers to New Competition*, p. 152. See also John S. McGee, "Patent Exploitation: Some Economic and Legal Problems," *Journal of Law and Economics*, 9 (October 1966), 150–160.

There is an ample if acrimonious literature on the innovative propensities of large vs. small steelmakers.[69] Our interviews uncovered no evidence contradicting and a fair amount supporting the dominant belief that smaller firms, in many instances well below the size of a single MOS plant by 1965 standards, have contributed a disproportionate share of the important technological innovations. Unlike their much larger rivals, even the most progressive ordinary steel producers with capacities of two million ingot tons or less support little or no basic research. However, such research was said to be quite unimportant to successful operation.[70]

There seems to be little one can do beyond routine quality control testing to improve portland cement as a product. What research the industry performs is focused mainly on process technology. Only the largest companies, usually operating on an international plane, maintain formal process design and development organizations. However, there are many cement plant engineering firms, captive and independent, competing for the typical new plant or plant expansion engineering contract. There are also very few trade secrets; cement mill operators regularly visit each others' plants to inspect new wrinkles. As a result, the firm without an in-house process engineering staff bears no discernible handicap relative to rivals supporting such a staff.[71]

In the refrigerator industry almost no research of a fundamental character is done. However, the costs of detailed design and testing prior to introducing a new model line can run into the hundreds of thousands of dollars. Even more important are the costs of tooling up for mass production, estimated by one manufacturer to be approximately $5 million for a completely new model. The most expensive dies and other tooling have useful lives of at least eight to ten years. The larger the production volume attained over the life of a design, the lower

69. See Edwin Mansfield, "Size of Firm, Market Structure, and Innovation," *Journal of Political Economy*, 71 (December 1963), 556–576; Walter Adams and Joel B. Dirlam, "Big Steel, Invention, and Innovation," *Quarterly Journal of Economics*, 80 (May 1966), 167–189; the comment by Alan K. McAdams and the reply by Adams and Dirlam in the *Quarterly Journal of Economics*, 81 (August 1967), 457–482; and G. S. Maddala and P. T. Knight, "International Diffusion of Technical Change—A Case Study of the Oxygen Steel Making Process," *Economic Journal*, 77 (September 1967), 531–558.

70. See also *Science and Government Reports*, November 10, 1971, indicating that U.S. Steel was drastically cutting its basic research expenditures.

71. Note that we disagree with the assertion by H. C. Eastman and S. Stykolt in *The Tariff and Competition in Canada* (Toronto: Macmillan, 1967), p. 150, that multi-plant cement firms achieve economies in the course of designing and building replications of a plant. The learning economies appear to be embedded in the engineering and design organizations, not in the operators who hire their services.

unit development and tooling costs will be, ceteris paribus. From this it does not necessarily follow that broad-line multi-plant firms have a unit cost advantage over specialists offering some narrow line in substantial quantities. But to the extent that refrigerator makers are compelled to manufacture a broad line, modest unit development and tooling cost economies undoubtedly persist all the way out to the size of the largest multi-plant operators. Assuming an eight-year model life, the company which averages only 75,000 units of some box size per year rather than 150,000 bears a cost penalty of roughly $4.00 per unit, or about 2.3 percent of wholesale value. It is doubtful whether large firms enjoy any further advantages in refrigerator design and innovation. There were inconclusive indications that smaller firms completed new model design efforts more quickly and less expensively than large rivals.

Our interviews yielded little information about the relationships between size and automobile battery R&D, mainly because there was little to talk about. Even in the sizeable multi-plant companies we visited, the central research and development laboratories were quite small. Materials suppliers make new technology available to small firms and large alike. There is some trade secrecy concerning production processes, but international technical exchanges among noncompeting firms are extensive. Somewhat more ambitious research and product engineering programs were said to be supported in the industrial storage battery field, but that segment of the industry was touched upon only peripherally in our interviews.

In cigarettes, brewing, weaving, and shoemaking, expenditures on R&D are very low and play only a small role in corporate strategy. All U.S. cigarette companies support defensive research inspired by the concern over cancer. What will come of it in an environment of skepticism as to whether a problem actually exists remains to be seen. Medium-sized Brown & Williamson and Lorillard led the way to "modern" filter-tip and mentholated cigarettes. All the companies to whom we talked relied upon independent machinery suppliers for the design and development of rolling and packaging machines.

Research in the brewing industry appears to be confined largely to undramatic yeast and malt analyses. Firms producing fewer than two million U.S. barrels per year evidently find it difficult to support more than the most routine quality control functions. With an annual volume of four million barrels it is possible to justify maintaining a laboratory fully equipped for special chemical and taste tests. The largest U.S. firms displayed an edge over small brewers in automating their brewhouses, but this was apparently because only they had been building new breweries. In Europe, a company with an annual output of less than three million barrels was found to be making comparable strides toward automation as it closed down small old plants and built anew.

All large- and some medium-sized textile companies support modest R&D efforts covering a wide range of product and process technology problems. However, research appears to be an unimportant strategy option. Much more important are the design and styling of new cloths, at which very small firms are at least as facile. For the most part, the development of new machines is left to specialist machinery suppliers, and chemical companies do most of the fiber and dye R&D.

The shoe industry is similar to textiles. Although a few small firms have made significant technological contributions, only the largest companies regularly support anything resembling a formal research and development program, typically at expenditure levels low in relation to sales. Most shoemakers rely almost exclusively upon the shoe machinery supply industry for their process technology. The principal exceptions are a few of the very largest companies. The leader in this vein was the Bata Organization, the world's largest shoe manufacturing firm, with two machinery plants in France, one in Canada, and one in India. Bata representatives stated that they, unlike smaller firms, could afford to support an integrated machinery development effort because of the high shoe production volume over which development costs were spread. Rivals confirmed that Bata had set the pace of innovation in some areas, but imitation from other shoe machinery makers had been rapid. As a result, Bata was believed to enjoy no significant process technology advantage over shoe producers relying entirely on outside machine suppliers.

Table 7.4 summarizes the implications of the interview and related evidence along two judgmental dimensions. The first column estimates how many MOS plants a firm must operate before reaching that threshold at which it has no impairment of incentive to conduct a thorough-going research and development program and experiences no significant unit cost disadvantage in supporting that program. The second column evaluates the R&D-related strategic handicap borne by a firm large enough to operate only one MOS plant. In only four industries are the adverse consequences of single-plant size more than slight, and only in the antifriction bearings industry does extensive multi-plant operation appear to yield important R&D advantages. Single-plant firms are not significantly handicapped in several other fields, despite a high indicated R&D threshold, because technological innovation is unimportant or unnecessary to success in the market or because specialist suppliers from other industries provide good access to the latest process and materials technology.

Table 7.4. Size Thresholds above which Companies Experience no Significant Research, Development, and Innovation Scope or Size Handicaps, Estimated from Interview Evidence.

Industry	Number of MOS plants to size threshold	Adverse strategic consequences of being large enough to operate only one MOS plant
Brewing	1	None
Cigarettes	1	None
Broad-woven fabrics	20–35	Very slight
Paints { trade	2–3	Very slight
Paints { industrial	2–3	Moderate
Petroleum refining	2–4	Slight
Shoes	20–50	Very slight
Bottles { including basic research and major developments	10–20	Fairly serious, compared to three-plant firm; slight thereafter
Bottles { orthodox product and process development	3–4	
Cement	20–30	Very slight
Steel	½–2	Slight
Antifriction bearings	5–8	Moderate to fairly serious
Refrigerators	1–3	Slight to moderate
Automobile batteries	4–6	Slight

The Economies of Multi-Plant Operation in Perspective

This exhausts the evidence we have been able to assemble from interview and parallel sources. Table 7.5 provides a summary evaluation of the advantages enjoyed by multi-plant firms in eleven functional categories. The judgments cover two dimensions: the extent to which a general-line producer with one plant of approximately optimal scale by 1965 standards operates at a disadvantage relative to firms realizing all the benefits of multi-plant operation, and (in parentheses) the number of MOS plants a firm must operate to realize *all* the advantages of size. The single-plant relative disadvantage estimates range from "none" through "little or none," "very slight," "slight," and "moderate" to "severe." Beyond this rank ordering, not much quantitative significance can be attached. The attributes evaluated have many intangible facets, and the judgments are necessarily subjective and impressionistic.

Several assumptions were nonetheless applied consistently. For one, the single-plant firm whose relative handicap is evaluated is assumed to supply general-line products, although not necessarily a full line of those products. Single-plant firms in several of the industries can unquestionably offer certain specialty items at no disadvantage at all even though they suffer a handicap on main-line products. Also, the environment assumed is the U.S. market as of 1970, with its own peculiar geographic configuration, real income levels, tastes, susceptibility to product differentiation, information processing capabilities, and (compared to Europe, modest) propensity toward market failure. Some of these environmental factors are not necessarily stable over time and, as we have seen repeatedly with respect to the market failure problem, the estimates may be extremely sensitive to changes in the factors.

Table 7.6 advances to an even more heroic plane of generalization, attempting to evaluate the *overall* disadvantage of general-line single-MOS-plant firms and to estimate how many MOS plants a general-line firm must operate to experience at most a slight disadvantage vis-à-vis companies realizing all the benefits of multi-plant operation. The descriptive adjectives used are the same as those presented in Table 7.5. Unlike Table 7.5, however, the judgments in Table 7.6 are based upon some implicit quantitative ranges reflecting the price premium advantages (net of promotional costs) sacrificed and/or the unit cost penalties borne by single-plant operators. Less than one percent translates into "very slight," one to 2 percent "slight," 2 to 5 percent "moderate," and more than 5 percent "severe." We have not recorded percentages directly in Table 7.6 because we are acutely aware how impressionistic our judgments are and we have observed with horror what flights of gullibility otherwise prudent readers can sustain when seemingly precise figures are dished up. Those who wish to make the quantitative leap must do so therefore at their own peril.

An additional element of subjective judgment embodied in Table 7.6 but not in Table 7.5 is the weights assigned to the various functional categories. We have been guided by what we observed through interviews to be important. Thus, for the brewing industry heavy weight was placed on the "advertising and image differentiation" facet, while specialization and lot-size economies received substantial weight for the antifriction bearing and refrigerator industries.

For seven of the industries we have been able to do no better than present a range of estimated single-plant firm disadvantages (in column (1) of Table 7.6). This partly reflects inherent judgmental uncertainties. The main reason, however, is that the handicap of a single-plant firm is sensitive to environmental and hereditary variables, and to ignore differences in those variables would be inappropriate. Thus, somehow or other Coors and certain smaller regional brewers have managed to

Table 7.5. Summary Evaluation of the Number of MOS Plants Required to Realize Multi-Plant Scale Advantages under U.S. Market Conditions and the Extent to which Efficient Single-Plant Firms Are Disadvantaged, 1970.

INDUSTRY	Advertising and image differentiation	Access to markets; distribution channels	Procurement of materials	Vertical integration into key inputs	Outbound transport pooling
Beer brewing	(1–5) Slight to severe	(1) Little or none	(1–2) Very slight	(1) None	(1) None
Cigarettes	(2) Slight to moderate	(4) Slight	(1) None	(1) None	(1) None
Fabric weaving	(Up to 20) Very slight to moderate	(6–15) Slight to moderate	(5–10) Slight	(3–5 weaving mills) Slight to moderate	(3–6) Very slight
Paints	(3–4) Slight	(1) None	(2–3) Slight	(3–5) Moderate	(1) Little or none
Petroleum refining	(1–4) Slight to moderate	(1) None	No evidence; probably none	(2–5) Moderate	(1) None
Shoes	(4–8) Moderate	(3–5) Slight to moderate	(3–5) Slight	(2–4) Very slight	(5–8) Slight
Glass bottles	(1) None	(1) None	No evidence; probably none	(3) Very slight	(1) None
Cement	(1) None	(1) None	No evidence; probably none	(1) None	(2–4) Slight
Steel	(1) Very slight	(4) Very slight	No evidence; probably none	(1–3) Slight for inland taconite users; none for coastal mills with competitive world market	(1) None
Bearings	(4) Slight	(4–8) Moderate	No evidence; at most slight	(1–5) Very slight	(2–5) Very slight
Refrigerators	(1–3) Slight	(up to 12, including other appliances) Moderate to severe	(1–2) Slight	(2–3) Slight to moderate	(up to 5, including other appliances) Moderate
Storage batteries (automobile)	(3–5) Slight	(5) Moderate	(1) Little or none	(1–3) Little or none	(2–3) Slight

Note: Figures in parentheses indicate the number of MOS plants a firm must operate to realize *all* the advantages of size.

Peak spreading, risk spreading, and other massed reserves	Acquisition of capital	Optimal investment staging	Product specialization and lot-size economies	Managerial and central staff economies	Research, development, and technical services
(2–3) Moderate	(no clear limit) Slight	(4–5) Slight to moderate	(2–3) Very slight	(2–3) Slight to moderate	(1) None
(2) Moderate	(no clear limit) Slight	(1) None	(1–3) Slight	No evidence	(1) None
(5–15) Slight	(no clear limit) Moderate	(1) None	(1–12) Slight to moderate	Multi-plant size probably disadvantageous	(20–35) Very slight
(2) Slight	(no clear limit) Slight	(1) None	(3–5) Slight	(2–3) Slight	(2–3) Very slight (trade) to moderate
(2–3) Slight	(no clear limit) Moderate	(2–3) Slight to moderate	(1) Little or none	Multi-plant size probably disadvantageous	(2–4) Slight
(3–5) Moderate	(no clear limit) Slight	(1) None	(3–5) Slight to moderate	Beyond several plants multi-plant size probably disadvantageous	(20–50) Very slight
(2–3) Slight	(no clear limit) Slight to moderate	(2–3) Very slight	(2–3) Very slight	(3–4) Slight; beyond 4–6 plants, size is probably disadvantageous	(3–4) Severe
(1–3) Slight	(no clear limit) Moderate to severe	(2–3) Very slight	(1) Little or none	(2–5) Very slight	(20–30) Very slight
(1) Little or none	(no clear limit) Moderate	(2–3) Slight	(1–3) None to slight	Multi-plant size probably disadvantageous	(1–2) Slight
(1) Little or none	(no clear limit) Slight to moderate	(1) None	(3–8) Moderate to severe	No evidence	(5–8) Moderate
(1–2) Little or none	(no clear limit) Slight	(1) None	(2–3) Moderate	Doubtful whether multi-plant size confers any advantage	(1–3) Slight to moderate
(2–3) Moderate	(no clear limit) Slight	(1) None	(2–3) Slight	Multi-plant size probably disadvantageous	(4–6) Slight

Table 7.6. Summary of Single-Plant Firm's Overall Relative Disadvantage and the Firm Size Required to Experience Not More Than Slight Price/Cost Handicaps.

Industry	(1) Overall disadvantage of representative general-line single MOS plant firm	(2) Number of MOS plants needed to have not more than "slight" overall handicap	(3) Share of U.S. market required in 1967	(4) Average market share per U.S. Big Three member, 1970
Beer brewing	Slight to severe, depending upon inherited brand image	3–4	10–14%	13%
Cigarettes	Slight to moderate (borderline)	1–2	6–12	23
Fabric weaving	Very slight to moderate, depending upon product line	3–6	1	10
Paints	Slight	1	1.4	9
Petroleum refining	Very slight to moderate, depending upon regional market position and crude oil access	2–3	4–6	8
Shoes	Slight to moderate, depending upon product line	3–6	1	6
Glass bottles	Slight to moderate, depending upon location and products	3–4	4–6	22
Cement	Slight	1	2	7
Ordinary steel	Very slight	1	3	14
Bearings	Slight to moderate, depending upon product line	3–5	4–7	14
Refrigerators	Moderate (incl. other appliances)	4–8	14–20	21
Storage batteries	Slight	1	2	18

develop a premium product image equal to that enjoyed by the leading national brewers. Those so blessed suffer at most a slight price/cost disadvantage relative to Anheuser-Busch.[72] But most regional brewers with sales equivalent to the output of an MOS plant or less have not been able to maintain such an image, and their handicap runs into the "severe" range. Single-plant weavers supplying fashion-sensitive dress goods experience at worst a very slight handicap relative to much larger firms, while small companies selling bed sheets and similar end consumer products suffer disadvantages at the upper end of the "moderate" range. Brand differentiation and access to crude oil are key strategic considerations for refineries. The regional refiner processing not more than 200,000 barrels per day can compete on equal terms with the giants if it has a sizeable position in its home market and good access to crude supplies, while a firm of similar size could be squeezed badly in tight markets if it must rely upon integrated companies for crude oil. These judgments, it should be noted, are sensitive to changes in such institutions as the depletion allowance laws, crude oil import quota systems, and the nationalization policies of OPEC (Organization of the Petroleum Exporting Countries) nations. Abolition of depletion allowances for both domestic and foreign crude operations would undoubtedly narrow the differential between nonintegrated refiners and the integrated giants. In the shoe industry, the disadvantage of single-plant firms attempting to offer a line of medium-priced family shoes or children's shoes is much greater than that of companies emphasizing fashion-sensitive women's shoes, work shoes, or top quality men's shoes. Bottle makers favorably located to serve packers and wine bottlers with simple, unchanging requirements suffer only a slight disadvantage at single-plant size levels, but when the array of products is more complex or a broader territory must be served, the handicap widens. In bearings there are narrow markets that can be served as well by single-plant firms as by the industry leaders, but problems multiply as the small company attempts to cover a fuller general line. We have resisted a temptation to widen the battery industry range to "moderate" on the assumption that most gasoline and auto supply chains presently exhibiting transregional preferences would buy on a regional basis at very small price differentials.

Column (2) of Table 7.6 estimates how many MOS plants a general-line producer must operate to bring its cost and/or price disadvantages to somewhere near the bottom of the "slight" range. The estimates here

72. Obviously, one cannot simply acquire the Budweiser or Schlitz image by building four new MOS breweries. Our estimates here compare going concerns, not hypothetical firms entering at inconceivably large scales.

assume a firm that is *not* serving offbeat niches in which disadvantages can be compensated by spatial or physical product differentiation. Despite this homogenizing assumption, a range is again given for seven industries to reflect remaining product line strategy variations and estimation uncertainties.

Column (3) translates these multi-plant figures into estimates of how large a percentage share of 1967 U.S. production a general-line supplier needed to experience at most slight cost and/or price handicaps.[73] They in effect summarize the combined scale economy imperatives for national market concentration. In most cases, realizing the main advantages of multi-plant operation does not necessitate high seller concentration at the nationwide level. Only in the refrigerator, brewing, and (less certainly) cigarette industries do scale economies compel anything approaching moderately tight oligopoly.

A less sanguine view emerges when we take into account the industries' regional and product line structures. Oligopoly may be mandated by the interaction of scale economies and high transport costs in sparsely populated cement markets, in markets for gasoline and fuel oil lacking good pipeline and water transport connections, and in all but those glass bottle markets with a high concentration of demand.[74] For important steel products such as hot-rolled strip, heavy plates, and large structural members fairly tight oligopoly is also implied, since optimal rolling mills are large and specialized and it is difficult to serve much more than a fourth of the continental United States economically from a single site. In the bearings industry, shipping costs do not necessitate national market segmentation, but product differences and associated equipment and skill specialization do. Our estimates in column (2) assume a firm specializing in ball, roller, or tapered roller bearings; not all three. Since substitution from one type to another is usually difficult on both the demand and supply sides, the estimates in column (2) and the demand patterns of the late 1960s imply middling oligopoly levels in the ball and roller market segments and high levels in such segments as tapered and needle bearings. Similar market segmentation exists in textiles, but equipment and skills are sufficiently transferable that the estimates in column (3) reflect the long-run structural imperatives better than upward-adjusted variants would. The national market share estimate for brewing is also unchanged when regionalization is taken into account because our column (2) range assumes a multi-plant firm

73. They are derived by dividing the estimates in column (2) by the U.S. industry SIZE variable in Chap. 6 and then multiplying by 100.

74. Our 3- to 4-plant estimate for a bottle firm assumes a regional posture permitting exploitation of logistic and massed reserve interactions.

deployed spatially to serve most of the national market economically.

When these complications are recognized, we find moderate or tighter oligopoly to be unwarranted for the vast bulk of production in four industries: shoes, batteries, paints, and fabrics; and for substantial fractions of two more: petroleum refining and cement. Cigarettes lies at the oligopoly threshold. For steel, bottles, and bearings, our estimates imply four-firm concentration ratios of 50 or more in significant regional or product submarkets. In brewing and refrigerators, *national* market concentration ratios of 50 to 70 are indicated. In no U.S. industry or major subsegment is anything like natural monopoly or total dominance by two or three firms compelled.

Column (4) provides a different perspective on the seller concentration question, presenting the actual average 1970 national market shares of companies counted among the U.S. industry Big Three. In only three industries, brewing, refrigerators, and petroleum refining, are the observed leading firm market shares of about the same magnitude as the "required" estimates of column (3). In weaving and storage batteries, actual shares exceed "required" shares by roughly ten times; in paints, shoes, bottles, and steel, by four to six times; and in cigarettes, bearings, and cement, by two to three times. To the extent that our estimates are valid, national market seller concentration appears in most industries to be much higher than it needs to be for leading firms to take advantage of all but slight residual multi-plant scale economies.

To this conclusion several comments must be appended. First, the plant numbers in column (2) of Table 7.6 and the market shares in column (3) assume that at most "slight" scale economy sacrifices are accepted. Yet the mind would no doubt boggle over the deeds some entrepreneurs would do for a one percent price or unit cost advantage on annual sales of, say, $100 million. Society too cannot be indifferent to real economies amounting to one percent of costs, though it might well be willing to trade off that percentage point for the allocative, political, and social benefits of more dispersed economic power. On this we shall say more in the last chapter.

Second, in some respects the estimates in Table 7.6 give the benefit of the doubt to multi-plant operators. That is, we have assumed that multi-plant firms actually take advantage of the specialization, transport pooling, investment staging, and other economies which our interviews showed to be attainable. Yet some large firms might fail to exploit their opportunities fully because of sluggishness or managerial deficiencies, in which case their relative advantage is overestimated. We have also not deducted from the estimated advantages of multi-plant size a penalty for the difficulties of managing very large organizations, primarily because there is so much seemingly random variation in the quality of management that we were unable to discern a clear central tendency.

The "required" market share estimates of Table 7.6 assume that individual plants are of a minimum scale optimal in 1965. For steel and cement in particular the MOS has risen significantly since then—in the case of steel, to a size two-and-one-half times that assumed in column (3). No new steel mills of this scale have been built by U.S. companies, but in the very long run scale imperatives will exert upward pressure on concentration, especially if demand grows only slowly.[75]

All the estimates in Table 7.6 consider the various advantages of size—real and pecuniary, private and diffused—as if they were homogeneous. If value judgments are to be made, however, this simplification may be unacceptable. Especially in the brewing, cigarette, and petroleum refining industries but to a lesser degree also in weaving, shoes, and refrigerators, image and advertising factors are an important component of the multi-plant firm's advantage. Many advertising economies are real, in the sense that a firm with a large market share needs to send fewer messages per million dollars of sales to achieve a given level of audience coverage. But the rewards are apt to be taken in the form of supranormal profits for the companies involved, which may offend our sense of distributive equity. And one might object even more strenuously to their whole basis in highly advertising-prone industries like cigarettes, beer, and gasoline, where vast resources are devoted to assaulting consumer preferences and making people perceive differences which do not exist or which by "objective" criteria are trivial.

One further qualification must end our list. Our focus has been on the handicaps of "general-line" single-plant firms. It bears repeating that many small firms survive and even do well supplying specialized products or serving geographically isolated market niches. Obversely, in industries where we have found the disadvantages of single-plant size to be substantial, the general-line single-plant operator may be a nonexistent construct because its handicaps do not permit it to survive. Or if such firms exist, they may do so only because they still operate plant and equipment acquired long ago at preinflation prices, but they count the days until obsolescence forces them to exit. Recognition that there are so many ways to survive and even prosper despite what appear

75. On the other hand, the spatial economics of future steel mills may change radically. Blast furnaces, converters, and primary slab and billet casting units will probably be pulled to deep-water coastal locations, while final products rolling may be decentralized to market-oriented mills. This will have complex repercussions on concentration, depending in part upon whether a nonintegrated competitive market for primary products develops.

to be serious obstacles has left us skeptical of simple generalizations like those offered in Tables 7.5 and 7.6. It is at least as important to know *how much* of an industry's output can profitably be supplied by small firms playing a niche-filling game and *how rapidly* disadvantaged producers will lose position, given the magnitude of their disadvantage and the optimal pricing response of larger firms realizing all scale economies.[76] We believe the theory and evidence developed in this volume are sufficient to support reasonable answers to such questions in concrete individual cases. But we do not know how to put the whole enormously complex mosaic together in a way which will allow sweeping quantitative generalizations.

As an additional source of perspective, it is worthwhile to compare our Table 7.6 estimates with those made by Bain from his study focusing on early 1950s conditions.[77] Our samples overlap for five industries. His conclusions on the advantages of multi-plant operation can be summarized as follows:

Industry	Unit production and physical distribution cost advantage of multi-plant enterprise	Number of MOS plants to realize all production and physical distribution advantages	Does multi-plant firm realize significant promotional advantages?	Does multi-plant firm have superior access to important natural resources?
Cigarettes	Slight	3–4	Yes	No
Petroleum refining	None	1	No	No
Shoes	Small (2–4%)	3–5	Yes, for some products	No
Cement	Small (2–3%)	3–10	No	No
Steel	2–5%	1–8	No	Yes

Our estimates and Bain's agree well for cigarettes and shoes, especially in view of the fact that his MOS estimate for a shoe plant brackets ours, while his estimated MOS for a cigarette plant implies only half as much output as ours does. For petroleum refining he finds no significant economies of multi-plant operation while we do. We share his judgment where crude oil markets function competitively and competitive product market transactions make optimal internal multi-plant investment staging

76. See Darius W. Gaskins, Jr., "Dynamic Limit Pricing: Optimal Pricing under Threat of Entry," *Journal of Economic Theory*, 3 (September 1971), 306–322.

77. *Barriers to New Competition*, esp. pp. 85–88, 137–138, and 152–154.

redundant. The rising scale requirements for crude oil exploration as inland reserves have become exhausted, the imposition of mandatory import quotas from 1959 to 1973 and the more recent tightening of domestic crude markets, and the rise of national television advertising directed toward increasingly mobile consumers may represent sufficient changes to explain the differences in our evaluations. For cement and steel Bain finds multi-plant economies while we do not. Bain's estimates for both industries were subject to an especially large margin of uncertainty, with some steel industry respondents denying that any multi-plant economies existed while others claimed sizeable advantages.[78] We believe our research has pinned down the issues with sufficient clarity that much greater confidence is warranted. A shift to taconite has also lessened the natural resources advantage Bain attributed to the leading multi-plant steel companies.

Multi-Plant Size and Profitability

Tables 7.5 and 7.6 estimate the cost economies and price premia available through multi-plant operation. If multi-plant firms in fact enjoy these advantages, we should expect to find them reflected in profit differentials. Also, if we have correctly identified the thresholds at which multi-plant size ceases to yield more than slight incremental advantages, a leveling off of profit differentials should be evident. In this section we inquire whether and to what extent recorded data on U.S. company profits are consistent with our estimates.[79]

For profits, unlike multi-plant operation advantages, one can open a book and extract clean, precise data. It hardly needs to be said that this precision could be spurious. For our present purposes four main sources of imprecision are particularly relevant. First, profit data are no better than the accounting conventions upon which they are based. Especially large firm-size-correlated differences are observed between the profits claimed by petroleum refiners in their annual reports and those published in U.S. Internal Revenue Service reports, since the latter have been offset by large depletion allowance claims. Second,

78. Ibid., pp. 87–88.

79. In making such a comparison, it is important to avoid having the subjective multi-plant advantage estimates be influenced by the profit data. To minimize the probability of such a linkage, most of the profit data collection task was carried out by a research assistant, James M. Kennedy. Final data clean-up and analysis were delayed until Tables 7.5 and 7.6 had been completed. We then scrupulously resisted temptations to change the table estimates. This, of course, does not guarantee the absence of reverse causality, since preparation for our interviews involved among other things analysis of company profit histories. It only minimizes the biasing effect of *systematic* profit comparisons.

reported profits are often influenced by the historical mix of capital vintages and the rules adopted in charging for depreciation. Firms operating plant and equipment acquired long ago at preinflation prices and now largely depreciated may record accounting returns on invested capital higher than those they could sustain indefinitely, especially in industries like paints, shoemaking, cigarettes, and batteries, in which productivity-increasing technological changes have been modest. Third, profits have until recently been reported only on a companywide basis by most U.S. corporations, but activity in the domestic industries of interest here may comprise only a small part of total company operations. This conglomerate reporting problem will be a serious one for several industries. Finally, there is evidence that the relationship between firm size and profitability varies over the business cycle. The largest enterprises tend to do relatively better when business is depressed or "normal" than when boom conditions prevail.[80]

Some of these difficulties cannot be avoided. We have tried to minimize biases due to the conglomerate reporting and business cycle problems by our choice of time periods. Our focus is on the years between 1961 and 1967. After then, conglomerate mergers made it increasingly difficult to get usable profits data for many companies, especially in the brewing, cigarette, paint, bottle, and battery industries. To test for sensitivity to macroeconomic fluctuations, we divide the data into two periods, covering roughly 1961–1964 and 1965–1966— the first characterized by soft to "normal" business conditions; the second encompassing the upswing of the boom stimulated first by tax reforms and then by increases in Vietnam war spending, but ending before the war-induced inflation was strongly in motion.

For these periods, we analyze after-tax returns on stockholders' equity reported by corporations of diverse sizes. The data come from two main sources. When an industry included a substantial number of companies, many too small to be tracked by the standard financial reporting sources, we have used the comprehensive aggregations in the Internal Revenue Service's *Statistics of Income* series.[81] That series covers corporation fiscal years ending during the IRS fiscal year ending June 30. We lacked access to the special tabulation for IRS fiscal year 1963. Therefore, our data for the first ("normal") period are a size-weighted average of the two fiscal years ending June 30, 1962, and June 30, 1964; while the later (boom) period includes the 1966 and 1967

80. See J. L. McConnell, "Corporate Earnings by Size of Firm," *Survey of Current Business*, 25 (May 1945), 6–12; and Scherer, *Industrial Market Structure and Economic Performance*, pp. 80–82.

81. Cf. n. 37 *supra*.

IRS fiscal years. Companies are classified according to size only by assets in the IRS series; assets therefore is the size measure used in all IRS-based analyses and, for consistency, on all but three of the non-IRS analyses. When the number of firms in an industry was small and/or when most of the multi-plant operators had assets within the largest IRS size category of $250 million and over, a list of companies operating primarily in the industry was compiled and profit data were drawn from the annual *Fortune 500* listings and *Moody's Industrials*. The intervals covered are calendar years 1962 through 1964 and 1965 through 1966. Simple averages of company rates of return across these years were taken. Corporations deriving less than half their sales from the industry in question or from vertically related activities were excluded from the *Fortune* and *Moody's* analyses. Except in one extreme case, no such selectivity could be exercised with respect to the IRS data.

The evidence is summarized in Figures 7.1(b) through (k), with Figure 7.1(a) providing for perspective IRS-based profit averages on the cohort of all manufacturing corporations. For the IRS-based analyses, asset sizes are presented (on the horizontal axis) in ranges—usually from $1.0 to 2.5 million through $250 million and over. Except in Figure 7.1(a), whenever a profit figure represents an average over more than one company, the number of company observations averaged is indicated by a circled numeral at the appropriate data point locus. When the observations for two time periods lay too close together to be registered clearly, the single circled numeral indicates the *smaller* of the two population counts.

Just above the horizontal axis of each industry diagram are numerals enclosed in rectangles. These indicate the approximate correspondence between company size and the number of 1965-vintage MOS plants compatible with that size. They are in most instances based upon an estimate of the capital cost of a new 1965-vintage plant (the CAP variable of Chapter 3), divided by two to reflect the average extent to which the original book value of companies' plant and equipment had been depreciated, and multiplied by one plus the industrywide ratio of inventories to land and depreciable assets as of December 31, 1964. These multi-plant size indicators must be viewed as very crude. They suffer from two particularly severe measurement difficulties. For one, the 1965 capital cost estimates reflect prices prevailing at that time, while company assets reported in financial statements include much plant and equipment acquired in earlier years when price levels were generally lower. Therefore, the rectangular multi-plant count indicators tend ceteris paribus to be biased downward, that is, located too far to the right on the firm size scale. This need not be so, however, if technological progress made it possible to acquire a given amount of production capacity at falling or constant cost per unit despite rising input price trends. Some compensation for the downward bias is also provided by our neglect of the cash, accounts receivable, and other noninventory components of current assets in our MOS plant capital cost estimates. Second, the reported assets on the basis of which firms are classified into size groups include assets for vertically related activities (such as malt plants, textile finishing plants, or retail shoe outlets) and also unrelated (conglomerate) activities of the firms surveyed. The single-plant capital cost estimates on the other hand pertain only to those operations likely to be incorporated at a typical main-line manufacturing site. To the extent that firms are conglomerately or vertically integrated beyond the manufacturing stage on which we focus, the multi-plant count indicators are biased upward, that is, located too far to the left on the firm size scale. The net effect of these diverse biases can only be guessed on a case-by-case basis.

Partly because of these data deficiencies, partly because the Internal Revenue statistics provide only limited clues concerning the variance from observed central tendencies, and partly because the number of observations in key size classes is extremely small, we attempt no tests of statistical significance. A sophisticated analytic approach would at best merely reinforce one's a priori conviction that the prevailing patterns

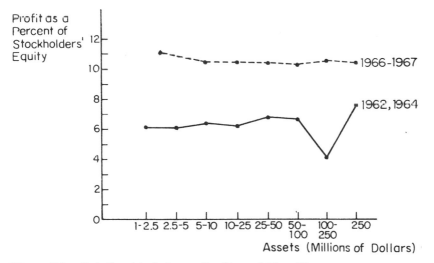

Figure 7.1.   Relationship between Profits and Firm Size.
Figure 7.1(a).   All Manufacturing.

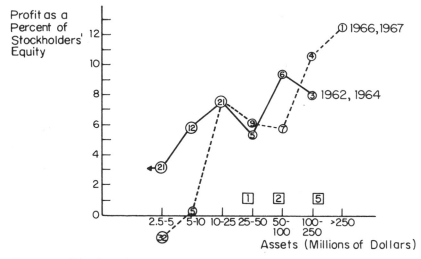

Figure 7.1(b).   Brewing.

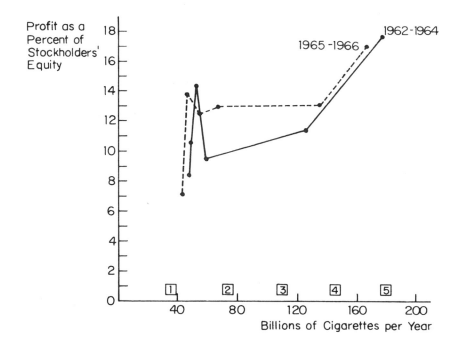

Figure 7.1(c).   **Cigarettes.**

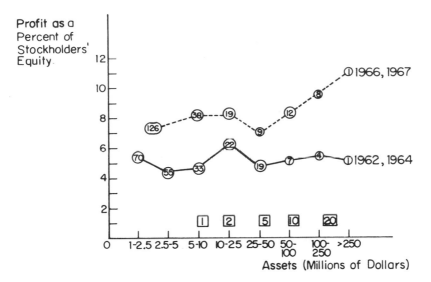

Figure 7.1(d). Cotton and Synthetic Woven Fabrics.

are tenuous. At worst, it could encourage unwarranted confidence in relationships that could be spurious.

With these caveats in mind, we turn to the data, taking up each industry's profit diagram in turn.

Surveying all manufacturing corporations, Figure 7.1(a) shows the sharp difference in average profit levels between the 1962–1964 period and the more boomish 1966–1967 period. There is a hint of size-profit curve tilting in favor of smaller corporations as business conditions improved, although the pattern is marred by the striking 1962–1964 profit slump in the $100–250 million asset range, encompassing some 182 corporations.

Figure 7.1(b) reveals that multi-plant brewing companies earned generally higher profits than firms with assets large enough to operate only one MOS brewery. The low returns which drove out many brewers with very small plants are clearly visible. There is a distinct increase in the implied advantage of the largest brewers from 1962–1964 to 1966–1967. This, we believe, reflects the secular trading-up of consumers to premium image beers and early results of the drive by Anheuser-Busch and Schlitz to open new, efficient, geographically decentralized breweries.

Reynolds, the largest U.S. cigarette seller, enjoyed a consistent and sizeable profit advantage over all its smaller rivals. Lorillard, the north-westernmost observation on both curves, did much better than its three rivals of similar size, presumably on the inherited strength of its Kent

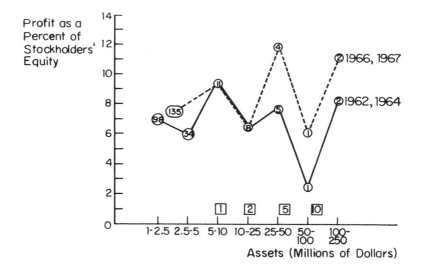

Figure 7.1(e). Paints.

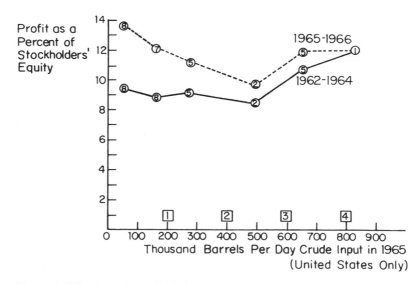

Figure 7.1(f). Petroleum Refining.

brand.[82] The evidence suggests that firm size may confer more than slight advantages beyond the two MOS plant threshold indicated in Table 7.6 but that other factors less clearly associated with size are also at work.

For the weaving industry, firms in the $25–50 million asset range, or those large enough to operate three to six MOS spinning-weaving mills by our capital requirements estimates, turn out to be among the *least* profitable during both time intervals. This plus the steady upward progression of returns for larger corporations during booming 1966–1967 (when military uniform orders had to be allocated by government directive among overloaded textile makers) inspires little confidence in our Table 7.6 estimate that all but slight multi-plant advantages are exhausted within that size range. Some solace is found in the fact that the most profitable firms on average during the 1962–1964 period were those with assets of $10–25 million. This range implies one to three MOS plants by our 1965 estimates, but possibly up to twice as many for plants built at earlier capital goods prices with less capital-intensive equipment than the Sulzer looms assumed in our computations.

The paint industry size relationships are highly variable.[83] Since firms large enough to operate multiple MOS plants were uniformly less profitable on the average than those in the single-plant range for 1962–1964, and since the advantage of larger firms in the later interval was erratic, the evidence cannot be considered inconsistent with our Table 7.6 conclusion that larger firms enjoy no more than slight advantages over companies with a single MOS plant.

Figure 7.1(f) uses 1965 U.S. refinery input data to group petroleum companies. The *least* profitable size group in both periods coincides with the midpoint of the range Table 7.6 estimated to be the threshold at which all but slight size advantages are realized. Smaller refiners, including those with capacity equal to only half an MOS refinery, realized returns higher than those of medium-sized companies. Evidently, in those days of abundant crude oil, they suffered little from the crude oil squeeze danger given heavy weight in our estimates. Inspection of the underlying data also reveals that the average returns among smaller

82. The data on Brown and Williamson are for British-American Tobacco's combined North American operations, on which separate reports were published beginning in 1964.

83. The IRS data include one firm in the over $250 million asset range—presumably National Lead. That observation has been excluded because National Lead derived only about 10 to 15 percent of its sales from paints.

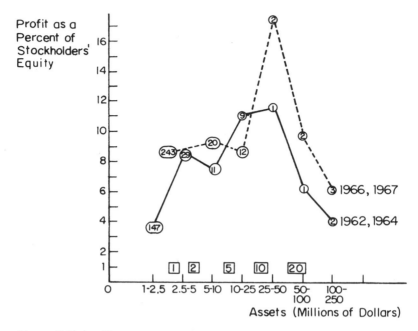

Figure 7.1(g). Shoes.

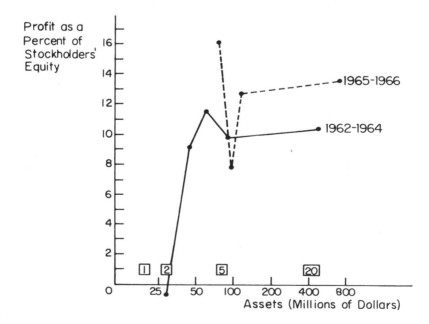

Figure 7.1(h). Glass Bottles.

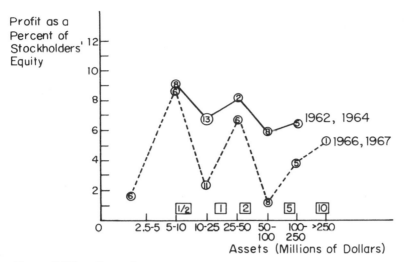

Figure 7.1(i).   Cement.

companies were pulled up by a few firms with very favorable crude production stakes, for some of which refining may have been only an afterthought. Interpretation of profit relationships among firms at the other end of the size distribution is complicated by the fact that most had major investments in crude oil production and refining ventures outside the United States. The plant count rectangles therefore understate those firms' overall size by a wide margin (although use of an assets measure would show little change in company *rankings*). And more important, it is difficult to tell how much the largest firms' profitability is attributable to U.S. as distinguished from overseas operations.

Shoe manufacturing corporations with assets of $1.0-2.5 million, barely enough to finance one MOS plant, fared much less well than larger rivals during the early 1960s but earned similar returns during the subsequent boom.[84] One possible interpretation could be that the product differentiation and market access advantages given heavy weight in our Table 7.6 estimates fade in a sellers' market. It seems clear that the very largest shoe companies operate at a net disadvantage. Interpreting the implications of the midcurve profit peaks is made difficult

84. The multi-plant indicators in this case are based on industrywide IRS asset/sales relationship data rather than the CAP variable of Chap. 3 because many shoe manufacturers lease most of their equipment and often their factory buildings. To the extent that all-industry asset figures are pushed upward by vertical integration and conglomerate activities, the plant count indicators may be too far to the right for smaller firms and too far to the left for the largest, more diversified corporations.

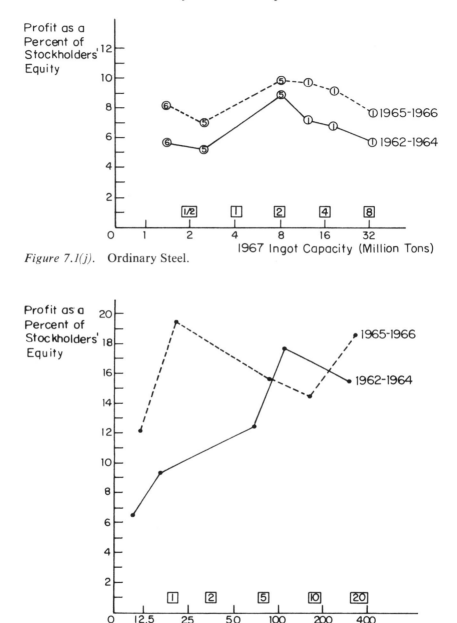

Figure 7.1(j). Ordinary Steel.

Figure 7.1(k). Bearings.

Note: Sources for Figures 7.1(a)-(k) are U.S. Internal Revenue Service, *Source Book of Statistics of Income* (Washington: microfilm or computer printout), tax years ending in 1962, 1964, 1966, and 1967; *Moody's Industrial Manual* (New York: Moody's Investors Service, Inc., various years); *Fortune's Directory of the 500 Largest Industrial Corporations* for 1962 through 1966; and company annual reports.

by the paucity of observations and by the fact that many medium-sized shoe companies operated shoe chains and had various conglomerate interests, so their asset figures may overstate the extent of multiple shoe plant operation.

For the glass bottle industry we were able to obtain usable data for only five firms, the smallest of which exited by merger in 1965 after running at an average loss over three years. The most that can be said is that industry leader Owens-Illinois was not noticeably more profitable than companies in the three to eight MOS plant range.

During both time intervals, marked by emerging excess capacity and eroding prices, the most profitable cement companies were those with assets of $5–10 million.[85] By our capital requirements estimates, this implies firms with only one-third the capacity of an MOS plant. But since a plant at the midpoint of the size distribution for the U.S. cement industry in 1969 had only 47 percent of an MOS plant's capacity, and in view of the ancient vintages of many U.S. cement mills, such firms probably operated one "typical" plant. It is clear that firms with extensive multi-plant operation were not more profitable than much smaller producers, and thus the evidence is completely consistent with Table 7.6.

For the steel industry the highest average returns are found among the firms with approximately 8 million ingot tons capacity, or about the capacity of two 1965-vintage MOS works. Within this group, the most profitable firm was National Steel, with two main plants, and Inland Steel, with one. No evidence on the profitability of 4 million ton producers is available because there were no companies in that size range.

The bearings industry leader, New Departure-Hyatt, and two of the next five sellers were subsidiaries of much larger parent corporations. The figures on five less conglomerate firms in Figure 7.1(k) can only whet our appetite for richer data. In the earlier period the companies of multi-plant size appear to enjoy a distinct advantage. But during the 1965–66 boom, which favored the automobile industry, the bearing producers' best single market, no clear size relationship can be discerned.

No meaningful analysis of profits in refrigerator manufacturing is feasible, since three of the four largest producers (General Electric, Frigidaire, and Westinghouse) were relatively minor components of giant corporations and the fourth, Whirlpool, had the lion's share of its sales in other appliance lines.

Finally, acceptable profit data could be obtained for only four storage

85. For 1962–1964 only one company was listed in the $2.5–$5.0 million size range. It reported a net loss of 16 percent on stockholders' equity.

battery producers, ESB, Gould, Globe Union, and General Battery; and reports of the first two are heavily tainted by activities outside the storage battery industry. Therefore no diagram is presented. All four had battery production several times the volume of a single MOS plant. No systematic profit-size associations are evident among them.

The degree to which our Table 7.6 multi-plant scale economies exhaustion threshold estimates are consistent with the observed profitability relationships are summarized as follows:

Brewing	Fully consistent.
Cigarettes	Erratically consistent, but multi-plant threshold underestimated.
Weaving	Possibly consistent for "normal" year if allowance made for capital estimate errors, but multi-plant threshold underestimated for boom year.
Paints	Consistent, though relationships erratic.
Petroleum refining	Inconsistent; advantages of multi-plant operation overrated by Table 7.6.
Shoes	Roughly consistent, but multi-plant threshold may be underestimated.
Glass bottles	Consistent with very weak profit evidence.
Cement	Fully consistent.
Steel	Roughly consistent, but profit data on predicted size threshold firms unavailable.
Bearings	Consistent for "normal" year, inconsistent for boom; evidence very weak.
Refrigerators	No evidence.
Storage batteries	Evidence too scant to analyze.

For four of the ten industries on which usable data were available—brewing, paints, bottles, and cement—the multi-plant advantage estimates are completely consistent with the profit evidence. For several others they are partly or roughly consistent. The greatest disparity occurs for petroleum refining. Perhaps as significant as the only fair concordance between subjective estimates and "objective" profit patterns is the wide variability of the profit relationships across size classes and over time. This would appear to confirm other important interview lessons: that the links between multi-plant size and scale economies are complex; that firms of quite diverse sizes can often find ways to adapt profitably to their market environments; and that the potential advantages of multi-plant size may not always be exploited fully.

8

Optimal Unbalanced Specialization in a Multi-Plant Framework

In policy judgments on the desirability of large enterprises, special weight may be accorded the *real* economies associated with organizing production at multiple locations. Some of the most interesting but least explored possibilities for achieving such economies involve geographically unbalanced composite specialization. Multi-plant firms in transport-cost-intensive industries, Chapter 7 brought out, frequently centralized the production of low-volume items subject to appreciable run-length economies while simultaneously decentralizing the manufacture of high-volume items. Company representatives believed they were realizing significant cost savings through this assignment strategy. Yet they were seldom able explicitly to estimate their quantitative magnitude.

Here the unbalanced composite specialization question is pursued further in three ways: describing a new method for computing optimally unbalanced product specialization assignments, using that computational algorithm to find the optimal product assignments in a number of contrived but realistic cases, and estimating the cost savings attributable to optimal unbalanced specialization as compared to autarkical full-line production by regional plants. Fringe benefits will include insights into the sensitivity of costs to variations in market shares and to nonoptimal geographic dispersion of plants.

The Computation of Optimal Specialization Patterns

When plant-specific and product-specific scale economies exist, total cost functions are concave downward, so conventional linear or convex programming methods cannot be used to find least-cost solutions. The state of the concave programming art is advancing rapidly but is still rudimentary. There is an extensive literature on methods of solving the so-called "plant location problem," that is, finding the optimal number, sizes, and locations of plants in geographic space, given economies of scale in production.[1] However, to the best of our knowledge, nothing has been done about the problem of multi-product plants with scale economies embedded in the production of each individual product as well as in overall plant cost functions.[2]

The principal method used in this chapter is adapted from a branch-and-bound optimum-seeking algorithm first proposed for the single-product, multi-location case by Richard Soland, but untested computationally until applied by us.[3] One computational requirement is that total costs be separable with respect to plant-product pairs. We therefore formulate a firm's total cost function so that it is the sum of three separate components: product-specific production costs, plant-specific production costs, and outbound shipping costs. Concretely, where there are $i = 1, \ldots, n$ possible plant sites shipping $k = 1, \ldots, p$ products to $j = 1, \ldots, m$ markets in the quantities X_{ijk}, the objective is to minimize the concave total cost function:

$$(8.1) \quad C = \sum_{i=1}^{n} \sum_{k=1}^{p} f_{ik}(S_{ik}) + \sum_{i=1}^{n} g_i(Y_i) + \sum_{i=1}^{n} \sum_{j=1}^{m} \sum_{k=1}^{p} t_{ijk} X_{ijk}.$$

1. An important early statement of the problem was Tjalling Koopmans and Martin Beckmann, "Assignment Problems and the Location of Economic Activity," *Econometrica*, 25 (January 1957), 53–76. See also Thomas Vietorisz and Alan S. Manne, "Chemical Processes, Plant Location, and Economies of Scale," in A. S. Manne and Harry Markowitz, eds., *Studies in Process Analysis* (New York: Wiley, 1963), pp. 136–158; E. Feldman, F. A. Lehrer, and T. L. Ray, "Warehouse Location under Continuous Economies of Scale," *Management Science*, 12 (May 1966), 670–684; M. A. Efroymson and T. L. Ray, "A Branch-Bound Algorithm for Plant Location," *Operations Research*, 14 (May-June 1966), 361–368; Kurt Spielburg, "An Algorithm for the Simple Plant-Location Problem with Some Side Conditions," *Operations Research*, 17 (January-February 1969), 85–111; and Graciano Sá, "Branch-and-Bound and Approximate Solutions to the Capacitated Plant-Location Problem," *Operations Research*, 17 (November-December 1969), 1005–1016.

2. An exception is Leo Polopolus, "Optimum Plant Numbers and Locations for Multiple Product Processing," *Journal of Farm Economics*, 47 (May 1965), 287–295. His nonlinearities however are not embedded in the individual product volumes.

3. Richard M. Soland, "Optimal Plant Location with Concave Costs," paper presented to the 39th meeting of the Operations Research Society of America, May 1971.

The first term $f_{ik}(S_{ik})$ denotes the product-specific cost of producing

$$S_{ik} = \sum_{j=1}^{m} X_{ijk}$$

units of the kth product in the ith plant. The second term $g_i(Y_i)$ reflects the plant-specific cost of producing a total output volume Y_i at plant i, where Y_i is the weighted sum of individual product output volumes

$$\sum_{k=1}^{p} w_k S_{ik},$$

the w_k being weights giving the relative importance of individual product units' contribution to total plant-specific costs. The third term embraces total out-shipment costs, t_{ijk} being the cost of transporting a unit of product k from plant i to market j. Scale economies will be explicitly embodied in the $f_{ik}(\cdot)$ and $g_i(\cdot)$ functions, but we assume for simplicity no cost advantages in amassing large shipments, so the out-shipping cost function is linear. Total cost function (8.1) is minimized subject to the constraints that no X_{ijk} be negative and that for every market j and product k the demand requirement d_{jk} be exactly satisfied by the production from one or more plants. It can be shown through a standard theorem of concave programming that under certain conditions which our problem in fact satisfies, each market's requirements for a given product will be served by a single plant.[4]

The basic principle of Soland's branch-and-bound algorithm is to converge iteratively upon the optimal solution by solving a series of linearized branch subproblems.[5] At any stage in the algorithm, linear underestimates of total cost are made by linearizing the total plant-specific and product-specific cost curves. The resulting linearized costs are minimized subject to the constraint set, yielding cost estimates which serve as a *lower* bound upon the optimal solution. "Branching" then takes place; that is, the solution space is divided into two sub-problems based upon that plant or product where, at the currently prevailing solution, the linear underestimate of costs is most severe. Two new linear estimates are then formed, one defined on the interval for output volumes less than the current solution at that plant or product, the other defined on an interval for greater output values. Total cost is then minimized for the two branch problems, and the linear solution

---

4. See George Hadley, *Nonlinear and Dynamic Programming* (Reading, Mass.: Addison-Wesley, 1964), pp. 91–93, for a proof.

5. For further details, see Alan R. Beckenstein, "An Optimization Approach for Evaluating Multi-Plant Scale Economies," unpub. diss., University of Michigan, 1972.

which has the lowest linearized cost is selected from the choice set consisting of the two new branch solutions plus all past linearized solutions from which branching has not yet occurred. (Such past solutions are called "intermediate nodes.") The cost associated with this chosen solution serves as a new lower bound on the problem's objective function value. Also, at any stage in the algorithm, the solution encountered with the lowest total *real cost* (based on the actual nonlinear functions) is deemed the "best-yet" solution, serving as an *upper bound* on the problem's objective function value. If the lower bound exceeds or equals the upper (real) bound value, the "best-yet" solution is optimal. If this criterion is not satisfied, the process continues, taking the lowest-linear-cost solution as the branching point for a new stage.

Crucial to the algorithm's functioning is the convergence, preferably quickly, of successively defined linearized cost estimates upon the optimal real cost upper bound. Sequencing is governed by the criterion of choosing at each stage as the target of branching that plant-product pair or plant for which the linear underestimate of real (nonlinear) costs is largest. This ensures that the branching sequence will proceed in the proper general direction. In his original conceptual paper, Soland has proved that the algorithm must in fact converge upon the global optimum after a finite (though possibly large) number of stages.

As in most complex nonlinear programming problems, however, there is a hitch. To ensure sequencing which leads eventually to the globally optimal solution, all intermediate nodes must be stored along with considerable supplementary information. For problems with many markets, potential plant sites, and products, storing this information either in fast memory or on computer disks is quite expensive. Therefore, a compromise may be required. Testing of bench mark problems showed that storage and processing time costs could be held in check by storing only the twenty "currently-best" (least linear cost) intermediate nodes while allowing the program to get very close to what was believed to be the optimal solution.[6] Yet with this limited storage approach, it is pos-

6. With total IBM 360–67 computer outlays of approximately $1000, more than 30 runs were made on cases involving 17 plants, 16 markets, and from one to four products. In nearly all cases, the solution obtained had a total real (nonlinear) cost within one-half percent of the lowest cost attainable through further heuristic adjustments, and presumably also of the true minimum cost. In several test runs involving 5 or fewer plants and markets and only one product, the program always converged upon the solution shown by enumeration to be optimal.

To test the implications of the intermediate node storage constraint, several runs were made with very large (and expensive) storage allowances. In such cases, parallel runs were also made with the "twenty-best" storage limitation. The cost differences between solutions were trivial.

sible that an intermediate node which at some stage in the run is not eligible for storage might later qualify for branching. Once such a node is lost, there is no way of getting it back. The result could be that the "final" computed solution leaves an isolated plant producing at a very small scale despite clear cost disadvantages because the algorithm is unable to return and reallocate the plant's production to some larger neighboring plant.

To deal with this problem, a second "cleanup" program was developed which permitted the user to sit at a computer terminal, make minor production reallocations heuristically, and immediately observe the results. The use of this program led in from one to fifteen iterations to production assignments upon which no further real cost-reducing improvements could be made, and which were therefore believed to be (although cannot be proved to represent) the true optimum optimorum. Still it is conceivable that wholly different and nonobvious lower-cost solutions might have been overlooked because an intermediate node was discarded prematurely. The most we can say is that extensive experimentation provided no indication that significantly lower-cost alternatives were overlooked. *If* they were, the consequence would be an underestimation of the composite specialization economies reported in a subsequent section.

Cost Functions and Other Model Components

We now define the cost functions and other parameters of equation (8.1) in sufficient detail that solutions to realistic cases can be computed.

Production Costs

In our production cost functions we wish to incorporate economies of scale. The Soland algorithm requires specifically that marginal cost be nonincreasing. Since product-specific scale economies are often related to fixed setup costs, a realistic and flexible cost function which includes the necessary properties can be defined as:

$$(8.2) \qquad UPSC = MUPSC + \gamma \left(\frac{1}{S}\right)^{\alpha}; \gamma > 0; 1 \geq \alpha > 0,$$

where $UPSC$ is product-specific cost per unit, S is the output of the product at a given plant, $MUPSC$ is the asymptotic minimum unit cost level, and γ and α are parameters. It is assumed that unit costs continue declining out to very large volumes, equaling $MUPSC$ only for $S = \infty$. While this seems realistic, it is convenient to be able to refer to a finite minimum optimal scale volume. We therefore define the product-specific **MOS** as that volume at which unit product-specific cost exceeds the asymptotic minimum $MUPSC$ by some arbitrarily small fraction η, say, by 2 percent. The strength of product-specific scale economies can then be characterized by a parameter ϵ, measuring the fractional elevation of unit costs due to producing a volume one-tenth the MOS volume as compared to the MOS output. From empirical data the values of $MUPSC$, S_{MOS}, ϵ, and η can be estimated; and given them, α and γ can be determined.

Plant-specific scale economies are attributable primarily to indivisibilities in equipment, administrative and custodial functions, and management. For most plants, especially in the industries we shall emphasize in subsequent computations, it is plausible to assume that plant-specific economies are exhausted at finite total output levels. We therefore define the unit plant-specific cost function:

$$(8.3) \qquad UPC = \begin{cases} Z - \beta \ln (Y + 1) & \text{if } Y < Y_{MOS}, \\ Z - \beta \ln (Y_{MOS} + 1) & \text{if } Y \geq Y_{MOS}, \end{cases}$$

where Z is the cost axis intercept, Y is the weighted index of plant output, Y_{MOS} is the MOS output, and $\beta > 0$. The magnitude of plant-specific economies is reflected by a parameter δ, measuring the fractional elevation of unit costs due to producing a volume one-tenth Y_{MOS} as compared to the MOS volume. By prespecifying Z, δ, and Y_{MOS}, we can derive a unique value for β.

Plant and Market Sites

A uniform set of seventeen potential plant sites will be used for all analyses. The sites are major industrial cities, chosen to provide reasonably complete coverage of the Continental United States. They are:

Boston	Chicago
New York City	St. Paul
Richmond, Va.	Kansas City
Atlanta	Dallas
Tampa	Denver
Pittsburgh	Los Angeles
Cleveland	San Francisco
Louisville	Portland, Ore.
New Orleans	

While other sites might be named, an alternate list would at best be only marginally better, given the generality of our analysis. Although it would be possible to use a different production cost function at each plant site to take into account differences in wages and material costs, we shall for simplicity assume that cost conditions are identical at each site.

A set of sixteen Continental U.S. market demand territories is also identified. The list is arbitrary, but it tries to compromise realism and analytic tractability as well as possible. For each territory, it is assumed that shipments are made to a more or less centrally located warehouse (conceivably on the same site as an operating plant), from which final breakdown by destination and shipment will take place. The central warehouse sites and the state (or state fraction) markets they serve are:

1. Boston: Maine, New Hampshire, Vermont, Massachusetts, Rhode Island, and one-third of New York state (excluding New York City).
2. New York City: New York City and one-third of the remainder of New York state, New Jersey, and Connecticut.
3. Pittsburgh: Pennsylvania, Delaware, and one-third of New York state (excluding New York City).
4. Washington, D.C.: District of Columbia, Maryland, Virginia, and West Virginia.
5. Atlanta: North Carolina, South Carolina, and Georgia.
6. Tampa: Florida.
7. Nashville: Kentucky, Tennessee, Alabama, and Mississippi.
8. Dallas: Texas, Louisiana, Arkansas, and Oklahoma.
9. Toledo: Ohio, Michigan, and Indiana.
10. Peoria: Illinois, Missouri, and Iowa.
11. St. Paul: Wisconsin, Minnesota, North Dakota, and South Dakota.
12. Denver: Nebraska, Kansas, Colorado, and Wyoming.
13. Phoenix: New Mexico, Arizona, Utah, and Nevada.
14. Los Angeles: lower two-thirds of California.
15. San Francisco: upper third of California.
16. Portland: Washington, Oregon, Idaho, and Montana.

Each territory's share of national (48 state) demand is assumed to be proportional to its 1970 population share. Total national demand, that is, the scalar by which the individual territory shares are multiplied to obtain the product-market requirement coefficient d_{jk}, will vary from case to case.

Transportation Costs

The third major component of costs in equation (8.1) is the unit cost t_{ijk} of shipping output from plants to regional warehouses. (Since products are assumed to be transported from the warehouses in any event, regardless of the plant sites chosen, final distribution costs are invariant with respect to the plant allocation choices and hence can be ignored.) Because, at least in principle, any plant can supply any demand node, a complete matrix of all possible plant-demand node pair costs is required. The basic matrix from which all internode transport cost figures were derived is presented in Table 8.1. It gives the estimated shipping cost in cents per dollar of F.O.B. mill product value for a composite bundle of steel mill products in 1966, assuming the geographic structure of rail carload rates prevailing for steel mill products at that time and our Chapter 3 bench mark estimate that shipping a dollar's worth of steel mill products over the 350-mile haul from Chicago to Cleveland cost 7.5 cents.

The geographic rate structure statistics on which Table 8.1 is based were taken from the Interstate Commerce Commission's sample of freight carload waybills for 1966.[7] Steel products were selected largely because the ICC data for them are especially comprehensive. Even then, there were gaps in the matrix, so it was necessary to interpolate, assuming (after analyzing the available data) that rates were proportional to the logarithm of distance. One further, more arbitrary assumption was that transfers from a plant to a warehouse in the same city involved a minimum handling charge of 1.75 cents per dollar of product value. Thus, the internode rates range from a floor of 1.75 cents per dollar to 40.54 cents (for a shipment between Tampa and Portland, Oregon).

Again, the rates in Table 8.1 were derived by bench marking the actually observed or interpolated *rail* carload rates to the Chapter 3 estimate that a 350-mile shipment from Chicago to Cleveland cost 7.5 cents per dollar of product value *by the mix of carriers actually employed* in 1963. Variations to describe the transport cost relationships in other industries are effected by multiplying the Table 8.1 matrix by the ratio of that industry's Chicago-Cleveland bench mark cost to the 7.5 cent steel industry bench mark. Thus, Table 3.14 in Chapter 3 shows a 350-mile transport cost of 2.2 cents per dollar of value for paints. The transport cost matrix for the paints industry is therefore obtained by multiplying the basic Table 8.1 matrix by 2.2/7.5. We assume furthermore that the product is sold at an F.O.B. mill price equal to the sum of plant-specific and product-specific unit costs at the MOS output volume.

Multi-Product Demand and the Economies of Unbalanced Specialization

The principal objective of our analysis is to estimate quantitatively the savings attributable to optimal geographically unbalanced composite specialization. To do so, we need interesting and realistic assumptions about the distribution of demand between high- and low-volume prod-

---

7. U.S., I.C.C., *Carload Waybill Statistics: 1966* (Washington, 1968).

ucts. We assume, consistent with independent evidence, that the size distribution of product demands is log normal.[8] To keep computation costs within reasonable bounds, analyses of the multi-product case uniformly assumed that there were four representative products: one with 60 percent of total demand, one with 31 percent, one with 7 percent, and a very low volume product accounting for 2 percent of total demand. This implies somewhat less concentration of output in the higher-volume product range than the 80–20 rule would, under which the best-selling of four products (representing 25 percent of the total number of items) would have to account for more than 80 percent of total sales volume. To be sure, if there were more items in the product line, each individual product would command a smaller share of the total volume than assumed here. It is a simple matter, however, to ensure that any desired fraction of total production be distributed in sub-MOS quantities by adjusting total market demand in relation to the assumed plant-and product-specific MOS values.

To measure the cost savings available to multi-plant firms practicing unbalanced specialization, we compare the total costs such firms incur satisfying a given matrix of product and geographic market demands with the costs incurred to satisfy the same demands through optimally dispersed autonomous plants, each forced to produce all four products. It is important to recognize that the optimal number and locations of optimally specialized plants may not be the same as that set of locations which minimizes costs for plants constrained to supply a full line. Therefore, separate optimization runs are required to determine where the full-line plants will operate and which markets each will serve.

This was done by assuming that the full-line plants produce a single composite product with total national demand equal to the combined demand for the four products actually supplied. The product-specific MOS volume for the single composite product case is then adjusted upward so that total national demand is the same multiple of the composite-product MOS as the largest-volume product's demand in the four-product case is to its product-specific MOS. This is done so that the market allows the same number of high-volume product MOS assignments in each case. For example, if total national demand for all products is 50,000 units, demand for the best-selling product is 30,000 units, and the product-specific MOS is 6,000 units, the market potentially provides room for 30,000/6,000 = five plants to realize virtually all product-specific scale economies in supplying at least the most popular product.

8. See John F. Magee, *Physical Distribution Systems* (New York: McGraw-Hill, 1967), p. 38.

Table 8.1. Unit Transport Costs between Plants and Markets: Steel Products. (cents per dollar of product value)

Plants	Atlanta	Boston	Peoria	Toledo	Dallas	Denver	Los Angeles	Nashville
Atlanta	1.75	19.64	13.13	13.59	15.68	23.20	31.99	6.62
Boston	19.63	1.75	21.02	13.56	27.96	29.64	38.93	21.19
Chicago	14.09	18.32	4.50	5.21	16.94	18.47	31.18	9.62
Cleveland	14.40	13.02	11.00	4.03	20.36	21.86	33.72	11.62
Dallas	15.68	27.96	14.32	19.14	1.75	15.87	22.63	14.04
Denver	23.20	29.64	15.90	20.13	15.87	1.75	21.65	19.81
Kansas City	16.47	23.50	6.75	13.32	10.34	12.40	27.08	12.34
Los Angeles	31.99	38.93	29.78	32.46	22.63	21.65	1.75	30.53
Louisville	10.10	18.94	5.85	7.64	16.36	21.38	32.28	4.45
New Orleans	10.35	23.85	15.60	19.50	10.58	21.46	27.13	11.87
New York	15.95	5.27	19.43	12.16	24.53	28.04	38.83	17.54
Pittsburgh	14.91	13.93	12.32	6.55	21.16	22.71	34.36	12.90
Portland	36.37	38.60	29.39	32.54	31.18	22.64	21.38	33.15
Richmond	11.70	11.51	17.80	12.83	22.85	27.50	36.27	13.38
St. Paul	20.34	22.62	9.68	12.70	18.64	16.83	30.20	15.58
San Francisco	35.33	39.37	30.28	32.93	27.99	22.67	10.34	33.49
Tampa	11.72	23.04	20.84	21.25	21.95	29.96	35.80	16.04

Plants	New York	Pittsburgh	Portland	Washington D.C.	St. Paul	San Francisco	Phoenix	Tampa
Atlanta	15.95	14.91	36.37	13.08	20.34	35.33	27.80	11.72
Boston	5.27	13.93	38.60	9.62	22.62	39.37	36.35	23.04
Chicago	16.80	10.15	30.79	15.28	8.71	31.68	26.67	21.66
Cleveland	11.42	3.13	33.51	9.39	15.02	34.36	30.71	21.91
Dallas	24.53	21.16	31.18	22.56	18.64	27.99	19.33	21.88
Denver	28.04	22.71	22.54	26.85	16.83	22.67	21.13	29.96
Kansas City	21.26	16.45	28.54	20.30	9.84	28.57	21.90	22.48
Los Angeles	38.83	34.36	21.58	37.05	30.20	10.34	8.19	35.80
Louisville	16.08	9.14	32.47	13.16	13.82	32.50	28.35	18.97
New Orleans	21.68	20.74	35.52	20.07	20.37	32.40	24.54	15.58
New York	1.75	9.61	39.15	5.85	20.86	39.95	30.06	19.86
Pittsburgh	9.61	1.75	34.68	7.59	16.00	35.50	31.02	20.51
Portland	39.15	34.68	1.75	38.12	26.68	13.64	23.54	40.54
Richmond	7.67	9.09	39.00	3.28	20.13	39.63	33.78	16.10
St. Paul	20.86	16.00	26.68	20.90	1.75	29.72	27.65	26.15
San Francisco	39.95	35.50	13.64	38.61	29.72	1.75	15.53	38.63
Tampa	19.86	20.51	40.54	17.75	26.15	38.63	31.36	1.75

For our single composite product analog, total demand would be set at 50,000 units and the product-specific MOS output defined as 10,000 units, permitting five plants to operate at the minimum optimal scale.

A further adjustment to the composite product-specific cost curve is required to reflect the fact that the three lower-volume products cannot in fact realize scale economies to the extent assumed in setting the MOS. At all output levels the cost curve must be shifted upward. The magnitude of this shift at the assumed MOS output level depends upon the difference between the average cost of producing each lower-volume item at some fraction of the MOS volume and the unit cost at the MOS volume. The total shift is the sum of these differences, each multiplied by the fraction of total output that the product represents. To return to our example, total demand is taken to be 50,000 units, distributed into 30,000 units of Product One, 15,500 units of Product Two, 3,500 units of Product Three, and 1,000 units of Product Four. The product-specific MOS for individual (noncomposite) products is 6,000 units. To obtain the unit cost at a composite volume of 10,000 units for the contrived single-product case, we calculate:

(8.4) $UC(10,000) = UC(6,000) + [UC(3,100) - UC(6,000)]$
         (composite)   (four-product)   (four-product)

$\cdot \dfrac{15,500}{50,000} + [UC(700) - UC(6,000)] \cdot \dfrac{3,500}{50,000}$

(four-product)

$+ [UC(200) - UC(6,000)] \cdot \dfrac{1,000}{50,000}.$

(four-product)

The terms on the right-hand side represent in order the average product-specific cost when producing Product One at MOS volume, the volume-weighted cost sacrifice associated with being able to operate at only 51.7 percent of the product-specific MOS for Product Two, the sacrifice from being able to operate at only 11.7 percent of MOS for Product Three, and the volume-weighted sacrifice from being able to operate at only 3.3 percent of MOS for Product Four. A similar adjustment can be computed for the one-tenth MOS output level. Given these calculations, the single composite product cost curve's parameters α and γ can be defined.

This adjusted product-specific cost function is used with the plant-specific function and transportation cost matrix to find the optimal number, location, and markets of plants forced to supply all four products. The four individual product-specific cost functions are then substituted into the resulting constrained-optimal set of production assignments along with the plant-specific and transport cost functions to determine the *actual* total cost of satisfying the assumed demand requirements from autarkic full-line plants. This solution is then compared with the total cost from the optimal unbalanced specialization solution. The difference between the two total cost values is an estimate of the economies attributable to optimal unbalanced multi-plant specialization.

Several strong assumptions affect the validity of such estimates. First, we have assumed the matrix of demand requirements to be fixed. No allowance is made for the possibility that quantities demanded might be affected by the prices set, which in turn are apt to be influenced by the costs incurred under alternate patterns of production organization. To the extent that the demand for low-volume products supplied by autarkic full-line regional plants is reduced because such plants must quote relatively high prices owing to their higher unit costs, our estimates of the economies credited to optimal compositely specialized multi-plant operation are biased upward.[9] Second, we have assumed that full-line regional suppliers must produce what they supply. As was seen in Chapter 7, the economies of composite specialization shrink toward zero if regional producers are able and willing to obtain their low-volume items from centrally located specialists. Third, we assume that multi-plant firms in fact organize their production assignments optimally. If they fail to do so because of dulled incentives or limited analytic capability, our multi-plant economy estimates are biased upward. Finally, it is possible that some of our analyses failed to find the true unbalanced specialization optimum optimorum, in which case our savings estimates are biased downward. Since the first three biases seem likely to be of greater magnitude than the last, it is probable that our results provide upper-bound estimates of the economies attributable to unbalanced composite specialization by multi-plant firms, given the cost and demand parameter assumptions.

Total Demand, the MOS, and Scale Economies

A critical assumption in our multi-plant savings estimates is the level of demand and its relationship to the plant-specific and product-specific minimum optimal scales. We begin the subsequent analyses with an assumption that demand is sufficient to permit the operation of as many equal-sized MOS plants as the average number of plants operated by a U.S. Big Three producer in the appropriate industry during 1970. Similarly, the product-specific MOS will be set at a volume such that the

9. As a first approximation, the amount of the upward bias is given by the area of a triangle whose height is the difference between the unit costs (including transportation) with optimally unbalanced as compared to autarkic full-line production and whose base is the reduction in quantity demanded owing to the required price premium.

highest-volume product (accounting for 60 percent of total demand) can be produced in MOS quantities at the same number of plants. Thus, if total demand is 50,000 units and the average Big Three firm operated ten plants in 1970, the plant-specific MOS is set at 5,000 units and the product-specific MOS at 3,000 units ($= 50,000 \times 0.6/10$).

Once we have computed "base case" solutions assuming a relationship between demand and the MOS volume sufficient to support the number of equal-sized plants actually operated by average Big Three members, we vary the quantity of demand downward. In this way we can estimate the difference in total costs from having a lower share of the market, all else equal. The scale economy sacrifices so estimated are not multi-plant economies in a strict sense, since equally low costs might be experienced by regional specialists with base-case *regional* market shares who, if need be, buy low-volume items at competitive prices from centralized specialist suppliers with the same *national* market share. That is, the estimates for the most part reflect the advantages of having a larger share of an appropriately defined market rather than the advantages of multi-plant operation per se, although the two cannot be divorced completely when market failure compels full-line production by regional firms.

Finally, we shall also test the sensitivity of total production plus transportation costs to extreme errors in plant assignment strategies, such as serving the whole national demand from a single central location or the opposite extreme of operating decentralized full-line plants at each of the seventeen possible sites.

The Industrial Case Analyses

We now analyze concrete cases conforming as closely as possible to the cost relationships observed in real-world industries. Data and computer budget limitations precluded covering all twelve interview sample industries. We have therefore focused on a subset of the most interesting cases. We exclude for example cases with a combination of strong scale economies, low transport costs, and nationwide demand small in relation to the MOS volume (as in refrigerators) because the optimal solution characteristically involves a high degree of production centralization. Since production of even the highest-demand items is centralized, centralization of low-volume products under an unbalanced specialization strategy can contribute at most only trivial incremental economies. Likewise, industries such as petroleum refining and cement manufacturing with negligible product-specific scale economies, high transport costs, and relatively large regional demands for even the lower-volume products are not particularly interesting, since the decentralizing pull of transport costs will severely limit tendencies toward geographically unbalanced specialization.

Our emphasis therefore will be on variants of the cost and demand conditions observed in two especially interesting industries: paints and glass bottles. Transportation costs are high enough in both cases to pull toward decentralization, but product-specific scale economies are important enough to encourage at least some centralization. By varying the production and transport cost parameters from their observed values, the analysis is then extended to encompass a wider range of qualitatively similar but quantitatively different situations.

The Paint Industry

From a leading manufacturer we obtained detailed data on the relationship between unit mixing and can-filling costs and lot sizes for five representative paint types. This evidence was used to estimate the parameters of the product-specific cost function, given the further assumption (based upon Census and other data) that 90 percent of all in-plant costs were product-specific, but that only 40 percent of the product-specific costs were subject to lot-size economies (much of the remainder being materials costs).[10] Costs subject to plant-specific scale economies were assumed to comprise the remaining 10 percent of total in-plant costs. The plant-specific cost function was then estimated to have a shape such that a plant one-third the minimum optimal scale suffered a unit cost penalty of 4.4 percent, as reported in Table 3.11, relative to *total* (plant-specific plus product-specific) unit costs at MOS volume. The minimum optimal plant scale was set at 10 million gallons per year, consistent with Table 3.11, and the MOS product-specific volume was set at 6 million gallons per year. Given these assumptions, the following compatible cost function parameter estimates were obtained: $\epsilon = 0.056$; $\eta = 0.020$; $\delta = 0.500$; $MUPSC = \$2.210$; $Z = \$0.904$. The transportation cost matrix was bench marked to reflect the 2.2 cent per dollar of F.O.B. plant value estimate of Table 3.14 for a Chicago-Cleveland haul, assuming furthermore (with some violence to reality) that the F.O.B. mill price equals the unit cost at MOS production volume.

The average number of plants operated by the leading three U.S. paint manufacturers in 1970 was 9.7. We round this to 10.0 and set total national demand for our base-case firm at approximately 10 × 10

10. We have assumed in all analyses that materials are purchased at constant unit prices. As was seen in Chap. 7, there are economies of large-scale purchasing in the paint industry. But they do not appear to be related in any close way to the geographical allocation of plants and products in a sizeable multi-plant firm.

million = 100 million gallons; that is, enough to support ten equal-sized MOS plants, each producing Product One in product-specific MOS quantities.[11] By our log normal product demand size distribution assumption, this means that the firm's nationwide demand is sufficient to support a product-specific MOS production volume in only five plants for Product Two, one plant for Product Three, and in no (or more precisely, only one-third) plant for Product Four.

The best unbalanced specialization solution found for this base case is summarized in Table 8.2. Six plants manufacture Products One and Two, two plants Product Three, and only a single plant (at Cleveland) Product Four. To the extent that our scale economy and transport cost parameter estimates are accurate, Big Three members actually practiced somewhat more decentralization in 1970 than was optimal. The continuing fall in unit product-specific costs beyond the MOS volume appears to pull sufficiently toward centralization that all six plants exceed the plant-specific MOS volume. Total plant outputs vary from 11.5 to 25.7 million gallons. Since no paint plant in any of the countries covered by our research had actually attained the upper end of this size range by 1970, it is possible our assumptions encourage too much concentration of output by ignoring managerial diseconomies of scale.[12]

Unit plant-specific costs were identical to the MOS output values for all six plants in the Table 8.2 solution. Unit product-specific costs ranged from 0.75 percent less than the unit cost level at MOS volume for the production of Product One at New York City to 1.77 percent above the MOS value for the production of Product Four at Cleveland.

When each plant was forced to produce a full line, the optimal number of plants turned out to be six, and the optimal locations were identical to those in the best unbalanced specialization solution. Total production plus transportation costs in serving an identical set of product and spatially distributed demands from balanced full-line plants were 0.109 percent higher than with the best unbalanced specialization solution. Evidently, the lot-size economies afforded through centralization of low-volume production were largely offset by increased transport costs,

11. When the total demand requirement was allocated among the 4 products and the 16 markets, rounding caused the sum of the individual demand figures to differ slightly from 100 million gallons (or other total requirements assumed in subsequent analyses). Since the differences were quite small and individual demand allocations were identical in all cases compared, our scale economy estimates are not affected.

12. It should be noted that no U.S. company actually enjoyed a demand of 100 million gallons in 1970, although one firm came close. The absolute demand volumes assumed are irrelevant, however. What matters is the ratio of demand to the assumed MOS volumes.

Table 8.2. Plant Locations and Product Volumes in the Base Paint Case Solution.

Plant	Thousands of gallons of product number				Total plant output (thousand gallons)
	One	Two	Three	Four	
Atlanta	9,454	4,874	0	0	14,328
Chicago	8,358	4,308	0	0	12,666
Cleveland	11,854	6,110	5,712	1,996	25,672
Dallas	7,596	3,912	0	0	11,508
Los Angeles	9,262	4,770	1,300	0	15,332
New York City	13,478	6,950	0	0	20,428
Total	60,002	30,924	7,012	1,996	99,934

leaving the net savings attributable to optimal multi-plant specialization quite small.

To test sensitivity to plant location errors, total costs were computed for cases in which all production was centralized at the optimal single location (in Chicago) and also with full-line plants located at sixteen different sites, each serving the market nearest it. Compared to the best unbalanced specialization solution, the additions to total costs for these decidedly nonoptimal allocation patterns were: total centralization, 1.57 percent, and total decentralization, 1.52 percent. Apparently, the production and transportation cost characteristics of the paint industry, at least as we have estimated them thus far, are such that it is hard for a leading U.S. firm to make really bad plant location and product assignment decisions.

To investigate the effect of commanding a smaller market share and hence having a smaller volume of demand in relation to the minimum optimal scales, another case was run in which the subject firm's total demand was cut to 50 million gallons, all other parameters remaining equal. Table 8.3 summarizes the results. With half the base case demand, only four plants produce Products One and Two, two Product Three, and one (in Chicago) low-volume Product Four. When balanced full-line production is forced, the optimal locations turn out to be identical. Total costs under full-line autarkic production (computed by using the appropriate product-specific and plant-specific cost function for each plant-product pair and plant) are 0.123 percent higher than with the best unbalanced specialization solution—a slightly higher premium than in the full-demand case, but still quite small. The total cost premia under

Table 8.3. Plant Locations and Product Volumes in the One-Half Demand Paint Case Solution.

Plant	Thousands of gallons of product number				Total plant output (thousand gallons)
	One	Two	Three	Four	
Atlanta	7,594	3,913	0	0	11,507
Chicago	10,106	5,209	2,856	998	19,169
Los Angeles	5,562	2,865	650	0	9,077
New York City	6,739	3,475	0	0	10,214
Total	30,001	15,462	3,506	998	49,967

complete centralization (at Chicago) and sixteen-plant full-line decentralization strategies are: total centralization, 0.93 percent; and total decentralization, 3.74 percent. The adverse consequences of extreme decentralization are more serious than in the full-demand case because of the greater scale economy sacrifices implied, but they are still not earth-shaking.

A further interesting comparison is between the costs of meeting a national demand volume of 100 million gallons per year through one optimally specialized firm, as in the Table 8.2 full-demand case, and two optimally specialized nationwide firms, each serving half that demand volume by duplicating the plant structures described in Table 8.3. The average unit cost disadvantage of the half-demand producers is 0.94 percent. This provides insight into the advantages of having a large market share and adapting to it optimally. As noted earlier, the observed cost savings are not economies of multi-plant operation in the strict sense, since single-plant specialists with similar *regional* market shares could supply at least Products One and Two at unit costs equivalent to those of the full-demand multi-plant operator.

Most of the computer runs for this chapter were executed before the compilation of data for Chapters 3, 5, and 6 was completed. In the process of cross-checking data for Chapters 3 and 5, it was learned that an error had been made in estimating the transportation cost per dollar of product value for paints. The correct estimate is the 2.2 cent figure used in the first two cases here. Our earlier computations assumed a shipping cost of 3.2 cents per dollar of value on the basic Chicago-Cleveland haul. This assumption was not altogether infelicitous, since the 2.2 cent estimate may well be biased downward, given other assumptions embodied in the present analysis. The 2.2 cent figure relates to F.O.B. mill product value, while our transportation cost matrix was built up by multiplying Table 8.1 entries by 2.2/7.5 and then multiplying further by in-plant unit production costs at plant-specific and product-specific MOS volume. Yet in-plant MOS unit costs underestimate F.O.B. mill prices because actual prices are set to cover the costs of low-volume products turned out at suboptimal volumes and because they exclude selling, central staff, and R&D costs (amounting to roughly 27 percent of sales in 1969 for a cross section of ninety-two paint companies.)[13] Also, our transportation cost estimates exclude the capital cost of inventories while they are in transit. Consequently, the 3.2 cent estimate may actually depict reality better than the 2.2 cent estimate. Whether or not this is true, we summarize the results from runs assuming a 3.2 cent bench mark.

Table 8.4 describes the best unbalanced specialization solution for a case exactly analogous to the full-demand case of Table 8.2, except that Chicago-Cleveland transport costs are assumed to be 3.2 cents per dollar of in-plant MOS volume unit cost. The higher transport costs encourage greater decentralization—seven plants instead of six for Product One, and for lowest-volume Product Four it becomes advantageous to maintain a second production source on the West Coast. When autarkic full-line production is forced, plant locations are the same as in the unbalanced specialization solution, except that no facility is operated

Table 8.4. Plant Locations and Product Volumes in the Full-Demand Paint Case with Bench Mark Transport Costs Increased to 3.2 Cents.

Plant	Thousands of gallons of product number				Total plant output (thousand gallons)
	One	Two	Three	Four	
Atlanta	9,454	4,874	1,778	0	16,106
Chicago	8,358	4,308	0	0	12,666
Cleveland	11,854	6,110	3,934	1,688	23,586
Dallas	7,596	3,912	0	0	11,508
Los Angeles	7,212	3,714	1,300	308	12,534
New York City	13,478	6,950	0	0	20,428
Portland	2,050	1,056	0	0	3,106
Total	60,002	30,924	7,012	1,996	99,934

13. National Paint, Varnish, and Lacquer Association, *Operating Cost Survey for the Year 1969* (Washington, August 1970), p. 12.

at Portland. Total production plus distribution costs are 0.090 percent higher than with optimal geographically unbalanced specialization. The cost premia for cases of extreme centralization (at Chicago) and full-line decentralization are: total centralization, 2.66 percent; and total decentralization, 1.18 percent. Again, the consequences of poor decisions are found to be modest.

Table 8.5 shows the distribution of production assignments when the subject firm's demand is one-half the base case level, or 50 million gallons per year, all else equal; and Table 8.6 the results for a national demand volume of 25 million gallons. As one would expect, there is progressively more centralization as demand is reduced in relation to the minimum optimal scale. The cost sacrifices incurred when the same quantities and spatial distribution of demand are satisfied from autarkic full-line regional plants are: full demand case, 0.090 percent; one-half demand case, 0.025 percent; and one-fourth demand case, 0.022 percent. The more centralization there is of high-volume products in this

Table 8.5. Plant Locations and Product Volumes in the Half-Demand Paint Case with Bench/Mark Transport Costs Increased to 3.2 Cents.

| Plant | Thousands of gallons of product number | | | | Total plant output (thousand gallons) |
	One	Two	Three	Four	
Atlanta	4,727	3,913	889	0	9,529
Chicago	10,106	5,209	1,967	998	18,280
Dallas	3,798	0	0	0	3,798
Los Angeles	4,631	2,865	650	0	8,146
New York City	6,739	3,475	0	0	10,214
Total	30,001	15,462	3,506	998	49,967

Table 8.6 Plant Locations and Product Volumes in the One-Fourth Demand Paint Case with Bench/Mark Transport Costs of 3.2 Cents.

| Plant | Thousands of gallons of product number | | | | Total plant output (thousand gallons) |
	One	Two	Three	Four	
Cleveland	12,221	6,299	1,753	499	20,772
Los Angeles	2,780	1,432	0	0	4,212

instance, all else equal, the smaller the marginal gains from *further* unbalanced centralization of the lowest-volume products appear to be.

The increases in total cost attributable to extreme centralization at Chicago and extreme decentralization to sixteen plant locations are:

	One-half demand	One-fourth demand
Total centralization	1.69 percent	0.50 percent
Total decentralization	3.06 percent	5.30 percent

The unit cost penalties borne by optimally specialized firms with a national market share one-half and one-fourth the market share of base case (Table 8.4) firms, ceteris paribus, are: one-half the base case market share, 1.3 percent; and one-fourth the base case market share, 2.9 percent.

Our final two paint industry cases embody assumption modifications which do violence to reality and therefore provide insight into the effects of unbalanced specialization in rather different industries. For the first, all parameters are identical to those for the half-demand case (Table 8.5) except that unit transport costs on a Chicago-Cleveland haul are raised to 6.4 cents per dollar of MOS production cost. The objective is to see how, relative to the full-demand case, halving demand and doubling transport costs simultaneously affect the optimal solution. Decreasing demand should cause more centralization, while increasing transport costs should induce more decentralization. The results are summarized qualitatively in Table 8.7. The two opposing forces balance out almost perfectly. The solution is identical to that of base case Table 8.4 except that Product Three is produced at three more plants. When the autarkic full-line solution is computed, production is optimally located at the same seven plants as in the unbalanced case, and total costs are 0.054 percent higher than with the best unbalanced allocation. This is less than in the full-demand case with 3.2 cent transport costs, evidently because higher transport costs eat up more of the savings

Table 8.7 Plants Producing in Best Solution to the One-Half Demand, Double Transport Cost Paint Case.

Product One	Product Two	Product Three	Product Four
Atlanta	Atlanta	Atlanta	
Chicago	Chicago	Chicago	
Cleveland	Cleveland	Cleveland	Cleveland
Dallas	Dallas	Dallas	
Los Angeles	Los Angeles	Los Angeles	Los Angeles
New York City	New York City	New York City	
Portland	Portland		

from unbalanced centralization, but it is greater than in the 3.2 cent, half-demand case, in which centralization is much higher for *all* products. For this 6.4 cent shipping cost example, the cost penalty borne by a producer centralizing all operations at Chicago is 5.26 percent compared to an optimally located and specialized manufacturer. The penalty for total decentralization of production at sixteen plants is 1.99 percent.

Finally, Table 8.8 summarizes the plant and product assignments when the product-specific scale economies parameter ϵ is doubled to 0.112, Chicago-Cleveland transportation costs are 3.2 cents per dollar

Table 8.8. Plants Producing in Best Solution to the One-Half Demand, Double Scale Economies Paint Case.

Product One	Product Two	Product Three	Product Four
Los Angeles	Los Angeles		
Louisville	Louisville	Louisville	Louisville
New York City	New York City		

of in-plant unit cost at MOS, and total demand is 50 million gallons (half the base case). Here the centralization forces are particularly strong; only three plants produce the higher-volume items and only one Products Three and Four. When balanced full-line supply is forced, plants at the same sites have total production plus distribution costs 0.462 percent higher than plants practicing unbalanced specialization. This is by a substantial margin the highest specialization economy estimate discovered for any computed variant of the paint industry case. It shows the sensitivity of savings to the steepness of the product-specific unit cost function. Premium costs attributable to adopting a highly decentralized sixteen full-line plant structure are also considerable: 9.20 percent of total costs under optimal unbalanced specialization. A single plant at Chicago incurs costs 1.00 percent higher than does the plant structure of Table 8.8.

The Glass Bottle Industry

The glass bottle industry has production and transportation cost conditions sufficiently different from paints to provide interesting additional insights. The product-specific cost function was estimated assuming fixed setup costs like those described in Chapter 7.[14] We assume further that plants with more annual output of a given product have proportionately longer average production runs; that product-specific costs

14. Cf. p. 304 *supra.*

comprise 90 percent of total in-plant costs; and that product-specific costs subject to setup economies represent only 40 percent of all product-specific costs (the balance involving raw materials, shipping cartons, and packaging labor). As in Table 3.11, *total* unit production costs are assumed to be elevated by 11.0 percent in plants constructed to produce only one-third the MOS output. These assumptions led to the following parameter estimates: $\epsilon = 0.187$; $\eta = 0.025$; $\delta = 1.676$; $MUPSC = 0.900$; $Z = 0.823$. Comparison of the ϵ and δ values for bottles with those assumed for the paint industry reveals that the scale economy effects in bottles are more than three times as strong as those in paints. Also, rounding the Table 3.14 estimate upward, we assume the shipping cost between Chicago and Cleveland to be 10.0 cents per dollar of unit cost at MOS volume, compared to the 2.2 or 3.2 cent figures assumed for paints.

The average number of plants operated in 1970 by the leading three U.S. glass bottle firms was thirteen. We therefore set the total national demand for Product One to be thirteen times the product-specific MOS, arbitrarily taken to be 13,000 units (say, in units of 10,000 tons). The plant-specific MOS is assumed to be $13,000/.6 = 21,667$ units and total national demand for all products thirteen times that quantity.

Table 8.9 describes the plant location and production assignments for the best computed unbalanced specialization solution to this base bottle industry case. Nine plants supply Products One and Two, while manu-

Table 8.9 Plant Locations and Product Volumes in the Base Bottles Case Solution.

| Plant | Output of the individual products | | | | Total plant output (10,000 tons) |
	One	Two	Three	Four	
Atlanta	20,956	10,805	3,116	0	34,877
Chicago	15,576	8,028	0	0	23,604
Cleveland	33,389	17,210	6,648	4,755	62,002
Dallas	21,396	11,019	2,501	0	34,916
Los Angeles	20,315	10,462	3,053	868	34,698
New York City	37,964	19,576	4,433	0	61,973
Portland	5,774	2,974	0	0	8,748
St. Paul	7,966	4,107	0	0	12,073
Tampa	5,673	2,924	0	0	8,597
Total	169,009	87,105	19,751	5,623	281,488

facture of the lowest-volume product is concentrated at only two sites.[15] A striking feature is the wide variation in optimal Product One and total production volumes between plants. Three plants operate at less than the plant-specific MOS output, and Product One is turned out in less-than-MOS volumes at the same three plants. This demonstrates that when transportation costs are substantial, there is no such thing as *the* minimum optimal scale, taking both production and shipping costs into account. The optimum varies with the density of regional market demand.

Plant-specific unit costs for the bottle production allocations shown in Table 8.9 range from the level consistent with an MOS plant (in six cases) to 67.5 percent more than the minimum MOS unit cost value (at Tampa). Product-specific unit costs are 1.57 percent below the assumed MOS value for the manufacture of Product One at New York, 2.87 percent above it for the production of Product One at Tampa, and 28.5 percent above it for the supply of Product Four from Los Angeles.

When bottle plants are constrained to produce a full line, the optimal geographic organization involves seven plant sites. Total costs are 0.270 percent higher than with the unbalanced specialization pattern of Table 8.9. Total centralization of production at Chicago increases costs by 10.47 percent relative to the best unbalanced specialization solution. Full-line decentralization over sixteen sites raises costs by 1.64 percent.

For the computations underlying our final example, described in Table 8.10, demand was halved, all other parameters remaining the same. As one would expect, substantially more centralization occurs. Compared to this unbalanced solution, the cost sacrifice borne by six optimally located full-line plants is 0.516 percent—the largest nonoptimal specialization cost premium found for any case studied. Unlike the 3.2 cent transport cost cases, we observe a negative correlation between the magnitude of unbalanced specialization economies and the ratio of national demand to the MOS volume. Apparently, production of high-volume items continues to be sufficiently decentralized that a substantial imbalance between high- and low-volume assignments can be achieved in the half-demand case. And strong product-specific economies combine with the fairly high incidence of sub-MOS production to make the cost savings from centralizing lower-volume product assignments larger than when demand is relatively strong.

15. If *different* low-volume product designs are demanded in the various regional markets, such centralization will of course be impractical and our multi-plant specialization economy estimates will be biased upward.

It should be noted also that the bottles case, unlike paints, departs rather severely from reality in its assumption that demand is distributed spatially in proportion to population.

Table 8.10. Plant Locations and Product Volumes in the One-Half Demand Bottles Case Solution.

Plant	Output of the individual products				Total plant output (10,000 tons)
	One	Two	Three	Four	
Atlanta	13,314	6,865	2,503	0	22,682
Chicago	11,771	6,067	0	0	17,838
Cleveland	16,695	8,605	5,541	2,811	33,652
Dallas	10,698	5,509	0	0	16,207
Los Angeles	13,044	6,718	1,831	0	21,593
New York City	18,982	9,788	0	0	28,770
Total	84,504	43,552	9,875	2,811	140,742

For the half-demand case, the cost penalties associated with extreme centralization and decentralization are: total centralization, 8.36 percent; and total decentralization, 7.59 percent. The increase in costs owing to having the full base-case demand satisfied by *two* optimally specialized nationwide suppliers, each with one-half the market share assumed for the Table 8.9 base-case firm, is 2.3 percent. These diseconomies of a halved market share are nearly twice as great as those observed for the paint industry with 3.2 cent Chicago-Cleveland transport costs (that is, from comparing the Table 8.4 and 8.5 solutions). Stronger plant-specific and product-specific scale economies for bottles as compared to paints are the reason.

Conclusion

Table 8.11 summarizes our estimates of the cost penalties avoidable through optimally unbalanced specialization as compared to autarkic full-line production for nine cases. The values range from 0.02 percent to one-half percent of total costs. They tend in general to be quite modest, indeed, much lower than we had anticipated on the basis of qualitative evidence compiled through interviews. It would of course be possible to find larger values, for example, by assuming even higher scale economy parameters and somewhat lower transport costs than in the half-demand bottle case. Also, the estimates are no doubt sensitive to our unvaried assumption concerning the distribution of demand among low-volume and high-volume products—that is, in the base demand cases, that nationwide demand is one-third to one-half the product-specific MOS for Product Four, accounting for 2 percent of total unit demand for all

Table 8.11. Comparison of the Unbalanced Specialization Economies Computed for Nine Cases.

Table	Bench Mark transport cost (cents per dollar)	Product-specific scale economies parameter ϵ	Plant-specific scale economies parameter δ	Demand assumption	Percentage increase in cost owing to balanced as compared to unbalanced production assignments
8.2	2.2	0.056	0.500	Base paint	0.109
8.3	2.2	.056	.500	One-half base paint	.123
8.4	3.2	.056	.500	Base paint	.090
8.5	3.2	.056	.500	One-half base paint	.025
8.6	3.2	.056	.500	One-fourth base paint	.022
8.7	6.4	.056	.500	One-half base paint	.054
8.8	3.2	.112	.500	One-half base paint	.462
8.9	10.0	.187	1.676	Base bottle	.270
8.10	10.0	.187	1.676	One-half base bottle	.516

products, and 1.16 to 1.52 times the product-specific MOS for Product Three, accounting for 7 percent of total demand. Still these assumptions do not appear to undershoot by any wide margin the actual shares of low-volume products encountered in transport-cost-intensive U.S. industries. The chances of a bias toward underestimating the relative importance of low-volume items appear particularly remote in the cases for which national demand has been halved or quartered. It seems quite clear that the economics potentially attainable through optimal geographically unbalanced specialization in a multi-plant context are much less important than the advantages of having, say, a market share twice that of rivals, for which savings ranging from 0.9 to 2.3 percent of total cost were estimated.

The unbalanced specialization economy estimates, it bears repeating, are biased downward to the extent that our computational algorithm failed to converge upon the optimum optimorum. However, a more serious bias in the opposite direction may be imparted by our assumption that regional suppliers must produce their own low-volume products, rather than buying them from centralized specialists. All in all, the analysis suggests that the economies attributable to optimal unbalanced specialization by multi-plant firms must be quite small in relation to total production and physical distribution costs.

9

Conclusions

In this concluding chapter we recapitulate the principal substantive findings, restate the emerging themes in a more unified way, and point out broader implications.

The Main Findings in Perspective

Our research began in response to a puzzle: why plants seemingly too small to realize all scale economies coexist so frequently with extensive multi-plant operation by leading firms. Part of the answer turns out to be disappointingly simple: The paradoxes which originally fired our curiosity were to some extent a fiction of measurement biases. By comparing the sizes of the leading twenty plants in each industry across nations, Bain systematically understated the sizes of "representative" plants in smaller nations. There is also reason to believe that, contrary to his findings, the extent of multi-plant operation adjusts to the difficulty of securing scale economies at the plant level, and in particular, that leading companies operate fewer plants in small markets than in large. Thus, there is less small-scale plant operation *and* less multi-plant operation in small nations than Bain's 1966 study led us to believe.

Nevertheless, a substantial fraction of the production in many industries does take place in plants too small to achieve all scale economies, especially in the smaller nations abroad but also in certain U.S. industries. And suboptimal plant scales do coincide frequently with multi-plant operation. Thus, the paradox survives, albeit in attenuated form.

There are numerous reasons for the persistence of small plants. Without doubt the most important is that markets in small nations like Sweden and Canada frequently do not provide much breathing space. In some national markets there is insufficient room for even a single plant of minimal optimal scale. In many additional instances, markets large enough to accommodate a very few MOS plants are fragmented further, among other reasons to satisfy buyers' desire for variety and security against monopolistic exploitation. Second, when outbound transportation costs are substantial in relation to product value, regional fragmentation occurs. That is, plants too small to minimize production costs are often optimal in the sense of minimizing production *plus* shipping costs in geographically vast and/or sparsely populated markets. Third, our statistical analysis suggests that suboptimal scale operation is more likely when the long-run unit production cost function is relatively flat than when unit costs fall sharply with increased plant size. To the extent that this is true, there may be self-regulating checks on the magnitude of efficiency losses attributable to the operation of small plants. There is also limited evidence that the growth of plants toward efficient scales is faster when plants are relatively small and therefore bear relatively high production cost penalties. Fourth, many small plants, and particularly those in the small plant tail of size distributions, are a rational response to the problems of manufacturing specialty products with volatile demand or other features requiring close managerial supervision or technologies well suited to low-volume production. Historical legacies from periods when "best-practice" scales were much smaller also help explain the persistence of small plants, especially in industries with durable, capital-intensive production equipment. The speed at which such legacies are shed appears to depend importantly upon the vigor of competition: Tough domestic or import competition stimulates modernization while cartelization, by dulling incentives, retards it. Finally, there are all sorts of ad hoc reasons for the survival of sub-MOS facilities, such as strong local product preferences, taxes graduated in favor of small suppliers, governmental constraints on the closing of plants, and a conscious choice by certain producers to concentrate on serving a limited home market and avoid the rough-and-tumble of export markets.

One of the most interesting and potentially most controversial results from our statistical analysis of plant sizes concerns the role of seller concentration. By bringing together insights from other analyses it can now be put in clearer perspective. We found in Chapter 3 that a regionally adjusted index of seller concentration had a powerful influence in "explaining" plant size variations, especially for the European nations but also for the United States and Canada. There were unambiguous indications that this effect involved a multiplicative interaction with the national market size variable: The larger the market (measured in terms of MOS plant equivalents) the leading three sellers controlled, the larger were average Top 50 Percent plant sizes. The problem in interpreting this relationship is that a consistently defined set of market size, concentration, and multi-plant operation variables "explains" plant size variations definitionally. Our variables were not so consistently defined, and no multi-plant variable was used in the plant size analysis, so an identity system was not formed. Yet in Chapters 5 and 6 we learned, contrary to conventional wisdom and expectation, that no simple statistical association exists between seller concentration and the extent of multi-plant operation. If in fact multi-plant operation does not vary systematically with concentration, then in a market of given size, an increase in concentration must, at least on the average, be accompanied by an increase in the size of leading sellers' plants. In this restricted sense, and to the extent that there is substantial overlap between the cohort of largest plants in an industry and leading sellers' plants, the observed positive association between plant sizes and concentration does have a definitional character.

Definitional it may be, but not behaviorally trivial. If other things (such as the extent of multi-plant operation) tend to be equal, fragmenting a small market into numerous small seller shares means that plants will be smaller on the average than they would be if sales were spread among fewer sellers. And in this respect we cannot escape the conclusion that concentration and plant sizes are linked meaningfully, or at least, meaningfully enough that one would be wary of measures which encourage or perpetuate structural atomization of smallish markets if one placed much weight on securing the scale economies associated with large plants.

This may be a sufficient answer to the question of causality in a static context, but it does not resolve the more important dynamic issues. Specifically, is high concentration on average a *prerequisite* to the building of efficient-sized plants? And if concentration is permitted or encouraged (for instance, through public policy measures) to increase, will increases in the realization of plant scale economies follow?

Here our cross-sectional statistical analyses provide no conclusive guidance, but interview evidence helps fill the gap. If sellers are willing to struggle for scale economies, investing in large plants or plant expansions and competing vigorously, on the price dimension among others, to absorb the attendant output increments, high concentration is *not* an essential precondition. In small markets it may be a *consequence* of such behavior, but it has no inherent causal significance. If on the other hand sellers accept accustomed market shares and avoid expansionary moves which upset the status quo but defend their traditional shares by expanding in pace with demand growth, a dynamics will exist under which high concentration encourages the achievement of scale economies while fragmentation discourages it. Through our interviews we observed many variations and combinations of these polar behavioral modes. Simple generalizations are not easily posited, but two variables appear to be important in explaining which mode predominates. First, reluctance to upset the price and market share status quo is greater in markets that are tightly oligopolistic than in either atomistically structured markets or those so concentrated that a single seller dominates. Given a tight oligopoly structure, large capacity expansions are more apt to be undertaken in relatively large markets than in small. Second, differences in the "animal spirits" of entrepreneurs plainly matter. Some producers appear more willing to struggle for position than others. This might at first be dismissed as a random variable outside the bounds of an economist's search for systematic and measurable associations. Yet we received the impression through our interviews that the spirit of independent struggle was distinctly weaker in Europe, and especially in France, England, and Germany, than in the New World. The more powerful explanatory role of the seller concentration variable for the European nations in our plant size analysis is consistent with this qualitative impression, and it is difficult to find an alternate explanation for the international statistical differences.

Indeed, the statistical results for market size and concentration together are consistent with, even though they cannot "prove," the hypothesis that dynamically as well as statically, concentration may under certain conditions contribute to the achievement of plant scale economies. Concretely, when competition fails because markets are so small in relation to the minimum optimal scale that tight oligopoly is inevitable and/or because there is a failure of nerve on the part of entrepreneurs—permitting still higher seller concentration levels to develop (for example, through merger) can lead to the construction of larger units. Concentration in effect provides a second-best solution to the plant-specific scale economies problem.

We turn now to the factors influencing the extent of multi-plant operation. As noted already, one variable which does *not* appear to be systematically related except in tautological ways is seller concentration. Economists have wrongly presumed that a positive relationship existed because they have implicitly accepted Ralph Nelson's erroneous assumption that an index of the *percentage* of all industry plants operated by the leading sellers adequately measures the *extent* of multi-plant operation. All that remains of the conventional wisdom is the fact that the leading firms in many concentrated industries do operate multiple plants, from which it follows that if there were less multi-plant operation, all else equal, concentration would be lower.

What systematic variables do then account for the observed variations in multi-plant operation? The most consistent explanatory factors appear to be market size and the relative importance of transportation costs. Multi-plant operation proliferates more in large markets than in small, and firms are drawn toward geographically decentralized multi-plant postures more strongly when transport costs are high in relation to product value than when they are low. There is weaker evidence that multi-plant operation is inhibited more when the pull of plant scale economies is strong than when it is weak. The combination of these three results implies that when national markets are large, enterprises expand to serve them on a nationwide plane, adopting a plant numbers, size, and location strategy which tends to minimize combined production plus physical distribution costs. Qualitative analyses suggest that the advantages of specializing plants in narrow product line segments underlie considerable multi-plant operation, although the statistical manifestations are elusive. Much multi-plant operation is also attributable to undigested, unrationalized mergers, but again, confirmation of this historical observation does not emerge readily from the cross-sectional statistical investigations.

More important to the policy debate is the question of what advantages multi-plant operators enjoy which are not available to firms maintaining a single plant of optimal scale. The problem, we have stressed repeatedly, is extremely complex, and we cannot pretend to have learned everything one would like to know. Yet some rather clear generalizations do emerge.

It has been well known that multi-plant size can confer risk-spreading, capital-raising, materials procurement, research and development, and (especially in consumer goods industries) sales promotional advantages. Our interview data generally confirm this view. If they add anything new, it is mainly an appreciation of how complicated the sales promotional scale economy relationships are and how often the advantages of large size can be offset or neutralized by small firms using promotional methods peculiarly well adapted to their market positions. Capital-raising advantages persevere out to very large firm sizes, although the handicap borne by a firm large enough to operate only one MOS plant in most of the industries covered by our study does not appear to be very great quantitatively. Except in a few areas, single-MOS-plant firms also hold their own in securing the advantages of large-scale purchasing. Multi-plant size makes it easier to support vigorous programs of technical research, development, and customer engineering in most of the industries studied, but in only three or four are such advantages strategically important, and they tend to be exhausted when two to four MOS plants are brought under a single corporate umbrella.

Where the most serious knowledge void has existed is on the links between multi-plant operation and production costs. It is here that our interview research focused most intensively. In most of the twelve industries we found evidence of a potential for achieving production cost savings through multi-plant operation. This potential was successfully tapped in a smaller proportion of cases. The extent of its realization depended upon a number of factors.

For one, running a multi-plant production network efficiently requires a more effective managerial information and control system than operating a single-plant enterprise. Many multi-plant firms failed to realize their potential because they were unable to cope with the managerial challenges.

Transportation costs are a second major variable. When they are high in relation to product value, the production cost savings from coordinating a multi-plant network optimally tend to be dissipated in outlays for increased cross-shipping. When they are very low, production tends to be pulled toward a central location unless other considerations (such as managerial control loss or labor market imperfections) intervene. Some of the most interesting opportunities for multi-plant production economies exist, therefore, in industries with intermediate levels of transport cost per unit of product value: roughly 3 to 12 cents per dollar on good-sized 350-mile shipments.

Third, the realization of multi-plant economies appears to depend in an absolutely critical way upon the workability of market processes. When markets are functioning well, the benefits of multi-plant operation tend to be small. When they are functioning poorly because of monopolistic pricing behavior or product complexities which preclude arm's-length transactions, the benefits can be substantial.

This theme has been a recurrent one. In investment decisions, we observed, appreciable cost savings can be realized when the expansion of plants serving regionally dispersed markets is coordinated optimally, *assuming* that demand must be satisfied with supplies produced within one's own plant system. But the more readily firms can cover temporary deficits by buying supplies at competitive prices from other companies or work off surpluses by selling to capacity-short rivals, the less important the economies of optimal *internal* plant network coordination tend to be. Likewise, multi-region suppliers can produce a full line of products at lower cost by centralizing the manufacture of low-volume items while decentralizing high-volume production—a strategy not open to single-location firms. The savings from such unbalanced specialization tend to be surprisingly small, our Chapter 8 analysis revealed. Yet they vanish altogether if regional plants, whether owned by single- or multi-plant firms, can obtain low-volume items at competitive prices from centrally located independent specialists. It is only when such competitive sources are lacking that multi-plant economies arise. In industries with relatively low transportation costs and complex product arrays, the operation of multiple plants, each specialized in a narrow line of items, may confer lot-size economies of appreciable magnitude *if* there are compulsions to offer a broad line, either because customers demand it or because the breakdown of price competition undermines incentives to specialize. But if markets are working well, rewarding those who offer selected price concessions to achieve longer production runs and letting sellers fill out their lines through competitive purchases from specialist suppliers, the incremental savings attributable to multi-plant product specialization dwindle. For a fourth illustration, market failure in such important, high-scale-economy primary input sectors as crude oil extraction, paint pigment manufacturing, and refrigerator compressor production may induce vertical integration and simultaneously increase the number of plants needed at the next stage downstream to have a balanced operation. Again, if the input markets could be made to work competitively, multi-plant operation would be less advantageous.

Given certain kinds of market failure, multi-plant producers are in the best position to compensate. The most significant potential production cost savings associated with multi-plant operation turn out with surprising uniformity to be "second-best" economies. This was surely one of the most unexpected but important discoveries emerging from our interview research. But because predicting the incidence of such market failures is such a complex task, requiring the whole theoretical apparatus accumulated by industrial organization economists and perhaps more, estimating the production cost economies attributable to multi-plant operation is formidably difficult. This complexity, we believe, plus a methodology which ignored feedbacks from conduct to structure, is what prevented Bain from reaching consistent, confident conclusions in his pioneering twenty-industry study.

Antitrust Policy Implications

All this has crucial implications for antitrust (or in Europe, "competition") policy. Structural and conduct-oriented measures enforced under the aegis of antitrust can improve industrial efficiency, impair it, or simultaneously engender mixed effects. To illustrate, permitting a sizeable horizontal merger may increase long-run production efficiency if the potential merger partners have such strong respect for their mutual interdependence that they would not build full-sized new plants independently for fear of either depressing prices or carrying too heavy an excess capacity burden, or if they decline to compete on a price basis to accumulate longer production runs and enhance their specialization. But such mergers could alternately strengthen respect for interdependence, making specialization-increasing and competitive expansion moves all the more unlikely or dampening those competitive pressures which would have stimulated independent efficiency-seeking behavior. Similarly diverse consequences could follow the implementation of a cartel with production rationalization features.

The economic theory underlying United States antitrust policy has in our judgment been overly simplistic, tending to deny categorically that real benefits can come from concentration-increasing mergers or cartels. This oversimplification appears to have two main roots: inadequate insight into the determinants of plant size decisions, plus an almost total preoccupation with plant-specific production economies and concomitant neglect of product-specific economies.

Failing to recognize the existence of a phenomenon is no serious sin if the phenomenon is quantitatively unimportant. The crucial policy questions are therefore: How often can concentration-increasing mergers or rationalization cartels lead to production efficiency gains? How large are the gains? What are the side costs? And how can one distinguish the cases in which benefits will exceed costs from cases of the opposite genre?

The answers to the first two questions turn, as we have seen, on the extent to which certain kinds of market failure occur. If such market failures are rare, concentration-increasing mergers and specialization agreements are apt to yield plant- and product-specific economies infrequently and of generally small magnitude. If they are widespread, a more ample benefit estimate is warranted.

For a nation like the United States, with markets characteristically large in relation to optimal plant- and product-specific scales and a relatively heterogeneous, independent-minded population of industrial chiefs, most production takes place under conditions sufficiently competitive that the benefits from further concentration or cartelization must on average be quite small. If one must choose between global policy alternatives—maximum emphasis on a first-best competitive regime vs. a tolerant attitude toward concentration and cartels with possible second-best benefits—the first-best strategy appears unambiguously superior. Although market failure is more widespread in member nations of the European Community, the failures are the result more of alterable tradition, permissive laws or regulation, and incomplete development of intermember trade than of any structural necessity, and over the long run a first-best policy emphasizing competition seems likely to yield higher levels of economic efficiency. But for relatively small nations like Canada isolated by trade barriers or (in the case of Sweden) whose trading bloc partners are also small and geographically scattered, it is much less clear that single-minded reliance upon competitive forces is the best policy. In such nations there almost surely exists a substantial array of cases in which mergers or specialization agreements could lead to larger, more efficient plant scales and production lots.

To be sure, these gains would not be a free good. One offsetting social cost might be the increase in prices and decrease in allocative efficiency traditionally associated with enhanced monopoly power. This, however, is probably a minor consideration. As we have argued, concentration-increasing multi-plant mergers or specialization agreements offer few incremental production efficiency benefits unless market failure is already present, and, under those conditions, prices are already apt to be hovering at levels which, if exceeded, would stimulate a surge of imports or new entry. Also, as Oliver E. Williamson has shown, a one percent across-the-board reduction in production costs more than offsets the allocative efficiency losses from an increase in prices well above one percent under nearly any plausible set of assumptions.[1] Much more important are the income redistributions caused by increased monopoly power, the impact widespread cartelization can have in dampening entrepreneurial vigor, and the social and political malaise that follow from excessive concentration of economic power. How much weight one wishes to place on such social costs is a question of values, and we doubt whether we could progress very far toward measuring the costs even if the weights were clearly articulated. We can only say that they are not insubstantial. Yet we feel certain that the efficiency benefits from mergers or specialization agreements in small, sheltered national markets can be sufficiently compelling in at least a subset of cases that policy-makers ought not to reject all such possibilities out of hand.

Even in nations like the United States with large and for the most part workably competitive markets, there exist isolated instances of market failure where appropriate second-best remedies might lead to

---

1. "Economies as an Antitrust Defense: The Welfare Tradeoffs," *American Economic Review*, 58 (March 1968), 18–34. See also n. 2, Chap. 7 *supra*.

net efficiency gains. The principal examples that came to light through our interview research are steel and antifriction bearings. In both, respect for mutual interdependence in pricing and/or broad-line coverage incentives have frustrated the development of optimal specialization patterns, leading to a substantial incidence of inefficiently small-lot production. Our best guess, and it is no more than that, is that production costs could be reduced by 5 to 10 percent on something like a fourth to a third of those industries' output through well-conceived, effectively executed specialization agreements. Potential savings of this magnitude in such important industries are hardly to be ignored. One might argue too that as long as the cases are indeed exceptional, the off-setting social costs would be modest, for a few islands of cartelization in a largely competitive sea are not apt to have much adverse incremental impact on the distribution of income and the maintenance of entrepreneurial vigor. Shouldn't such cases therefore be viewed sympathetically? And as a prerequisite, shouldn't the per se prohibition of market-dividing and other collusive agreements in U.S. antitrust law and the emerging per se presumption against substantial horizontal mergers be rescinded so that the cases can be judged on their merits?

To these questions both specific and general answers are required. On the specifics of the steel and bearing industries, we doubt whether specialization agreements would on balance be a good thing. There is clearly an efficiency gain potential, and it should be evident from the fact that we conducted this study that we place appreciable weight on achieving industrial efficiency. Yet we are by no means confident that the potential would be translated into actuality. The U.S. steel industry in particular, although the most efficient in the world until recently, has less than a peerless record of implementing needed efficiency measures when they were needed. It is far from certain that the result of specialization agreements which reduce competitive pressure would be a vigorous drive toward efficiency, and not a resting on one's oars. We are also fearful of the costs. Few industrialists have recognized as clearly as U.S. steelmakers the profitability, when one enjoys monopoly power but no cost advantage, of setting prices at levels which encourage new entry and the erosion of one's market share.[2] Given the pricing latitude specialization cartels would confer and the higher production costs of domestic as compared to foreign producers, it is likely the U.S. steel industry would set prices at levels encouraging growing imports,

2. See Darius W. Gaskins, Jr., "Dynamic Limit Pricing: Optimal Pricing under Threat of Entry," *Journal of Economic Theory*, 3 (September 1971), 306–322; and George Stigler, "The Dominant Firm and the Inverted Umbrella," *Journal of Law and Economics*, 8 (October 1965), 167–172.

thus accelerating its long-run demise. Similar import entry encouragement dangers exist for a cartelized bearings industry. Also, we attach considerable value to maintaining a diversity of supply sources, however little genuine price competition the suppliers might provide, and we admit the liberal's dread (on largely noneconomic grounds) of concentrating so much power in so few hands. So while we would listen attentively to rationalization proposals with provisions designed to maximixe expected benefits and minimize the probability of adverse side effects, our predisposition would be skeptical.

The second, more general problem is the difficulty of administering a "rule of reason" successfully. If governments agree to consider concentration-increasing mergers and rationalization cartels on their merits, there are bound to be numerous petitions. Some, if a correct reckoning of benefits and costs could be made, ought to be approved; some (and in nations with generally workable competition, most) ought not. But how to separate the wheat from the chaff? We were not greatly impressed with the average quality of merger and cartel approval decisions where industries covered by our research operated in a "rule of reason" jurisdiction. There are severe limits on the ability of judicial and regulatory bodies to make sound decisions concerning complex economic issues when the proponents of a monopolistic scheme have a commanding advantage in knowledge of and insight into the intricacies of their industry.[3] The opportunities for bamboozlement and coöptation are great, as is the probability of "wrong" decisions. We would like to believe that scholarly works like ours will improve the decision-making process by illuminating the fundamental conceptual relationships and suggesting the appropriate factual questions. Still, we are not really very optimistic.

For small, sheltered nations, we see no way these dangers can be avoided without foreclosing unacceptably many efficiency gain opportunities. Some rule of reason is virtually essential. For large nations like the United States or trade areas like the European Community, the choice is closer. We would like to think that a rule of reason could be administered intelligently enough to approve the relatively few competition-limiting actions promising benefits well in excess of costs while disallowing all the others. If however we are overly sanguine on this point, it is undoubtedly better to adopt tough per se rules prohibiting all market division cartels and horizontal mergers tending substantially to lessen competition.

3. Cf. Derek C. Bok, "Section 7 of the Clayton Act and the Merging of Law and Economics," *Harvard Law Review*, 73 (December 1960), 291–299.

Structural Fragmentation

While concentration may be too low to permit maximum efficiency under some circumstances, it could in other cases be higher than it needs to be to maintain the optimal balance between structural efficiency and competitive vigor. What do our research findings imply about the desirability of structural fragmentation—breaking up large multi-plant firms whose size has little or no efficiency justification?[4]

Since we have found *some* multi-plant economies in nearly every industry studied, it seems clear that breaking up large firms whenever high concentration and multi-plant operation coincided would necessitate scale economy sacrifices. The key questions are again matters of degree: How sizeable are the benefits of multi-plant operation? How many plants must be combined before marginal gains become inconsequential? And what is the nature of the economies which might be sacrificed through dissolution?

Referring to the judgmental estimates in Table 7.6, we recall that in four of our twelve sample industries—paints, cement, steel, and storage batteries—the overall scale economy disadvantage of a firm large enough to operate only one MOS plant was at most slight. In nearly all the other industries, the number of plants required to experience no more than a slight handicap under U.S. market conditions was typically small, ranging between two and six. Perhaps more telling, in the storage battery and weaving industries, actual average U.S. Big Three market shares in 1970 were roughly ten times as large as they needed to be to permit the realization of all but slight residual multi-plant economies; in paints, glass bottles, shoes, and steel, leading firm shares exceeded "required" shares by four to six times; and in cement by three to five times. These estimates suggest that in more than half the industries covered by our research, substantial deconcentration could be effected while forcing at most slight scale economy sacrifices.

Here, however, we encounter again a paradox discovered in our statistical analyses. Of the seven industries singled out for their high ratios of actual to required concentration, only three, bottles, steel, and storage batteries, had national market four-firm concentration ratios exceeding 40 in 1967. The two *most* concentrated U.S. industries in our sample, cigarettes and refrigerators, had actual to required ratios of from 2 to 4 and 1.0 to 1.5 respectively, with the ranges reflecting measurement uncertainties. National market concentration and multi-plant operation beyond thresholds required to realize the most important scale economies are *not* closely correlated.

4. On leading proposals in this vein, see n. 10, Chap. 1 *supra*.

To be sure, concentration is higher when appropriate regional market definitions are adopted for the cement industry and narrower product lines are considered in weaving, shoes, and paints. Yet for at least the last three high multi-plant industries, it would be hard to argue convincingly that there exists a concentration problem sufficiently serious to warrant wholesale dissolution and divestiture actions. And in cement, the plants of leading U.S. producers are typically so widely scattered that divestiture actions would lead to increases in competition mainly at the fringes of regional markets. The costs in terms of foregone scale economies would be low, but the gains in competition would also be much less than the sheer number of cement plants involved might suggest.

Although cement should not be dismissed completely as a candidate, especially in view of its long collusive history and its technological backwardness compared to counterparts abroad, this preliminary screening on the basis of actual vs. required concentration ratios points most sharply toward glass bottles, steel, and storage batteries. Determining how much economic good could be done through deconcentration actions in those industries would require a more far-reaching investigation than we have undertaken. Some skepticism is warranted in every case.

In batteries, where the most sweeping divestiture program would be feasible, the principal performance problems appear to lie in the industrial battery submarket, served by many fewer plants; the vertical integration of General Motors into battery making; and the private-label stocking policies of retail gasoline chains. Price and quality competition at the wholesale level is fairly vigorous. In glass bottles, as in cement, geographic scattering of plants and high transportation costs would limit competitive benefits. It is ironic, too, that the second most vulnerable firm, Brockway, attained a substantial part of its multi-plant posture through government-approved mergers. The steel industry poses still more difficult judgmental problems. Steel's performance in terms of pricing, technological innovation, capacity utilization, and success in damping inflationary pressures leaves much to be desired.[5] Yet it is doubtful whether the residual fragments of an atomized United States Steel Corporation or Bethlehem Steel would be able and (given output absorption concerns) willing to carry out the relocation and rebuilding programs needed to make the U.S. steel industry internationally competitive in coming decades. It is equally questionable that they will make such investments if left alone. If a potent deconcentration law existed, it

5. In an expert panel experiment conducted by Steven R. Cox, steel received the second worst consensus performance ranking of 14 U.S. industries. Only contract construction fared worse. Cox, "An Industrial Performance Evaluation Experiment," *Journal of Industrial Economics*, 22 (March 1974), 205.

might be applied to greater public advantage by threatening the steel industry's leaders: "Set in motion an investment program guaranteeing that the United States will have a modern, efficient steel industry by 1990, or we will atomize you."

By focusing on industries in which actual market shares greatly exceed the market shares required to attain all but slight incremental multi-plant economies, we may however have misdirected our search. Such an approach implies among other things that all scale economies are equally desirable socially. This is debatable. One might in particular be willing to sacrifice brand image and sales promotional advantages of considerably greater magnitude on the presumption that they confer little or no real social benefit. If so, brewing joins the list of prominent divestiture candidates, for the most important persistent multi-plant advantages enjoyed by the leading U.S. brewers are promotional.[6] Cigarettes would join too, had industry leader Reynolds not concentrated all its production at a single site in Winston-Salem, making dissolution difficult. Another strong contender would be petroleum refining, particularly if parallel policy changes eliminate crude oil supply distortions. Still, strong value judgments are required before one can be prepared to ride roughshod over existing beer, cigarette, and gasoline brand preferences and perhaps to intervene and curb the advertising escalation probable when divestiture actions create a host of new brands. Like most economists, we take a dim view of high-pressure advertising and superficial brand differentiation. But we confess no great desire to be in the (nationally branded?) shoes of the senator or congressman running for reelection after fathering a bill depriving home-state consumers of their Budweiser and Schlitz.

In the final analysis, such value judgments must carry the day. Given *our* social welfare function, which places much more weight on investment, production, and physical distribution economies than on promotional advantages, refrigerators and antifriction bearings are the *least* promising candidates for structural fragmentation. Specialization economies interact in sufficiently important ways with broad-line compulsions to warrant an extremely cautious tack. Even there, however, and certainly in all the other industries, the production and physical distribution economies of multi-plant operation are not so great that they unambiguously dominate all other considerations. Excluding the unmeasurable loss of consumer satisfaction brand image fragmentation

6. It is probably true that without their brand image advantages, Anheuser-Busch and Schlitz would have been less likely to build a network of decentralized, modern, large-scale plants. But now that the plants exist, the investment economies are "sunk," and opportunities for *further* investment economies are much more limited.

might temporarily cause, the worst scale economy sacrifices attributable to a thoroughgoing but intelligently executed deconcentration program could hardly exceed a good year's productivity growth increment, and for most of the twelve industries it would be much less. That is not an exhorbitant price to pay *if* high utility is attached to creating a society in which economic power is dispersed to the maximum practical extent.

The critical question is, how seriously is such a society desired? More on sociopolitical than economic grounds, we rank the dispersion of power high among our goals—high enough that we would be willing to accept modest efficiency sacrifices to achieve it. We therefore believe a well thought out deconcentration program would more than justify its costs. Yet this must be regarded for what it is, a choice reflecting our personal values. On such global policy judgments, unlike cigarettes, everyone must roll his own. The most we as economists can do authoritatively is supply the high-scale economy inputs—a comprehensive theory of multi-plant economies and evidence on their approximate magnitude.

International Trade and Integration Implications

The decade preceding our interview research saw a radical lowering of tariffs and other trade barriers for the four European nations in our sample and for parts of the Canadian and U.S. bearing and battery industries. Our research findings reveal that, especially for smaller nations, increased international trade can make an important difference in unit production costs by enhancing the attainment of scale economies.

Three mechanisms deserve special mention. First, our statistical analysis of plant sizes suggests that leading plant sizes increase much more than proportionately with increases in exports as a percentage of domestic production. Although one cannot be sure of the true causal chain, it seems reasonable to presume that export-expanding policies, by broadening market horizons, have a favorable impact on the incentive to build large, efficient plants and plant additions. Second, there is no significant statistical evidence of an offsetting shrinkage of plant sizes in response to greater import penetration, so reciprocal trade increases do not merely cancel out each other's scale economy effects. Indeed, interview evidence suggests that in at least certain industries, increased imports have been a stimulant to the construction of modern plants. Third, the broadening of market horizons through trade barrier removal creates opportunities for further product specialization and the exploitation of product-specific scale economies.

We were not surprised to discover these three effects. What was surprising, at least for Americans with only superficial prior insight into the European Community and European Free Trade Association developments, was to see how much trade continued to be inhibited by both artificial restraints national governments imposed and tacit or explicit spheres of influence understandings among potentially competing national industry groups. Granted, institutions and industrial structures built up over decades of protectionism cannot be done away with in a few years time. Yet it is important to recognize that appreciable potential efficiency gains remain unexploited, awaiting a sustained effort to remove further trade barriers and upset international market division agreements.

Managerial Implications

While creating scale economy opportunities, the reduction of tariffs and growth of international trade also pose new business organization and management challenges. One response has been the growth of multi-national firms. Companies operating in several member nations of a free trade area are in an especially favorable position to pursue cost-saving product specialization strategies. In a few instances uncovered by our interview research, this was done with considerable success. But in other cases, we were surprised to observe how slowly the specialization process was proceeding. Some companies had not even begun to think about the problem. It seems clear that special organizations and skills must be developed to take full advantage of the product-specific scale economy opportunities a multi-national, multi-plant production structure offers. Successful operation requires that a delicate balance be struck. As long as nationalism and cultural differences persist, on-site operating efficiency is likely to be enhanced by letting native managers run national plant networks with maximum possible autonomy. To implement an optimal product specialization plan and to exploit the massed reserves potential of multiple plants distributed throughout a free trade area, however, requires centralized management and control. Compromising these conflicting mandates is not easy. Inability to find the right balance impeded the realization of economic integration economies in some multi-national companies. The problem is a continuing, important one.

Another barrier to the realization of specialization economies, even in large but relatively homogeneous markets like the United States, is the inability of multi-plant firms to cope with the information processing requirements. Here, we believe, change is inevitable. As the capacity of electronic data processing equipment grows and as persons trained to use that capacity analytically flow from the universities into industry, the ability of multi-plant, multi-product firms to solve complex production assignment and scheduling problems is bound to increase. One significant by-product may be an increase in the cost savings realizable through multi-plant operation. To be sure, we were impressed at how well certain managers did in deciding multi-plant investment staging sequences, centralization vs. decentralization of low-volume item production, and similar matters on largely intuitive bases. Our numerical analysis of the optimal unbalanced specialization problem also revealed that total costs may not be highly sensitive to the exact solution chosen over at least a wide range of interesting parameter values. We nevertheless believe that there is much unmined gold left in the hills, and that multi-plant firms are going to develop better ways of extracting it.

Further Research Avenues

We have learned a great deal in the course of this project, but too much remains to be learned. In this final section we note some of the problems on which, we believe, further research is most urgently needed.

The variables associated with differences in plant sizes have been analyzed cross-sectionally, and hence in effect statically, fairly thoroughly. But more light needs to be shed on the dynamics of the processes by which different plant size distributions are generated. The causal role of concentration deserves special attention. On a related dimension, we have seen that new firms and firms expanding into new geographic markets frequently enter with plants smaller than the minimum optimal scale. Much more research, both statistical and qualitative, is needed to illuminate this entry phenomenon, which is absolutely fundamental to the functioning of industrial markets. The links between export performance and plant sizes should also be investigated through statistical analyses with more sophisticated lag structures than those we postulated.

Perhaps the most important gap in our understanding of multi-plant production and physical distribution economies concerns the relationship between firm size, market shares, and the average lengths of production runs. Are larger firms and companies with larger shares of their markets better able to put together longer, more economical production runs? The evidence we gathered shows no strong relationships, but the issue was brought to focus relatively late in our interview program, and we ought to know much more about both cross-sectional patterns and the dynamics of the processes by which product specialization emerges.

We have learned that many of the production and physical distribution economies of multi-plant operation are second-best benefits, realizable because the market mechanism fails as a coordinating and specializing instrument. There have been numerous contributions to the economic theory of second best since the pioneering article by R. G. Lipsey and Kelvin Lancaster in 1956, but almost no attention has been paid to the kinds of production efficiency breakdowns identified in this volume. Further work on both the pure theory and the numerical analysis of plausible first- and second-best tradeoff possibilities is warranted. We would not be surprised if simulation analyses showed that the tradeoff surface is quite flat, in the sense that similar output bundles can be attained with given resources through either first-best competitive market processes or second-best solutions involving nonmarket coordination within the confines of powerful multi-plant firms. It may, however, be difficult to take into account in such analyses the higher probability that monopolistic enterprises will operate completely off (that is, within) the potential tradeoff surface owing to deficient cost reduction incentives or control loss.

From a similar but more applied perspective, better estimates of the potential savings attainable by operating multi-plant complexes optimally can be derived through further large-scale computer model testing in the spirit of our Chapter 8 analyses. On the economics of reserve massing in geographic space a special void exists. Models are needed which combine orthodox investment, production, inventory, and transportation cost variables with random and cyclical demand variation. The Chapter 8 analysis might also be extended in interesting ways by postulating different product demand size distributions and by introducing inventory carrying costs, transportation costs varying with shipment volume, lot-size decisions varying with annual production volume, and alternative warehousing strategies.

As Chapter 6 observed, our interview research sample was biased in favor of industries with relatively extensive multi-plant operation, at least in the United States. A more complete picture of how market size, plant sizes, and the extent of multi-plant operation interrelate awaits a careful international comparisons analysis of those variables for a much larger sample.

Finally, it is remarkable that although an enormous amount of research is done on capital markets, there is little comprehensive evidence on how large an advantage giant firms enjoy relative to small companies in raising capital. The quantitative analysis in Chapter 7 represents a beginning, but no more than that. More empirical work is needed. It should also be recognized that this advantage of multi-plant firms is another second-best benefit, attributable to imperfections in the functioning of capital markets. Efforts to perfect capital markets and hence to move toward first-best solutions deserve continuing attention.

Appendixes
Indexes

A

The Sources of Employment Size Distribution Statistics

There are two main ways of obtaining data on plant size distributions. One is to use the standard compilations prepared by the census or statistical authorities of most industrialized nations. These are almost always based upon employment counts, although sales distribution statistics are also encountered occasionally. A second approach is to consult specialized trade journals, some of which publish plant capacity or output statistics regularly, or to go directly to governmental regulatory agencies, industry trade associations, or the firms themselves for information. Particularly for the process industries, on which employment data measure true plant sizes most inadequately, we were in effect compelled to emphasize the second method. The sources of data were so diverse that no simple summary could do justice to them. We shall gladly provide further details privately for scholars interested in specific industries. Census compilations underlay the employment size distribution comparisons in the early pages of Chapter 3 and roughly half the plant size observations used in our multiple regression analyses. Since they are the most abundant source of data for international comparisons, it seems appropriate to spell out more fully where they can be found and what some of the main obstacles to comparison are.

Surely the most difficult single problem is the widely varying industry definitions and degrees of aggregation found from one nation to the next. As Chapter 3 noted, our solution approach has been to combine the richly subdivided United States data to match as closely as possible the particular definition employed by another nation's census authorities. To carry out such a matching effort, knowledge of the language, the technology, and national industry peculiarities is important.

All the nations covered by our study except Germany based their plant employment compilations on the notion of an "establishment," defined by the U.S. Census Bureau as "a business or industrial unit at a single physical location which produces or distributes goods or performs services." There appears to be fairly general agreement among the census authorities of various nations as to what an establishment is. Except in Germany, plants operated by a single company at two physically separate locations in the same city would normally be counted as two separate establishments. There is nevertheless latitude for minor interpretational differences both internationally and within a given nation. The usual criterion for determining whether units share the same physical location is whether they report the same address. It is possible that separate buildings on a geographically contiguous plot of land might be reported as having separate addresses, and hence would routinely be counted as distinct establishments. A U.S. Census Bureau official stated that the Bureau does not try to enforce strict uniformity in such cases, but allows firms some discretion to define establishments in whatever way most closely corresponds with the realities of their operation. When distinctly different activities, each sizeable, are pursued at a single location, the normal U.S. and foreign practice is to encourage subdivision into multiple establishments for reporting purposes. Again, however, some discretion is permitted; if there is unified control and accounting and the records kept do not permit such subdivision, all activities will be counted under the heading of a single establishment, which will then be classified to that industry in which sales or employment are greatest.

The main unit of reporting for the German *Zensus im Produzierenden Gewerbe* is the *produzierende Betrieb*, which might best be translated as a works. The concept is in most respects similar to that of an establishment. Thus, when related production activities are all located on a spatially contiguous site, they are reported under the heading of a single *Betrieb*. The main difference is that employment in affiliated administrative and auxiliary activities (but not separated headquarters) is also credited to the *Betrieb* as long as it takes place in the vicinity of the main production operations, even if its site is not physically contiguous to the production site. The German *Betrieb* tends therefore to be somewhat more inclusive than the establishment of the United States and other nations, with an upward plant size measurement bias of unknown but probably small magnitude resulting. The most recent *Zensus im Produzierenden Gewerbe* available at the time of our Chapter 3 analysis was for 1962. However, more current size distribution data were obtained, also on a *Betrieb* basis, from the Statistisches Bundesamt series, *Die Industrie in der Bundesrepublik Deutschland*, Series 4.

The sources of plant size distribution data for some 420 U.S. manufacturing industries is the *Census of Manufactures*, conducted twice each decade by the Bureau of the Census. The data are published in the complete bound Census report series and in a special preliminary paperback volume usually entitled *Size of Establishments*. As we have already brought out for Germany, an important source of methodological variation between nations concerns the handling of employment in central offices, auxiliary service installations (such as research and development laboratories, repair shops, warehouses, and garages), sales offices, and the like. For the United States such activities are uniformly excluded from plant employment distributions if they are located at sites physically segregated from the production sites. If they occur on the same site as a production operation, their employment is likely to be counted as part of the production establishment's employment unless they are sufficiently sizeable and distinct that the company chooses to report them as separate establishments. Whenever they are reported separately, their employment is not counted as part of the four-digit manufacturing industry's size distribution, but it is included in employment totals at the two-digit level of aggregation.

Beginning with the years 1969 and 1970, detailed establishment size distributions for all Canadian manufacturing industries have been gathered together in a summary publication entitled *Type of Organization and Size of Establishments*. Data by industry for earlier years are found in the individual industry reports published, usually annually, in connection with the Census of Manufactures. Employment in physically separate headquarters offices, sales offices, and auxiliary installations was not included in the production establishment size distributions, but was tabulated separately for each industry.

Establishment size distribution data for United Kingdom manufacturing industries are presented in the individually bound industry reports of the series, *Report on the Census of Production*. For 1963 there were reports for 125 different manufacturing industries. They were issued irregularly over a period of roughly two years, with issue announcements appearing in the monthly catalogue of Her Majesty's Stationery Office. Other censuses have been conducted in 1954, 1958, and 1968, among others. The 1968 census was just becoming available in 1972, when our statistical analysis of plant sizes was completed, so older data had to be used. The treatment of employment at central offices, research laboratories, and other "common service" facilities is unique. Even when such employment occurred at physically distinct sites, it was either included in the figures for a company's main establishment or apportioned among the company's production establishments in proportion to the number of operatives employed at each, except for companies with activities so diverse that no sensible allocation was feasible. The effect of this convention is to bias plant size estimates, and especially leading plant size estimates, upward. Indeed, the bias is probably more serious than under the assumptions adopted in Germany.

For eighty-eight Swedish manufacturing industry groups, size distributions based upon the number of *arbetare* (wage earners) are released every two years by the government's central statistical agency (Statistiska Centralbyrån) in the comprehensive volume *Industri*. The data can also be found in the more accessible *Statistisk Årsbok*. Workers occupied in central offices and various auxiliary activities at a plant site are, as in other nations, counted with production workers at that site. When home offices or repair shops clearly associated with an industry were located at separate sites, they were counted as additional establishments within the relevant industry. The effect is to overstate the number of establishments and, since employment at such facilities tends to be lower than at leading production plants, to pull down average Top 50 Percent plant size estimates. However, a comparison of census plant counts with counts based upon interviews and other sources revealed that the number of additional establishments created in this way is very small, at least for the industries covered by our study. Geographically separate warehouses and sales offices are not counted as additional production establishments, nor is their employment allocated to production units.

The source of employment size distribution data for French manufacturing establishments was *Les Etablissements Industriels et Commerciaux en France en 1966*, published by the Institut National de la Statistique et des Etudes Economiques. The industry classification is unusually rich, richer even than that provided by the United States Census in many instances. Similar compilations were published for 1962, 1958, and 1954, but we were warned by the National Statistical Institute that the industry classifications and plant assignments were changed greatly between census years. A serious problem in using the data for any year is that physically separate central offices, warehouses, sales offices, garages, and similar service units were counted indiscriminately along with production units as establishments. The effect again is to extend the small-establishment tail of the size distribution and to bias Top 50 Percent plant size estimates downward. However, the National Statistical Institute kindly prepared for us a special tabulation covering twenty industries, including all our sample industries, making it possible to exclude all such auxiliary establishments from the size distributions.

B

Derivation of the
Transportation Cost
Variable Estimates

To assess the impact of outbound shipping costs on multi-plant operation patterns for the industries analyzed in Chapter 5 (and on a more limited scale, Chapters 3 and 6), it was necessary to estimate the F.O.B. plant price per pound of the principal products associated with each four-digit industry and the cost per hundredweight of shipping those products in carload or truckload lots over a specified distance. The relative importance of final product shipping charges is then estimated by the ratio of the freight rate to the products' value per pound.

A prime source of information for value per pound estimates was the 1963 *Census of Manufactures*, which presents value of shipments figures for numerous seven-digit products within four-digit Census industries. The necessary freight rate information was obtained from official tariffs published by various regional rate bureaus and from publications of the Interstate Commerce Commission's Bureau of Economics.

Deriving reasonably accurate value per pound figures proved to be difficult in a number of industries because of deficient information or inappropriately broad Census industry classifications. For the products comprising many four-digit industries, the *Census of Manufactures* discloses only the total value of shipments without revealing the physical quantity of units shipped. Without quantity data, one cannot directly establish wholesale unit value. There are in fact relatively few industries for which both value and quantity statistics are available on all the products spanned by the four-digit classification. But in many cases it was possible to establish a representative unit value figure because the omitted products were either similar to other industry products or accounted for a small fraction of total industry shipments. There remained, however, a substantial number of industries for which five- and seven-digit product groupings were so heterogeneous, or the quantity data were so sketchy, that reliable unit value figures could not be derived. This is one reason why virtually all of the catch-all N.E.C. (not elsewhere classified) industries have been omitted from the final sample.

For 101 major four-digit industries, the data were of sufficient quality to estimate unit value figures with fairly high confidence. In 54 of them, the Census unit of measure was either tons or thousands of pounds. In such cases deriving a product's value per pound was simply a matter of dividing the dollar value of shipments by the total weight of the shipments. For 47 other industries, the Census Bureau's quantity measure was the number of physical units (or, in the case of certain liquids, the number of gallons or barrels) shipped in 1963. Household refrigerators and freezers (S.I.C. 3632) illustrates the problem. In 1963, 4.1 million household refrigerators valued at $687.9 million were shipped from U.S. plants.[1] Thus, the average refrigerator carried a wholesale price of about $170. But there is no clue in the Census data as to the shipping weight of a typical refrigerator.

Fortunately, detailed shipping weight information for refrigerators and many other consumer products can be found in the Sears Roebuck mail order catalogue. According to Census data, the largest selling household refrigerator model in 1963 had two exterior doors and a storage capacity of from 13.5 to 14.4 cubic feet. Since 1,175,378 of these refrigerators valued at $226,451,000 were shipped in 1963, their unit value was $192.70. Sears lists the shipping weight of its middle-line 14.2 cubic foot, two-door model as 330 pounds. Our best estimate of the value per pound of a typical household refrigerator is therefore $192.70/330 = $0.58. In order to obtain the appropriate value per pound figure for the entire industry, it is necessary also to derive an estimate for a representative household freezer and compute the mean value for refrigerators and freezers, using their respective sales volumes as weights. These calculations yield a figure of $0.50 for freezers and a final value per pound rating of $0.57 for the entire four-digit industry, reflecting the fact that the sales of refrigerators in 1963 were 4.8 times those of

1. U.S., Bureau of the Census, *Census of Manufactures, 1963* (Washington, 1966), Table 6A-1, B-18, p. 36.

freezers.[2] The Sears catalogue proved invaluable in establishing value per pound estimates for forty-one consumer-oriented industries. In each case the rating was derived in the same general manner as for refrigerators and freezers. For six other industries (flat glass, industrial gases, electric lamps, flavoring extracts, metal containers, and glass containers) shipping weights were obtained directly from manufacturers or by weighing representative items (including standard shipping containers) on scales inspected by Bureau of Standards personnel.

For another 54 industries, product lines were so complex and Census data so limited that neither of these product value estimation approaches was feasible. In those cases total outbound shipment tonnage estimates from the 1963 *Census of Transportation* were matched with *Census of Manufactures* sales data to calculate the desired value per pound estimates. Since the industry definitions used by these two sources do not always match perfectly, since the *Census of Transportation* data are subject to sometimes substantial sampling errors, and since certain on-site transfers may have been recorded as sales but not as outbound tonnage shipments, these estimates are a good deal less reliable than those for the 101 industry subsample.

The final step in deriving the sought-for transportation cost indices was compiling rail and truck freight rates for products representing the 101 industries on which relatively accurate value per pound estimates were available. At the time this part of the project was initiated, it was not clear whether class or commodity rates ought to be stressed. Rail and motor class rate schedules are particularly well suited to determining rates for large numbers of products over a given shipping distance. The rail and motor class rate schedules are identical in form. Each consists of two volumes. The first carefully indexes articles for easy reference and assigns "ratings" for carload and less-than-carload shipments. Each rating, or class, is some fraction of a base rating of 100.[3] The first section of the second volume lists shipping distances between various points of origin and destination; Section Two then reveals the actual rate in cents

2. The largest selling freezer in 1963 was an upright model in the 15.5 to 17.4 cubic foot range; it had a unit value of $158. There were 2 Sears freezers in this size range: a 15.8 cubic foot model weighing 305 pounds and a 333 pound, 17.0 cubic foot model. The average weight of these 2 freezers, 319 pounds, combines with the unit value figure of $158 to yield a value per pound estimate of $0.50.

3. To illustrate, magnesium pipe fittings received a carload rating of 65 in 1963. The final freight charge per 100 pounds for magnesium pipe fittings and all other articles with ratings of 65 was thus 65 percent of the charge for products assigned a rating of 100. See *Uniform Freight Classification 6* (Chicago: Edward Keogh Printing Company, 1961), p. 289, item 29720.

per hundred weight for shipping an item with a given class rating over a given distance.[4]

Although the class rate information is complete and accessible, it is not truly representative of prevailing shipping costs. Only a small percentage of freight traffic by ton-miles actually moves under class rates; commodity rates are clearly more important. Trucking companies and railroads establish commodity rates for items which move regularly in substantial quantity between two specific locations. The origins of such shipments are points where manufacturing or warehousing of the commodity is conducted in considerable volume; the destinations are volume consuming points. Class rates are quoted only on shipments so sporadic or of such small tonnage that establishing a separate commodity rate would not be justified.[5]

Commodity rates are thus unquestionably a better measure of the *level* of outbound freight charges incurred by major manufacturing firms. Whether or not there are substantial differences between the *structure* of commodity and class rates could not be determined conclusively until the necessary rate data had been collected. Officials of Associated Truck Lines stated that each commodity rate is determined by applying a fixed percentage reduction to the corresponding class rate, regardless of the length of haul. For example, during 1970 the motor commodity rate for plastic bottles moving between any two points within the Central States Territory was 85 percent of the relevant class rate. If all motor commodity rates were 85 percent of class rates, and if rail commodity rates were also some fixed fraction of class rates, an index of transportation costs based upon the lower commodity rate would be merely a linear transformation of the class rate index. However, an Associated representative stated that the percentage differentials between class and commodity rates do vary considerably from item to item. Given the likelihood that the commodity and class rate structures differ significantly, an attempt was made to obtain rail and motor commodity rates for products in the sampled industries, using the public files of the Interstate Commerce Commission in Washington, D.C.

It soon became apparent that the hundreds of rail commodity rate tariffs were too complex and poorly indexed to permit accurate inter-

4. Rail classification and tariff catalogues were obtained from the Tariff Publishing Officer of the Uniform Classification Committee. Associated Truck Lines of Grand Rapids, Michigan, furnished the corresponding motor freight catalogues. All were current in 1963.

5. The tariff manager of Associated Truck Lines reported that a special 3-day study of Associated's traffic disclosed that only 30 percent of the truckloads surveyed were class-rated.

pretation in a reasonable amount of time. The chief of the I.C.C.'s Economics Bureau suggested that a workable alternative source would be the Bureau's one percent samples of carload waybill statistics for 1966. The series discloses the average freight rate per ton-mile actually paid by shippers, as specified on the sample waybills for products in two-, three-, and in some instances four-digit industries. Four-digit industries are covered most completely in the series of publications classifying origins and destinations on a state-to-state basis. In this series average freight charges have been calculated from waybills for all sampled carloads involving similar products between points in any two specified states. Thus, the average ton-mile freight charge listed on waybills for cars carrying steel mill products between stations in Illinois and Ohio (an average distance of 335 miles) was $0.017 in 1966.[6] Since the bulk of the sample's tonnage was presumably governed by commodity rates, we infer that the carload commodity rate charged volume shippers of steel mill products in 1966 was roughly equal to this figure. Ideally, we would have preferred data current in 1963 and not subject to sampling error. But if the I.C.C. samplings were at all representative they should provide satisfactory estimates of the interindustry structure of rail commodity rates prevailing during the period spanned by our analysis.[7]

Variations in ton-mile rates among product groups would be hopelessly obscured if the waybill data used were based on hauls in different sections of the country or on hauls of differing length. The section of the country within which products are shipped is relevant because the general level of rates varies among the five major rail rate territories. The length of haul is also important since, as a general rule, ton-mile rates decline as the distance shipped increases. The ton-mile rate for a product shipped between California and New York is likely to be lower than that of almost any product moving between New York and New Jersey, regardless of the relationship between the two rates over the same length of haul.

It was therefore hoped that the I.C.C. state-to-state series would disclose for each four-digit industry ton-mile rates charged on shipments moving within the same rate territory and between the same two states—specifically, Illinois and Ohio, an important medium-length haul of about 335 miles within the Official Territory. Unfortunately, for many industries the sample of freight carloads moving between Illinois and Ohio was too small to allow reliable estimates. Nor were there any other

6. I.C.C., Bureau of Economics, *Carload Waybill Statistics, 1966: State-to-State Distribution* (Washington, 1968), Statement SS-6, p. 47.

7. According to the chief of the I.C.C. Economics Bureau, rail freight rates were quite stable over the 1963–1966 period.

two states for which rate information was available on every industry in the sample.

However, another I.C.C. series of waybill samplings helped provide the missing information. The Bureau of Economics' Mileage Block data include average ton-mile rates within each of the five rate territories on the basis of distance shipped. For a given territory it is possible to find ton-mile rates over a constant haul length for almost every industry in the Bureau's sample. However, far fewer industries are covered at the four-digit level by the Mileage Block series than in the state-to-state data.

To assure that rates compiled from the two sets of data were as comparable as possible, the Mileage Block figures were based on hauls of 350 miles within the Official Territory (which spans the northeastern United States, including North Carolina and Tennessee and more northerly states, extending to a narrow strip along the west bank of the Mississippi River). Rates drawn from the two series are about evenly represented in the final rail commodity rate index, though the Mileage Block rates are not as finely detailed. Many of the Mileage Block rates are based on three- (and in a few cases two-) digit industry classifications, and consequently a number of four-digit industries in our sample share the same ton-mile rail commodity rate.

Since the I.C.C. does not sample truck waybills, it was necessary to obtain motor commodity rates directly from the published tariffs. Fortunately, these tariffs are thoroughly indexed and relatively easy to interpret. The only serious difficulty was the familiar problem of adjusting rates for differing shipment distances. Truckload rates for the 350-mile run between Chicago and Cleveland were used whenever possible. However, there remained many products which do not move in large volume between Chicago and Cleveland, so that commodity rates had not been established. In such cases the only alternative was to choose the closest approximation to a Chicago-Cleveland haul from among the various intercity runs listed, and then to adjust the rates for that haul to a corresponding distance of 350 miles. Following the advice of an experienced motor freight traffic manager, this was accomplished as follows: The unadjusted commodity rate was divided by the motor class rate for the applicable item between the two cities in question. This established the proportional relationship between the product's commodity rate and class rate for any desired length of haul. The resulting fraction was then multiplied by the class rate for the product between Chicago and Cleveland to estimate the commodity rate that would have been established had the product been shipped in sufficient quantity between those two cities.

Appendix Table 3.1. Industry Definitions and Plant Size Measures: United States.

Industry	1957 S.I.C. codes	Data year	Size measure	Average size of Top 20 plants[a]	Average Top 50 % size	Midpoint plant	No. of plants to Midpoint
Beer brewing	2082	1967	Employees	1,565	1,693	840	18
Beer brewing	2082	1967	U.S. bbl. output	3,057,000	3,246,000	1,427,000	18
Cigarettes	2111	1967	Employees	2,288[16]	5,719	2,900	4
Cotton & synthetic weaving	2211 2221	1967	Employees	3,379	1,497	800	104
Paints & allied products	2851	1967	Employees	542	248	125	133
Petroleum refining	2911	1967	Employees	2,134	1,694	800	32
Petroleum refining	2911	Jan. 1969	Stream bbl./day capacity	236,217	194,238	101,000	31
Shoes, except rubber	3141	1967	Employees	963	564	365	176
Glass containers	3221	1967	Employees	1,431	1,258	770	27
Hydraulic cement	3241	1967	Employees	403	340	220	48
Hydraulic cement	3241	1969	Barrels per yr. capacity	6,610,000	4,800,000	3,300,000	52
Blast furnaces & steel mills	3312	1967	Employees	12,475	11,900	6,610	23
Ordinary steel works	33122	1967	Ingot short tons per yr. capacity	4,344,000	4,915,000	2,933,000	15
Ball & roller bearings	3562	1967	Employees	2,000	2,673	1,620	11
Household refrigerators & freezers	3632	1967	Employees	2,630	7,160	4,240	4
Household refrigerators & freezers	3632	1967	Units/year	325,000	806,000	500,000	4

| Storage batteries | 3691 | 1967 | Employees | 524 | 571 | 260 | 17 |
| Storage batteries | 3691 | 1967 | Automobile battery equiv. units/year | 1,600,000 | 1,700,000 | 910,000 | 17 |

Sources: U.S., Bureau of the Census, *Census of Manufactures, 1967*, vol. I: *Summary and Subject Statistics* (Washington: USGPO, 1971), chap. 2; Research Company of America, *Brewing Industry Survey: 1968* (New York, 1969); U.S., Department of the Interior, *Certified "Refinery Inputs" by Individual Refineries* (Washington, loose-leaf, circa 1969); "Large Cement Plants in North America," *Rock Products* (May 1969), pp. 50–52; *Iron and Steel Works of the World*, 5th ed. (London: Metal Bulletin Books, Ltd., 1969); miscellaneous trade sources; company annual reports; interviews.

[a]When the industry included fewer than 20 plants, the number of plants is given in subscripted parentheses.

Appendix Table 3.2.   Industry Definitions and Plant Size Measures: Canada.

Industry	1957 S.I.C. codes	Data year	Size measure	Average size of Top 20 plants[a]	Average Top 50 % size	Midpoint plant	No. of plants to midpoint
Beer brewing	2082	1967	Employees	356	844	410	5
Beer brewing	2082	1967	U.S. bbl. output	n.a.	1,045,000	454,000	6
Tobacco products	2111 2121 2131	1967	Employees	376	941	753	4
Cotton spinning & weaving	2211 2281	1967	Employees	696	1,017	814	8
Paints, varnishes, lacquers	2851	1967	Employees	215	255	152	14
Petroleum refining	2911	1967	Employees	364	520	300	9
Petroleum refining	2911	Jan. 1969	Stream bbl. day capacity	54,472	75,628	58,950	9
Nonrubber shoes & slippers	3131 3141 3142	1967	Employees	320	264	188	37
Glass containers	3221	1969	Employees	770(9)	1,179	1,040	3
Hydraulic cement	3241	1967	Employees	168	230	175	8
Hydraulic cement	3241	1969	Barrels per yr. capacity	3,870,000	5,790,000	4,190,000	7
Iron & steel works & steel foundries	3312 3313 3316 3323	1967	Employees	2,063	11,930	7,200	2

Ordinary steel works	3312	1968	Ingot short tons per yr. capacity	$673,000_{(18)}$	3,675,000	2,600,000	2
Ball & roller bearings	3562	1970	Employees	$400_{(5)}$	775	700	2
Household refrigerators & freezers	3632	1967	Units/year	$49,800_{(12)}$	100,000	80,000	3
Primary and secondary batteries	3691 3692	1967	Employees	115	221	188	5
Storage batteries	3691	1967	Automobile battery equiv. units	$265,000_{(18)}$	630,000	450,000	4

Sources: Dominion Bureau of Statistics, Manufacturing and Primary Industries Division, *Annual Census of Manufactures: 1967* (Ottawa, usually 1969) (appears in individual industry reports); Canadian Manufacturers Association, *Canadian Trade Index* (Toronto, various years); Research Company of America, *Brewing Industry Survey: 1968* (New York, 1969); *Oil and Gas Journal*, 67 (March 24, 1969), pp. 135–137; D. H. Stonehouse, "Cement," special report, Mineral Resources Branch, Department of Energy, Mines, and Resources (Ottawa, 1969), p. 5; miscellaneous trade sources; company annual reports; interviews.
^aWhen the industry included fewer than 20 plants, the number of plants is given in subscribed parentheses.

Appendix Table 3.3. Industry Definitions and Plant Size Measures: United Kingdom.

Industry	1957 S.I.C. codes	Data year	Size measure	Average size of Top 20 plants[a]	Average Top 50 % size	Midpoint plant	No. of plants to midpoint
Beer brewing & malting	2082 2083	1963	Employees	1,568	1,145	510	38
Beer brewing	2082	1967	U.S. bbl. output	919,300	957,000	418,500	22
Tobacco products	2111 2121 2131	1963	Employees	1,884	2,812	1,700	8
Cotton & synthetic weaving	2211 2221	1963	Employees	917	391	218	124
Paints and printing ink	2851 2893	1963	Employees	889	718	324	30
Petroleum refining	2911	1963	Employees	1,079 [19]	3,417	3,000	3
Petroleum refining	2911	Jan. 1969	Stream bbl./day capacity	104,835	259,710	210,500	4
Nonrubber shoes & slippers	3131 3141 3142	1963	Employees	938	478	260	105
Glass containers	3221	1954	Employees	876	1,236	638	10
Hydraulic cement	3241	1963	Employees	471	559	350	13
Hydraulic cement	3241	1963	Est. barrels/yr. capacity	n.a.	4,275,000	2,940,000	13

Iron and steel works, steel foundries, and forge shops	3312 3313 3316 3323 3391	1963	Employees	6,182	5,706	3,000	24
Ordinary steel works	33122	1967	Ingot short tons per year capacity	1,435,000	2,128,000	1,512,000	8
Ball & roller bearings	3562	1969	Employees	1,369	3,160	2,800	5
Household refrigerators & freezers	3632	1967	Units/year	111,000(9)	167,000	120,000	3
Storage batteries	3691	1967	Automobile battery equiv. units	330,250	1,865,000	1,000,000	3

Sources: Board of Trade, *Report on the Census of Production: 1963* (London: HMSO, 1968–69), Parts 18, 21, 23, 31, 37, 77, 101, and 105; idem, 1954, for glass containers; T. A. J. Cockerill, private communication on brewery outputs; *Oil and Gas Journal*, 66 (December 30, 1968), refinery capacity survey; *Iron and Steel Works of the World*, 5th ed. (London: Metal Bulletin Books, Ltd., 1969); British Iron and Steel Federation, *The Steel Industry* (London, July 1966), pp. 92–95; Monopolies Commission, *Report on the Supply of Electrical Equipment for Mechanically Propelled Land Vehicles* (London: HMSO, 1963); miscellaneous trade sources; company annual reports; interviews.
ªWhen the industry included fewer than 20 plants, the number of plants is given in subscripted parentheses.

Appendix Table 3.4. Industry Definitions and Plant Size Measures: Sweden.

Industry	1957 S.I.C. codes	Data year	Size measure	Average size of Top 20 plants[a]	Average Top 50 % size	Midpoint plant	No. of plants to midpoint
Beer brewing	2082	1967	Production workers	133	146	92	16
Beer brewing	2082	1967	U.S. bbl. output	103,033	184,750	101,200	7
Tobacco products	2111 2121 2131	1967	Production workers	222(5)	360	264	2
Cotton & synthetic spinning & weaving	2211 2221 2281	1967	Production workers	338	543	343	8
Paints, varnishes, lacquers	2851	1967	Production workers	89	159	90	7
Petroleum refining	2911	1967	Production workers	125(5)	337	337	1
Petroleum refining	2911	Jan. 1969	Stream bbl./day capacity	49,642(5)	92,105	84,000	2
Nonrubber shoes & slippers	3131 3141 3142	1967	Production workers	131	126	74	22
Glass containers	3221	1967	Employees	340(6)	713	600	2
Hydraulic cement	3241	1967	Production workers	179(9)	338	291	3
Hydraulic cement	3241	1968	Barrels per yr. capacity	3,950,000(7)	5,770,000	4,400,000	3

	Codes	Year	Unit				
Iron & steel works; steel castings & forgings	3312 3313 3323 3391	1967	Production workers	1,679	3,478	2,027	6
Ordinary steel works	33122	1967–68	Ingot short tons per yr. capacity	271,000(15)	913,000	726,000	2
Ball & roller bearings	3562	1967	Employees	3,420(2)	5,580	5,580	1
Household refrigerators & freezers	3632	1967	Units/year	18,100	106,200	97,300	2
Storage batteries	3691	1967	Automobile battery equiv. units	279,000(6)	562,000	394,000	2

Sources: Statistiska Centralbyrån, *Industri: 1967* (Stockholm, 1969), pp. 388–391; Alf Carling, *Industrins Struktur och Konkurrensförhållanden* (Stockholm: Statens Offentliga Utredningar, 1968); Gunnar Ribrant, *Stordriftsfördelar inom Industriproduktionen* (Stockholm: Statens Offentliga Utredningar, 1970); Sveriges Industriförbund, *Svensk Industrikalender* (Stockholm, 1969); *Oil and Gas Journal,* 66 (December 30, 1968), refinery capacity survey; miscellaneous trade sources; company annual reports; interviews.
[a]When the industry included fewer than 20 plants, the number of plants is given in subscripted parentheses.

Appendix Table 3.5. Industry Definitions and Plant Size Measures: France.

Industry	1957 S.I.C. codes	Data year	Size measure	Average size of Top 20 plants[a]	Average Top 50 % size	Midpoint plant	No. of plants to midpoint
Beer brewing & malting	2082 2083	1966	Employees	429	377	205	26
Beer brewing	2082	1967	U.S. bbl. output	503,300	575,000	247,136	16
Tobacco products	2111 2121 2131	1966	Employees	455	551	475	9
Cigarettes	2111	1968	Billion units/year	4.73[13]	6.82	5.93	5
Cotton & synthetic weaving	2211 2221	1966	Employees	717	409	236	85
Paints, varnishes, lacquers	2851	1966	Employees	317	232	106	39
Petroleum refining and lubricant blending	2911 2992	1966	Employees	825	1,413	1,050	7
Petroleum refining	2911	Jan. 1969	Stream bbl./day capacity	108,227	216,780	131,000	5
Nonrubber shoes	3131 3141	1966	Employees	345	451	202	76
Glass bottles, other than handblown	3221	1966	Employees	825	1,653	1,000	5
Hydraulic cement & lime	3241 3274	1966	Employees	360	324	197	27
Hydraulic cement	3241	1969	Barrels per yr. capacity	5,370,000	5,550,000	3,810,000	18

Industry	SIC codes	Year	Unit				No. of plants
Iron & steel works & steel foundries	3312 3313 3316 3323	1966	Employees	5,920	6,918	4,650	14
Ordinary steel works	33122	1968	Ingot short tons per yr. capacity	1,196,000	2,318,000	1,653,000	6
Ball & roller bearings	3562	1966	Employees	615	1,736	1,050	4
Household and laboratory refrigerators & freezers	3632	1966	Employees	200	817	600	3
Household refrigerators & freezers	3632	1967	Units/year	115,000[a]	287,000	200,000	2
Storage batteries	3691	1966	Employees	309	638	540	5

Sources: Institut National de la Statistique et des Etudes Economiques, *Les Establissements Industriels et Commerciaux en France en 1966* (Paris, 1968); special tabulations supplied by the Institut National de la Statistique; *Oil and Gas Journal*, 66 (December 30, 1968), refinery capacity survey; *Iron and Steel Works of the World*, 5th ed. (London: Metal Bulletin Books, Ltd., 1969); Communauté de Travail des Brasseurs du Marché Commun, *Combined Statistics: 1967* (Brussels, n.d.); miscellaneous trade sources; company annual reports; interviews.
[a] When the industry included fewer than 20 plants, the number of plants is given in subscripted parentheses.

Appendix Table 3.6. Industry Definitions and Plant Size Measures: West Germany.

Industry	1957 S.I.C. codes	Data year	Size measure	Average size of Top 20 plants[a]	Average Top 50 % size	Midpoint plant	No. of plants to midpoint
Beer brewing	2082	1967	Employees	947	482	235	95
Beer brewing	2082	1966	U.S. bbl. output	812,570	410,160	168,730	79
Cigarettes	2111	1967	Employees	701	1,377	806	6
Cotton & synthetic weaving	2211 2221 2281 2282	1967	Employees	1,798	1,097	590	57
Paints, varnishes, lacquers	2851	1963	Employees	732	362	80	52
Petroleum refining	2911	Jan. 1969	Stream bbl./day capacity	96,010	124,360	92,500	10
Nonrubber shoes & slippers	3141 3142	1967	Employees	1,112	553	275	82
Pressed and blown hollow glass	3221 3229	1961	Employees	1,364	1,573	570	16
Hydraulic cement	3241	1967	Employees	546	580	330	18
Hydraulic cement	3241	1968	Barrels per yr. capacity	4,686,000	4,665,000	3,284,000	21
Ordinary steel works	33122	1968	Ingot short tons per yr. capacity	2,225,000	3,852,000	3,087,000	6

Ball & roller bearings	3562	1970	Employees	1,997	c. 3,285	c. 3,000	7
Household refrigerators & freezers	3632	1967	Units/year	n.a.	570,000	370,000	2
Storage batteries	3691	1967	Employees	652	2,433	1,500	3

Sources: Statistisches Bundesamt, *Zensus im produzierenden Gewerbe: 1962*, vol. 3 (Stuttgart and Mainz, August 1968); Statistisches Bundesamt, *Die Industrie in der Bundesrepublik Deutschland*, Fachserie (subject matter series) D, various issues; Deutscher Brauer-Bund e.V., 8. *Statistischer Bericht* (Bad Godesberg, 1967), pp. 66ff.; *Oil and Gas Journal*, 66 (December 30, 1968), refinery capacity survey; Siegfried Mängel, *Technischer Fortschritt, Wachstum und Konzentration in der deutschen Zementindustrie* (doctoral diss. of the technischen Hochschule, Aachen, privately published, 1971), p. 184; *Iron and Steel Works of the World*, 5th ed. (London: Metal Bulletin Books, Ltd., 1969); miscellaneous trade sources; company annual reports; interviews.

Appendix Table 3.7. Regression Analysis Independent Variable Values: Six Nations, Twelve Industries.

Nation	Industry	MS3	GROWTH	MOS GROWTH	EX-PORT	IM-PORT	TAR-IFF	LOY-ALTY	PHYS-DIFF	PROD3	EMP	CAP	MOS-UP	MOS-DOWN	ADJ	SIZE	CONC	MERG
U.S.	Brewing	67	1.6	0.41	0.1	0.8	n.a.	2	1	4	2235	60	1	0	0	28.8	39	0
U.S.	Cigarettes	66	2.2	0.30	4.4	0.0	n.a.	2	2	12	2275	40	0	0	0	15.9	68	0
U.S.	Weaving	28	0.8	3.56	5.1	3.9	29	1	3	6000	600	9	0	1	0	447.2	30	0
U.S.	Paints	26	1.3	0.77	1.4	0.0	13	1	1	2333	450	6	1	0	0	70.8	26	0
U.S.	Petroleum	34	3.1	1.26	0.6	0.4	14	1	1	12	1900	200	0	0	0	51.7	25	0
U.S.	Shoes	22	1.0	4.99	0.4	3.3	14	1	3	2167	250	1	0	1	0	493.4	17	0
U.S.	Bottles	65	3.3	1.69	1.7	0.2	27	0	0	5000	1000	22	0	0	0	66.5	65	0
U.S.	Cement	65	3.3	1.57	0.2	0.9	4	0	0	5	160	42	1	0	0	58.6	20	0
U.S.	Steel	45	2.0	0.65	2.2	5.0	9	0	0	1333	9000	1200	0	1	0	35.4	42	0
U.S.	Bearings	50	4.6	2.31	7.2	2.3	19	2	1	3333	800	20	1	0	0	73.5	43	0
U.S.	Refrigerators	66	-1.0	-0.08	3.8	0.7	15	2	2	70	2650	45	0	0	0	7.2	64	0
U.S.	Batteries	51	1.9	0.68	0.9	0.8	21	1	1	168	300	4	1	0	0	53.6	54	0
Canada	Brewing	89	3.4	0.08	1.4	0.1	n.a.	2	1	33	2235	60	1	0	0	2.9	89	0
Canada	Cigarettes	89	5.8	0.05	0.2	0.4	n.a.	2	2	16	2275	40	0	1	0	1.3	90	0
Canada	Weaving	93	1.8	0.19	4.0	31.7	27	1	3	2000	600	9	0	0	1	12.4	67	0
Canada	Paints	32	3.8	0.17	0.6	5.2	21	1	1	1500	450	6	1	0	0	6.0	40	0
Canada	Petroleum	73	7.5	0.24	0.5	5.3	8	1	1	12	1900	200	0	0	0	5.6	64	0
Canada	Shoes	14	2.4	0.96	1.9	5.5	26	1	3	667	250	1	0	1	0	48.4	18	1
Canada	Bottles	100	3.5	0.18	0.3	15.0	22	0	0	2733	1000	22	0	0	1	6.9	100	0
Canada	Cement	92	7.1	0.32	3.7	0.7	6	0	0	5	160	42	1	0	0	6.8	65	0
Canada	Steel	81	6.8	0.11	14.1	12.0	13	0	0	500	9000	1200	1	1	0	2.7	80	1
Canada	Bearings	90	4.8	0.10	11.7	63.8	18	2	2	1067	800	20	0	0	0	2.5	89	0
Canada	Refrigerators	50	6.3	0.03	4.8	4.7	22	2	2	37	2650	45	1	0	0	0.7	75	0
Canada	Batteries	77	4.5	0.11	2.1	5.8	23	1	1	87	300	4	1	0	0	4.4	73	0
U.K.	Brewing	31	1.0	0.09	1.3	4.3	n.a.	2	1	25	2235	60	1	0	0	10.6	47	1
U.K.	Cigarettes	97	0.9	0.03	6.2	0.7	n.a.	2	2	24	2275	40	0	0	0	3.6	94	0
U.K.	Weaving	11	-4.5	-2.58	25.2	30.0	24	1	3	2000	600	9	0	1	1	34.0	28	1
U.K.	Paints	40	2.4	0.24	11.4	1.7	13	1	1	2333	450	6	1	0	0	8.4	40	0
U.K.	Petroleum	95	12.2	0.40	26.9	33.5	0	1	1	12	1900	100	0	1	0	7.8	79	0
U.K.	Shoes	15	1.7	2.46	7.0	9.7	14	1	3	633	250	1	0	1	0	149.3	17	0

Chapter 6 Variables

Country	Product																	
U.K.	Bottles	54	2.3	0.21	3.9	1.3	25	0	0	3833	1000	22	0	0	0	73	11.5	0
U.K.	Cement	88	2.7	0.30	2.3	1.8	5	0	0	5	160	42	1	0	0	86	16.6	0
U.K.	Steel	45	2.5	0.16	14.7	6.8	12	0	0	800	9000	1200	1	1	0	39	7.4	1
U.K.	Refrigerators	59	4.9	1.23	17.0	10.5	20	2	1	3600	800	20	1	1	0	82	24.3	1
U.K.	Batteries	30	5.4	0.04	22.0	3.9	15	2	2	21	1700	45	0	0	0	65	1.2	1
U.K.	Batteries	77	4.1	0.14	26.0	2.6	7	1	1	148	300	4	1	0	0	75	10.1	0
Sweden	Brewing	58	1.5	0.01	0.4	2.2	n.a.	2	1	6	2235	60	1	0	0	70	0.7	1
Sweden	Cigarettes	100	4.8	0.01	0.7	9.8	n.a.	2	2	25	2275	40	0	0	0	100	0.2	0
Sweden	Weaving	65	-1.0	-0.07	17.3	46.7	14	1	3	1167	600	9	0	1	1	50	6.2	1
Sweden	Paints	38	5.5	0.10	5.1	14.1	7	1	1	933	450	6	0	0	0	92	1.7	1
Sweden	Petroleum	100	11.5	0.03	12.6	89.7	0	1	1	9	1900	100	0	0	0	100	1.1	0
Sweden	Shoes	23	1.0	0.13	4.0	28.6	14	3	3	110	250	1	1	0	0	37	13.4	1
Sweden	Bottles	100	7.9	0.07	12.3	11.1	12	0	0	700	1000	22	0	0	0	100	1.7	1
Sweden	Cement	100	4.0	0.10	3.0	0.6	9	0	0	5	160	42	1	0	1	100	3.9	0
Sweden	Steel	39	7.5	0.06	21.2	24.5	5	0	0	467	9000	1200	1	1	0	63	1.1	0
Sweden	Bearings	100	4.2	0.26	70.2	18.1	10	2	1	7000	800	20	0	0	1	100	8.6	0
Sweden	Refrigerators	75	8.7	0.02	22.0	17.0	10	2	2	8	1700	45	1	0	0	89	0.5	0
Sweden	Batteries	78	8.3	0.05	21.0	2.5	10	1	1	107	300	4	1	0	0	100	1.7	1
France	Brewing	24	5.6	0.16	1.8	2.1	n.a.	2	2	14	2235	60	0	0	0	63	4.4	1
France	Cigarettes	100	4.0	0.05	6.4	3.3	n.a.	2	2	31	2275	40	0	0	0	100	1.6	0
France	Weaving	18	0.6	0.31	19.3	7.2	23	1	3	3333	600	9	0	1	1	23	59.9	1
France	Paints	14	7.7	0.30	6.4	4.7	19	1	1	2000	450	6	1	0	0	14	6.7	0
France	Petroleum	80	9.7	0.38	19.3	12.1	8	1	1	12	1900	100	0	0	0	60	8.0	1
France	Shoes	10	6.9	4.80	19.3	5.6	23	3	3	1158	250	1	0	1	0	13	139.8	0
France	Bottles	46	5.9	0.28	8.7	1.7	23	0	0	2233	1000	22	0	0	0	84	7.1	0
France	Cement	82	7.1	0.95	5.9	0.4	10	0	0	5	160	42	1	0	1	81	25.3	1
France	Steel	45	5.1	0.21	30.1	23.0	10	0	0	933	9000	1200	1	1	1	84	6.6	1
France	Bearings	80	7.8	0.71	12.3	16.2	28	2	1	2033	800	20	0	1	0	80	16.1	0
France	Refrigerators	51	11.4	0.06	14.8	25.7	15	2	2	12	1700	45	1	0	1	100	0.9	1
France	Batteries	74	10.3	0.32	1.0	0.6	20	1	1	147	300	4	0	0	0	94	13.1	1
Germany	Brewing	7	8.5	0.73	1.3	0.5	n.a.	3	2	63	2235	60	1	0	1	17	16.3	1
Germany	Cigarettes	93	8.8	0.13	2.7	0.1	n.a.	2	2	28	2275	40	0	0	0	94	2.8	1
Germany	Weaving	15	2.2	0.91	20.3	25.6	11	1	3	3333	600	9	0	1	1	16	50.2	1
Germany	Paints	26	9.1	0.59	5.3	1.7	9	1	1	2333	450	6	1	0	0	32	9.1	1
Germany	Petroleum	72	18.8	0.48	11.0	32.8	4	1	1	12	1900	100	0	0	0	47	8.4	0

Appendix Table 3.7 (Continued) Regression Analysis Independent Variable Values: Six Nations, Twelve Industries

Nation	Industry	MS3	GROWTH	MOS GROWTH	EX-PORT	IM-PORT	TAR-IFF	LOY-ALTY	PHYS-DIFF	PROD3	EMP	CAP	MOS-UP	MOS-DOWN	ADJ	Chapter 6 Variables SIZE	CONC	MERG
Germany	Shoes	20	3.3	3.62	3.8	10.5	11	1	3	900	250	1	0	1	1	175.0	20	0
Germany	Bottles	95	7.5	0.35	6.2	2.5	14	0	0	2400	1000	22	0	0	1	8.0	93	1
Germany	Cement	47	7.3	1.38	2.7	1.2	2	0	0	5	160	42	1	0	0	32.5	54	0
Germany	Steel	45	6.5	0.44	24.9	16.1	6	0	0	1400	9000	1200	1	0	0	12.4	56	1
Germany	Bearings	88	10.0	n.a.	19.6	8.7	11	2	1	3333	800	20	0	1	1	52.0	90	0
Germany	Refrigerators	70	23.6	0.13	21.0	2.6	4	2	2	30	1700	45	1	0	0	3.3	72	1
Germany	Batteries	85	13.0	0.36	21.1	10.3	7	1	1	183	300	4	1	0	1	7.8	82	1

Appendix Table 5.1. Transportation Cost Data for 101 U.S. Industries.

S.I.C.	Industry description	Value per pound	Rail class rate[a] (cents)	Rail commodity rate[b] (cents)	Truck commodity rate[c] (cents)	Composite freight index[d] (cents/dollar)
2011	Meat slaughtering plants	$0.37	145	48.0	70.0	1.72
2013	Meat processing plants	.44	100	43.0	71.0	1.36
2015	Poultry dressing plants	.27	133	43.0	65.0	2.35
2021	Creamery butter	.60	133	40.0	61.0	0.93
2024	Ice cream	.20	186	40.0	100.0	5.00
2026	Fluid milk	.09	186	40.0	120.0	13.33
2032	Canned specialties	.19	93	39.0	56.0	2.43
2033	Canned fruits and vegetables	.16	93	39.0	56.0	3.04
2034	Dehydrated food products	.27	87	39.0	66.0	2.19
2035	Pickles and salad dressing	.20	93	39.0	56.0	2.61
2037	Frozen fruits and vegetables	.23	100	39.0	77.0	2.85
2041	Flour mills	.056	86	33.0	50.0	6.38
2042	Prepared animal feeds	.036	86	29.0	50.0	11.76
2043	Cereal preparations	.27	106	43.7	56.0	1.64
2046	Wet corn milling	.06	93	40.3	53.0	6.98
2051	Bread	.16	93	50.0	104.0	6.50
2052	Biscuits, crackers, and cookies	.30	93	50.0	104.0	3.47
2062	Cane sugar refining	.11	93	31.0	57.0	3.86
2063	Beet sugar	.09	93	31.0	57.0	4.72
2071	Confectionary products	.38	106	47.0	66.0	1.79
2072	Chocolate products	.35	106	47.0	81.0	2.32
2082	Malt liquors	.06	73	38.0	60.0	9.12
2085	Distilled liquor	.45	133	38.0	73.0	1.30

Appendix Table 5.1. (Continued)

S.I.C.	Industry description	Value per pound	Rail class rate[a] (cents)	Rail commodity rate[b] (cents)	Truck commodity rate[c] (cents)	Composite freight index[d] (cents/dollar)
2086	Bottled and canned soft drinks	.05	73	38.0	53.0	10.60
2087	Flavorings	.12	93	38.0	71.0	5.83
2092	Soybean oil mills	.05	70	29.0	65.0	6.52
2095	Roasted coffee	.72	86	35.3	64.0	0.76
2096	Shortening and cooking oil	.15	100	35.0	56.0	3.30
2111	Cigarettes	1.50	146	67.0	69.0	0.45
2272	Tufted carpets and rugs	2.10	186	65.0	104.0	.47
2515	Mattresses and bedsprings	0.45	146	106.0	195.0	4.27
2611	Pulp mills	.05	73	37.5	58.0	8.24
2621	Paper mills	.12	86	41.3	59.0	3.78
2631	Paperboard mills	.053	93	33.0	58.0	7.64
2641	Paper coating	.22	86	43.4	71.0	2.44
2643	Bags	.12	86	43.4	73.0	4.90
2647	Sanitary paper products	.18	93	57.0	73.0	3.55
2649	Converted paper products	.32	106	57.0	73.0	1.96
2651	Folding paperboard products	.17	93	46.5	73.0	4.08
2653	Corrugated shipping containers	.11	93	84.0	73.0	6.79
2812	Alkalies and chlorine	.02	80	35.0	69.0	22.87
2813	Industrial gases	.01	133	55.6	78.0	70.16
2816	Inorganic pigments	.23	93	40.0	67.0	2.24
2819	Inorganic chemicals NEC	.025	93	31.5	67.0	19.70
2821	Plastics materials	.59	120	40.3	61.0	0.90
2822	Synthetic rubber	.23	93	46.6	67.0	2.45

2823	Cellulosic man-made fibers	.49	106	46.6	73.0	1.34
2824	Noncellulosic organic fibers	1.18	106	46.6	73.0	0.56
2841	Soap and other detergents	0.24	93	40.0	53.0	2.08
2842	Polishes and sanitation goods	.20	93	40.0	53.0	2.50
2844	Toilet preparations	1.19	133	40.0	69.0	0.55
2851	Paints	0.24	93	40.0	55.0	2.25
2871	Fertilizers	.037	53	31.0	52.0	10.88
2892	Explosives	.14	93	40.0	140.0	8.00
2911	Petroleum refining	.023	93	31.5	56.0	23.71
3011	Tires and inner tubes	.59	100	73.6	94.0	1.43
3111	Leather tanning	.45	100	51.4	84.0	1.85
3161	Luggage	1.60	186	61.4	84.0	0.50
3211	Flat glass	0.09	146	47.7	54.0	5.71
3221	Glass containers	.06	93	53.3	55.0	9.12
3231	Products of purchased glass	.33	106	47.7	54.0	1.56
3241	Hydraulic cement	.01	60	27.2	55.0	51.54
3272	Concrete products	.02	60	33.0	51.0	24.78
3275	Gypsum products	.02	60	34.0	51.0	18.79
3291	Abrasive products	.14	60	40.0	58.0	4.01
3312	Blast furnaces and steel mills	.056	93	41.5	48.0	8.00
3315	Steel wire drawing	.165	93	44.0	67.0	2.62
3321	Gray iron foundries	.14	93	41.3	67.0	4.35
3322	Malleable iron foundries	.185	93	41.3	67.0	3.29
3323	Steel foundries	.304	93	41.3	67.0	2.00
3331	Primary copper	.303	93	45.4	60.0	1.59
3333	Primary zinc	.12	93	45.4	60.0	3.97
3334	Primary aluminum	.224	93	45.4	67.0	2.35
3351	Copper rolling and drawing	.462	120	40.6	60.0	1.19

Appendix Table 5.1. (Continued)

S.I.C.	Industry description	Value per pound	Rail class rate[a] (cents)	Rail commodity rate[b] (cents)	Truck commodity rate[c] (cents)	Composite freight index[d] (cents/dollar)
3352	Aluminum rolling and drawing	.37	120	40.6	67.0	1.63
3356	Rolling and drawing NEC	.72	120	40.6	60.0	0.75
3361	Aluminum castings	.65	120	40.6	67.0	.97
3362	Brass, bronze, and copper castings	.69	120	40.6	60.0	.85
3369	Nonferrous castings NEC	.54	106	40.6	67.0	1.23
3391	Iron and steel forgings	.25	93	41.3	77.0	2.51
3411	Metal cans	.21	146	108.0	86.0	4.46
3441	Fabricated structural steel	.15	93	42.4	77.0	3.84
3443	Boiler shop products	.16	93	42.4	77.0	4.55
3444	Sheet metal work	.18	93	42.4	77.0	4.09
3446	Architectural metal work	.26	100	42.4	77.0	2.79
3452	Bolts, nuts, rivets, and washers	.33	93	47.0	67.0	1.87
3493	Steel springs	.17	100	95.0	77.0	4.74
3494	Valves and pipe fittings	.81	93	95.0	75.0	0.97
3498	Fabricated pipe and fittings	.25	93	95.0	75.0	3.13
3585	Refrigeration machinery	.82	120	68.0	137.0	1.43
3623	Electric welding apparatus	.28	93	111.5	77.0	3.07
3631	Household cooking equipment	.59	120	111.5	94.0	1.78
3632	Household refrigerators	.57	146	98.3	137.0	1.85
3633	Household laundry equipment	.52	160	98.3	115.0	1.98
3635	Household vacuum cleaners	1.21	120	111.5	131.0	1.16
3641	Electric lamps	1.20	160	111.5	154.0	1.11
3651	Radio and television sets	1.33	186	111.5	148.0	1.05

3652	Phonograph records	1.63	120	111.5	120.0	0.74
3671	Electron tubes	2.93	186	111.5	204.0	.59
3679	Electronic components NEC	0.41	186	111.5	80.0	1.98
3691	Storage batteries	.24	186	111.5	77.0	3.22

Sources: See the discussion of methodology in Appendix E.

[a]Rail freight rate per cwt of class-rated shipment between Chicago and Cleveland in 1963.

[b]Rail freight rate per cwt of a commodity-rated shipment over a 350-mile haul in the Official Territory for 1966.

[c]Motor freight rate per cwt of a commodity-rated shipment between Chicago and Cleveland as of 1963.

[d]Ratio of freight cost per cwt to F.O.B. product value per cwt, in cents per dollar of value.

Appendix Table 5.2.   Variable Values for Industries with Complete Transportation Cost Data.

S.I.C.	MPCEN4	MPCEN8	MPDER4	MPDER8	C4	VA63 ($ million)	RPS	LOCAL
2011	91	109	36	67	31	1908	0.005	36.6
2013	29	44	12	21	16	563	.007	9.0
2015	60	76	21	33	14	411	.005	11.7
2021	27	33	11	22	11	133	.007	54.0
2024	84	138	66	99	37	433	.005	11.7
2026	259	336	234	380	23	1515	.001	10.1
2032	14	26	12	21	67	541	.063	26.3
2033	62	127	33	56	24	1029	.005	33.6
2034	17	28	7	15	37	116	.040	62.0
2035	18	30	9	14	36	249	.019	10.2
2037	27	51	16	33	24	550	.008	34.4
2041	56	78	24	46	35	373	.011	34.5
2042	85	135	45	69	22	984	.003	21.8
2043	11	19	12	25	86	365	.167	36.7
2046	7	12	6	11	71	291	.125	38.0
2051	232	347	88	173	23	2404	.002	9.0
2052	31	39	20	29	59	627	.036	13.0
2062	11	17	10	14	63	254	.063	42.0
2063	41	62	19	58	66	201	.040	39.0
2071	6	23	5	11	15	635	.011	12.0
2072	7	11	6	10	75	185	.221	56.0
2082	23	37	9	20	34	1286	.028	16.0
2085	28	37	15	24	58	624	.042	24.0
2086	77	121	32	53	12	1234	.001	18.0
2087	18	26	35	45	62	400	.019	13.8
2092	31	39	20	33	50	152	.003	51.2
2095	21	39	17	34	52	616	.030	29.2
2096	23	43	14	25	42	265	.028	20.0
2111	9	14	5	14	80	1310	.167	76.0
2272	9	16	6	12	25	259	.030	58.5
2515	26	42	16	24	26	286	.007	6.5
2611	11	17	7	13	48	296	.063	60.0
2621	45	74	23	39	26	1857	.011	17.0
2631	33	46	11	21	27	1186	.019	36.3
2641	28	39	11	21	30	457	.018	22.2
2643	38	54	11	27	22	370	.010	17.7
2647	21	28	16	25	62	370	.046	16.3
2649	15	22	9	15	23	303	.014	14.6
2651	25	50	12	30	21	477	.010	10.4
2653	100	176	40	88	20	804	.004	5.5
2812	19	24	10	20	62	389	.071	27.6
2813	285	343	183	285	72	260	.007	13.2
2816	19	27	12	22	68	286	.071	12.6
2819	75	113	14	33	31	1903	.014	27.1
2821	21	47	14	28	35	1202	.017	13.0

Appendix Table 5.2.   (Continued)

S.I.C.	MPCEN4	MPCEN8	MPDER4	MPDER8	C4	VA63 ($ million)	RPS	LOCAL
2822	9	14	8	12	57	330	.070	52.4
2823	14	19	13	19	82	412	.061	61.5
2824	14	18	14	19	94	922	.071	50.0
2841	25	42	25	37	72	1137	.040	14.6
2842	14	18	13	21	34	420	.017	17.7
2844	14	20	11	18	38	1233	.031	26.6
2851	38	74	27	52	23	1112	.005	9.0
2871	72	106	15	46	34	288	.014	47.8
2892	25	31	15	26	72	166	.063	17.9
2911	45	79	16	36	34	3138	.017	43.5
3011	32	48	17	34	70	1322	.053	29.6
3111	17	34	10	23	18	273	.011	25.5
3161	5	9	6	10	31	113	.030	29.0
3211	20	28	19	25	94	364	.077	20.0
3221	40	61	18	45	55	630	.022	16.8
3231	13	18	12	17	43	310	.028	25.8
3241	56	95	19	38	29	786	.013	24.0
3272	104	173	38	64	17	540	.003	19.6
3275	56	67	45	65	84	260	.028	26.5
3291	14	20	10	18	58	416	.068	31.5
3312	57	79	34	52	51	7700	.015	35.0
3315	15	21	8	14	28	253	.022	26.4
3321	23	34	13	23	28	1168	.010	31.7
3322	7	12	7	11	46	205	.050	48.4
3323	24	34	10	18	23	587	.015	25.3
3331	22	28	20	32	78	286	.050	51.8
3333	9	15	6	11	57	99	.090	21.3
3334	20	23	12	23	100	500	.070	46.4
3351	24	34	15	30	45	478	.030	29.1
3352	33	44	23	36	68	721	.037	21.9
3356	11	16	8	15	46	251	.056	11.7
3361	14	20	12	20	33	344	.014	19.5
3362	12	17	7	13	18	144	.013	19.6
3369	7	11	6	10	18	169	.017	29.2
3391	7	14	6	12	30	395	.024	33.7
3411	113	143	81	114	74	831	.015	12.6
3441	32	41	18	27	15	815	.005	8.7
3443	27	46	17	28	25	770	.008	12.5
3444	33	48	9	17	11	632	.009	8.0
3446	6	12	5	9	13	149	.008	11.9
3452	23	32	9	16	18	695	.011	24.3
3493	6	12	6	11	44	69	.070	36.1
3494	20	34	8	14	13	943	.010	13.8
3498	6	18	4	9	17	145	.020	20.0
3585	10	16	5	12	25	893	.023	17.9
3623	5	12	6	12	41	162	.061	35.5

Appendix Table 5.2.   (Continued)

S.I.C.	MPCEN4	MPCEN8	MPDER4	MPDER8	C4	VA63 ($ million)	RPS	LOCAL
3631	8	13	6	12	51	230	.080	18.6
3632	6	10	5	10	91	631	.150	50.0
3633	8	16	8	15	78	354	.105	33.2
3635	4	8	4	8	81	116	.233	33.8
3641	33	37	31	36	92	362	.030	18.4
3651	11	19	6	14	41	912	.056	30.4
3652	13	17	12	16	69	125	.060	38.9
3671	13	20	12	17	87	251	.074	26.2
3679	19	38	9	18	13	1457	.006	20.0
3691	49	71	28	50	59	129	.024	10.9

Sources: U.S., Senate, Committee on the Judiciary, Subcommittee on Antitrust and Monopoly, *Concentration Ratios in Manufacturing Industry: 1963*, Part II, 90th Cong., 1st Sess., 1967; and U.S., Bureau of the Census, *Census of Manufactures, 1963*, vol. I:, *Summary and Subject Statistics* (Washington: USGPO, 1966).

Appendix Table 5.3.   Variable Values for Industries with *Census of Transportation* Value per Pound Estimates.

S.I.C.	Industry description	Value per pound	MPCEN4	MPCEN8	MPDER4	MPDER8	C4	VA63	RPS	LOCAL
2099	Food preparations NEC	0.09	64	78	22	37	24	850	0.006	5.2
2271	Woven carpets and rugs	1.56	9	15	8	13	65	120	.100	40.0
2522	Metal office furniture	0.40	12	21	5	11	33	228	.046	30.8
2531	Public building furniture	.39	7	12	5	11	24	142	.022	24.2
2541	Wood partitions and fixtures	.84	4	9	7	13	4	219	.003	12.3
2542	Metal partitions and fixtures	.32	6	12	6	11	23	214	.020	23.6
2591	Venetian blinds and shades	.20	8	23	8	15	37	94	.073	15.3
2834	Pharmaceutical preparations	1.00	13	25	5	10	22	2596	.030	30.0
2861	Gum and wood chemicals	0.07	11	16	12	18	63	100	.100	68.0
2891	Glue and gelatin	.24	33	54	12	25	28	147	.015	10.3
3069	Rubber products NEC	.83	21	38	9	23	23	1427	.010	22.1
3229	Pressed and blown glass NEC	.16	26	39	21	31	68	472	.039	40.4
3253	Ceramic wall and floor tile	.20	17	26	9	17	49	111	.051	10.8
3255	Clay refractories	.02	36	58	10	27	41	118	.031	15.7
3261	Vitreous plumbing fixtures	.43	13	23	11	18	57	102	.056	10.7
3271	Concrete block and brick	.01	15	19	10	16	5	246	.002	35.5
3292	Asbestos products	.12	28	51	22	36	56	269	.029	11.9
3293	Gaskets and insulations	.60	10	14	7	13	35	161	.033	26.7
3423	Hand and edge tools	.56	14	22	9	17	21	364	.016	20.9
3431	Metal plumbing fixtures	.16	8	13	7	12	49	140	.071	20.2
3433	Nonelectric heating equipment	.42	11	24	9	16	16	496	.012	23.3
3442	Metal doors	.37	11	21	7	12	8	570	.004	5.1
3461	Metal stampings	.50	19	26	7	14	13	1369	.005	25.2
3511	Steam engines and turbines	4.20	10	14	10	14	93	380	.090	35.3
3522	Farm machinery	0.53	25	41	18	30	43	1328	.021	45.1
3531	Construction machinery	.30	17	26	12	22	42	1301	.025	49.4

Appendix Table 5.3. (Continued)

S.I.C.	Industry description	Value per pound	MPCEN4	MPCEN8	MPDER4	MPDER8	C4	VA63	RPS	LOCAL
3534	Elevators	1.08	11	17	9	15	62	202	.070	45.2
3541	Metal-cutting machine tools	3.01	10	15	6	11	20	699	.022	47.8
3542	Metal-forming machine tools	0.55	6	12	5	10	22	281	.033	31.5
3551	Food products machinery	3.91	17	34	7	14	22	380	.014	21.2
3552	Textile machinery	0.69	14	29	6	17	35	314	.033	45.2
3561	Pumps and compressors	.87	15	23	9	16	26	769	.016	17.5
3562	Ball and roller bearings	1.12	23	31	13	23	57	628	.050	31.8
3566	Power transmission equipment	0.52	10	20	8	13	24	556	.019	32.3
3571	Computing machines	7.68	19	32	15	24	67	1101	.057	17.9
3572	Typewriters	1.44	7	11	5	10	76	143	.191	86.5
3581	Automatic vending machines	1.29	11	17	9	16	55	121	.063	20.3
3582	Commercial laundry equipment	0.47	11	15	9	14	47	71	.050	17.2
3611	Electrical measuring instruments	3.75	13	19	6	13	34	505	.033	26.6
3613	Switchgear and switchboards	0.97	41	61	23	40	51	648	.023	23.3
3621	Motors and generators	.66	35	43	24	34	50	993	.023	19.5
3622	Industrial controls	2.16	12	17	7	13	56	451	.080	37.0
3661	Radio and telegraph apparatus	12.05	24	32	22	27	92	1014	.042	27.3
3662	Radio and communications equipment	12.36	28	49	13	24	29	4328	.020	26.5
3672	Cathode ray picture tubes	4.49	6	11	7	12	91	128	.215	38.0
3674	Semiconductors	30.40	5	17	5	13	46	467	.069	20.0
3692	Primary batteries	0.61	24	28	18	26	89	114	.050	9.0
3694	Engine electrical equipment	1.37	11	16	7	14	69	497	.100	49.0
3722	Aircraft engines and parts	4.18	15	32	7	17	56	2244	.050	43.5
3741	Locomotives and parts	1.10	5	9	4	8	97	186	.285	35.0
3811	Scientific instruments	6.30	5	9	6	10	29	359	.025	11.1

3861	Photographic equipment	1.97	10	25	9	19	63	1270	.070	52.0
3941	Games and toys	3.24	10	19	6	10	15	444	.013	31.7
3982	Hard surface floor coverings	0.25	5	9	5	10	87	119	.174	67.0

Sources: U.S., Senate, Committee on the Judiciary, Subcommittee on Antitrust and Monopoly, *Concentration Ratios in Manufacturing Industry: 1963*, Part II, 90th Cong., 1st Sess., 1967; and U.S., Bureau of the Census, *Census of Manufactures, 1963*, vol. I: *Summary and Subject Statistics* (Washington: USGPO, 1966).

Author Index

Subject Index